A NASTY BUSINESS

A NASTY BUSINESS

S M Barron

J&J

First published in 2014 by Jarndyce & Jarndyce
6 Ashgrove Cottages Ruscombe, Nr Stroud, Gloucestershire GL6 6BY
smbarron17@gmail.com

Distributed by Gardners Books, 1 Whittle Drive, Eastbourne,
East Sussex, BN23 6QH
Tel: +44(0)1323 521555 | Fax: +44(0)1323 521666

www.amolibros.com

British Library Cataloguing in Publication Data
A catalogue record for this book is available from the British Library.

ISBN 978-0-9575745-0-2

Typeset by Amolibros, Milverton, Somerset
This book production has been managed by Amolibros
Printed and bound by T J International Ltd, Padstow, Cornwall, UK

This book is dedicated to all those who have been badly served in today's civil justice market, and also to those law practitioners and decision-makers who work to make our system for resolving civil disputes fit for purpose.

Acknowledgements

We are grateful to many people for their help in producing this book. Some will be unaware that their blogs and websites, papers and books have helped to inform much of the content, others have been most generous with their time and given much needed wise counsel. To those who have read the drafts, revised, corrected and advised many, many thanks.(In particular thanks go to Christine, Michael, Sue, Janet, Roger, Tom, Rachel, Ros and Simon.) A very special thank-you goes to Peter – the book would not have been produced without his ready encouragement, advice, and constant supply of coffee, tea and the odd (medicinal) glass of wine. Thanks too to Peter Down for his witty, clever cartoons and to Jane Tatam for her support and indispensable guidance.

Contents

PART ONE		1
One	2001–2002	3
Two	2002: June–September	21
Three	1983–1984	35
Four	1984–1985	50
Five	September 2002	68
Six	September–October 2002	88
Seven	October 2002	106
Eight	November 2002–January 2003	121
Nine	February 2003–August 2003	139
Ten	September 2003–November 2003	158
Eleven	November 2003–July 2004	166
Twelve	August 2004–December 2006	189
Thirteen	2003–2006: the Attack	196
Fourteen	2007	218
Fifteen	2007–September 2008	227
Sixteen	October 2008–2010	258
PART TWO		281
Seventeen	Recovery	283
Eighteen	Recovery 1: Solicitors Professional Indemnity Insurers	293
Nineteen	Recovery 2: The Law Society's Complaints Service (dec'd)	302

Twenty	Recovery 3:The Bar Council's complaints service (also dec'd)	308
Twenty-one	Recovery 4: The Bar's Professional Indemnity Insurance	324
Twenty-two	Recovery 5: Mediation	330
Twenty-three	Recovery 6: Legal Expenses Insurance (LEI)	337

PART THREE 349

Twenty-four	Who judges the judges?	351

PART FOUR 369

So, what's to be done? 371
Blogs, books and contacts 379
Footnotes 383
Cast List 395

Introduction

'This is a court of law, young man, not a court of justice.'

Oliver Wendell Holmes –
US Supreme Court Judge (1841–1935)

So, where do we go for justice?

When courts are called civil justice centres, justice is what we might quite reasonably expect them to provide, otherwise they could be caught by the Trade Descriptions Act 1968 (as amended 2008). Litigants, clients, consumers – people usually go to a civil court for justice not for law: after all, law is the means to an end not the end itself, and even if there is, eventually, some agreement in a civil courtroom about what the law says, justice may still be elusive.

Law is often a delight to those skilled in the trade; many of them are captivated by it. The rest of us acknowledge that it is an essential, valuable tool, and find the intricate body of law constructed by lawyers and legislators over the centuries impressive. But if law is used in such a way that it obstructs a just outcome – justice – then it is not such a delight, it is a public hazard and somebody with the power to do something about it, should do something.

In any market for goods and services, other than justice services, we consumers play a vital role in supervising quality simply by taking our business elsewhere if dissatisfied, complaining, telling others or demanding our money back. If the dissatisfaction is general and voiced loudly enough, useful laws can be brought in to address the dissatisfaction. These days, if goods or services are viewed as essential, like energy, health, food and finance, we consumers also have a voice on official bodies charged with regulating them. In order to play our essential regulating role in whatever capacity, we need to be confident, and for that we need a transparent market, information and easy access to fair and prompt redress if things go wrong.

Clients of law services – as distinct from the justice service – have very recently been given a small voice in a new system for regulating them and better access to redress. So maybe, in time, a new client-focussed law market will emerge responsive to customer and public need. On the other hand, clients of the civil *justice* service have very little hope of directly influencing the quality of the service itself. And they certainly cannot take their custom elsewhere or get easy access to redress. So they can do little to encourage the justice service-providers (the judges, the courts, the parliamentarians) to respond to their concerns, and when they encounter a problem with the service they can only hope that someone with the power to do something, does something.

Judges arrive at their powerful positions via the law route, that's what they know and feel comfortable with. Justice, on the other hand, can be more challenging and, despite what the prospectus might have said, was not the prime focus of their training and work experience. The best way to arrive at justice is via truth and the road to truth in our adversarial civil justice landscape, as many have observed, can be challenging, difficult to discern, time-consuming and uncomfortable. If law and the rules of the court provide efficient transport to as near to truth and justice as reasonably acceptable all well and good but, unfortunately, that is not always where law is headed despite what it might say on the front of the bus.

Nobody goes happily to court, except possibly, those who earn their living there – lawyers, ushers, cleaners, judges and so on – most of the rest of us would rather avoid those arenas of mystifying conflict. Especially the criminal courts: murder, fraud, rape, treason are courtroom dramas best enjoyed in fiction form, or media reports. The civil courts are rarely fun either; usually duller, but still best avoided if a hassle-free life is the objective. And if avoidance is possible. Most people will try to find some other way of sorting out a civil dispute, and there is an increasing number of alternatives to battling it out in front of a judge. Nevertheless, court is still unavoidable as the last resort when all else fails – or if you are summoned.

Debts, real or otherwise, and family problems make up much of the action in civil courts, but there are plenty of other ways to encounter a Kafka moment or two: 24/7 partying neighbours, speed cameras, neglected rail-track, fences, disputatious cars, the wrong trade name, employer, doctor, bank, airline, insurer, planning authority, lawyer, bottle of ginger beer … the list is endless. You don't have to do anything wrong, you don't have to be careless, vexatious, a bully or plain silly. You can be eminently sensible and accommodating and still end up there. Most people manage to avoid the experience. The less imaginative among them may smugly believe they're safe since there are easier routes to resolving disputes and they are unaware that, in many instances, luck rather than good judgement has saved them. But what about the unlucky ones?

The usual advice is to find yourself a good lawyer. There are some very good ones out there, but until there is a sure-fire way of knowing who is a good lawyer for you before you've spent your entire year's housekeeping on mysteriously high legal bills (and a disappointing outcome), it's a gamble. Some people can afford it and some can find someone else to pay, but many have to find at least some of the costs and some pay all. So, you'd best avoid choosing the wrong solicitor or, possibly worse, the wrong barrister. If it does all go wrong, you must also be very careful to avoid finding yourself in court in front of the wrong judge, or even the right judge on his off day. That really is unlucky.

There are people who see large cheques in a hot cup of coffee spilt in a careless moment and rush headlong to embrace the compensation culture. Legal Aid, insurance or 'no-win, no-fee' will cover the costs, they think, if the threat of court action doesn't extract the desired result. However, successive governments have tried to restrain the cost of Legal Aid and the excesses of the claims management business and both have recently been reined in. Besides, courts are really only fun for the professionals and some spectators: rather too often amateurs will find courts are joyless casinos. Far better stick to roulette or horses. If you have the choice.

They tell us that 'every man [sic] deserves his day in court'. 'They' are those very same people who earn their living there. Of course, the gamble may pay off, you may be the lucky one to hit the jackpot and come out with a surprised and happy smile, better off than you expected, or you may actually get what is promised on the packet and enjoy a smug 'I told you so' grin. You may just come out even, not much better or worse money-wise than when you went in, but a good deal wearier and not really persuaded that you have been supplied with what you went there for in the first place, willingly or unwillingly: truth and justice.

It is also possible that you'll find yourself trapped in *Bleak House* or a spirit-destroying, dark, cold labyrinth of incomprehensible rules, regulations and laws in a language that sounds familiar but seems to mean something different. You could get to lose an awful lot and not just money and sleep. Civil court visits can end in prison. Civil court combat can end in death. Rarely, it's true to say, and sometimes the rare prison stay is deserved. Death is not.

Big, high-cost civil cases get the attention: celebrity divorce, business shenanigans, high-profile challenges to decisions by high-handed powers, but every day the civil courts deal with cases that will never make the headlines not only because the players are unknown, not only because the dispute may seem, and even be, trivial, but often because the case becomes tied up in legal complexity and, therefore, to the indifferent observer, tedious. Nevertheless, it is in those civil courts that so much damage can be done to very ordinary people who really do not deserve it. Unnecessary damage. Damage that could be avoided if the professional players would so choose.

The top providers of our civil justice service, the judges, can be very serious people who expect to be taken seriously and who can be observed frowning on courtroom games or slipshod arguments. As they see it, they are following ancient traditions honed over the centuries from the mists of early human society to keep our present society in order, the final guardians against anarchy. They are carefully selected by their peers, having dedicated years to absorbing the skills and knowledge of the law passed down through time to earn the mantle of guardian, keeping even kings and presidents in check. They are skilled in what should be a high and noble profession, uniquely protected and privileged to deliver an essential service. We need to give them authority in return for what they might offer: truth, justice and an ordered society. Along with those other essential services, we want and need justice: a just society with just laws justly observed.

As the civil justice service is carefully cocooned from market forces, its clients have little choice: it's a case of take it or leave it. Except that some clients can't leave it. Moreover, they don't have a watchdog to advise and speak for them. Dissatisfied customers of judge performance have no OfJudge to fight their corner. Nor are they asked to complete client satisfaction forms – an amusing idea easily dismissed with the explanation that the successful litigant will be happy and positive, the unsuccessful unhappy and negative. This unsophisticated view of consumer research ensures that the customer has little or no say in improving the service. If dissatisfied customers have any energy, time, or money left they are told to appeal within the very system they have found wanting. The only way clients can hope to have any effect is to challenge the service-provider in his chosen arena: appeal to his colleagues in a higher court. Not quite a friendly and mutually beneficial exchange of views and ideas then, more a gladiatorial battle between unarmed, inexperienced, puny, little litigants and experienced, muscled professionals in full battle dress. Not quite the level playing field they are so keen on – in law books. The statistics on appeals are hardly encouraging. If you get to the appeal stage you really are gambling with the dice loaded against you.

The one constant observation to be heard about our justice system in England and Wales is that it is the best in the world, an observation made most often by the highest lawyers in the land, so the incentives necessary to get the service-providers to improve performance are rather feeble. Is it any wonder that the civil justice business still serves the interest of those service-providers and that customers can only hope the roulette wheel will spin in their favour? They must place their hopes in Parliament, where the legal profession is disproportionately represented, to act on their behalf.

These mutterings are not new. Our judges and lawyers have heard them before, for hundreds of years. Some may even agree, but many will protest that the civil justice system *does* focus on the public need for justice and is constantly under review. It is certainly true that there is a steady stream of reports, articles, papers, surveys and conferences. Legal experts produce expensive research which some people might read and then some very important person might make a speech about to a very senior audience, arguing for reform of this or that rule, procedure or Act.

In fact, in 1998 a brand new rule book for civil disputes in the courts of England and Wales appeared. The new book of rules, which is practically readable and tries to establish sensible overriding objectives for delivering civil justice, may not be perfect but is quite a step in the right direction. The Great and the Good had been tinkering with the rules for well over a century, but although they knew they should do a proper overhaul sometime, once they looked at the job they decided that perhaps they'd better just do some make do and mend until they could find time to tackle a proper job. Finally, at the close of the 20th century, they made a seriously determined effort and produced the new set of rules. Rules which could have taken the civil justice system into a new landscape, where the search for truth and the fair apportionment of justice prevailed. It is somewhat regrettable that it has proved so hard for the key players, the lawyers (especially those who become judges) to break from their old habits and keep their eyes on the overriding objective of the reformed civil law. Only they can do it. Consumers of this expensive public service do not stand a chance of getting their voices heard and opinions heeded, at least not without exposing themselves to the risk of losing money, patience, friends, time, good health, reputation and happiness.

★

Here are a couple of stories to tell. True stories: all the files and records are available to check. One dates from before the reforms and one after. Together they show that despite the new rule book, our civil justice system can be perverted by overindulgence in law to attack rather than defend good citizens and even aid and abet wrongdoing, stifling truth and denying justice. These stories are told in the hope that a study of the anatomy of civil justice failures in two relatively simple civil cases will provide useful guidance for service-providers and useful warnings and guidance for the rest of us. Of course, all names and descriptions of people and places have been changed – for the usual reasons.

PART ONE

ONE
2001–2002

'Good fences make good neighbours.'

Seventeenth-century proverb

Lucy and Max bought a house in the country. It is an interesting, original house about one hundred years old. It had been built on a steep hillside covered in ash and beech trees, brush and bracken which tumble down to a beautiful river. A small terraced garden has been created out of the wildness and there are paths criss-crossing the land, some following the contours and others leading down to the water.

When they were buying their new home, Homestead, Max and Lucy were focussed on the house itself which needed work, so when they moved in September 2001, some five months after their offer was accepted, they were very busy finding builders and electricians, painters and decorators and a reliable, affordable plumber. This was challenging in a busy housing market, particularly as Max and Lucy knew little of the area and no one to advise on local tradesmen, but they were retired and had lots of ideas and some experience of house renovation. They liked that sort of thing.

Their new home is on a road that runs across the hillside, parallel with the river and then loops round and down to a track running alongside the riverbank. For the first couple of months after they moved in Max and Lucy had no reason to walk that way. They were busy and always turned left to drive to the nearest towns.

On first viewing the previous April, they had admired the garden but only peeped at the some three acres of woodland. They had also walked up the road to see the properties around. Homestead was not overlooked and no neighbour was near enough to cause noise problems. They contracted a surveyor to check out both house and land, but he felt the land was too demanding for a man of his age and pointed out that the property had the security of the Land Registry's guarantee.[1] It had been registered for the first time just two years earlier when the owners, the Swales, bought the property. *They* had moved out after barely a year there (for work-related problems, the agent told Lucy), leaving the house empty. It had been on the market for over a year and no one had made an offer. To be on the safe side Max agreed to meet with a woodland manager, a Mr Jenkins, who had been engaged briefly by the Swales during their one year of ownership, to look at the land.

On a day of torrential rain Max and Mr Jenkins met, and slipping and sliding on the steep hillside leading down to the riverbank they decided to stick to the main paths running across it, but that evening Max reported back to Lucy on what he'd seen and, despite the awful weather, had liked. He was somewhat concerned about an old concrete cistern on the riverbank which might be a dangerous public hazard bearing in mind that it was just by the one *public* footpath running across the property along the river's edge. The other paths were private although one had a right of way for neighbours in two houses along the road, a house called Dunroamin' and another called Honeysuckle Cottage.

Max also mentioned he'd been shown some dozen or so felled trees which Mr Jenkins had told him had been felled illegally by a neighbour a year or so before, adding that there had been something of a scene. Lucy and Max decided that they would make further enquiries, but were not too concerned because they knew that some of the land was in the process of being sold to a neighbour, and the woodland manager wasn't too sure of the background details and had no up-to-date information, *and* they had Land Registry's guarantee. Nevertheless, Lucy added another question to the long list she'd prepared for their young conveyancing lawyer, Daisy Hoople. 'Check on disputes.'

Since she was young and not fully qualified, Daisy was supposed to be supervised. A senior partner at the firm took over the work briefly when she went on holiday, so he knew that the purchase was out of the ordinary with a public footpath and ancient rights of way over the land and so on, but he seemed assured by the fact that the property was registered. Unfortunately, he didn't stay with it and he didn't spot that most of the early deeds were missing from the bundle forwarded to him by the Swales' solicitor. So, both members of the firm Max and Lucy had engaged to conveyance this purchase treated a complex property as standard which it wasn't.

Lucy was liaising with Daisy to avoid duplication and confusion as Max was busy moving his business. She wrote her list of questions, starting with those about the house, then the paths, then the cistern and then added one about 'the scene'; could Daisy check if there were any disputes? Then she waited for her response. After several days Airfixed to the telephone, Lucy finally made contact, and stifling any suggestion of impatience started to work her way down the list.

When she raised the query about a possible neighbour dispute she was told of the response by the Swales on the General Enquiries Before Contract Form – the SPIF[2] – which every seller has to complete, which said on disputes: 'We have not been notified of any.'

'Is that the standard answer?' Lucy asked.

'Sounds a bit over-cautious, perhaps,' was the reply, 'but you don't have to worry, the Title is protected. Your Title is registered with the Land Registry guaranteed by the Crown – and the vendors would be in trouble if they lied on this form. They're using a reputable firm of solicitors, it's not as though they're doing the conveyancing themselves. Next question.'

'Don't fuss,' Lucy wrote on her list and moved on to the next question.

Lucy reckons she's quite good at spotting potential trouble but she had no such intimations here. The tree felling had happened over a year earlier and the presumed tree-felling neighbours were buying the land anyway, the sale to be concluded before their purchase. The Title was registered with Land Registry. On neighbour disputes she felt confident that they didn't have to fuss. Open cisterns, dodgy verandas, penetrating damp and ancient Agas were another matter. The surveyor's report added yet more, but nothing serious enough to cause alarm, let alone abandonment of the purchase, particularly as Lucy's sale was on track at a higher price and the Swales had agreed a reduction in theirs.

They met Mr and Mrs Swale once on another visit to Homestead in torrential rain. The family was no longer living there; they had moved out nearly a year before and only came back from time to time. On this occasion they had come back to continue packing up and Max and Lucy both managed to make time to squeeze a visit there together to meet them and discuss the property. They had allowed two hours but it took over four, there was so much to check out. The Swales also confirmed that there were some ruined buildings on the land and an abandoned plot further along the road for parking cars, all on the property plan. There was even a rumour of fishing rights. The Swales seemed somewhat distracted – hardly surprising really, they'd had less than a year in the house before they had to move out and it had hung on the market for yet another year, and here they were packing up to move again with their young family, who now grizzled around bored with little to do but get in the way, locked indoors by the rain.

The Swales mentioned the two acres of woodland to be transferred to neighbours. They told of the deer that visited from time to time and about the birds to be seen and heard in the area. They told of the trees they had asked Mr Jenkins to fell in order to open up a view of the river. This prompted Max to ask about Mr Jenkins's story of the 'illegal' tree-felling incident. Was it still a problem?

'No,' said Mrs Swale, who was getting somewhat impatient with an unhappy little daughter perfecting her economy moan, the one that can be sustained for hours if not nipped in the bud. They were running very late and as the monsoon showed no sign of abating they abandoned their plan to walk down the road that curved back to the river and check on the cistern. A most unfortunate decision as it turned out.

On the day of Lucy's move there was one last-minute hitch caused by the solicitors. Daisy was on holiday again and the finance manager who took over on the day managed to keep all the monies paid at the time arranged by Lucy's purchaser, in her firm's bank account without quite getting around to passing the substantial sum on to the Swales by close of business, despite increasing protests from her clients, so no house-key was released, and Lucy and Max had to spend the night in a local hotel while the long-suffering removal men had to sleep in the cab. After two days' work and a six-hour journey they still had a sense of humour. Lucy and Max appreciated that.

Late October. Max and Lucy finally found time to go for that walk to check on the riverbank and the hazardous cistern for the first time. They started down the road which eventually curves round on itself to the river. Deep in conversation they were practically past the next house on the road before it occurred to both of them there was something wrong. Something decidedly different from what they'd seen on that same walk the previous April. They returned a bit of the way and pondered. There was a brand new fence along the road. Six feet high and 11 fence panels long: 66, say, 70 feet of brand new fence on what looked like their land.

They decided to check the plans and phone Land Registry to see what had happened to their registered Title document. They had had to prod Daisy to forward the deeds to the nearest Land Registry district office. Maybe the land sale included a tranche they had not been told about. They didn't think so but maybe they'd got it wrong. They had only walked that way once. Could this be something to do with the cheeky tree felling? Most unlikely as they knew that the trees were felled on another part of the land. This curious new fence seemed to be part of a house called Blackstone Cottage, the first house on that side of Homestead. They returned home immediately and scrambled over the junk shop of furniture, rolled carpets, redundant TVs, books and more books, and pulled open still unpacked boxes to finally find the plans they'd been sent before they moved in. They went back up the road. They looked at the plans. They looked at the fence. No question, there was certainly something wrong.

Land Registry, once prodded, sent their Title with its plan in a few days. As they suspected, no other tranche of land had been conveyed. Title plan to hand they went back up the road to Blackstone Cottage. There were the 11 new fence panels. Poking behind the fence they could see a shed, a brand new, large chalet-style shed and a compost box behind it and the wild scrubland they'd seen in April tamed with paths and some plants. At a rough estimate looking at the plans and the length of fence, over 4,000 square feet of their land had been taken and developed by the people in Blackstone Cottage. There must be some misunderstanding, surely?

They phoned Mr Jenkins who told them how in September 1999 he and Mr Swale had come across men felling trees on Homestead land, how they had called on the tree-felling neighbours and shown the lady who answered the door the plan of Homestead they had with them, pointing out that it was a registered Title. He told of the conversation that had then taken place. He had thought the lady rather unfriendly and rather too keen to let them know that she and her husband were lawyers. He said that the message was clear, well at least to him: 'Don't mess with us, we're lawyers.' He remembered that she had agreed to meet Kevin Swale again to 'sort out the confusions and look at plans.' That was as far as he was able to go with his story. He offered to put it all in writing. He lectured in woodland management and took a dim view of what he suspected the owners of Blackstone Cottage had been up to, particularly if they were lawyers.

Then Lucy phoned the Swales. Mrs Swale answered. She listened to the report and, according to Lucy, responded with a sharp intake of breath and, 'What bloody cheek! The cheeky cow!' She confirmed that it was the owners of Blackstone Cottage, with the name of Ogmore, who had been caught taking down Homestead trees, not the Ackroyds who owned Dunroamin' and who had bought a couple of acres of Homestead land.

Kevin, her husband, and Mr Jenkins had caught the tree fellers at work and immediately gone to see the Ogmores. Only Mrs Ogmore was there and when they had shown her Homestead's Title plan she had told them she owned all the land down to the first path where the felled trees lay, some 200 feet downhill from the road. When they had pointed out the registered plan gave Blackstone Cottage only a 50-foot downhill boundary she had told them their Title plan was wrong. At this point Mrs Swale paused in her report as if checking herself. She became rather vague. She wasn't too sure but Mrs Ogmore *may* have mentioned she and her husband were lawyers but she wasn't there at that first confront…er…meeting. Mrs Swale continued (cautiously) to report that she and the family had visited Mrs Ogmore later, possibly months later, to try to understand what this neighbour and presumably her husband, neither of whom they'd met in the previous six months, were up to. Kevin had had a beer and the kids some cola. Only Mrs Ogmore was there. She was welcoming and friendly but although she had had many weeks, a couple of months in fact, to prepare for this rather important meeting she had not quite managed to acquire her deeds, or so she told them. Important meeting, important documents to compare and one side, a professional solicitor, just happened to forget them. This is what Mrs Swale told Lucy on the phone. That's the same Mrs Swale who had answered the questions about disputes on the Seller's Property Information Form with, 'We have not been notified of any'. Assurances and a glass of beer are all well and good, but the point of the meeting between the Swales and Mrs Ogmore had not been entirely social but to look at documents and try to sort out the 'misunderstanding' according to Mrs Ogmore – presumably by the Swales – and 'confusions' according to the Swales. The Swales left Mrs Ogmore with a copy of their Land Registry plan. As Lucy recalls, Mrs Swale paused and seemed to be pondering a thing or two. Perhaps Kate Swale was thinking about the answer they had given to the questions about disputes on the SPIF. Not so much a confusion, more a contradiction. Lucy was pondering too. Kate Swale may well have been pondering the trouble they could be in. Lucy was pondering the trouble the Swales could have left for her and Max to deal with. Kate Swale wanted an end to this difficult conversation. She told Lucy to get in touch with the Ackroyds at Dunroamin', 'They know all about it,' she said.

Max and Lucy had a look on the internet to find out about squatters and the rules governing squatters. There was talk of changes in the law coming in 2002,[3] but in 2001 the rules were: those hoping to grab somebody else's property without their permission and hold on to it, must do so openly, so people know about it; they must make sure they have exclusive use, so that the rightful owner cannot have access to it; and they must hold on to it unchallenged in those ways for 12 years; and they must make proper use of the property, it's not enough to park a car on expropriated land, or light bonfires, or throw rubbish there.

So, the new fence along the road was open to every passer-by to see. It prevented anyone from accessing the land from the road. But the fence did not enclose the land; the more adventurous could brave the scrubland round the end of it for access. Max and Lucy could do this more easily from a narrow rough track which ran parallel with the road, just 15 feet below it, leading up to the very new-looking compost bin and the very new and very smart chalet-shed. The track was overgrown with weeds, brambles and nettles and blocked by a fallen tree but negotiable and, although only they and previous Homestead owners – and possibly the Ogmores, would know of its existence, it still prevented the purloined land from being 'exclusive'. The shed was clearly using the land, but both fence and shed were brand new, not even 12 months, let alone 12 years on the annexed land. Neither was seen by Max and Lucy the previous April. Lucy remembered noticing the terrace of Blackstone Cottage as they walked by that day; now it could not be seen from the road – hidden by a very new-looking six-foot high fence.

The Ackroyds, who lived in the next house along the road, the other side of Blackstone Cottage, were away but their daughter was able to fill in more details. She and her parents had watched the actions of the Ogmores with dismay. Mr Ogmore did not appear to be around much but Mrs Ogmore was a very determined lady in her opinion and might prove difficult. The Ackroyds had discussed the tree-felling incident with the Swales during negotiations to buy the couple of acres of Homestead land when, soon after that incident, they had met the Swales on the ancient wide path running across the land and parallel with the river some 200 feet below the road. The owners of Dunroamin' had right of way on part of it. The owners of Blackstone Cottage did not, besides they couldn't access that path from their land.

When the Ackroyds returned from holiday they added more details. The Ackroyds had been dismayed at the actions of their mutual next-door neighbour when they saw the landscapers moving in on Homestead territory. They had a copy of Homestead's Title plan so knew that territorial expansion was taking place and suspected it was not authorised. They had noticed that the Ogmores had stuck a small, white marker down on the wide lower path, with the name Blackstone Cottage on it but Mrs Ogmore had actually told them only a month previously that her land didn't go down as far as that path and they knew it didn't according both to their deeds and Homestead's registered plan. It seemed to them highly likely that the Ogmores were squatters. If so Max and Lucy had squatters who were lawyers.

So a picture began to emerge of this lady who lived next door and wanted to live even closer. She knew the land she had had developed recently had been registered to Homestead. She claimed her deeds showed a different boundary to the one on the Homestead Title plan, but at an informal meeting arranged with several months' warning, claimed that she couldn't show hers – for some reason. She hadn't contacted Land Registry – for some reason. She hadn't contacted the Swales after their 'amicable' meeting – for some reason. She had taken advantage of the fact that Homestead was empty to hire a landscaper to make over what was legally Homestead land, to create terraces and paths and erect a shed. She had an above-average knowledge of the law and access to free advice but had behaved like a land thief.

Any ordinary person in her circumstance would move with speed to contact Land Registry and sort things out, this person was clearly not ordinary. She had done nothing – apart from clearing and planting more of the land she knew was being conveyed to new owners who had yet to move in.

'The Swales should have done something,' said Dick Ackroyd, 'they should have sorted it out.'

'They should have admitted there was a dispute,' agreed Alice Ackroyd.

Neither Max nor Lucy was seriously worried. From their increasing knowledge of the rules on trespass and squatting it seemed to them that the Ogmores would have a hard time holding on to the land. If they had any evidence supporting a claim to it, they had had plenty of opportunity to show it.

Max checked again with Land Registry who confirmed that Blackstone Cottage was not registered and that they had received nothing from the Ogmores, so Max decided the time had come to write to the lady. Reviewing the way the Swales seemed to have been taken in, Max wanted to make clear he would not be so easily bamboozled. His first letter was brief and unequivocal. It pointed out their concerns, made clear they'd spoken to the Swales and asked that she remove the trespass. As there was no reply after two weeks and she was clearly in residence, he wrote again. A brief reply acknowledged receipt and promised to be in touch later. Why the delay?

Max and Lucy found a local surveyor, Mr James Nunn, who inspected the roadside fence and confirmed that according to Homestead's Title plan there was 'encroachment' of well over 100 feet along the road and around 60 feet downhill on the terrain he couldn't access, so the encroachment was a fair-sized plot. A week later Lucy noticed a plume of smoke from a bonfire Mrs Ogmore had lit on Homestead land close to some trees. Max wrote again, protesting.

Then a few days later when they were deeply engrossed in renovation projects for their entrance hall, they became aware of someone fumbling at their front door. A woman was looking for a letterbox in their letterbox-free door. The post-box was at the top of the drive. They invited Mrs Ogmore in.

They saw no evidence of the sociability the Swales said they had encountered on their family visit. Perhaps not so surprising in light of the tenor of the short, perfunctory letters Max had sent. They offered a drink. It was refused. She said she did not want to have a dispute and they agreed. She said that she hoped matters could be kept away from the neighbours. She said she wanted to stay in Blackstone Cottage for many years and she would not have bought the property had it come without the land shown by her deeds. They asked if they could see the deeds. She said she had had to retrieve them from the building society for her surveyor. She had commissioned a survey and was now awaiting his conclusions. There was no question, she said, but that she legally owned all the property bounded by her new fence and possibly more further Homestead way. They said that they would expect both surveyors, hers and theirs, to come to the same conclusion if they were working from the same plans. She had copy of their Title plan, could she please let them have copy of any plans she relied on? She asked if they had seen their first deer.

Her plot of land had been part of Homestead until the summer of 1963 when Homestead's then owner sold it and the 'Black Hut' erected on it. According to all the conveyance plans for Homestead since that sale including one just months after, Blackstone Cottage had just a small looped boundary which appeared to follow a contour in the hillside. They found her claims confusing. How come she had commissioned a landscaper to carry out all the work: clear land, build an elaborate chalet-shed, remove trees, plant shrubs, make paths, erect a large compost bin and a substantial length of fence without first retrieving and checking her deed plans – particularly as the Swales had given her Homestead's Title plan and she believed the plans gave her property different boundaries? What plan had she provided for the work? What plan had she now provided for her surveyor? What had these two solicitors done to check the boundaries before they purchased? What did the property particulars say at the time? Why could she not show the Swales her deed plan and why was she delaying in showing it now?

Only now, *after* the landscaping and after new owners had reopened Homestead and started to question her actions did she get round to checking the key document – apparently. She admitted that the Swales had raised the matter with her in late 1999 and had appeared at her house with their plans. Kevin Swale, she said, had not taken the matter further. Lucy began pointing out that it was for her to 'take the matter further', but Max intervened. The conversation had been civil so far and he wanted it to stay that way. She asked them not to fell any more trees near her house. They pointed out they hadn't felled any trees near her house, but they had been told that she had had trees felled – trees that were not on her land. She said nothing on that, but stressed her concern not to lose the privacy provided by the trees. Max and Lucy said nothing on that, but suggested they wait for the results from both surveyors, hers and theirs.

After she left they read the letter she had been trying to post. Lucy says, 'We might have been less civil if we'd read it earlier.' Mrs Ogmore's note on file makes no apology for anything but states that her surveyor would *define* the boundaries to Blackstone Cottage and then, 'we will meet to discuss matters.' Well, they had met and although the discussion had been polite, it had lacked substance. The substance that could only be provided by her.

'We would never have bought the property if we only had that necklace boundary to our property,' she had said.

Max and Lucy then progressed to correspondence and calls to Land Registry. The Assistant Registrar they spoke to had told them that Blackstone Cottage was not registered and that he had heard nothing from the Ogmores, but that as the land grab had taken place very recently squatter's rights would be difficult if not impossible to establish. Lucy says that when asked what exactly the word 'guarantee' meant on Title documents the Assistant Registrar gave a nervous laugh. 'It's not an absolute guarantee,' he said, 'we do have to rectify the register from time to time if we find there's been a mistake. If we do you'll be compensated for any loss of land.'

Max wanted to know what Land Registry did before first registering a property and was told the Registry relied on the deeds the owner sends. This gave rise to the obvious question:

'What if they're in conflict with deeds of other properties?'

'If the other properties are registered conflicts are sorted out beforehand.'

'But what if the other properties aren't registered?'

'Well, we can't do much then can we?'

'Couldn't you do what planning authorities do when a planning application comes in, couldn't you post a notice? Couldn't you send notices to neighbouring properties?'

'No we couldn't do that. Too expensive; too time-consuming. The rules don't require us to do that.'

‘So, not so much couldn’t as don’t have to. You could but you don’t, why not?’

Nervous giggle again. ‘Well, we never do that. The rules don’t require us to.’

If the ‘rules’ *had* required them to take the same measures as planning authorities, the chances are that the unpleasant predicament Max and Lucy now found themselves in could have been avoided. To this day no one has explained why such a relatively simple precaution is not part of ‘the rules’.

They had given their surveyor, Mr Nunn, all the Homestead plans they had dated after May 1963 when Blackstone Cottage was sold off as a separate property from Homestead, but discovered that the bundle of documents sent to them by their solicitor didn’t include any conveyance for that actual 1963 sale or any documents from before that date. A copy of the original conveyance in 1963 should have been in their ‘bundle’. It clearly had been in their bundle until recently as several documents, called ‘extracts’, recorded that it had been seen by solicitors carrying out the five or six sales of Homestead which had taken place since 1963, but now it had very inconveniently disappeared. Inconveniently for Max and Lucy. The first conveyance they had showing Blackstone Cottage as a separate property was dated nine months later and that showed Blackstone land exactly as on the *Homestead* Title plan.

The solicitor who’d acted for the Swales told them he’d sent everything his firm had, but that did not include anything prior to 1964. It was curious that he knew he had not seen any deed for a near hundred year-old house prior to 1964 and had not chased up the missing documents. He suggested Max write to the solicitors who’d acted for the Swales when purchasing Homestead in 1999, when it was first registered. The Swales hadn’t used the same solicitors just two years later when selling to Max and Lucy. Both solicitors practised in the same city. The city the Swales now lived in.

After the standard lawyers’ procrastination, the previous solicitors admitted that they still held all the earlier deeds for Homestead. Nobody had asked for them, why did Max want them? Max says, ‘He actually sounded distrustful as though asking for the deeds to our home was suspicious! What did he think we wanted them for, how long would he have held on to them and what would have happened to those interesting old documents if we hadn’t needed to hunt them down?’ These solicitors insisted that they had to have the Swales’ permission to release them. ‘Whose deeds are they, anyway?’ Max asks. He wanted an end to further procrastination so he said, with some truth, that he wanted to trace the history of the old house and the lawyer agreed to send them – if the Swales agreed! Max simulated fulsome gratitude and eventually all the earlier deeds arrived.

All except the crucial one for the first sale of the Black Hut in 1963 describing a necklace of land around it. Clearly it had been there during the 40 years since then as the extracts testified. They now had conveyances, beautiful, old, waxed documents in elegant script, dating back to the 19th century but not the crucial 1963 conveyance.

Meanwhile they were pressing ahead with plans for the house and land, in between family and friends and residual careers. They called on a few landscaping companies and were well on the way to selecting a local one with a good reputation when the man took a closer look at the plan of Homestead land.

'So, is this your land?' he asked, 'What is this plan exactly?'

According to Max, when he was told it was the Title plan of Homestead, the landscaper went rather quiet, staring at the plan and land. Max thought he was considering the landscaping challenge on wild terrain with a 40° gradient. Then the landscaper left promising to get back to them. They never managed to make contact with him again and it took a long time for the penny to drop. This was the man who had carried out the land-grab makeover for their next-door neighbour less than a year before. He wanted nothing more to do with the problem he'd helped – unwittingly – create.

It was February 2002 before they heard any more. A letter from Land Registry enclosed a copy of a conveyance, dated May 1963, which had been sent to them by Mrs Ogmore showing a parcel of land with a hut on it – the Black Hut – originally part of Homestead. There was nothing in the *wording* of the conveyance to indicate how much land went with the Hut but there was a plan attached. A crude child's drawing of a plan with wobbly lines showing a rectangle and the outline of the hut – and a scale: 1:2,500. There were two measurements written on the oblong of land: one for the short sides going downhill and one for the longer boundaries running parallel with the river, but this second measurement had been altered. Whatever measurement had originally been written, the first digit had been overwritten several times and then crossed out and the number '2' written above in a different colour ink. There was also a wonky arrow pointing to the corner of the rectangle near Homestead on the riverside away from the road and the words 'telegraph pole', suggesting that a pole had marked that end of the riverside boundary. Neither side of the crudely-drawn rectangle scaled to the measurements written there. In fact they scaled more or less to the measurements on Homestead's Title plan suggesting a somewhat smaller plot but a rectangle – not one with a curved boundary.

This was the conveyance Mrs Ogmore had been keeping from everyone for two years. It was easy to see why, but she had also sent Land Registry a much newer plan. This was another drawing of the plot of Blackstone Cottage land from an older and more artistic child. One who could use a ruler. It showed the outline of the house. It showed trees, steps and paths and it showed the new chalet-shed and the septic tank, but it didn't show the large compost box at the back of the shed some 10 feet or so more on to Homestead land, because although the drawing suggested the chalet was on Blackstone Cottage land, it also suggested that it was right up against the downhill boundary and there was no room for the compost bin.

From this newer plan Max and Lucy detected that Mrs Ogmore was admitting some trespasses on neighbours' land. The conifers the Ogmores had planted on the Ackroyd's land were shown as trespassing and another trespass, this time on Homestead land, by a stretch of path built in the farthest downhill riverside corner of the plot and out of sight to anyone including Max and Lucy. Nothing else apparently existed outside the boundaries of Blackstone Cottage according to this nice little gardening magazine drawing. Blackstone Cottage floated in a land, a world, a universe of its own without giving any useful indication of how Blackstone Cottage land related to Homestead and Dunroamin' land. This was strange bearing in mind that the artist, one Mr Hammer, had not only the copy of Homestead's Land Registry plan which had been given to Mrs Ogmore over a year earlier, but he also had access to several Ordnance Survey maps which showed how all three properties fitted together in the jigsaw. Even more curious, his new plan showed the roadside boundary as longer than the riverside boundary. The artist, Mr Hammer, had *marked* the end point on that roadside boundary, but had then ignored his mark and taken another point further on – just by a telephone pole. This extension allowed room for the chalet wholly inside Blackstone Cottage territory.

If the boundary had started downhill from the correct point it would run through the shed/chalet as drawn on his plan. There was no report accompanying this sketch to explain what Mr Hammer had been asked to survey and how he had carried out his task. No explanation. Certainly no explanation as to why Mr Hammer had added extra feet to the roadside boundary allowing him to draw a boundary line Homestead side of the brand new chalet.

This was a fiddled plan. A plan that did Mr Hammer's professional reputation (whatever it was) no favours. It was not a plan to hold its head up proudly in court. Amateur landscape gardeners would like it. To avoid showing the shed encroaching on Homestead land the plot shape was not a rectangle or a parallelogram – it was an amusingly contrived rhomboid. Not a plan to be taken seriously.

The Registrar (Assistant) wrote pointing out that unless Max and Lucy could produce their version of the May 1963 conveyance and it confirmed the looped boundary to Blackstone Cottage shown on their 1964 conveyance, the Ogmores' conveyance prevailed because it predated theirs.

A month or so later, however, Mr Assistant Registrar (Max and Lucy now called him Mr Beige) raised all the questions they had asked themselves about the Ogmores' conveyance and Mr Hammer's plan: the discrepancy between the scaled boundary lines and the figures written by them, and the clear fact that one had been altered. 'It does raise questions,' he wrote, and he did not seem to buy the notion that even if that conveyance plan had to be taken as the correct authority, the plot was anything other than a rectangle, so bearing in mind the altered figure and the scale provided on the plan, he was not persuaded by the measurements or the rhomboid pretension. The chalet trespassed on Homestead land. The roadside boundary was the only one accessible to measure and if it was not the same as the riverside boundary the conveyance would have recorded what it was. There was nothing in the wording of the conveyance itself about measurements. All the questions came in his letter written just before Max and Lucy were about to leave home for several weeks for research work that Max was still involved with. They needed to get their surveyor, Mr Nunn, back to do a survey and provide a report with photographs to help the gentlemen at Land Registry understand what they were dealing with. Land Registry told them that they had the right to claim back any costs they might incur if there was an error in the registration and reminded them that if they lost land as a result of that error they would be compensated. So! No worries then!

Mr Nunn sent in his report with supporting photographs based on Max and Lucy's plans. He had had to carry out the survey without access to Blackstone Cottage but, nevertheless, he confirmed serious encroachment. Everyone seemed to have difficulty working out the points of the compass. What was north to Blackstone Cottage was south to Homestead. This, and Mr Hammer's need to include the Ogmore chalet in Ogmore land, together with the somewhat impenetrable land itself and the confusions with angles, seemed to tie the opposing surveyors in knots. One, single, independent non-schizoid surveyor would have coped. Shame Mr Beige didn't propose it, better still insist on it. They would need to tie that floating garden down into the real physical world. Land Registry knows a bit about maps and suchlike – and about squatters. They have their own surveyors who would come to see for themselves how the land lay. Max and Lucy were confident their surveyors could sort it out. Nobody, Max and Lucy assured themselves, would be taken in by tricky plans and dubious conduct. Even if her figure for the roadside boundary was finally determined as correct, there were still five or more encroaching fence panels to explain.

Max wrote again to Mrs Ogmore pointing out that it was clear encroachment had taken place. He said no more than that on the subject. However, they got a very sharp reply 10 days later asserting that they did not own all the land they thought they owned as their Land Certificate was incorrect, and until a 'final determination' was made by Land Registry they were hardly in a position to make further assertions. The final paragraph gave an intimation of what was to come.

She regretted that, 'despite my attempts to conduct matters in a neighbourly way, by calling on you personally …'!

'So,' says Lucy, 'when we caught her trying to post her unfriendly letter in our non-existent letterbox and invited her in she was, in fact, calling on us personally in a neighbourly way.'

The letter continued, 'and offering a meeting with experts [Max and Lucy's proposal] you have chosen to continue to deal with matters in such a belligerent manner.' Belligerent was certainly how both Max and Lucy felt after reading that. If they ever imagined that this lady was going to feel embarrassment, and try to wriggle out of the trouble she was in without losing face, they were now finally disabused. Lucy felt more threatened by that dishonest account and what it revealed about the talents of their adversary than she did by the land theft. As things turned out she was right to do so.

Mrs Ogmore followed up that letter with an email complaining that a tree on Homestead land by the road had been blown over on to the overhead telephone wires. She informed them this was because of the 'hacking, chopping and sawing of trees, shrubs and branches by you and your agents'. Max and Lucy had not hacked, chopped or sawn anything within 100 feet of the tree. She also informed them that she had always treated that tree as the boundary between the properties. So, the end of her brand new encroaching fence was not the limit of her ambitions: the fallen tree was yet a further 40 feet into Homestead land. She instructed them to take action on the fallen tree immediately.

They let her know they had already taken action. She had another go repeating her exposition on the cause and informing them that she would hold them responsible for any loss or damage caused by 'you/your agent's act/s' which now posed a danger to her property (could that be the shed?) to the public and the BT service. This did not establish better neighbourly relations. Max, who had been so diplomatic when she made her 'neighbourly' visit now laid it on the line, pointing out that the property she referred to was illegally on their land and that they had asked her to remove it on more than one occasion.

He also rejected somewhat pedantically any analysis by the 'ill-informed and inexpert of the life cycle of trees and their morbidity'. BT removed the fallen tree free of charge.

It is undeniable that relations started off on the wrong foot: Max and Lucy didn't like the brazen theft. She didn't like the threat of having to move her shed and hand land back – or pay for it. No meeting of minds there. This, of course, is the stuff of neighbour disputes and only much later did it occur to Max and Lucy that there was a deliberate strategy to raise hackles and up the ante. Their 'firm' response played straight into the hands of the enemy; by making their strategy one of uncompromising determination to make her remove the trespass, of standing up to bullies, lawyers and courts would see only battling neighbours, six of one and half a dozen of the other. Lucy and Max would be tarred with the Ogmores' brush.

Faced with conflicting plans, Land Registry decided to join in and sent their own surveyor. Max and Lucy invited the Ackroyds to meet Land Registry's man as they would also be affected by the outcome, since they found themselves living a little too close for comfort to a territorially ambitious neighbour. They parked their cars just by Ogmore's car port and the houses were not that far apart. Other neighbours Max and Lucy had got to know had noted the land grab and some even offered to write Statements to that effect. Visitors from other parts of the country, particularly town dwellers, were shocked at the 'blatant cheek of it!' These visitors didn't know that the area was one of the last in the country to require land registration and was dotted with scorch marks from fireballs of boundary disputes blazing up and down the riverbanks. They knew of three in 2002 and several more have been added since, just in that small locality. There was at least one coolly organised squatter action which didn't last long but was certainly dramatic with police and hospitals involved, most of the others were or are boundary disputes based on deeds good and bad, and they tended to last until financial exhaustion or the courts, which often means both, put an end to the misery.

The Ackroyds had played quite an important role so far. They had told Max and Lucy what had been going on before they moved in. They reported that there was no sign of Mr Ogmore and that his wife had made no effort to speak to them until just after they had started to report what she had been up to. They were amused that she should now want to make friends with them. They had learnt that she could be very civil.

Max asked the Land Registry surveyor to mark on the roadside fence where the boundary to Blackstone Cottage ended according to his registered plan, and also where it ended according to the Ogmore's deed plan. All four of them then left him to his own devises – or so they thought. They thought wrong. They'd actually left him in the hands of the mysterious *Mr* Ogmore. Lucy saw this unknown neighbour, a solicitor in London they had been told, arriving by car as she walked back home. 'That was at 10 in the morning,' she said, 'so we were just a little surprised when the Land Registry man turned up in late afternoon to say that he had finished. How could it have taken so long to measure the plot according to the two different plans?' Three years later they found out how.

Mr Beige made it clear that Mr Hammer's plan was only useful for identifying very roughly where paths and trees, house and shed were and also the parking bay wall at the other end of the property which divided Blackstone Cottage from Dunroamin', 'but it is not a reliable plan to assist the determination of boundaries to Blackstone Cottage,' he wrote in a letter to both sides. The report produced by the Land Registry's surveyor was not impressive either, although the plan was an improvement on Mr Hammer's and did at least include the other properties around.

In the meantime Max and Lucy decided this was a quarrel between Land Registry and the Ogmores who were, after all, contesting Land Registry's registration. All the squatters had to do was fill in the form, pay the fee, provide their evidence and make their argument. Mr Hammer's imaginative plan had not quite done the job Mrs Ogmore had paid for. The man at HM Land Registry was not impressed by rhomboids designed to encompass trespassing chalet-sheds. He agreed with Max that the rules of geometry prevailed and rectangles, however crudely drawn, with measurements on two sides had the same measurements on the other two sides unless there was compelling evidence to the contrary, and there was no compelling evidence. Mr Beige was not persuaded by her attempt to argue that a reference to a telegraph pole on the riverside boundary actually meant a telephone pole on the road. As the dispute was with the rather laid-back gentleman at Land Registry and not in the fraught, adversarial combat zone of the courts where rhetorical skills, bullying by costs and disingenuous argument can be an effective tactic, Max and Lucy remained as relaxed as the man at the Registry. This claim was being investigated. Plans were being studied, surveyors were involved and so far no costs were building up for them to pay as Land Registry offered indemnity. Lawyers they might be, but the Ogmores could not exploit their superior fire power against their enemy if the threat of financial ruin by legal costs was not a weapon to hand. The battle was in the investigative Registrar's office not an adversarial court.

Max pointed out to both the Land Registrar and to Mrs Ogmore that even if her questionable deed plan prevailed, her Mr Hammer had come up with a very odd interpretation of it, and even according to his plan she was encroaching over the Ackroyds' land and Homestead land and further along the road.

She replied stating that she had every confidence in her highly respected and experienced surveyor. In fact Mr Hammer was an architect and building surveyor, not a qualified land surveyor at all, which explains the pretty garden plan he'd provided but does not excuse the consequences of his unprofessional involvement. By now it was clear that Land Registry did not share her confidence and, noting her approach, her manner over the previous months, sensibly urged Max and Lucy to reach an agreement with her. They were about to leave so they thought they'd make a start by writing to her to propose that everyone agreed certain ascertainable facts. She dismissed the idea of ascertainable facts. Only Mr Hammer's plan would do.

Max and Lucy decided that the only way she was going to get what she wanted was if she claimed squatter's rights – *adverse possession*[4] in legal speak. They could recall hints at that in some of what she had said when she was caught trying to post her unpleasant letter through their letterbox-free door and in the contents of her unfriendly letter. She had repeated the claim that she had gardened in the area she had seized for over 12 years, on more than one occasion. Max and Lucy really hoped she wouldn't try that claim as it could get very messy and pit her word against the words of their witnesses. They decided they would have to get their Witness Statements in writing when they returned from their travels.

They were hopeful that by the time they got back the following June she would have been persuaded by Mr Beige to finally make her formal claim to their land, with her evidence and with proper plans. Nothing could progress unless and until she did that. They assumed that her paperwork would include copies of her instructions to said 'expert surveyor' and his reports explaining his curious interpretation of her 1963 plan. They assumed that as it was a matter between her and Mr Beige he would ensure that she got on with any claim she wanted to make. An unwise assumption. She did not want to make any claim. She was in possession of their property and she was not going to do anything that might allow them to prise her hands off it any time soon. On the contrary, their absence was very helpful in the growing season. It is a mistake to go away for a lengthy period when there's a potentially serious dispute around, but that lesson took Max and Lucy a long time to learn.

TWO
2002: June–September

'Matilda told such Dreadful Lies
It made one Gasp and Stretch one's eyes.'
Hilaire Belloc, Cautionary Tales – Matilda

When they returned in early June they were immediately immersed in their building and gardening projects, and the permanent fixtures of family and friends. Summer brought more visitors. As far as the land grab was concerned, they waited for action from the Ogmores and Her Majesty's Land Registry. They admit with hindsight leaving the matter entirely in their hands was not altogether wise. Many people would have had the foresight to anticipate that. Max and Lucy can list a lot of hindsight observations in what follows and few moments of foresight.

In other circumstances they would have opted to negotiate a deal to get rid of this bother before it became yet more of a nuisance, but Mrs Ogmore did not seem to want any sort of negotiation. She seemed keen to seize every opportunity to cause antagonism by clearing and using more of Homestead land. They could see what she was up to by peeking behind her trespassing fence running along the road, but they could see it far more clearly from the other path, the one running parallel with the road just 15 feet below it, right up to the compost box and shed. When they started to collect Witness Statements they met a local who had carried out a lot of work on Homestead for the family who had owned it from the early eighties until they sold to the Swales in 1999. He confirmed that the path had always been there and that Rick Stone, his employer, used to run his dogs along it right up to Blackstone Cottage's terrace and the roadside conifers. He was adamant that there had been no shed, paths or fence while he worked there, that the land was just wild hillside and that neither the Ogmores when they moved to the area, nor the previous owners objected to Rick Stone's dogs on the land. Lucy later made contact with Mr Stone who emphatically agreed with his ex-employee.

Mrs Ogmore's letters to the gentleman at Land Registry quite subtly projected an image of innocent victim who had always lived in peaceful harmony with her neighbours. This was somewhat disingenuous. Whereas most of the neighbours Max and Lucy met confessed they did not know the couple, the one or two who knew something of her had other views. It was most unreasonable, she complained, that she was having to cope with uncalled for unfriendliness from these newcomers, it wasn't as though she knew anything about their registered Title until she was shocked to receive their letters last November! So – a difficult lady and an amnesiac.

However, the correspondence from Mr Beige seemed to suggest that all these attempts at image projection were becoming increasingly redundant as he became more aware of the facts. Mrs Ogmore may have begun to suspect that she wasn't going to get what she wanted by relying on Mr Hammer's plan and as things stood she wasn't able to exploit her superior fire power as a legal professional dealing with amateurs because the matter was not being litigated – expensively litigated. It was not going to plan. Ironically, if she had thought Max and Lucy were after ransom strip money she would have been wrong. This business may have been the most important item on her agenda, she and her husband may have been planning the land grab for a long time, evidence suggested they had certainly planned it for a few years before Max and Lucy bought Homestead, but it wasn't much more than an irritant to them – at the time, and a very good story for friends, family and their new neighbours.

Maybe she and her invisible husband had decided to pin their hopes on a squatter claim.[1] Apart from anything else this would add further delay, allowing time for all sorts of land 'rectification' and could perhaps lead to the courtroom where she could hope to use her superior fire power. Land Registry was taking things slowly but she did need more time, an adverse possession claim needed serious titivation of the wild land: spraying to clear the weeds and undergrowth, then some odd judicious felling and lopping, and then planting.

It was unfortunate for her that the new owners of Homestead did not have a mortgage so the Title deeds were theirs to inspect at any time. If they'd had a mortgage their Title deeds would be held by a building society or bank and they'd not be in a position to realise what was going on until the jungle on the land she wanted was transformed to look like an established garden and thus at the very least, confuse and confound. Her pranks were not original. Stealing bits of neighbouring property when that property was in the process of changing hands was not unknown in the area. And the Ogmores benefitted from the dense woodland and the steep hillside hiding the annexation as it gradually progressed. The new owners wouldn't know where their boundaries were precisely – or even imprecisely. The terrain allowed for all sorts of mischief. Even with the plan and without the Ogmores, it would have taken some time to know where Homestead's unfenced boundaries were.

Lucy wrote again to the Swales to find out more about their encounter with the lady at Christmas or New Year 1999/2000. Somewhat to her surprise their account stayed almost unaltered. They admitted that they had come across the tree-felling by chance and immediately spoken to Mrs Ogmore, but now they were careful to avoid any description of that encounter as heated and forgot to recall that Mrs Ogmore had told them about her profession and her claim to own far more land, as described by the other witness, the impartial one, Mr Jenkins. They also described their later visit to Mrs Ogmore which was, according to their account, amicable. Whereas over the phone months earlier they had expressed strong disapproval of Mrs Ogmore's actions, now they described a scene of friendly neighbourliness. Amicable or not, they admitted they had left her copy of their Title plan and that she had said that her deeds showed something different but could not let them see the documents. They had put their house on the market just a month or so later and seemingly quite forgot about that meeting when answering the SPIF question on disputes.

At the end of June came Mrs Ogmore's letter claiming adverse possession. Not just the land she/they had already taken but a lot more besides. 'I have always viewed this land as mine. I have been gardening here since 1988.' She claimed more than 4,000 square feet extra of Homestead land. The extra square feet were added by selecting another roadside pole as a boundary marker, even though no one was persuaded that any post on the roadside marked the boundary. Poles were dotted all along the roadside, some usefully carrying power or telephone connections, others in permanent retirement with wires cut. This new marker pole was a very old redundant electricity pole with the cut wires pointing down the hill and sharply angled towards the riverside boundary of Blackstone Cottage. It could well have linked with another pole down the hillside. It could well have linked with a pole at the boundary edge of Blackstone Cottage: the one described on Blackstone Cottage's 1963 roughly drawn plan.

Mrs Ogmore decided that this dead pole on the roadside was the one shown on her plan. Her new choice of pole gave the Ogmores a roadside boundary of over 150 feet more than Homestead's Title plan suggested. This new boundary marker pole more than doubled the size of her plot. It was difficult to see what gardening had been done with the jungle in this newest claim. It was on the steepest area of the hillside – practically a cliff. Apart from an old Homestead hedge along the roadside right up to the Ogmore's new fence, no cultivation had ever taken place on that 'cliff'side.

Another survey was on the way. The cool Mr Beige had decided that in the light of the latest claim, Ordnance Survey experts should be called in. Max wrote trying to persuade Hazel Ogmore to explain her claims both old and new, but as elaborate confusions began to unfold, he set to work to persuade her to meet at her place and explain in situ. It took two weeks but they finally succeeded. And they actually got to shake hands with the elusive Mr Ogmore. He was not unpleasant, a bit nervous perhaps, a bit on edge, but he left it mainly to his wife giving the impression that this was her battle and he was keeping out of it. Max and Lucy later surmised that this might be because he had a reputation to protect. They could not have been more wrong.

This new Mrs Ogmore did do smiles. The visitors got the Swale treatment this time. Did they want to sit outside on the patio or in here? Would they like a drink? They opted for inside and tea.

'And now,' she said, leaning forward hands on knees like an infant school teacher talking to toddlers, 'the ball is in your court.' A curious statement, but decidedly friendly.

'Well,' said Lucy, 'we've come to talk over your claim.'

'Ah,' she said, still smiling, 'it seems you don't accept that your registration is wrong – so we seem to have a disagreement, a dispute.'

Max replied, 'You're disputing our registration so you need to make your claim to Land Registry, don't you, and provide supporting evidence? When you do that we can get the ball rolling. We don't have any dispute with them but we do think you should lodge your claim, provide your evidence. We're prepared to wait a bit more but we can't wait forever. It's a couple of years since the Swales gave you a copy of Homestead's plan and nine months since we asked you to remove the trespass and,' Max added, 'the land doesn't stand still – it keeps changing.' The infant school teacher leant back. The smile disappeared. These toddlers were obviously rather naughty; they needed firm handling and the withdrawal of special privileges. No more smiles. And no afternoon drink either it seemed. Max and Lucy persevered. They wanted to extract as much information as they could. Why, Lucy asked, didn't they look at their deeds before they bought? Surely they checked them when the Swales gave them a copy of Homestead's registration plan especially as they disputed it? Why had they commissioned the tree felling without checking their deed plan? Why did they still go ahead and have landscaping done without sorting out any conflict between their deed plan and the Homestead registered plan, if they thought Land Registry had made a mistake? Why didn't they get in touch with the Registry immediately they saw that land they believed theirs was registered to Homestead?

Max pointed out that as they were lawyers they would know the problems ahead and how important it was to sort things out as soon as they were alerted to a possible conflict. He asked them to explain all this and also why they believed the land they had taken was theirs. But it was clear that Mrs Ogmore spotted irony when she heard it and was still withdrawing privileges.

Mr Ogmore intervened then. He said that they didn't look at the deed plan to Blackstone Cottage before they bought. They relied on another plan. When they came to buy the vendor had been very vague and had just waved his hand at the panorama and told them the boundary was at a path way down through the trees towards the river and Mr Ogmore waved his hand vaguely at the panorama down through the trees towards the river. Max and Lucy remembered what the Ackroyds had told them about the peg that had suddenly appeared on the path running some 200 feet below the road. The peg with 'Blackstone Cottage' written on it. As for the tree felling – apparently they believed the land belonged to them. But why?

The Ogmores avoided the question. Mrs Ogmore immediately suggested they looked at the garden and Max and Lucy followed her down a long, narrow staircase to their terrace. Like many houses on the hillside, Blackstone Cottage is a bungalow at road level but has one storey below built into the hillside at half the depth of the road-level living rooms. She led them to her chalet. Lucy says it is an exceptionally nice, large chalet-shed with French windows, a short veranda and hanging baskets and so on. All very new with garden table, chairs and parasol.

Once there Mrs Ogmore seemed to have little to say. Max and Lucy knew from their neighbour witnesses that first an old shed had been erected down the hillside almost out of sight from the road and then about a year ago the land had been terraced and this new chalet built in its present position. Max prompted her by saying, 'So you put a shed down the hill first, a year or so ago, and then you had this bit landscaped last year establishing a flat terrace on the hillside and built this new one here – to get more sun – is that it?' She seemed surprised. Perhaps she didn't know that informants had briefed them so well. 'I've been gardening this area for years and years – ever since we moved here in 1988. I love gardening. I had a small shed on our patio for the first 10 years.'

Lucy pointed out that they didn't make sheds like the one they were now looking at until recently. She added that the Swales and the previous owners, the Stones, certainly would have noticed it and the neighbours too, of course. 'And as you may know, Rick Stone had Homestead surveyed just three years ago when he was selling up. All the neighbours we've asked say the chalet only appeared last summer and all this was jungle. They've put all that in writing. Of course, they can't see the shed now. Now you've put the fence up.'

Mrs Ogmore's eyes widened. She would like to see those Statements. She then told them that she would get Statements too confirming that she had always gardened there. According to both Max and Lucy she pointed to fledgling plants installed obviously very recently around the area of the chalet. Max suggested that they save a lot of time and hassle and exchange their Witness Statements. Apparently she blanched at that and started to walk back to the house. 'All in good time,' she informed them, adding, 'Perhaps I should see your Statements first.'

Max was unimpressed with that and reminded her that it was up to her to act; her argument was with Land Registry, not them. She should send her evidence there and as soon as possible. It was seven months since the Registry had been alerted to the problem, but they couldn't do anything until she lodged her claim and provided her evidence. Mrs Ogmore said that Land Registry was dealing with the matter. Max insisted that they were unable to deal with the matter until she made her claim and in the meantime here she was trespassing on Homestead registered land. What did she want – a court case?

She responded with, 'Land Registry is the judicial authority in this matter, they are dealing with it.' She spoke with firm authority and continued her way back to the house. Max and Lucy were being dismissed. She held the front door open and Max, who admits he was a little angry with her arrogance by now, tried again asking if she was sure she wanted a serious, formal dispute adding, 'As lawyers you'll know what that can lead to, we know something about it ourselves.' Time to worry them a bit he thought. She gestured towards the front door, 'Your ownership is disputed,' she said, 'and Land Registry is the judicial authority dealing with it.' Class dismissed.

Far from sorting things out, this meeting left them feeling vulnerable. Lucy began to suspect that this neighbour dispute would not be so easy to resolve. The Ogmores occupied the land, had time on their side and gold-medal obfuscation skills.

Mrs Ogmore wrote to Land Registry saying that she and her husband had had a meeting with Max and Lucy which was 'unproductive'. 'Like a factory on strike is unproductive,' said Max. It was all too clear that the

Ogmores intended to delay matters as long as possible. The creeping fear was that the Ogmores *wanted* a battle and one using their weapon of choice: litigation. Lucy and Max still had some confidence it would not come to that as Mr Beige was dealing with things and he, not a judge, was 'the judicial authority'. To ensure that Land Registry's man was up to speed, Max sent him a copy of his letter to the Ogmores pointing out that the purpose of the meeting had been to provide evidence supporting their claim to Homestead land and they'd failed to provide anything.

Max also gave some useful consumer advice pointing out that if it were true, as they claimed, that they'd had the entire fence creosoted because it was rotten and needed protection, and not because they wanted to confuse witnesses, they should have creosoted both sides and not just the side visible from the road. He also suggested that they could have a claim against the supplier for the largest and most recent section of fence as it should not have rotted in a year. He then took his tongue out of cheek and repeated for the umpteenth time the instruction to remove the trespasses. He asked why two solicitors would fail to take the basic precaution of checking plans before purchase, particularly as the land was unregistered and was unfenced on at least three sides. 'After all, this is contrary to lawyers' standard practice to advise purchasers of unregistered property to check boundaries against the conveyance and attached plans.'

He went on to ask why they did not register the property. It was not compulsory[2] in that region in 1988, but there was nothing to stop them registering it as a sensible precaution and was also considered good practice. He then asked the sort of questions they would want answers to if, as seemed increasingly likely, they were forced to get Land Registry's solicitor to help. He finished with a reprise of the questions which should have been answered at the meeting if they really wanted to avoid entanglement in courts. Most lawyers make a point of avoiding courts in their personal lives. They knew what a gamble it can be. But these two were not the usual kind. Max and Lucy feared the Ogmores would do nothing unless forced to. They were in possession of Homestead land and every week they were altering it to convey the impression they had, indeed, been gardening there for years.

The warning that witnesses can dissolve into thin air when asked for signed Statements had proved groundless, and Max and Lucy had four or five from witnesses to the very recent unilateral annexing of Homestead territory. After refreshing his memory with a visit, Mr Jenkins had put his report in writing, including his recollection of Mrs Ogmore's claim that she and her husband were lawyers. He took exception to that. Would the Swales have acted differently if they had remained ignorant of the fact that their potential opponents were lawyers? Then there was the unequivocable Statement from Rick Stone's handyman: 'I can state that the area behind the new fence was undeveloped while I worked on Homestead. There was no fence, no shed, no paths and no cultivation.'

As the Swales had only been in Homestead for less than a year, it seemed a good idea to contact the previous owner, Rick Stone. He would have had something to do with the first registration of the property in April 1999. Max and Lucy had had good reports from the locals about him. He was well known, being a bit of a celebrity, and well liked. He'd moved out of Homestead after some 16 lively years there during which time he had renovated much of the property. He hadn't wanted to sell Homestead at first so he let it from time to time for a few years before finally deciding to part with it permanently.

Tracking him down wasn't easy but when they finally succeeded, he offered to write confirming that there had been no shed or extended fence when he sold in 1999, and that as far as he was concerned the Ogmores owned hardly any land on Homestead side of their house, the boundary was just as shown on all the previous deeds, the plan his solicitors sent to the Swales, the plan sent to Land Registry for first registration. He was absolutely certain he would have known if the boundary was anything different. He told Lucy that his dogs enjoyed a run along the higher woodland path running from his outbuildings right up to the conifers on Blackstone Cottage's roadside boundary, just below the road and parallel with it, and no one questioned them running on land the Ogmores were now claiming as theirs. As far as he was concerned there were just three or four fence panels indicating the extent of Blackstone Cottage's land on Homestead's side. Up until he moved out, Homestead's boundary with Blackstone Cottage was just as described on the registered plan and no previous Blackstone Cottage owner had objected – nor had the Ogmores.

It was in a later conversation with him that she learned why Mr Ogmore had hardly been around and why he left the action to his wife. Mr Ogmore *had* been a solicitor but wasn't any more. The Law Society had struck him off their list of acceptable members – following a stint at Her Majesty's pleasure. Neither Max nor Lucy is inclined to believe that anyone sent to prison – even for white-collar crime – is a scoundrel and guilty as charged, however… .

The Law Society confirmed the news and gave an indication of the reasons. As well as the usual use and abuse of clients' monies – and gross overcharging even by lawyer rates, there was also a reference to accounts being 'inappropriately' written and documents that had been altered. Max and Lucy should have followed that up immediately and paid the £25 demanded for a copy of the Society's report and adjudication, but they didn't, not immediately. They had suspicions about the authenticity of the Ogmore conveyance plan, as it had clearly been altered and there was disparity between the measurements and the scaling and now they knew he had done a stint in prison for (among other crimes) playing around with documents. They had the case reference and thought that enough. Rick Stone added that he had nothing to do with 'those people' (but that his wife had) and advised Lucy to contact a solicitor he recommended in a nearby town. Advice they very unwisely ignored. Finding a good solicitor is very important but difficult. If you get a recommendation – take it, particularly if, like Lucy and Max, you want someone local and you're new to the area.

This was the first unwise decision they made. The second unwise decision had been to go away for six weeks expecting the correct action by the very people whose every interest lay in inaction, and Land Registry. Even if their adversaries had not been lawyers deficient in scruples, they should have treated this dispute as important business and asked family, friends and a few neighbours to keep an eye on things. Someone they could contact while away.

James Nunn, Max and Lucy's surveyor, wrote again after comparing the imaginative Hammer plan with the dodgy 1963 conveyance plan on which it was purportedly based, noting the lengthened roadside boundary on Hammer's version. The only fixed point on the plan was the point on the roadside where the Ogmore's carport wall met Dunroamin's boundary. But there was no fixed point at the other riverside end, so James Nunn sent an amended Hammer plan illustrating the splay of possible boundary lines radiating out from that fixed point to accommodate a sensible margin of error.

Lucy and Max had opted for the single, independent surveyor as the best bet for a timely and economical outcome, Land Registry's man having failed to fill that role. But then Mr Beige commissioned another expert, this time from Ordnance Survey, to survey Blackstone Cottage basing the work on one OS map.

Meanwhile Max and Lucy were busy trying to tame the wilderness around Homestead into a terraced garden. The house, too, was by now in full renovation mode and about to challenge structural engineering expertise with an extension out over the hillside to take better advantage of the spectacular view. Even so, they *could* make time to deal with the shenanigans from next door without losing sleep. Next door was about 100 yards away and invisible, lost in vegetation. So, this was not like neighbour disputes in a town or city where disagreements with next door can be more like a battle between conjoined twins.

Even though she could neither be seen nor heard, Mrs Ogmore still had a talent to annoy. Not only did they have to write long letters correcting her reshaping of reality, but she seemed impervious to the corrections, simply ignoring them. She exasperated rather than just irritated them. She informed them that, 'the Land Registry is being requested' (present continuous tense) 'to act as the judicial forum in which the boundary dispute is to be resolved and nothing further can be achieved by exchanging correspondence.' In other words she was not going to answer any of Max's questions.

Although there was no evidence that she was getting anywhere with Mr Beige, Max and Lucy decided after the OS survey that it would be worth the effort to visit him at his office some 60 miles away to get the results and speak to him face to face. They also wanted to see and feel this, so far, unconvincing 1963 plan. Was it really part of the 1963 conveyance? Was it genuine and even if it was were the two numbers part of the original or had they been 'inappropriately written' later – bearing in mind that nothing else in the conveyance nor any other evidence supported those figures?

The big steel and glass Land Registry office lay silent and still, cushioned in tasteful landscaping. Hard to believe anything went on there. But then if their experience was anything to go by, whatever did go on went on exceedingly slowly.

Mr Beige was very civil but the first alarming piece of information he gave them was that Hazel Ogmore had not formally lodged an application to have the matter investigated. Land Registry was not acting as the 'judicial forum'. Nobody was. She had lied. Things were moving very slowly because she hadn't pressed the start button, not even for her claim that the Homestead Title plan should be rectified according to her 1963 plan, and certainly not for this new 'adverse possession' claim. That was followed by the news that the 1963 conveyance had been forwarded to him 'by Mrs Ogmore's solicitors'! They pointed out that Mrs Ogmore *was* her solicitors and wondered if the mortgage company had realised that when they forwarded such a crucial document to her. Lucy remembered the scrupulous care taken 20 years earlier when she had gone to look at her deeds at her building society's office. Then she was never to be left alone with them. Now this couple with dubious scruples had had the documents in their care – for months … at least. Plenty of time for inappropriate writing.

The languid gentleman seemed unconcerned, however. He played with the original of the 1963 conveyance. Showed how it was tied together, scoffed at the scruffy plan but saw little chance that it had been inserted later. He expressed the view that the telegraph pole referred to on the plan was not a roadside telephone pole. No, Land Registry did not have the expertise to test the ink forensically. A private forensic laboratory might be able to. As for mediation … No, they don't offer mediation but they could pass all this over to HM Land Registry's solicitor, if both parties agreed. They couldn't see their neighbour passing things over to any impartial legal investigation without a lot of prodding. But how to prod and what with? Max had an idea of something electrical.

They feared the man might actually fall asleep before their very eyes until the moment they turned to the squatter claim. He sparked from beige to red. 'You must act and you must act soon. We can't do anything on that,' he insisted. 'You haven't made clear that as she has not made a claim for adverse possession that land is yours and she must remove herself and all her trappings. You must not be seen to tolerate it. See a lawyer. And soon. It's theft isn't it? She's trying to steal your land.' He showed them the two survey results making clear that everything outside their conveyance plan except the sewerage cover was very, very new. 'As you can't find your version of the 1963 plan, hers wins on paper, but if you can provide evidence to discredit it, you should do so. Apart from those numbers there's nothing in their conveyance to support those measurements. The plan has a scale and I scale the boundaries to less. In any case everything outside that rectangle is on your land. It looks as though she's trying to steal it. Happens a lot, squatting,' he said. 'Steal someone else's property. It's theft. And land is property. See a lawyer. We can't deal with an adverse possession claim. That's for the courts to decide. Either she lodges a claim and provides the evidence or she removes herself. She's playing for time. She's in possession and she's waiting for you to act. So act. See a lawyer. You are entitled to have the fence and shed removed.' He slowed, cooled down, 'If you believe she's squatting on your land, I couldn't possibly comment of course, but court action might get her to see you mean business. Think about it and see a lawyer.'

They got the message. On the journey home Max suggested they try to have the plan tested forensically. See if the writing was genuine 1963 vintage. 'We'll say we'll offer not to contest the rectangle once it has passed the forensic test.' Lucy agreed. 'And we'll see a lawyer,' she added.

And that is what they did.

Was it the threat of the forensic test? Was it what Max and Lucy did next on the advice of the lawyer they turned to? Or was it just that the Ogmores would have taken any opportunity to get things out of the hands of investigating Land Registry and into adversarial court confrontation no matter what? Mrs Ogmore objected strongly to their visit to Mr Beige and wrote a very terse letter to him complaining that, 'no doubt (they) had managed to glean, *free of charge*, useful information from somebody in your position and with such invaluable experience.' That letter copied by Mr Beige to Max and Lucy showed how displeased she was. Possibly because she did not expect them to take the initiative.

The next mistake Max and Lucy made was to try a local solicitor, not Rick Stone's recommendation, and without checking if he was a litigation specialist. They didn't know there was a distinction. They thought all lawyers did litigation. Max knew London 'Rottweilers' who would have done a proper job. They didn't think they needed a Rottweiler. Their position was so strong – particularly as the land they might lose if that dodgy rectangle plan prevailed mattered little to them. They had over three acres of land and Land Registry would compensate them for any losses. The squatter business was no threat at all. No court would give these squatters the time of day once they knew how they'd played the last three years and looked at the evidence. That is what they thought.

The local man, Julian Pilling, agreed that he would write the formula letter: Move in seven days or we will take action to move you. He also agreed that they should cut through the anticipated prevaricating games and show they meant business. He suggested removing a couple of trespassing fence panels themselves. He said that under the circumstances, as they'd asked the Ogmores often enough to either come up with a substantiated claim or remove the trespass, they were fully, legitimately, permitted to exercise self-help and remove the new section of fence their side of the mark made by the Land Registry surveyor.

And that is what they did. They removed just two of the eleven fence panels and the post between them on their side of the mark – just in case the 1963 plan prevailed. They put a note through the Ogmores' door saying what they had done pointing out that they had left the panel where the surveyor had marked the end of Blackstone Cottage's roadside boundary to await Land Registry's determination on the 1963 conveyance.

The next day a policeman called. He was a genial man and when he saw for himself the plans, heard something of the story and saw a couple of Witness Statements he was happy to advise. He knew a bit about squatting and was rather entertaining on the subject. 'It's your land,' he said. 'She's done nothing to lay claim to any this side of that mark. I suggest you take down the other panels on the squatter land. But no more sawing off the posts. Leave them,' he said and left. They went back up the road a few hours later and acted on his suggestion. They removed five more panels leaving the skeletal posts behind. A man driving by stopped. Both Max and Lucy remember the ensuing conversation.

'You're going to get yourself into trouble doing that,' he said. It was the

Ogmore's gardener. 'Why?' Lucy asked. 'Surely you're the one in trouble trespassing on our land. We told you to stop clearing it.'

'Oh ho! Ho! You're gonna be in trouble.'

'What – like your Mr Ogmore? Prison trouble?'

Pausing to take account of that, he then said, 'Mr Ogmore is very nice man.'

'Not everybody thinks so. There's surface nice and deep down nice,' Lucy replied as he drove away.

Mrs Ogmore got the solicitor's letter the next day advising that she remove the shed and other trespasses within seven days or they would be obliged to do it themselves and charge for the work. The proper conventional response was to reply asking for a stay of action and start negotiations. That is what any solicitor would propose if he or she were advising the Ogmores. That is the textbook, conventional set of responses according to the legal books and according to Julian Pilling, but the Ogmores are not conventional neighbours and they are not conventional lawyers either. Hazel Ogmore was her own solicitor acting for herself and she did not advise herself to act in the conventional way. Hazel Ogmore's response was a letter on her firm's paper informing Max and Lucy that she – er – her firm, Bulmer & Co., intended to apply for an injunction *ex parte*[3] against them entering any of the land she claimed, and named a court some 50 miles away. The letter informed them that, 'We are instructed by Mrs H. Ogmore to represent her in a claim for damages for trespass to her land.'

This was the first schizophrenic missive on that firm's headed paper the couple received. There were many more to come.

You might imagine that Max and Lucy would be quite pleased to get some judge sorting out the troublemakers. After all there was no doubt the Ogmores were trespassing even if the 1963 plan were accepted; Mr Hammer's plan had been well and truly hammered and they had enough Witness Statements to knock any further adverse possession/squatter claim on the head.

They weren't pleased. Not in the least bit. Quite the opposite. They, or rather Lucy, knew altogether too much about courts and lawyers playing around with neighbour disputes and she had no desire to refresh her knowledge. She knew too much because she'd been there before and she knew from experience once courts are involved complexity, confusion and costs in time and money were a dangerous possibility.

Twenty years earlier Lucy, along with quite a few others, had become convinced that as problem-solvers and dispute-resolvers, courts and lawyers were simply not 'fit for purpose'. You might think that this is the voice of someone who lost a case. You'd be wrong. They, that is to say, Lucy and her late husband,

Felix, won the case. She doesn't call the outcome a win, nor did Felix, nor did her family. Nor did Max. So they did not relish court combat over a boundary or an adverse possession claim with anybody at all, least of all with any version of Mrs Ogmore, Mistress of Confusion and Disingenuousness and, moreover, fee-free Solicitor in Person.

THREE
1983–1984

'The one great principle of English law is to make business for itself.'

Charles Dickens, Bleak House

So, here's the story.

Felix and Lucy bought a house in a city. A small, ancient city. They moved with their two daughters in the hot, sunny summer of 1976. It was a tall Edwardian semi-detached house with a long, thin garden and a narrow, fenced passage down the side allowing access for wheelbarrows, bicycles, balloons and so on. They liked the house and the friendly neighbourhood. 'Memories of our first seven years there are always sunny,' Lucy says.

Their house had a dilapidated, old brick-built shed which enjoyed the sunniest position at the south-facing back of the house. After seven years they finally started to knock it down to replace it with a sun-trap breakfast room. An architect designed what he described as a boring box and they decided, despite his protestations, to drop the floor level to that of the garden for the sake of the neighbours on the other side of the fence so that it would be less of an intrusion. They were not obliged to drop the level. Nor were they obliged to have an inappropriate flat roof, but they decided that it would also be less of an intrusion for next door.

It's not as though these particular neighbours were into the house beautiful. In fact when they came to view their future home before purchase Lucy remembers the condition of the house on the other side of the fence did give her pause for thought – but not for long. They'd lived in various houses in various communities and not encountered neighbour difficulties – quite the contrary. The forsaken house did not appear threatening, although a casual enquiry about it to their vendor at a pre-purchase viewing did not elicit the fulsome assurances they had anticipated. The elderly vendor avoided the enquiry, but her daughter assured Felix and Lucy that the neighbours were 'all right really'. Her mother became tight-lipped and said nothing. Later the daughter whispered that the neighbours in the dilapidated house weren't really a problem – any more. Her mother just didn't understand them. They were arty, and while the children were growing up they were rather wild and noisy, but the children had grown up and left home. Well, Lucy and Felix were quite 'arty' too, most of their friends were, so, no problem.

'Ted and Dorothy next door (the semi-attached) are lovely, perfect neighbours,' said elderly vendor as they left. And so they proved to be, even tolerating the house renovation work Felix and Lucy undertook late into the night. As for the arty neighbours, Felix soon established a good relationship. They seemed to Lucy and Felix Graham to be live-and-let-live people, just like most neighbours, just like themselves.

It took 11 court visits to teach them they were wrong. As the lessons progressed they observed that they were lucky not to live in those parts of the world or those epochs in human history where neighbour disharmony can mean something a little more serious than visits to the local county court, where it can lead to considerably less pleasant outcomes. Then they were thinking of Northern Ireland, the Lebanon, Israel and Palestine, Nigeria or North Africa. More places have been added since then – the former Yugoslavia, Rwanda, Chechnya, Sudan, Somalia, Sri Lanka, Iraq, Syria – the list goes tragically on and on. Instead of landing up in court, you could land in a coffin.

Most people escape any formalised antagonism, like a pogrom, ethnic cleansing or a court case over tall trees. Their story concerns a fence post. *One* fence post. The unpleasant business tended to teeter on the line between farcical and infuriating. On occasion it managed a good deal more than an irritation in the posterior.

The Graham family held the view that on the whole most people are live-and-let-live neighbours as they just want to get on with their lives and live as harmoniously as possible with those around them. People are perfectly pleasant and reasonable as long as you are perfectly pleasant and reasonable. However, if there's one thing a dispute with a neighbour reveals once you start to discuss it with others; it is how few escape any irritations at all. On the whole, it seems, we want and need people around, we just don't want them around too noisily or too visually ... too intrusively. We want them on our terms, or at least on a subtly negotiated compromise between two sets of terms – theirs and ours.

Drilling the partition wall at well gone midnight is very unreasonable behaviour. Felix apologised the next day and Ted and Dorothy made a joke of it. They were, indeed, good neighbours. They gave Lucy home-grown carrots and beetroots. She gave them home-grown tomatoes and apples. They baby-sat; Felix helped put up their fence. But they were never intrusive, saw gossip as demeaning and respected the privacy of others. They were there, friendly and helpful and the Grahams tried to reciprocate. Both couples thought that's what being good neighbours amounted to, that those were the unspoken rules of good neighbour behaviour.

Seven years later Ted and Dorothy moved away. The Grahams kept in contact. Unfortunately for them the new neighbour was unaware of the unspoken rules and fairly quickly established that she was not one for subtly negotiated compromises, but the Grahams didn't have time to think about her, they were trying to understand what on Earth was going on with their arty neighbours, Reg and Thelma Doyle, who appeared to be convinced that Felix and Lucy had put a fence post – *one* fence post – several inches on to their territory. The criminal post was in fact in line with all the other posts on either side of it and at equidistance from the flank wall of their house and it had gone in exactly the same place it had been fixed some 20 or so years earlier. However, neither Felix nor Lucy could tell them this because from the very first they absolutely refused to communicate, except through lawyers.

Eleven court visits over one fence post? Sounds like two sets of stubborn goats doesn't it? The lawyers would certainly like you to think so, but the truth is you don't need two lots. You only need one, add a few lawyers – and a judge short on common sense – or just in a bad mood, and you've got a perfect lethal mix. Just as you don't need two belligerent armies to start a war, you just need one to invade and the invaded can either defend or capitulate, so you only need one side to attack using the courts as a weapon. Litigation isn't necessarily a quarrel, six of one and half a dozen of the other, it can be an assault: Germany marching into Poland could hardly be described as 'a quarrel' because Poland didn't take kindly to the idea. Six of Germany and half a dozen of Poland? The choice is to capitulate and pay whatever is demanded or stand up to the bullies.

The Grahams thought the courts were their defenders; that courts would insist that they were used only as a last resort, only after honest and open discussion. They thought the courts would not indulge 'morons in a hurry' or be used to indulge what lawyers call 'vexatious behaviour', above all over a very trivial matter which could be sorted out in a visit to the site of the 'dispute'. A trivial matter where the evidence that no crime had been committed was literally concrete. They were wrong.

The problem arose from the building work on the flat-roofed sunroom. Just as most people know to keep away from courts, they know to approach a building project as you would a fetid river full of piranhas. You want to get to the other side but you appreciate there may be the odd challenge on the way. In the Grahams' case it was the classic stuff of freelancers working two or more sites at the same time with a freeloader's angle on the clients' budget. The contractor had 'personal problems' and in those days the Grahams believed they should show consideration for people with 'personal problems'. He was, after all, a friend. Always a big mistake. Never employ a friend, and certainly not a friend with personal problems. They stayed friends after the building work was finally completed but, according to Lucy, 'More because in those days we had an above average supply of consideration. We did not have an above average supply of either time or money.'

The infamous fence running parallel with their flank wall at a regular three feet from it was causing the two builder lads bother. The post had rotted at the base and the weight of the two panels was causing it to lean over into the passage. One Friday as they went off site they told Lucy that the coming Monday they were going to remove the post and the couple of fence panels and fix them back in the right place when the job was done. They showed bruised and scraped knuckles. The post had shifted with weathering into the concrete passage: the Grahams' passage being lower than the Doyles' path, which was wider at that point, and the fence veered away from their house.

Lucy was aware of a cooling in friendliness from Reg and Thelma Doyle since the building work started and suspected that they did not appreciate the sacrifices of the lower floor level or that awful flat roof. They didn't want any building work at all. They didn't like change which the Grahams had thought was rather quaint when they first met them. They liked people who wanted to preserve the past.

The following day Felix mentioned the builders' plan to Reg Doyle when they met at the local pub to alert him to the reason for the removal of the post and two attached fence panels. Lucy was focussed on other things when Felix returned and it was evening before she got round to asking about Reg and the fence post. Felix reported that Reg had responded rather oddly. He'd said he would have to ask Thelma. Lucy and Felix were mystified. What would he 'have to ask Thelma'? Felix had explained that the fence would be put back when the work was finished and both Grahams were beginning to regret mentioning it at all.

As Lucy says, 'People can run their lives as they like as long as they are pleasant, reasonable and don't interfere unreasonably in mine. The fence and post were our responsibility.' They decided they would ask the builders on Monday to put the fence dismantling off until the Doyles were happy. No builders Monday, needless to say, and Lucy forgot about the fence. Tuesday, the builders arrived unannounced and started on the fence but were stopped immediately by a very angry Reg Doyle.

Lucy was not too happy herself. She had a job to go to, and was reaching the limit of her consideration allowance. *If* the Doyles had queries they had had the weekend and Monday to raise them. Lucy did not need this interruption to the already delayed building work. She had no time to deal with it in detail but diplomacy called for a visit and a suggestion that they meet later. She found him still very cross. She didn't feel like saying anything which was fortunate because he had no intention of letting her. He informed her that under no circumstances were they to move that fence. He informed her he had consulted a lawyer.

Lucy was dumbstruck. The Doyles had consulted a lawyer without consulting them first over the temporary removal of a rotted fence post and fixing a replacement in its correct position. Had he gone mad? Why on Earth pay a lawyer before you've even discussed matters? Why pay good money when a word or two could explain things? What on Earth was going on here? They may be unhappy about the extension but they hadn't said anything. What's it got to do with lawyers? Retreat was the best option.

'I can see you're angry so perhaps we can meet later to sort this out,' she said.

'You people are making me angry. You do not touch that fence, unless you want to find yourself in court. We have taken legal advice, and I am warning you now. Tell those men of yours to leave the fence alone.' He was a big man with a very big voice. Further exchange of views seemed unlikely to be fruitful. Lucy was late for work anyway. Felix should take over when he got back in the evening. He knew the gentleman far better.

She talked the incident over with colleagues at work, one of whom was also a neighbour, and not surprised. The Doyles were seen as rather odd recluses and the fact that Felix had managed to befriend Reg Doyle had caused some amused surprise in the street. Colleagues advised that she go to see a solicitor as soon as possible and Lucy decided to follow their advice. Reg was a highly qualified man; it seemed most unlikely he'd rush into battle without checking his facts, so she'd better check too.

A solicitor friend confirmed that the Doyles had no right in law to prevent what the Grahams planned, as their Title was older and also the fence was theirs, but he added that he had seen some pretty odd people in his time and if these wanted to make life difficult using the law, they certainly could. Lucy gave some background information including the fact that the Doyles were going through a bit of a bad patch as Reg Doyle was fighting redundancy from his fairly prestigious job. Her lawyer friend warned that they could mean trouble. He offered to help all he could but this was not in his area of law. He specialised in criminal cases. Not mimsy-pimsy, middle-class neighbour disputes.

Lucy was dismayed. Surely it can't go any further. It couldn't possibly go to court. No court would take such a silly, unnecessary thing seriously and any judge would throw out a case brought by someone who didn't even try to talk things over before engaging lawyers. Her lawyer friend, Paul, agreed. 'Courts don't like vexatious litigation. You say you were on friendly terms. So, no ongoing antagonism. Odd. But those personal problems might have something to do with it. They're taking it out on you. I can't say how the Court would react to your situation. Trouble is a lot of time and money can be wasted and you'd have to put up with a lot of bother before you find out. What people don't understand is that it all depends on the judge. One judge might send them packing at the earliest opportunity; another might let the whole thing run its course before making any decision. Once these things go to court anything can happen. You could end up spending a lot of money with no guarantee that you will get it all back. And,' he said, 'you could be absolutely right about nearly everything and still lose in court. You'd have to be very unlucky but then you'd have to go to appeal. Do you have a way to pay for this by any chance?' Lucy wasn't sure they had a way to pay next month's mortgage.

This did not fit with her view of judges and courts. Judges wouldn't allow this sort of nonsense to disturb their busy enough lives. Losing money is bad but losing time as well! Neither Felix nor Lucy had any of either to lose, but they'd known Paul a long time, he was a highly regarded, very level-headed, reliable solicitor. He wouldn't stir up trouble, raise anxiety unnecessarily. Was he actually saying that courts *could* countenance vexatious, trivial litigation without being too phased by a refusal to talk first? 'Surely the first thing they'll do is come to look at the problem and they'll see what a nonsense it is? We're only 10 minutes from the Court.'

'I wouldn't worry needlessly,' replied Paul. 'Perhaps if Felix goes to see Mr Doyle this evening – and gives him some dignified way out, he'll have calmed down and it will all have been a storm in a teacup. It really does seem extraordinarily stupid. I wonder who he consulted. See if you can find out.'

Felix went round to have a word that evening. He reported Paul's advice about what he called prior rights (the Grahams' house and therefore their original conveyance was older than the Doyles') and about ownership of said fence post, pointed out the reason for the temporary removal, invited them to inspect site of same. They refused the invitation. They informed Felix that no one was to touch the fence post, because (curiously) their house value had to be protected for the sake of their grandchildren! And closed the door. Felix, who could when he chose, charm warring children and disputatious acquaintances into peaceful compliance, had failed to make any headway. The Doyles seemed determined to engage in battle but not to explain why, nor to investigate the facts. The Grahams couldn't take any further delay on the building work. Felix was away in the USA for the last six months of the year, and had quite enough to deal with organising that.

He phoned the builders and told them to move post and panels after he'd written to the next door neighbours. The building project was to be completed by the end of June, a mere three months over the target completion date. He delivered the letter next door explaining that the fence panels and post would have to be removed sometime and now would be right time for the sake of the builders, and that they would be put back when the work was completed with a new post to replace the rotten one.

No response after a week so two fence panels and the post, the rotten post between them, were removed.

The first solicitor's letter arrived by registered post after a couple of days. And so was war declared and lawyers' fun and funding began. At least it sort of began but in a half-cocked way, because the Grahams just failed to play the game as devised. It would have begun in earnest had they not been such awkward, distrustful, reluctant and eventually refusenik clients of the legal profession. They knew that once they were into spending money on this absurdity they'd be sucked into getting it back and that meant being sucked into a lawyer's sticky web and possibly court. War would be unavoidable.

They decided to try direct contact again. Felix went round a second time and came back smiling. At last a breakthrough of common sense. This time they did agree to meet on site. The date was set: 8th June. Felix cancelled an important meeting, reorganised a pressing work schedule and came rushing home. When he arrived Lucy reported that someone looking very like a solicitor had called next door a few hours earlier, stayed about an hour and left.

Reg and Thelma cancelled the meeting. Their 'lawyers had advised against it' and from that moment on they were all trapped. From cancelling that meeting the Doyles engaged egos and handed control to their lawyers letting them lead them deeper into the mire – and dragging the Grahams along with them. They would have to see this through or pay the Doyles what they demanded (well over £1,000) as well as place a knuckle-bruising post to impede the only passage between the front and back of the house.

Time was short. Felix's departure neared. They'd have to put the fence panels back before they left. They wrote suggesting the Doyles might like to agree the positioning. No answer. Building work finished and builders were about to go off site. Fence panels and post replaced meticulously in line with the rest of the fence.

The recorded delivery letter arrived the next morning. The first of many.

They dealt with the confusing letters as best they could before they left, as 'litigants in person', but the lawyer letters kept coming. The Doyles would not explain themselves or even say how much the post was trespassing. The Grahams proposed a site meeting with one independent surveyor, and met a barbed wire of negatives. With hindsight Lucy now says they should have left it there. They had done all that was reasonable and all was recorded in the burgeoning correspondence file. They should have written one last letter stating this adding in unequivocal terms that they would not respond to any further communication on the matter.

What they thought they needed was an outsider with some authority just to look at the site of this gigantic, time-wasting silliness. Someone with authority to look at the post and the passage, and put an end to it. The Grahams both had real jobs to do and people dependent on them doing them. They felt that as these neighbours wouldn't talk to them directly, only through their solicitor at Hassle Costa & Grabbe (Lucy's unoriginal choice of name), they'd try to reason with *him*. They naively hoped at the beginning he would put a stop to it for his clients' sakes and his own reputation. They thought he wouldn't want the embarrassment his clients would cause. They even imagined that his professional code would require him to steer his clients away from conflict. At that time they simply had no understanding of the overriding objective of many legal firms, what they are in business for. With blindly determined clients such firms are perfectly placed to attain that business objective. The Doyles' lawyer was now telling them how much they'd have to pay if they wanted to settle out of court. The sums increased alarmingly as the letters increased in number seeming to reflect what the Doyles were paying *them*. The Doyles wanted their foolish investment repaid by the Grahams.

From the start friends had come to solemnly study the post with the rotten bottom, the hole it had originally come from, the line of fence. The friends had laughed a lot, joked a lot, and most refused to believe the nonsense was anything to worry about. If anyone could be dragged into expensive time-wasting legal combat over something so clearly nonsensical, the law is a tormentor not a protector. Anyone could be vulnerable. Even sensible, level-headed, articulate, intelligent them. But there were some who didn't laugh. They knew there could be something to worry about. Those who didn't laugh had their own experiences, the stories came flowing whenever the Grahams began their tale. 'On occasion we didn't get to tell *ours*, which was really frustrating!' says Lucy.

Friends were comforting and some were encouraging, but none of them could put an end to it. What was needed was that authority to put a stop to the solicitor's letters that the Grahams thought always needed a reply, usually a rebuttal of something or other, banged out late at night on the old typewriter with a lot of Tipp-Ex, time-consuming, irritating and stressful. Lucy and Felix had their own lives to lead and resented what they saw as irresponsible and selfish behaviour with the potential add-on of expensive on the part of professionals who claimed to be in the business of resolving disputes. They wanted someone to step in and put a stop to it and let them to get back to their lives without having to buy off the aggressors. 'Taxes we pay – everyone has to, its a deal we're happy to make, a social contract, but handing over our hard-earned income to some lawyer to buy off an attack was paying protection money and not what we thought the legal service of an advanced, civilised, mainly law-abiding country was about,' says Lucy.

If not an arbitrator, then what they needed was someone sensible, someone with a talent for persuasion to come in, speak to the Doyles without a lawyer whispering in his ear, and put a stop to it. There was one possible player for that role, but only because he knew the Doyles and the Grahams had a smile-and-nod passing acquaintance with him. They had no idea whether he had any talent for it, and anyway it was a bit of a cheek to burden him with sorting out an embarrassing conflict like this. He could end up losing a friend and the smiles of some passing acquaintances. Gone are the days when one could turn to the parish priest. The Grahams didn't even know the name of the parish priest. They dithered.

The Doyles wanted the fence back, they were invited to negotiate where; they ignored the invitation. The builders closed the gap. They reckoned they could not have done more.

Another solicitor's letter demanding money with menaces arrived on the day of their departure. In the middle of the chaos of last-minute arrangements before leaving home to work abroad for six months, an aggressive, provocative solicitor's letter was not well received. They somehow made time to reply. They should not have bothered. They had entirely the wrong approach. They should have ignored the aggressors, but that was not their way, they could not consider ignoring such a letter. Paul, their solicitor friend, agreed to deal with things while they were away in the US reminding them that this was not his specialist area. He promised to fend the enemy off if necessary until Lucy returned in September. Felix and Emma were staying there and would not be back until Christmas. Claire was staying in England to await A-level results.

On Lucy's return more threatening letters arrived. Her proposals to meet on site and discuss the fence post were still ignored or rejected, but Paul managed to arrange a meeting with two senior officers on the other side of the line. He reported back that they wouldn't say much apart from stating that their clients' deeds showed a different boundary. However, Paul didn't know how different because, 'they'd forgotten to bring the documents with them.' You'll have noticed the ghost of Ogmore games to come. There are others. It is becoming clear why Lucy wanted to avoid the litigation and court route in dealings with the Ogmores. Time and again events with the Ogmores resonated with this earlier encounter with our civil justice system.

Paul pointed out that their failure to bring any supporting evidence meant at least one letter from him and at least one letter from the other side. All income generating for the law business and with clients like the Doyles they could go on prolonging things and adding to the costs which the Doyles or the Grahams will have to pay. Normally it is assumed that these things balance out. Disputing neighbours both share a vested interest in saving money. They can do that by talking to each other and trying to settle matters without lawyers present, but the Doyles didn't operate on those terms. Usually people in dispute try some face-to-face discussions, and usually when things are bad there is a history of long-term antagonism, but until the Grahams started building the extension both sides were on friendly terms and that happened at the same time as the Doyles were dealing with 'personal problems'. 'The friendly relations were down to Felix,' says Lucy, 'he was a very amiable man.'

The Doyles, or rather their solicitor, could withhold whatever information was needed until the Grahams paid for a court order forcing them to disclose whatever they claimed they had. These lapses of memory are certainly expensive for the client, and they could mean the lawyers don't have much confidence in their case. On the other hand, they may be supremely confident. They may have the killer fact and just want to milk the contest for all they can get. It's a gamble. Paul asked how good a poker player Lucy was. Lucy said she was useless at cards. Paul advised her to stay away from courts. She asked if she had the option. Paul said maybe not.

Lucy still had some confidence that a judge would come down very heavily on parties who refused to try to settle disputes sensibly and openly. Felix believed that too. Their friends believed it too ... except their friend Paul.

A further attempt to set up a lawyer-free meeting with the Doyles failed. Meanwhile, neither the Doyles nor their terrier were prepared to let go. Their solicitor, Mr Gee, was a fresh-faced young man with an innocent manner but nonetheless adept in the arts of his trade. Lawyers of the ordinary work-a-day kind can teach politicians, and journalists, quite a lot about spin. No one is surprised that so many politicians are lawyers by training.

The fact is the Doyles would not have been a problem without Mr Gee's help, and he didn't have to work too hard to bring in the fees. All he had to do was write letters for which he would be paid handsomely, and avoid any meeting on site to confront the concrete facts. He didn't have to know if he was right. The longer he avoided testing the facts the better from the point of view of income generation. As long as the clients continue to pay up he could keep it going indefinitely, forcing the Grahams (or so they thought) to write back with corrections, clarifications and so on. He could accuse the Grahams of anything he liked. Not murder, treason, rape or international terrorism perhaps, but only because these are criminal matters and would be dealt with by publicly-funded policemen on a wage, policemen who would object strongly to any time-wasting. So, he didn't really have to be that clever or that hard working. Just churn out the wordy letters, and keep the punter paying. The more letters generated, the more the essence of the matter is hidden in words and the costs and the blood pressure rise. The more the punters paid in money and emotion the deeper they were impaled on the hook of litigation. At some time the Grahams too would have to spend real money and at a certain level of expenditure they would want, need, to get it back.

Lucy says they were very aware that the intention was to hook them too. The Doyles had spent money and behaved rather badly, they had to justify the expenditure *and* save face. They had to live with themselves. Lucy said, '*Mea culpa*'[1] was an unlikely phrase on Reg Doyle's lips, but she was surprised at Thelma, a quiet, rather shy lady. As there seemed so little evidence to support their accusation and as they were continuing to pay to pursue it, Lucy feared they were being led into a trap, some legal trap. Now the Doyles were claiming that they had 'counsel's opinion'. Why would any barrister advise them to pursue such a case, unless he could see a cause? There *must* be more to it.

Felix was still in the US, so Paul told the other side to wait. But he also wrote a fairly formal statement to the Grahams in which he warned that the case could cost a sum which more or less equalled the amount Lucy would take home that year in her part-time professional job. As this was a friend who wasn't looking for work she took his warning seriously. She was shocked to think she was expected to hand over all the money she would take home in a year to lawyers over one fence post they had put in the right place.

After Christmas with the family all back things began in earnest. The Doyles issued their Claim in the local county court. They wanted the land, all postage stamp of it, and costs and a thousand pounds. That is to say they wanted the Grahams' postage stamp of concrete, the Doyles' lawyers' costs and the Grahams' thousand pounds. They did not provide evidence as to why.

Paul told them the other side was bullying, they wanted to frighten with costs, get the Grahams to pay to be left alone, and also recover some of what they'd so unwisely spent in the first place. Paul couldn't see their case. Even if their deeds showed a different boundary, the Grahams' deeds had precedence. He also reported that they still hadn't shown him their deeds, after seven months.

He then suggested that the Doyles might be trying for adverse possession:[2] the fence post had been out of line for 12 years or more and they've acquired ownership of the tiny triangle. He then came up with another warning, a danger that had not occurred to them. He said that everything could become too complex for the average judge to follow in the courtroom situation. Until that moment the Grahams had assumed that if the worse came to the worst they could at least rely on a judge to sort things out. Paul commiserated and told them they were left with only a few choices: pay something to the Doyles (more accurately their lawyers) and move the post to make them go away, or possibly pay something into court. He told them that if they paid something into court they'd still be trapped in litigation. If they were inclined to stand up to bullies they should counterclaim, make the Doyles a little more anxious.

Felix and Lucy did not like any of the options and were becoming angry with a justice service that appeared to be unable to protect them. If they counterclaimed it would just ratchet the whole dispute up a notch. Paul said that if they were not prepared to give in (pay up and move the post), and if the Doyles wouldn't talk to them and insisted on court action, a counterclaim for vexatious litigation over a trivial matter should get the Court to look at how they've behaved. He advised them to try to get the Claim struck out as trivial and vexatious.[3] Felix and Lucy felt that described the attack very accurately, but would have preferred Paul to be more confident.

Most people, non-lawyers like them, would expect the Court to protect them from this sort of mugging by litigation. Paul said it might in the end, but advised against suggesting what a court *ought* to do. In his view citizens could challenge big business, government, God himself, but not 'The Courts'. Judges, he told them, don't take kindly to anyone telling them what they ought to do. This was unfamiliar territory for the Grahams at that time. They had always thought that sound argument, evidence and good sense prevailed in the courtroom.They asked him if the Court would be concerned by the Doyles' refusal to discuss things with them, and he thought it should do but it depended on the judge. It was up to him.

'So that was it,' Lucy says. 'Not really an option was it? I was expected to work for many months and hand over my net pay to some young solicitor to buy off a mugging that in any other context would land the mugger in the police cells. It appeared Mr Gee looked forward to my hard-earned, honestly and honourably-earned income because he'd corralled two angry, frustrated and seriously misguided people and persuaded them to leap into the litigation hole.'

The Grahams were accused of trespassing by placing one post on to the Doyles' property. The Doyles seemed reluctant to answer questions and their hope that the lawyers would want to escape this soul-draining antagonism had long gone. They feared that the pleasant, open demeanour of the young Mr Gee was misleading. They decided to counterclaim. Their aim: to let the post stay where it was and not to lose a penny in the process. Given the facts, a reasonable aim, an attainable aim, you might think.

Lucy found it hard to believe that pride, personal angst and obsessive myopia were at the root of it. She suspected although they hadn't actually claimed adverse possession – squatter's rights – that must be their argument, but Mrs Britton, who had lived in the Grahams' house since 1934, insisted she would have noticed if the post was jutting out of line, and it never did. If that was the Doyles' claim why didn't they say so and show their evidence so everyone could see whether there was any substance in it? Just like the Ogmores they did no such thing.

Felix and Lucy continued to reply to the letters. Much as they valued Paul's help they couldn't afford to gamble on using it if there was, indeed, the possibility they would not be reimbursed. They didn't have any form of indemnity nor other financial help. They were too poor to pay lawyers and too rich for Legal Aid.[4] 'No-win, no-fee'[5] agreements were not on offer in those days. They did get a threatening letter from the Doyles' building society – 'our members, Mr and Mrs Doyle, inform us that you are trespassing on their land, etc., etc.,' Paul dealt with that one: 'Do come to see, my clients are not trespassing, and you're talking of no more that a pocket handkerchief of land at the most which cannot materially affect the value of their property. Do come to see.' They heard no more from that building society.

They decided eventually to take the advice freely given by friends and ignore next door and their obsession. 'It's their problem. Don't let them make it yours.' There was a lot of residual Sixties stuff around in their circle at that time. The Sixties had moved from drab, post-war, deferential Britain to free-fun-and-let's-go-do-something Britannia, but the legal profession and the legal system had not moved with the times.

They lived in a university town with a law library. Lucy decided to make a visit and dedicate an hour to reading up on boundary disputes. Many visits later she'd read of more or less every case that made even a passing reference to boundaries. She had found a good, readable book. Readable law books do exist and this one gave her enough relevant information to make any case made by the Doyles seem even more impossible. That was confidence building until the doubts crept in: if it was impossible why were they spending good money on it? They weren't known for being profligate. What were their lawyers, including counsel, counselling? The books confirmed that judges frowned on trivial, vexatious cases and Lucy decided she would not waste a minute more of her life on the machinations of lawyers, urged on by who knows what in the minds of their neighbours. She had far more urgent and real concerns, as had Felix.

But first they would take up Paul's recommendation of a local boundary expert and tell him the story – 'expensive but an expert'. They came out of their first meeting with Mr V.E. Solicitor hugely relieved. He may charge Lucy's weekly wage per hour but if he's even half as good as his fees he'd sort it in no time. He wasn't as it turned out. No time meant no fees. They went to a memorable second meeting with high hopes. As the expensive minutes ticked by they became more deflated. They found themselves telling him exactly what they'd told him at the first meeting. He'd forgotten most of it. Did he know about keeping notes and reading them *before* seeing his client? Great personality, but not value for money.

He came to look at the site of the crime and assured them that as soon as the judge – any judge – saw it, the matter would be thrown out. 'Good', they said, 'How soon can you get a judge to see it?'

'Ah, well,' he replied, 'it's a bit more complex than that. Your judge, whoever he turns out to be, will most likely come … in due course. You can't hurry judges and don't ever forget they are all different and respond in different ways to cases. You can never be sure what they will say. I do know a very good barrister who'll deal with the court appearances.' Lead entered their souls. Barristers now.

He wrote them a letter enclosing for their perusal his first invoice. The letter rehearsed what he'd said, most of which they knew, and pointed out that even if they won outright they should not count on getting back all their costs, that is to say, all his costs and his friend the barrister's costs. 'I shall of course endeavour to recover the maximum possible.'

They pondered this. At length. Anyone with a sense of justice might expect some compensation for this mugging with a court-shaped cosh: the stress, the work and so on. Far from being compensated, the victims lose money. Their new personality solicitor, local expert, was making them a no-win/no-win offer. Wasn't there something rather more attractive he could propose? Unfortunately, no.

The real deflator was the moment at the next meeting when he came up with advice. It was somewhat flawed. Lucy's excellent book in the law library told of a case, one V.E. Solicitor now cited to them, *warning* them the other side could rely on, 'Could be a breach in our defence,' he said. Lucy thought a bit and decided to disagree. She cited a case she had found which had overturned that 'precedent', making it a redundant precedent. She had the reference to hand. He paused, curious. He'd not heard of it. He was very interested. He had a boundary dispute of his own with a property somewhere in the West Country. Her cited case would be perfect for him. Would she give him the reference? So there they were giving *him* legal advice! Wasn't it supposed to be the other way round?

The summons to a pre-trial hearing arrived. Set for the New Year. They decided enough was enough, from then on they'd do it themselves, they'd act as litigants in person.[6]

FOUR
1984–1985

'"You're nothing but a pack of cards," said Alice.'
Lewis Carroll, Court Scene:
Alice's Adventures in Wonderland

They looked forward to meeting their first judge, fairly confident that he would put a stop to the nonsense. Judges come in various grades; this one was at the lowest level titled in those days 'Registrar' (now District Judge). They had every hope that their Registrar would grant their counterclaim or, at least be persuaded to look at the scene of the crime as soon as possible, and then, hopefully, throw out any accusation of wicked wrongdoing, bringing this un-amusing farce to a close on the grounds of triviality if not vexatious litigation.

They had to wait an hour for the delayed audience so they used the time attempting to encourage Mr Gee to negotiate a way out of the nonsense. They had little doubt that he would see it as a nonsense and indeed he did seem just a little bit embarrassed as he evaded and avoided, but despite their efforts, he insisted he could do nothing without his clients' agreement.

Many of the allocated 30 minutes in the small room where this hearing took place were spent listening to the Registrar telling himself what the Doyles' case was about while he read, they feared for the first time, their defence. He didn't quite get round to the counterclaim. He wanted surveyors in on the act. Felix pointed out that the evidence was clear on site for all to see, but the Registrar told him that it was a bit more complex than that. Felix pointed out that surveyors would escalate the dispute as they would want to recover the costs, so how about a judge looks at it to see if there's any mileage in the Claim in the first place before everything gets too expensive and the original Claim gets smothered under costs? According to Lucy, the Registrar looked at them in disbelief. Of course surveyors cost money, but that's what happens when neighbours disagree about boundaries. Felix pointed out that it was not a complicated land matter. Felix suggested that if there had to be surveyors in on it, how about a single independent surveyor?

The Registrar responded sniffily that that is not how the courts operated. He told them to find themselves a surveyor and get both surveyors to report back in a couple of months' time. He then came up with a series of directions and dates which the Grahams didn't quite follow, but he wasn't talking to them anyway. He directed all he had to say to young Mr Gee and the Grahams found themselves on the point of being ushered away without even a mention of their counterclaim, let alone an enquiry about what *they* had hoped would be done. Lucy said, 'He wanted us all to leave the room, but we asked him to look at our counterclaim. He sighed. He'd give us a minute but he was a very busy man. We requested an early visit to the site to see the cause of the dispute. Trivial, we said, and a waste of the Court's time. The Registrar ignored our invitation and then assured us that for small, tiny even, areas of land can go all the way to the High Court!' Was this supposed to *justify* continuing a trivial case?

He told them that there was a case concerning a trespass of just six inches. Felix asked if that was six inches of a boundary all the way along and the Registrar replied, yes, and the boundary was no more than 100 feet long. He was packing their papers away, but Felix persisted. 'But this is just one tiny triangle six or possibly just four inches deep maximum and just five feet long at most.' He then demonstrated the triangle on the tabletop.

The Registrar did pause again. He was obviously preparing for the next summary judgment,[1] by now he had the file for that out. 'But,' says Lucy, 'he did pause. Something flickered in his mind, very briefly … and then flickered out – much to the relief of Mr Gee who we could sense freeze at the door listening anxiously, eager to get away before something bad happened, like the Judge actually taking our counterclaim seriously.' For one nanosecond there had been the chance that their counterclaim[2] would be considered, the outside chance that they might persuade that Someone in Authority to visit the site, see for themselves the evidence, see the triviality and throw the whole vexatious nonsense out.

They were then into a surveyors' site meeting, plans, experts arguing. The same as lawyers arguing: nothing amounting to much, no deepening of understanding, no conciliation of aggrieved parties, but a lot of costs. They were where the lawyers wanted them; beyond the point of no return. Either they write off Lucy's net income for the year and put up with a permanent irritation in their side passage or see this through to the end. They later realised that the Registrar hadn't actually set a date for the surveyors' reports. A rather sad omission – for them.

The next hearing was some four months later before a different Registrar and in the company of a very different solicitor for the Doyles. Could this new solicitor explain what was happening? Could she explain why no report had been sent, why their surveyor's report had been ignored? She didn't know about that. In fact she didn't seem to know much about the case at all. She was not that certain of the names of 'her' clients. She was young, she was decidedly attractive. She had very long legs and a very short skirt.

The Registrar, too, was somewhat different from the desiccated, precise, rather prissy elderly gentleman they'd first encountered. Lucy's recall is quite detailed (she has a written report of what followed). 'He had quite a sparkle in those very blue eyes, set in a very tanned face, and that sparkle shone ever more brightly as those eyes encountered our new adversary, settling into her chair and crossing her very long legs. This time we expected to make the Registrar listen to how trivial, vexatious, time wasting this nonsensical claim was. We would tell him how since the surveyors' meeting the Doyles' surveyor had disappeared off the radar screen. We would urge him or any judge to visit the site with the surveyors and see for himself the evidence and the triviality of the whole dispute. The scene of the non-crime was only 10 minutes away from the Court.

'He listened to us, some of the sparkle gone. He said, "And Miss (Longlegs) what does your firm have to say to that?"

'Miss Longlegs said she didn't have instructions on the surveyor or on that precise proposal, but as her clients were still pursuing the Claim she was sure they were acting on their surveyor's advice. The Registrar looked disappointed for a moment. "I'm sure Miss (Longlegs) would argue that there is a matter of substance here which the Court has a duty to consider. Her clients have spent considerable sums of money so far and contend that the Defendants are trespassing. Their surveyor concurs." '

Was Twinkly Eyes working for the opposition? Felix recovered quickly to tell him that it was not clear that their surveyor *did* concur. When the surveyors met months ago, he did not seem convinced that this was a matter for the courts. Since that meeting he has been uncontactable. If the Plaintiffs[3] have spent a lot of money so far, it is hardly a reason for making them spend more when a site meeting by a judge or an arbitrator with the surveyors could settle it before even more money is wasted.' That dulled the twinkle somewhat.

Felix pointed out that Gee was demanding to see documents he had already been sent, but had failed to send his surveyor's report. Gee was delaying unreasonably while indulging in a 'fishing expedition'. 'We have been waiting months for that report. We need a site meeting as soon as possible.' Twinkly eyes lost interest. A smile and a nod to Miss Longlegs and they were dismissed – with another reminder that it was 'a bit more complex than that'.

Mr Gee claimed to be embarrassed by his elusive surveyor. The Grahams waited another month and then, three months after that all-important court-ordered site-meeting, having heard nothing, the Grahams wrote again suggesting the Doyles abandon the case and they would propose some compromise on their counterclaim – and costs.

Three more weeks passed and reply came there none. Then, into month five after the site meeting, a letter. The Opposition had at last their surveyor's plan and report. Could they look at the Grahams' deeds? It was all on again, tentatively. They already had photocopies of the Grahams' deeds.

Still no answers to their question as to precisely how far into the Doyles' territory they were accused of encroaching, let alone a theory for why the post should be anywhere else. Silence again from the Doyles. Before the Woolf reforms,[4] litigants could withhold information until the very last minute, by which time the other side would have banked higher levels of stress, anxiety, debts and unpaid overtime. Mr Gee could churn out letters on a regular basis, all seeming to require a reply. The Grahams were pleased they had decided to act as litigants in person; at least the correspondence only cost time, and irritation.

The promised plan did not materialise. Silence. The Grahams wanted an end to it, but they wanted their surveyor's costs back. They decided to ask the Court to propose arbitration. Arbitration is more user friendly than the courts, quicker and more likely to get at The Truth. The hearing is informal and the strict rules of evidence do not apply. Moreover, no solicitor's costs are allowed except for the costs stated on the summons, any costs of enforcing the award and 'such costs as are certified by the arbitrator to have been incurred by the unreasonable conduct of the opposite party.' This was a more attractive route than the confusions, delays, obfuscation and costs of the court's quaint way of settling matters. The other side seemed to be fading away, expensively, leaving an unresolved dispute and unpaid bills.

To their surprise they finally managed to persuade somebody to do something. The outcome of the third and final hearing before trial was a notice from the Court advising the matter *was* to be decided by arbitration. The Grahams' hopes were raised. But if it only takes one to drag a dispute into court, it takes two to go to arbitration. In less than a week they received the depressing letter from Mr Gee: 'We write to inform you that we intend to rescind the reference to arbitration as we do not consider that arbitration is the correct venue for the dispute between you and our clients.' Could it be the loss of costs (income) or the lost opportunity to confuse (games and costs) that they so lamented? Two days later the Grahams heard that the Court had put the matter down for trial.

The Grahams yet again tried to persuade Mr Gee and Co. on site to see what they intend to show the Court. All they wanted was their outgoing expenses paid: the surveyor, the lawyers and incidental costs. Request for site meeting denied. The Enemy had their barrister lined up for the job. 'Your suggestion amounts to a proposal to argue the merits of the case across the fence. The proper place for that is in court.' Difficult to see what was proper about a courtroom that was improper about the actual site: the post and fence the Court is being asked to give judgment on? Why so little interest in material facts?

The Grahams decided to ask Mrs Britton to act as a witness, and she agreed. Whatever had caused her dislike of the Doyles, it ran deep. The other side were a little alarmed at her possible appearance in court and wrote that if she did turn up she would be 'rigorously cross-examined', no doubt hoping the threat would be passed on to her. It was. The Grahams felt obliged to warn her, but it made her all the more determined.

In March 1985, just one week before trial, Mr Gee informed the Grahams that 'at last' he had received a report and plan from his surveyor! Moreover, he said, 'it is an *agreed* plan!!' Agreed by whom? Certainly not by their man who hadn't even seen it. Agreed by the clients perhaps after some tweaking here and there? So much for the independence of the expert witness. Their man wrote an angry rebuttal. 'Most untrue, not agreed. Not even seen. Most unprofessional.' The Grahams wrote a full frontal letter to young Mr Gee expressing strong disapproval and pointing out how they were forced to let other people down to attend court, to abandon their legitimate responsibilities on an expensive nonsense in court.

Just a few days before the first meeting in court before a proper judge it transpired that this claim was *not* a squatter claim. The Grahams discovered after months of time-wasting irritation and just days before trial, that the Doyles' claim was that the boundary *always* veered out of line at that one post and then veered back again. The whole matter hinged on the other side's refusal to look at the quarrel from the Grahams' side of the fence and see for themselves the concrete evidence. Now the Grahams understood why their opponents hoped to frighten Mrs Britton off. She'd lived in the house from before the war. She would know whether or not the fence had 'always' had a dog-leg at that post.

As the land on the Doyles' side of the fence was higher, about a foot higher, than on the Grahams' side, the concrete for the base of a coal bunker on the Doyles' side which had been placed there some 20 years earlier had squeezed, while still wet, under the gravel-board before it had set hard through to the Grahams' side. Once set, the rough concrete was held in place by soil and dirt a few inches above the original passageway on the Grahams' side. It cantilevered over the smooth path that had been laid when the Edwardian house was built. But the original path was still there hidden from sight under it. Lucy says, 'You could get your hand under the jutting concrete and feel the old path's smooth straight edge, continuing the line of our side passage a consistent three feet from the flank wall of our house, just as described in our deeds. The fence post had severed at ground level and shifted slowly our way dragging the two fence panels and gravel boards on either side with it to end up in line with the outside edge of the cantilevering, rough concrete.'

When the builders replaced the post and panels, the fence followed the line of the original path underneath just as it was supposed to do. No trespass. No crime. Looking over the fence from their side the Doyles only saw the jutting concrete suggesting a dog-leg at that post. They couldn't see the path underneath. They were told that if they could prove that the fence line legitimately jutted into the passage they might be able to get the whole extension taken down, because the Grahams wouldn't be able to meet the statutory three foot gap between building and boundary. Once they were hooked on the litigation they had started they couldn't get off without losing money and face, and they believed they were right and that both money and face would be saved. Their lawyers told them not to talk to their neighbours. They didn't take up any of the invitations to check their facts. They were enemies at war on a nonsense. The Grahams were sure any judge would see that it was a nonsense.

All the machinations, the 'he said/she said' of demeaning disputes could have been avoided if that meeting arranged two years earlier, had not been cancelled at the last minute on the advice of the solicitor, before the builders had taken the obstruction down. He had looked at the post from the Doyles' side of the fence. He had decided that the post was solidly placed in the position he saw it. He decided that it had been erected 15 or 20 years earlier in that position, that it was intended that the post should be in that position, out of line, because it had always been out of line. No matter that when he saw it, the post and two fence panels on either side were leaning over quite acutely, that the post was not attached to the ground – and wobbled. He saw no need to check his conclusions from the Grahams' side of the fence, and certainly not with the Grahams. His conclusions confirmed his clients' theory, so, 100% of the company present that afternoon was in agreement. You couldn't hope for better than 100%.

The damage his cavalier conduct had unleashed could have been limited had either one of those court Registrars taken the initiative and suspended their comfortable assumptions to spend an hour or two looking at the concrete facts on site, no more than 10 minutes away. They would have been in a position to understand something about the matter they seemed happy to burden the Court and, more to the point, *the Grahams*, with. After all, they did have the authority to put a stop to the nonsense.

A lot of people who had followed the story and seen the scene of the crime expected a quick and sensible outcome once it actually got into court. They were dismayed that it was still dragging on. The Grahams, on the other hand, had long lost their dismay capacity somewhere.

They had the distinct impression that the Registrars did not see them as clients, customers of the civil court system, but as nuisances who didn't understand the rules of the game, and prevented the efficient processing of the day's business. The Grahams lacked the good sense to engage their own solicitors, and the Courts are not there to protect cheapskates. *The Grahams*, on the other hand, reckoned that by acting for themselves, because it denied at least one set of lawyers the chance to confuse, obfuscate and delay, they saved everyone money and time. However, in the Court's view this was not the Small Claims Court, this was a court for grown-ups, and the Grahams had no business being there unaccompanied and should not expect any special allowances. It did not seem to cross the Court's mind that it was *their* job to understand their clients and help them in that alien environment, rather than the other way round. After all they were the paid professionals, the Grahams the unwilling customers.

Despite their experience so far the Grahams continued to believe the argument that originally persuaded them to act as litigants in person. They put their trust in judges.

So to trial. Their contest was booked for two days in early April. They estimated that was one day too many. However, it was not up to them and some players had a vested interest in extra days. The barrister for the other side was a youngish lady never without a cigarette, who told the Grahams she had seen the site. They knew she hadn't seen it from their side of the fence.

Lucy and Felix had been given an odd piece of advice by several solicitors, free of charge. 'Remember,' they were told, 'treat the Judge as though he was a not terribly bright 11 year old' (several lawyers – always an *11* year old).

Perhaps the loneliness of the man on the high chair deserves some sympathy. A judge could have a serious problem understanding what the antagonists might think is clear and obvious to them. The clients have been living with their cases for some time. The judges, up there on their own, must seem to be in control despite knowing less about the matter than most of the players down below, and they must decide what is relevant and whom to believe. They came from down there themselves; sometimes solicitors, usually barristers, and they will remember the judges who failed to attract their respect. Most of them will want to do better, but seeking out truth and delivering justice is a hard job for the type of judge who really wants to deliver just that in our adversarial system. They must rely on the lawyers for each side to help them, they are not supposed to ask too many questions, but the lawyers are not there to aid the search for truth, to identify a just outcome, they are there to win the case, score points and impress the spectators. They can and will confuse, distract and obfuscate, whenever they think necessary and possible – whenever they can get away with it.

Of course the hanging judge macho-types don't have a problem. They don't agonise, they see clearly (sometimes even before the trial) whose side they're on, and for them the power they can exercise, almost unchallenged, is quite pleasurable: 'I've decided and what I decide goes. If you don't like it you can appeal.' This macho-style judge is not an endangered species.

The conscientious ones can ask questions, but don't want to lose credibility and must be careful not to descend into the arena, be seen to lose their impartiality. Interrogation, inquiry, questions from the presiding judge – that's *not* how 'we' do it. It's the *adversarial* not the *inquisitorial*[5] tradition this side of the English Channel and wherever the English system operates. It is said that the judge is actually deciding who has the better lawyers. And here were the Grahams entering the arena on their own. No lawyer of any kind, good, bad or indifferent, to fight for them. They still held to the notion judges were trained and quality-controlled to limit any wild discrepancies and protect against whimsy, laziness, capriciousness and wild prejudice. *And* not to waste court time. But as the trial date approached Lucy and Felix were becoming just a little unnerved by the judges they'd already met and the attitude of the professionals they'd talked to.

Felix wanted a site visit on day one. How was this Judge, indeed any judge, going to understand about extruded concrete cantilevering over the evidence, and about severed fence posts, in a courtroom? The site was so very near. They could be there in no time. The Judge, an elderly, rather somnolent man, had no such plans for the day unfortunately.

The Doyles' surveyor arrived at court with another plan – plan B. Would they please dispense with the first plan – plan A? He had another theory . . . well, actually the same theory but different evidence. Would they mind? They minded. Ms Barrister promised she would explain it was a late arrival which their expert had not seen. How Judge Lethe responded to this carefully manipulated foul, the Defendants and their angry expert couldn't know, he showed no real concern.

The Grahams' expert told his clients that plan B was as much rubbish as plan A and he would easily rubbish it – as long as the Judge *did* sport the intelligence of your average 11 year old.

Day Two: The Plaintiffs' surveyor finished his evidence. It was now the turn of the Defendants' surveyor.

He had spent the previous night into the early hours, drafting rather beautiful, elaborate drawings to discredit the argument he'd only just got from his elusive opposite number. Did the elderly, rather somnolent Judge understand that neither plan A nor plan B had been agreed? The beautiful and elaborate drawings obviously impressed with their artistry and professionalism, but Lucy feared that the 11 year old above them was struggling to understand their meaning out of context. Their expert stressed that a site viewing would make all clear. As another day drew to an early close, three whole days were set down for further hearings. Five days on this nonsense. Felix argued that the remainder of Defence expert's evidence be heard on site. Judge Lethe did *not* agree. They would meet again in the courtroom after Easter. Lucy would have to let a few more people down at work, but the alternative was to delay proceedings for yet another month or possibly longer. She tried to stuff her exasperation out of sight. A seriously annoyed Felix was also going to have to juggle work commitments yet again. The Plaintiffs were time-rich, both being retired.

Day Three: Their expert concluded his evidence. His Honour was struggling; His Honour was not hiding *his* exasperation. He sighed, he pushed the drawings this way, he pushed the drawings that way and eventually he pushed the impressive works away. It seemed that the Defence expert had rather overestimated the talents of your average 11 year old. As far as Felix and Lucy could see, the drawings presented the argument with clarity. All rather alarming. Does the Judge think the Defence was trying to bamboozle him? Why does he make it so difficult for himself? Why doesn't he come and in his own time see on site what the drawings explained?

Day Four: The Doyles as witnesses. Now, at last, a chance to press the Defence's 'trivial, vexatious, unreasonable' accusation. Unfortunately, the way the Court had dealt with the matter itself weakened their argument. How can such a clearly complicated matter that has tied up the Court for four days and with three pre-trial hearings, be described as trivial? The judge finds it difficult to follow. So it must be complicated. The case was not unreasonable or trivial. Nevertheless Lucy and Felix remained confident. They had three killer questions lined up.

'Why,' Felix asked Reg Doyle, 'did you refuse to talk to us and refuse to try to sort things out before you consulted a solicitor?'

He waited for the answer – one eye trained on His Honour.

'I didn't think I had to,' came the reply. He was not denying the accusation, but what sort of an answer is that? Felix glanced again at Judge Lethe. The man in a wig nodded. *He* seemed to accept the eloquent argument. Felix soldiered on, optimism draining into the same place as exasperation. Try again. 'You are claiming that we have taken an area of land no bigger than this handkerchief, (handkerchief evidence shown to Court) you say you thought we had, but you couldn't know that. Not without checking. Wouldn't it have been better to check your facts before taking such drastic action? You are a highly educated man, degrees in physics; you are trained to check data, why did you treat this matter, which on your insistence has been dragged into Court, so casually without checking and clarifying?' His Honour showed less interest in this one.

Shrug from Reg Doyle.

Final go: 'Why did you refuse to let the matter go to arbitration?'

'We had confidence in the Court. The case was before the Court' (smile at His Honour). 'Two surveyors had surveyed the site. I could see no reason for taking the matter to arbitration.'

Questioning Thelma Doyle was even more challenging. As with so many neighbour disputes and many other disputes, family disputes, particularly divorces, muddying the waters is relatively easy. You can't keep records of everything that is said and done, written records, photographic records, electronic records, and any accusation will retain some suspicion of validity no matter how vigorously rebutted.

The facts remained: the Claimants had gone to court without ever discussing things with the Defendants or checking facts and then persistently refused both negotiation and arbitration. They had failed to provide their surveyor's argument until the first day in court. None of this was denied. Nor was it denied that the combatants were previously on friendly terms.

The lawyers could present themselves as above all this tasteless ding-dong. His Honour the Judge remained aloof and seemingly unconcerned. He asked no questions, made no comment. Was he in the Search for Truth business at all? Lucy had become convinced that Judge Lethe had decided on the 'six of one and half a dozen of the other' explanation. A temptingly easy option and not excusable. He would have to ignore the facts now admitted by the Doyles in court.

The Doyles had called a fencer as witness, but it became obvious he was not too sure why he was there or what he was expected to say. He seemed to be making the case for the Grahams, and Lucy noticed that Ms Barrister was quite relieved when he left.

Day Five: At last the Grahams' turn. But Judge Lethe seemed to have difficulty with plans and the decomposition of fence posts. He still hadn't seen what they were talking about. Had not even set a date to look at the facts. The weather was still good. If he had a problem he also had the solution. He *was* in charge.

The Grahams managed to jam four witnesses into their first go. Felix was the first, Lucy played barrister, and he seemed to clear up some confusion caused by the Doyles' expert. Judge Lethe did seem to follow what was being said, and wrote what he wrote with confidence. Of course nobody knew what he actually wrote. Nobody was going to see it and give it marks out of 10. Far from encroaching on the Doyles' land, Felix declared, as would be seen at the site visit, the fence post was more their side.

Paul agreed to give evidence for them. He recounted how Lucy came to see him the very day Reg Doyle shouted at the builders, he told of the early stages of the dispute and delicately described his meeting on site with the other side and how 'unfortunate' it was that they had forgotten to bring any documents. He stressed the Grahams' efforts to resolve things quickly, without giving in to the bullying. Felix and Lucy thought his evidence punched the message 'reasonable meets unreasonable' hard home. Later he told them that given the amount of court time already taken by this matter, the Judge will most likely assume that both parties were equally to blame. 'It's easier, you see.' They didn't see actually. Easier for whom?

Amateurs as they were, the Grahams broke convention and called Mr Gee. They wanted to expose his tactics. They were, in their determined search for truth and justice, losing the focus of their argument. Mr Gee was not accused of unreasonable behaviour, his clients were. It didn't help their case to show some of the unreasonableness was on the part of the Plaintiffs' solicitors and surveyors. This open-faced young man presented a very persuasive witness. Why had he evaded his duty to justify his clients' claim? Why had he refused to meet on their side with documents and reports? Why had he failed to show his clients' deeds until much later? Why had he advised his clients to cancel that crucial meeting and then advised them not to speak to the Grahams? Why did he not respond to their surveyor's report sent a year ago? Why had he waited until the trial began to show his surveyor's final plans and report?

He answered all the questions with equanimity and some of the questions with effective evasiveness, but he stressed that he hadn't advised his clients to cancel the crucial meeting, another member of his firm had. But why had he pursued a case he claimed he knew should never go to court? 'I had thought it was all over last summer,' he said, 'but Mr Doyle came hammering on my door, complaining about bad service, about negligence, and insisting that we continue.' That rang very true of Reg Doyle. Mr Gee was only doing his job. The other lawyer was called and Felix put the same questions to him. The answers came pat: there was no point in his firm's clients meeting them, nothing to be gained and it could have led to problems. Problems? What problems? Misunderstandings can occur when lay people talk to each other (careless talk cost costs?). His clients were being represented by his firm and they were wise to accept professional advice, and could and should trust their lawyers to best look after their interests. Lay people (that's *ordinary* people) should pay lawyers to do the talking it seems. Now, why should that be?

Felix put the questions, attacking the professional tactics of the legal professionals and His Honour, a superior legal professional, left him to it. He did not pursue the answers. Perhaps the Grahams were just a little unwise to ignore the possibility that the Masonry, informal if not sealed in blood, of the professionals would hold in that small-town legal coterie.

This lawyer was a Legal Executive.[6] Legal Executives could be the mainstay in the firm, usually knowing more of the gossip, sometimes knowing more of the law, certainly knowing more of the local courts, who to phone, who to whisper the odd word to, who has the ear of the judge, his likes and dislikes. Sensible young solicitors solicited their favour and their advice. This one was the 'expert' who visited right at the start, who looked at what the Doyles showed him and heard what the Doyles told him and who decided that he knew that the offending post offended. He it was who advised the Doyles what they wanted to be advised: 'Cancel the meeting.'

The builder witness Lucy called did, in the end, say what he was there to say: the post was rotten at the base, had fallen into the passage and he and his mate had asked to remove the encumbrance and later put everything back in exactly the right place. Unfortunately, by the time he got to the end he clearly found the whole experience far more challenging than he had anticipated. He began to look tired. As his confidence ebbed his credibility diminished. He said what he wanted to say, and repeated it often enough. He did not waver from the facts. Again, it wasn't evident that Judge Lethe had taken on board the technical evidence provided. This could and should have been crunch evidence. The Grahams had decided against calling any of the other witnesses to the same evidence because they believed one of the builders would be enough. Both had been keen to give support. They hadn't liked being shouted at and knew the Doyles' claim did not stand up.

The case was adjourned for three weeks; a further day was set down. Would this, finally, conclude the case? It might because this was the day Mrs Britton would give evidence, and this was the day the Grahams *would* persuade the Judge to visit the site.

Day Six: Mrs Britton was a perfect witness. The team from the other side had good reason to fear her appearance. It wouldn't do to 'cross-examine rigorously' a dignified (and determined) lady in her seventies. Her mind was sharp, she was not going to be confused or bullied. She gave the history of the fence. Made it clear that no post had ever been out of line while she lived there. She informed the Judge that were he to visit the site *as she had done on a few occasions recently* (strongly emphasised), he would see that the fence panel the Grahams had erected followed exactly the line of the original side passage, he would be able to feel *as she had*, the straight edge of that old concrete path under the jut of the newer, rough concrete.

Judge Lethe agreed to visit the site. But not that day. There was to be yet Another Day in Court! Lucy was the final witness on Day Six. Still more focussed on the vexatious harassment. Still, even then, fairly sure the Judge would understand their indignation, would agree the Doyles had behaved unreasonably and that he would disapprove. Felix was not so sure. Judge Lethe's attention span was poor; he seemed to be on the verge of falling asleep. Was he taking notes – or was he doodling? Of course he could have visited the site on Day One and then dismissed the Claim as trivial and vexatious, if he'd had a mind to. The Grahams feared that, by Day Six, His Honour himself, was sucked into the legal vortex whipped up by the other side, because an investment of three pre-trial hearings and six days in court over whether one fence post had moved just four inches or not, had to be seen through to the end. It had to be made to look serious. Otherwise the Court would look rather unwise, irresponsible, lacking in good judgment – just plain silly. The Court could lose credibility.

The Grahams had relied on the Judge coming to see for himself. The other side had resisted. 'It's a bit more complex than that,' Ms Barrister had said delaying this nemesis, but now that the site visit was agreed Ms Barrister was suggesting that the impending Courtly visit was their idea. The Grahams had noted other tweaking of the truth on minor matters by this lady but, whether she liked it or not, seeing is believing.

Day Seven: The Site Visit. The Doyles stayed indoors. As usual, Ms Barrister spoke first but this time very quietly, so the Grahams couldn't hear what she was saying into the ear of the Judge. They didn't ask her to speak up.

Finally the Grahams were given their chance. 'The Court' traipsed round to the Grahams' side of the fence. They all stopped at the offending post. Felix showed the extruded concrete. Lucy knelt to run her hand along the straight edge of that original path. Judge Lethe hitched up his robes. He knelt. He felt under the overlapping rough concrete the straight edge of the original path underneath. He looked at the offending post. There it was, perfectly in line with the Grahams' path. He gave nothing away. Had the point been made, finally? As it could have been made two years earlier?

Back to court after lunch for the summing up. Lucy had prepared a speech that was far too long. She was still so determined to emphasise the waste of everybody's time, the provocations, the escalation of costs, Mr Gee urging them to engage solicitors, 'We could tell Mr Gee ourselves why his clients were mistaken, and we didn't need to pay someone else to do it for us.'

'Boundary disputes can cost thousands of pounds and, win or lose the case, the client always loses money, only the lawyers win. Had our neighbours chosen to express their displeasure at our extension and attack us in any other way, we could have sought the Court's help to defend ourselves. Far from defending us, the Court was inadvertently aiding the attack. *It* was the threat that caused all the trouble, and litigation costs was the weapon our neighbours used to try to force us to do as they willed.'

She still agrees with every word of that little speech but, of course, should never have said it in court. A misjudgement made in the belief that judges understood how ordinary people think, that they saw it as their duty to prevent the courts from being used to bully, harass, mug and molest. Those words were very unwise a quarter of a century ago and regrettably they would still be very unwise in the 21st century, not least because they draw attention to the fact that the judge *is* in the arena whether he likes it or not. Wrong words for the wrong judge.

Ms Barrister had the final speech. She did point out how long the Court had taken to 'sort out' her clients' claim. Nothing taking so long could possibly be trivial, if it were, indeed, trivial, it would have been thrown out at the first hearing and never come to trial. Her clients were merely protecting their property from theft which could hardly be described as vexatious action and abuse of the courts, the Court had quite correctly recognised her clients' right to protect their property and agreed the matter should be decided at full trial. Her clients' surveyor was a highly experienced expert witness (he was a local estate agent with basic (interior) measuring skills). She emphasised how much her clients had paid to 'protect their property'. Once again the justification for all this waste of time and money was the waste of time and money. She very sensibly kept her speech short and delivered it with impressive theatrical skills. The Judge listened carefully, conscientiously, took notes (slowly) and – deferred judgment. For five and a half months. He deferred for five and a half months his decision on whether one fence post had been moved four inches into the Doyles' property. This was a long, marinating judgment. It should be rich in flavour, worth waiting for.

His judgment lasted nearly two hours and at the end few had much idea what it amounted to. The Opposition was prepared to propose (helpfully) that it was a fifty-fifty draw, 'and who knows where the post should be!' The ushers and clerks heard Felix's retort, 'Fifty-fifty! If that proposal succeeds we shall appeal.' He had listened rather more carefully. The Grahams' surveyor's work was preferred and Mrs Britton's evidence conclusive. The post was not trespassing. The usher and clerk disappeared and a little later everyone was summoned back to court. The Judge had returned. The post was in the right place and the Plaintiffs must pay costs, but only three-quarters of the Defendants' costs. Why? Well, that wasn't clear to anyone. The Grahams thought it was because he'd rejected their trivial, vexatious, etc., etc. claim, but later they decided it had something to do with a little, fanciful notion possibly whispered into his head by Ms Barrister at that site meeting, something they didn't hear and something never actually mentioned before, certainly not by his Lordship. Had they just listened to 'a fine mind unravelling', to an exhausted old man who had simply lost it … or a judge who had decided to abandon a life of conscientiousness and go for the hell of a joke as he neared retirement? The joke that may well have given His Honour a laugh was a nice little twist, one he'd dreamt up entirely on his own over those five and a half months. He decided that another post, a post nobody had claimed was a problem, encroached on the Doyles' land by *two inches*!

The Grahams did not find it funny. For several reasons. One: the post in question had also rotted at the base and had been reinforced with a concrete stay by the fencer working for the Doyles when they were out at work but the Doyles were at home. The Doyles had decided where it went. The fencer had said as much in his evidence. Two: He had concreted it in further into the Grahams' passage. They had had to chip a bit out to get the bike pedals through. The new concrete stay was two whole inches their way! Anyone who cared to look could see for themselves. His Honour had made it up and rather sneakily not let them in on his tricky plan until too late so the Grahams couldn't even protest, let alone show it was untrue. Judge Lethe left everyone confused.

Felix said, 'We were uncertain whether our sentences were concurrent, suspended or we'd been in the wrong courtroom.'

A local solicitor congratulated them on their 'success'. It seems they had, effectively, 'won' in the sense that the Doyles had to pay their own and most of the Grahams' costs and the post was deemed to be in the right place. People seemed to think that they had won but the Grahams did not share that view: too much nastiness.

Some of the Judge's tangle of words was recorded and some of the recording was transcribed. It still didn't make much sense. Mrs Britton seemed to be the star, the crunch witness. She said the Grahams had done no wrong, so they had done no wrong. The trespass claim failed. As to their vexatious, etc., etc. – well, they decided that must have failed too. No one could remember what he said about it, indeed if he said anything, there was nothing about it in the transcribed sections of his judgment that they received from Mr Gee.

Some time later they met young Mr Gee in town and asked whether he thought there was anything they could have done to prevent the whole sorry saga. Lucy says, 'He was a civil young man but utterly unable to see himself as a villain who'd fleeced his clients and bullied us. He was only doing his job.'

His answer? 'No, nothing. The Judge decides.'

THE FENCEPOST SAGA

THE FENCEPOST SAGA

'A lawyer with his briefcase can steal more than a hundred men with guns.' Mario Puzo (1920-1999) The Godfather. *(1969, Chapter One)*

FIVE
September 2002

Scientia potentia est – Knowledge is power.

So it was Lucy's experience of the civil courts over 20 years earlier that underlay her desire to avoid court action with the Ogmores, at all costs. Max had known Felix and knew the fence-post story and shared her view. Felix had worked professionally on mediated solutions to family disputes before he became ill, Max had joined a project to find mediated resolutions to international business disputes, Lucy had worked with like-minded people on alternative dispute resolution schemes. They were unenthusiastic litigants, they would far prefer some alternative to court where every effort is made to ensure that the 'parties' know as soon as possible what they are disputing, some way of resolving the matter not hamstrung by ancient precedents, irrelevant rules and regulations, bad judge management and litigation tactics driven by litigation costs – lawyers' income.

Lucy had had a look at the 1999[1] reforms which were supposedly revolutionising civil justice and the new rule book read well. The new rules might have prevented the worst of the fence-post saga had they been observed, but she felt it was too early to be confident they could put their trust in them. The reforms had been in place for three years and her enquiries on how they were doing did not encourage confidence, they did not seem to be making much of an impression. To have an effect the new system had to rely on altering the mindset of the practitioners, and old habits die hard. The protection offered by Land Registry indemnity was not enough in itself. There was still the threat of time-wasting games, unpaid work for Max and her and frustration.

Hazel Ogmore's threat (on Bulmer paper) of an injunction arrived on a Saturday. Max and Lucy's lawyer had shut the office. The following Monday was a bank holiday. He would open up again just as Ogmore, assistant solicitor at Bulmer & Co., was making her application at a court 50 miles away for an injunction to keep Max and Lucy off Homestead land. If successful she would be free to make further garden makeovers until Max and Lucy got it back.

In any event, if the Ogmores persuaded the Court to give the injunction, they would have succeeded in getting the whole business into court and out of the hands of Mr Beige, where things were not going so well for them. Max faxed a letter to the Court named by Ogmore. It was very brief: 'We deny the allegations. We object to any restrictions on access to our registered land. This is a matter for mediation not litigation.'

The faxed letter did not get to the Judge until days after he'd sent Ogmore and her barrister friend packing. The Judge was unimpressed by Ogmore's spurious allegations of threatened wanton and imminent destruction of her beloved shed. Apparently, she and her barrister had then tried a few more courts in the region but with no joy. Her claim of a threat to destroy her shed was hardly sustained by the evidence she tried to sell: a conventional letter from Max and Lucy's lawyer instructing her to remove the trespasses within seven days or failing that Max and Lucy would remove it themselves. A standard letter which should have received the standard response. She and her barrister accomplice did manage to persuade one court to set down a directions hearing for the following Friday but they did not want a directions hearing. A directions hearing would mean that Lucy and Max would be there telling the Judge what Ogmore and accomplice did not want him (or her) to hear. They wanted an *ex parte*[2] injunction hearing and pretty damn quick before Lucy and Max could find a lawyer to help.

Mrs Ogmore was not your standard squatter and her barrister friend was not your standard barrister. Whereas the judicial rebuffs would, with ordinary lawyers, have led to a change of direction, a reconsideration of the attractions of the standard response, these two decided to go for broke and lodge their application for an injunction at the Royal Courts of Justice in London. This time they succeeded. Or more accurately, Ogmore's barrister, Keith Stoat, succeeded and within 20 minutes of walking into the Judge's chambers and after a mere 10 minutes of playing with the verities unopposed by irritating facts, was able to fax his co-conspirator the good news. She had got her injunction and taken her squatter claim out of the hands of Mr Beige and into court.

How did Keith Stoat do this? Well, very simply he told the Judge, the High Court Judge, that there had been an 'argy bargy' on 'disputed' land the Monday before. The Ogmores' barrister was gambling, he could have been rumbled if the right questions had been asked. The disapproving High Court Judge did dismiss Stoat's attempt to distort the lawyer's letter, there was no imminent threat;

nevertheless he allowed the injunction preventing Max and Lucy entering their own land, while allowing the squatter free access for her landscape makeovers – to keep two battling parties apart.

Had either Max or Lucy known about all this court activity, had they known it had gone all the way to the Royal Courts of Justice, had the Judge at the Royal Courts insisted that he hear their side of the story, they would have been able to give a more accurate account of what had taken place just a few days earlier. It is highly likely that the outcome that day and all the days to come would have been very different. This is the report they would have been able to give—

The previous Monday, a bank holiday was a nice, warm, sunny, late August day. Lucy had finished painting some cupboard doors while listening to a Radio 4 afternoon play and Max had tidied the woodshed. There were no further diversionary activities they could pretend were an absolute imperative so there was nothing for it, they would have to get the job done and it would have to be done that day. Lucy collected the camera. Max picked up the secateurs. It was just after three by the time they set off. They were going to take photographs of their land in the event that the following day Ogmore would succeed with her injunction and they would be unable to access it. She would be able to continue spraying and clearing it to suggest she had 'always gardened there'.

Max and Lucy went up the road first, to check there was nobody around and take a few pictures down the steep hillside by the shed. Then they went back to approach their land from the woodland path running parallel with the road leading up a slope to the compost box and then the large chalet-style shed. It was the height of summer and the nettles and brambles were flourishing so Max went first with secateurs to cut them away and Lucy came behind using a garden fork for stability on that uncertain terrain. The first six months of walking on their steep hillside land had taught them to treat it with respect. Swollen ankles and unreliable knees threatened to cripple if they didn't take care.

They were fighting their way uphill through the summer jungle when they realised there was someone around after all. Mrs Ogmore was around. She was there ahead and above them on the path just by the compost bin. She was bent over and clapping her hands together like a young child – with the fingers splayed. 'Oh! Very clever, very clever', she said. Max and Lucy stopped, adrenaline rising, brains registering events a second or so late. What was 'very clever'? They stopped, but they did not retreat.

'Very clever!' she repeated. Max went forward. Lucy followed. Hazel Ogmore was trespassing but she was the one who now started to chant 'Get off our land'. Max ignored her and moved to the side of the trespassing compost box to make his way to the encroaching shed. Lucy most unwisely decided to put the camera out of sight in the undergrowth.

'Right,' said Hazel, 'I'm calling the Police.' And stomped off adding, 'Why don't you wait for the judicial process?' Yet again this 'judicial process' – which she had failed to trigger with Land Registry but seemed eager to throw at the Court. Max and Lucy weren't that concerned about the Police threat, Hazel Ogmore had already called the Police once too often and had credibility problems ever since the officers had seen the evidence confirming that her claims did not stand scrutiny. As she strutted back across her newly-acquired garden she passed a man coming across the grass towards Max and Lucy and spoke to him. Whatever she said caused Joe Ogmore to change gear from a walk to an attempt at a run, a sort of lumber, and grab something from the shed wall. Events which had been odd so far, then took a turn for the ugly.

Lucy was aware that Joe Ogmore now had something in his hand: metal, long, thin and bright silver. 'A knife flashed into my numbed brain,' she says, but it was not a knife. It was a long, narrow trowel. There was no time for further study as Ogmore had pushed Max hard in the chest forcing him to take a step back causing him to catch his heel on the edge of the wooden compost box. He landed with a heavy thud on top of dry weeds and twigs. Ogmore, a short, fat gentleman in a dirty, orange tee shirt was now towering over Max who was sitting hunched among the dry compost less than two feet off the ground while Ogmore was trying to wrestle the secateurs from his fist. Failing in that, Joe Ogmore started to hit Max on the head with the fist holding the trowel. One, two, three. Max started to put his hands up to protect his eyes. Four, five, six! Max was now hit on the inside of his protecting arms and Ogmore tried again to wrestle the secateurs from him. Max bent double linking his hands behind his head and dropped the secateurs behind him. Now Ogmore rained blows on the very vulnerable base of his skull. All this time he was chanting 'Get off our land! Get off our land!'

And what was Lucy doing? 'I was still trying to get my brain up to speed. Nothing in my life had prepared me for this.' It finally caught up as the attack on Max's neck gathered pace. She was standing on a narrow strip of grass just beside the compost box with a sheer cliff of cleared land less than a foot to her left. She knew she really ought to do something. She had the garden fork. Options flashed into her mind. A claymore-style swing to send Ogmore into the shed, a bayonet thrust of the fork's tines to the neck to send him into eternity.

She turned the handle of the fork towards him and prodded his large belly very gently, but enough to stop him hitting Max. He paused. He thought for a moment then he swung his fist and hit her hard on the side of her face pushing the pin of her earring into her flesh. She finally found words.

'You stupid man,' she said, 'you'll end up back inside!'

That stopped him. The chanting stopped. He turned to go back to the house and as he did so he said, 'You stupid women.' What did he meant by 'women'? Was he referring to his wife as well as Lucy? Had she suggested the attack when she spoke to him just before he launched himself at Max? Did she say, 'Start an affray', for example? Or was he disgusted by Max's lily-livered, pacifist response to his gung-ho attack on invaders, unaware, obviously, of Max's special training at Her Majesty's (Government) expense in techniques for dealing with the enemy, techniques not shown to ordinary national servicemen, techniques which did not involve weapons but could involve death. Max was a few years older than this assailant but far fitter. Ogmore had had a lucky escape. He didn't deserve it. As he walked back to his house he passed his wife again as she returned. Again they spoke. She seemed keen to console him. 'You did very well dear, very well,' they heard her say.

'I've called the Police,' she announced and, approached nearer still bent over like someone with indigestion, still with the splayed fingers. 'You think you're judge and jury. What are you afraid of? Why don't you wait for the judicial process?' Again this non-existent 'judicial process'.This was the process they could have avoided if Land Registry had done its job, or if the Swales had not lied about neighbour disputes, or if the squatters were ordinary squatters and not a pair of rogue lawyers.

Lucy said that they would wait for the Police and Hazel stomped back to Blackstone Cottage. As Max and Lucy were slowly regaining their wits, but before the shock effect hit them, they took advantage of the moment to inspect what the Ogmores had been up to in the time since they had last inspected their misappropriated land. Unfortunately, Lucy's wits were not fully regained; she forgot the camera.

Quite a bit of new land had been cleared by spraying and hacking but not planted or landscaped. Max and Lucy sat on the edge of the newly-created cliff and waited for the Police. Ten, 15 minutes they waited. The short deep cuts in Max's skull were still slowly dripping blood. The effects of the shock attack were beginning to tell. Ogmore must have left 20, 25 minutes earlier. They decided they would wait no more. They would return home along the path to call the Police themselves.

Lucy stopped the bleeding and Max went straight to bed on her orders. She tried to distract herself weeding. Not a good idea, weeding allows far too much time for thinking and the significance of what had happened was slowly beginning to sink in. This was a whole new revelation of the nature of their opponents. The Ogmores showed what Lucy's late husband, Felix, a psychotherapist, would have called 'borderline personality'. What sort of person in their sixties single-handedly attacks two people armed with secateurs and a garden fork yet seems fearless of their own danger? How fanatical is this man for land – their land?

It did not occur to either of them that day the attack may have been deliberate, strategic.

When Police Sergeant Edwards arrived an hour or so later Max was lying in bed. The bleeding from the short, deep cuts in his head had mostly stopped, but the bruises and contusions on his arms and neck were coming out and his right hand where Ogmore had tried to wrestle the secateurs from him was red and swollen. The side of Lucy's face and ear were still red and throbbing. She was trying to keep busy concerned that she had not shown the constraint Max had managed but had pushed the thug in the belly. She was pretty sure Ogmore would claim it was one against two and that she had struck him. Which she had. Not quite a strike, perhaps, more a push with the T handle of the garden fork. Nevertheless, she regretted that at this late stage in her life she had used force and to little avail, except that it did stop the dangerous attack on Max. She doubted she had made a mark on him whereas it was all too evident that he had made marks on both of them. She wasn't agitated, she wasn't angry, she wasn't even anxious. She was depressed and told the Sergeant so. She was depressed because she could see that this was going to be a dreadful business. They were up against two borderline cases who had the resources and the obsession to continue the games they had been playing for the previous nine months but far more intensely and on the playing field of their choice. It was now clear that they were quite capable of far more than just reordering land and distorting facts to protect themselves, and if they were successful with their injunction application the following day, the whole business would be in the hands of the Court. Courts mean money. Courts mean stress, and court combat with two tricksy lawyers mean both money and stress writ large.

The Police, however, had shown a different approach and different talents. So far they had not been taken in by the claims of the Ogmores, and this new policeman, Sergeant Edwards, was a good policeman. He told them he had been looking at the reports of the two earlier occasions when the Ogmores had summoned them. He didn't tell them what the reports said, but he did listen carefully to what he was now told. He looked at the cuts and bruises and recorded them and he wrote statements which he gave them to sign. It was interesting that both Max and Lucy who had hardly spoken to each other after the attack both described the instrument that caused the cuts in Max's head and contusions on the inner parts of his arms as a long, thin, silver trowel with a wiggle at the end. Neither of them could take in all that they'd seen so neither of them could be more precise about this weapon. Sergeant Edwards wrote out their statements in his own Tyneside voice, but neither Max nor Lucy felt inclined to object. The facts he recorded were correct. They did feel better by the time he left to drive up the road to Blackstone Cottage and the Ogmores.

It was some hours later when he phoned to say that he had brought Ogmore in for questioning and the following morning when he telephoned again to say that Ogmore had been held overnight and charged with Actual Bodily Harm on Max and Assault on Lucy.

'He did not have a scratch on him, yet he admitted that you two had between you a pair of secateurs and a garden fork. He seemed to think that as he believed you were trespassing on his land he had the right to physically 'escort you off it'. But even if it was his land he had no right to attack you like that. I noted all the injuries. If it had been the fight he claims he'd have been seriously discommoded against two well-armed adversaries. I'm sending a photographer round to record your injuries. My only problem is that I could not find that trowel with the wiggle you both described. I looked everywhere.'

'You couldn't look *everywhere*,' they assured him, 'they could easily have thrown it down the hill, the undergrowth is dense, they could have hidden it anywhere in the house. Even with a search warrant and a team of searchers that trowel would not be seen again,' they said. They were wrong, but by the time it *was* found Sergeant Edwards had moved back to Newcastle and this story had moved on.

Judges don't have time to check out the facts and if there's been an affray *and* an arrest they have a clear duty to keep the antagonists apart. To keep the peace. This Judge did not inquire why if there had been an affray *both* combatants had not been arrested. No doubt Keith Stoat would have had a ready answer. He wasn't asked. So it was that war was unleashed. The weapon was litigation and only one side was armed and knew the tricks of combat.

Lucy was woken at seven the next morning by Max informing her that there was a bailiff at the door with a court order. Lucy says that if there's one thing guaranteed to get her hackles up it's being woken up early in the morning (early for her, anyway) for no good reason. The Bailiff was, admittedly very embarrassed and apologetic. Ogmore started the harassment by the Court system that day. They were going to get used to it. They were also going to get used to visits from Mr Nelson, the Bailiff, that week, getting ever more embarrassed and apologetic each time he appeared. 'She doesn't know what she's doing. She's so strung out. I'm very sorry. Please don't think that the people in this county are all like this.'

'But she's not one of your people – she's a Londoner,' they assured him. She had made some mistake on the forms so they had to be delivered – in duplicate – three times. They contained an interim injunction preventing Lucy and Max from going on to their own land, so she had succeeded in getting over the first key hurdle. They didn't know at the time how, but they were still confident she'd get no further.

They phoned their solicitor. He couldn't help. He said he didn't do litigation. Why did he not tell them that when they went to see him? Now they had to find another solicitor who did do litigation, and in a hurry. He named a firm in another town to the north. They didn't know any law firms in the area North, South, East or West and didn't have time to make enquiries. They rearranged their plans for the day and went to see a Mr Cain at Cross & Cross & Co. Mr Cain was intrigued. He looked at the documents. He seemed to think their opponents would make interesting adversaries. He told them they should attend court that Friday in a town some 30 miles away for a hearing. 'Of this woman's injunction?' they asked. 'No, it's just a directions hearing. The injunction hearing is the following Wednesday.'

Lucy and Max were booked to go to London for the weekend: cricket at Lords. Max, a MCC member, had invited guests. He was not prepared to be bullied and inconvenienced by the dubious actions of the squatters; if this Friday's hearing wasn't that important they wouldn't go, but Mr Cain strongly advised that they went and also write their own application to try to get it heard at the same time the following Wednesday.

Hazel Ogmore tracked them down to Mr Cain and tried to get to speak to him. She left a message with the receptionist informing him that what Lucy and Max had reported was just a 'sob story' and to contact her to hear the 'facts'. He did not contact her.

Max rearranged plans for the weekend and wrote a couple of statements for the Friday directions hearing: 'the land is registered to us, unless and until Ogmore proves otherwise; for nine months we have been asking her to provide evidence of her claim to our land or remove herself and she has done neither, she *has* been clearing more and more of it; the Court should take note that Mr Ogmore has been arrested for his assault on both of us last Monday;' and finally, 'we don't think this is a matter for litigation in court. We think this is a matter for mediation and open disclosure of evidence.'

District Judge Dyer was a small, shiny-faced man with a ready smile which faded as Max read out their statement. He turned a less than friendly face to Ogmore. 'Well?' he said, 'what about it? Mediation?'

She didn't manage an answer. She just shook her head, and he said no more on that. Not another word on mediation. No attempt to persuade nor any question as to why she rejected it. He did make a note of her rejection. He then turned to directions. 'Well, then – directions ...' he started. Ogmore interrupted 'There's a hearing set for next Wednesday on my ... my *client's* application for an injunction.'

District Judge Dyer showed some impatience – 'So, what am I doing here?' he asked her. She shrugged. Clearly the Court staff hadn't noticed the duplication and Ogmore had failed to notify the Court and cancel this redundant hearing. Max and Lucy could have stuck to their travel plans after all. 'No directions,' he said and packed up to go. Thus ended their first experience of the new civil justice landscape with their squatter neighbour. A complete waste of time and two train tickets.

Back from their cricket weekend late on the Sunday night, they quickly drafted their own application for an injunction as Mr Cain had advised; modelling it on the one they'd received from Ogmore. They named Mrs Ogmore alone as the Defendant as she had named herself alone as the Claimant.

The next day they heard noises up the road and went to investigate. Ogmore's gardener was putting the fence panels back. She had an interim injunction and they couldn't stop her. In any event when Max and Lucy got there, Max with his camera, her gardener assured them that were they to try he'd use his hammer on them. They needed a sound recording of this. Lucy ran back to the house for the camcorder, but it took too long and the camcorder battery was dead. The gardener was still there, however, finishing up his illegal activities and he didn't know the camcorder was dead. 'So,' she said pointing it at him, 'you refuse to stop putting up that fence on our land and threaten us with violence if we try to stop you?' He looked awkward and mumbled, 'I don't know what you mean. I never threatened you.' This was Ogmore's reliable witness. 'Oh! So you *do* lie,' Lucy said. He looked shifty, stopped work, grabbed his tools and scarpered. Max had a few pictures and they returned home to finish their application to the Court adding a request that the Court order Ogmore to prevent her 'servants or agents' making further attacks or threats.

The following day, Monday, they drove a second time the 60-mile return journey to the Court to lodge their application. The Clerk was a very helpful young woman who was also sympathetic. Apparently she'd encountered Ogmore and her barrister friend when they'd tried to get the injunction at this Court and they had been distinctly unpleasant and angry when they were only granted the directions hearing. She told Max and Lucy that they tried to say that they'd only been rejected by the judges at the other courts because they'd applied to the wrong court, but this young lady, suspecting something was up, had phoned the first Court and been told that they'd been sent packing because they had not persuaded the Judge there was a need for an injunction. The young lady was pretty disgusted by their bullying manner and their misrepresentation of the facts. Max and Lucy drove home fairly confident things would soon be sorted out and Ogmore would have to either put her case or remove her trespass or, more likely, both.

They returned yet again to court two days later, Wednesday, for the injunction hearing, putting the rest of their lives on hold for what they hoped would be a crucial and final court appearance. This hearing was to be held in a real courtroom. As they waited among other litigants and representatives they noticed a short, overweight, balding man in barrister garb fixing them sternly and weaving his way towards them. He was trying so hard to impress by standing as tall as he could manage he was in danger of falling over backwards. He didn't introduce himself by name and refused to sit down. Having checked who they were, he asked if they had a solicitor present. 'We haven't had enough warning for our solicitor to attend. He's advised us not to agree to anything but wait until he checks out any proposals either from you or from us. We're awaiting confirmation from our legal expenses insurers and Land Registry on the detail of costs cover.' Lucy and Max had the satisfaction of the very slightest blink in his fixing eyes. He turned stiffly and returned to Ogmore. Lucy realised that they hadn't given him a copy of their prepared statement about land ownership. She found him sitting sprawled in a small room talking to Ogmore. She tapped on the glass of the door. Lucy says he turned slowly and flicked a finger which she assumed was an invitation to enter. Not a man overendowed with charm and good manners then. She handed him the statement.

The presiding Judge was a Circuit Judge. One up from a District Judge, who is one up from a Deputy District Judge. In clear contrast to Judge Number One (the one they were told was District Judge Dyer), he was tall and grey, pallid and grey. Not old – just grey. Lucy names him Judge Grey.

He gave the floor to Ogmore's man, Keith Stoat. The first thing Stoat did once proceedings started was throw in their direction a thick sheaf of papers. '*American Cyanamid*',[3] he said. Lucy had no idea what he was talking about. Later Lucy learnt that this was a case which established the legal precedent of *status quo* – leaving things as they are. In other words he was arguing that whatever the merits of the case or the legality of Ogmore putting her fence back on their land, things should stay as they are until the case is sorted. The fence should stay. And the injunction.

Neither Max nor Lucy had a hope of reading even the first page of the thick, small-print document there and then, let alone understanding it and deliberating on the best course of action. Of course, if Stoat had handed it to them while they were waiting to go into the courtroom, they would at least have been forewarned and had 40 minutes or so to consider objecting. They didn't even think to speak. But then they were over-confident, they had imagined that once a Judge in the new Woolf landscape had read their submission papers and looked at the exhibits attached, he would dismiss this injunction application in no time and Ogmore and her barrister would be sent packing again. Instead he sat high on his seat above them and gave a lecture on the obvious, intoning in a slightly bored but disapproving manner, 'These disputes can lead to enormous expense and stress, you both can't win, somebody has to lose in the end ... Now go away find yourselves a room and talk.' He had heard what Stoat had to say. He didn't invite either Max or Lucy to speak. They didn't need to be told what 'these disputes' could lead to. It is unlikely that any normal citizen would need the advice either, even without a fence-post experience.

Lucy and Max followed Stoat to a room. He was still trying to be dignified and intimidating, but Lucy couldn't lose that image of him nearly falling over backwards. Max started things off by reporting the incident with the gardener a few days earlier; pointing out that Ogmore had no right to put the fence back on their land. Stoat protested, 'But it's not your land. Mrs Ogmore states it's in her deeds.' Max corrected him dismissively. 'Even she doesn't claim that area of land in her deeds – you must surely know that?' Stoat exploded from his chair, 'Don't speak to me like that. Who do you think you are?' Lucy stopped being amused. Was this the bad manners and bullying the young clerk had taken exception to? What on Earth are they going to achieve with this man?

He remained standing. Lucy muttered her objection to his aggressive manner. He calmed a bit.

'Well,' he said, 'I suppose if we can all be civil we may get somewhere. You say in your Particulars of Claim[4] that you are prepared to leave the disputed land as recorded in the deeds – your deeds and Mrs Ogmore's deeds – to Land Registry to determine. We could call that land "the rectification land". We might agree to that.' Max and Lucy exchanged looks of relief and nodded agreement. 'That leaves the rest of the land Mrs Ogmore believes is hers, the land she claims she's acquired by adverse possession.'

'Yes', they said, waiting. Stoat was still standing. 'How about Mrs Ogmore offers to buy that land from you?' Max and Lucy exchanged smiles; this was more interesting, it could bring everything to an end in no time. All that potential for chicanery in an adverse possession claim cut off before it got started. Once the sale is done and dusted they need have no further dealings with this woman or her aggressive husband. 'Would you be interested?' he asked.

'To clarify,' said Max, 'the rectification land claim she's making is settled by Land Registry, and Ogmore, *Mrs* Ogmore, offers to buy the extra land she wanted to try to claim by adverse possession, the squatter land. That's sensible bearing in mind she doesn't stand much chance with that claim – as you must know.' Stoat did not respond. 'We just want these people out of our lives and behind a fence,' Lucy said. 'You know Joe Ogmore attacked both of us last week and the CPS are charging him with assault and actual bodily harm?'

Stoat sat down at last. 'I'm not representing Joe Ogmore. He's not my concern. I'm representing Hazel; I'm looking after Hazel Ogmore. As the Judge has warned these sorts of cases can prove very protracted and very expensive.'

'Of course we know that,' said Max. 'Why didn't your client get on with the process of sorting it out with Land Registry? That way was not expensive.'

Stoat shifted in his chair and changed mood again. 'It takes time. It's a bit more complex than that. You can't always keep at it. You know I've got a property in a village not far from here and my neighbour, an elderly lady, disputes my ownership of a bit of my land. She goes on the attack from time to time and then forgets about it, and then later starts all over again. It's been going on for years.' Was he now turning friendly, taking them into his confidence? 'I can see that you are obviously reasonable people, what do you think? Would you be prepared to sell her the land?'

'Well,' said Max, 'we'll certainly consider selling her some of the land, not all the land she seems to want if her letters are any guide, but some of it once

Land Registry has done the job it needs to do. The job they're offering to do according to the man we spoke to there. You understand that she hasn't made a claim not even for the rectification land?' Again Stoat did not respond. 'Well, if she comes up with a reasonable offer – yes, we'd certainly consider it.'

Stoat stood. 'Right. I'll go to see her now and see what she thinks of your proposal.' He left. Lucy turned to Max, '*Our* proposal? Why did he say that? It was his proposal and I didn't like his "I can see you're both reasonable people". That's exactly what Gee said to Felix and me on the one occasion we got to see him before the Doyles started court action. It disarmed us then. It's not going to disarm me a second time. This one seems to want to play hard games/soft games. That outburst was crazy, uncalled for. I don't trust him.'

'He's Ogmore's man and claims to be a friend of hers, of course we don't trust him, but he's all we've got and as long as Land Registry finally gets to see her claim and sort that out, things should be OK. We've told him we're not agreeing to anything until Cain has seen it.'

They should have spent the lengthy time Stoat left them on their own writing a record of the conversation. In fact they should have recorded everything that had taken place on a tape recorder. Instead, they waited, doing nothing. Half an hour passed. What was taking so long? Was she proving difficult to persuade?

It was getting to lunch time and Lucy had just decided to go to hunt some sandwiches when Stoat burst back into the room with the curious remark, 'Have you had enough time or do you want some more?' They were waiting for him, what was he trying to suggest? That the delay was due to them? 'We're wanted back in Court,' he announced. Bemused they asked if she's agreed to the proposal pointing out that they'd been twiddling their thumbs waiting for a reply. 'Yes, yes,' he said.

'Well, how should we value the land she may want to buy?' asked Max.

'Ah! Well,' said Stoat, 'willing buyer, willing seller.[5] What we'll do is you propose three valuers, she'll propose three valuers and we'll see if we can agree a valuer who will give a valuation.' They knew that this was a nonsense. If she wanted to buy and they were prepared to sell, they should bargain on a price Max and Lucy proposed. Besides, any agreement was dependant on advice from Mr Cain. Anyway, they had to wait for Land Registry's decision on the 'rectification' land first. For the same reason they didn't pay much heed to the next event. Stoat produced a copy of the Hammer plan. 'Let's look at what we're talking about,' he said.

'Not with that plan,' said Max.

'It'll do for now,' said Stoat and proceeded to mark off sections of land on it. He didn't explain he intended to hand the marked plan to the Judge and it didn't strike them as strange that he was marking a discredited plan when there were several OS plans available.

As they approached the courtroom Hazel Ogmore whispered something to her man and he came back to ask them if they would still let her have access to her shed and make bonfires on their land. In the new spirit of what they took to be good relations they agreed instantly, blissfully unaware of the games being played. Back in the courtroom Stoat did the talking. The Judge was now all smiles as though he was dealing with squabbling children who had made up.

'Subject to professional advice, the Defendants would consider selling some of their land to the Claimant, *willing buyer, willing seller* – the land marked on the plan.' The penny dropped. That's why he had marked plots on the Hammer plan. Max delved in their file and found their unmarked copy. Lucy tried to recall what Stoat had drawn on the plan and regretted they had paid no attention to his hurried scribbles, but then decided that it didn't matter as Land Registry would still have to do its work first, and Cain would ensure everything was correct.

Judge Grey was pleased with them. They were pleased with themselves – until, that is, the moment when the Judge turned in their direction and looked at them for the first time. He solemnly informed them that they were not to go on to the land marked on his copy of the plan handed to him by Stoat – on pain of prison!

Until that moment neither Max nor Lucy had spoken in court. They had not been invited to speak. Lucy's shocked intake of breath on hearing that threat was picked up by the microphone and the Judge heard. He turned back towards them.

'Can we speak?' she asked. He nodded encouragingly. 'We're not sure …' she began, mind whirling in confusion. She whispered to Max, 'But surely she has to make her case for any injunction against us?' Her whisper was picked up by the microphone and the Judge interrupted. He told them in quite a kindly way that it was simply a temporary measure until a decision was made about the land, until the dispute was settled. Lucy's mind blanked. Trying and failing to make sense of it, utterly confused, they filed out of court. Stoat was now all smiles and friendliness. Well, *he* seemed happy, no more tantrums and at least Hazel Ogmore was now prepared to let Land Registry get on with the job they should have completed months ago. Maybe those highly questionable figures on her deed plan will be tested forensically to see if they were genuinely written in 1963. Thank goodness Mr Beige of Land Registry had her deeds in safe keeping. Better still, she'd given up the pretence that she owned the squatter/adverse possession land by agreeing to buy the land she'd threatened to take through the court system. That had to be a better outcome. Not that the court system had gained Lucy's confidence. As she was leaving she turned to Stoat, saying: 'Well, I don't suppose we'll meet again but I think we've found a solution. Goodbye.' She even offered her hand, and he even shook it.

On the journey home reality kicked in. What on Earth was that Judge doing letting that woman have free run of their land and denying them access – to their own property? Didn't he read their submission? Did he know what he was doing? He had given Ogmore her injunction without hearing a word on the subject from their side. The depressing thought occurred to them – perhaps he hadn't read their work – all the work, and therefore he didn't know what he was doing. Then they realised that they hadn't managed to read out in court the prepared Statement Lucy had handed to Stoat, setting out the case for them to be granted an injunction, not Mrs Hazel Ogmore.

Then Max asked, 'Did you hear Stoat say anything to the Judge about Land Registry settling the "rectification land" question?' Lucy couldn't remember. 'You know, I don't think so.' The journey home got gloomy.

Once home things moved from gloomy to black. The post had been delivered. There was a letter from Mr Beige. Ogmore had written to him days before saying that everything was now with the Court and Land Registry no longer had anything to do with her claims so she wanted all her papers back. His letter reported that he had sent everything back – everything including the original conveyance with the original dodgy plan. The one they wanted tested forensically.

They phoned Mr Beige immediately. Why couldn't he have warned them? 'We made an agreement in court today based on the understanding that you would be adjudicating on the "rectification land". Nobody told us that she had withdrawn all her documents. Now she's got her plan back and we'll never be able to test its authenticity. What's more we'll have to fight it out in court at either our or Land Registry's expense. She'll not have to pay a penny to a lawyer because she *is* her lawyer.' Mr Beige stuttered his apologies. He couldn't do anything else he insisted. He didn't know about the injunction hearing and besides, he had to return everything when she demanded he do so. 'You could have alerted us,' said Max

She'd written to him five days earlier. He'd had plenty of time to let Max and Lucy know before he returned the deeds. He'd always copied correspondence to both sides previously – why not then? He knew they wanted the forensic tests. Mr Beige began to sound upset. He was fulsomely apologetic. They reminded him that he was the one who urged them to consult a lawyer and told him what the lawyer had advised. They told of Joe Ogmore's physical assault.

Mr Beige assured them that they would be indemnified by the Registry for 'all reasonable costs'. This should have pacified them a bit – but it didn't. The following day they wrote to the Court – to the Judge, as tactfully as they could, avoiding any hint of criticism of the way he had managed the hearing, enclosing the Statement they had given Stoat.

Their new solicitor, Robin Cain, met them the following week after they'd received copy of the order Judge Grey made. 'Looks a bit of a mess at the moment but good job you made clear everything was dependent on professional advice. You're not committed. I'm sure we can recover ground, if you'll excuse the pun.'

Over the next couple weeks some ground was recovered by Cain. They had stressed to him at their first meeting it was likely that he would encounter a challenging adversary with Ogmore acting for Ogmore. He may have to check things with them more often than is usual for a straightforward boundary dispute. It wasn't a straightforward boundary dispute. It was a squatter dispute with a dodgy solicitor and her ex-con, physically aggressive husband.

Robin Cain's sharp, admonitory letters to Ogmore overcame their misgivings about his ability to be forceful enough with their adversary. They stressed that the first thing they wanted corrected was that injunction. He was curious about Stoat's failure to inform them that Ogmore had got all her documents back. Neither Lucy nor Max was sure that Stoat knew. They couldn't say whether the barrister had knowingly withheld that information or whether his client had withheld the information from him. All they knew was that they had been misled. Also, they couldn't understand why the Judge had granted the injunction without even inviting them to speak. They gave their new champion the copy of the letter from Land Registry granting indemnity.

For some reason Cain was not encouraging on the matter of lifting the injunction. He wanted to know what inconvenience it was causing. Quite apart from the clear injustice, his clients thought she was still chopping trees and clearing the land, so he visited Homestead and armed with binoculars agreed she might well be in the process of clearing more of the land. He proposed they engage a barrister to represent them at the next hearing, a directions hearing. As Land Registry had confirmed that they would pay for a barrister's (reasonably priced) services, his clients agreed. They noted that many of the barristers' hourly rates he quoted were lower than his.

They'd been in the area no more than a year but they already knew two other couples with ongoing land disputes. One had been full of praise for their barrister. Word-of-mouth recommendation, just what they wanted. Such rare and valuable intelligence is difficult to find when it comes to legal services; nevertheless, Cain asked them to consider another barrister, one listed in two chambers, one in London and one in the West Midlands, who was running classes for lawyers on adverse possession. 'Nobody knows more about the law on adverse possession than Robert Tweed. Only recently called but already making quite a name for himself. It's quite a journey but I'm attending his courses on land disputes – young, ambitious with a nimble mind.'

They dithered a bit as Lucy was reluctant to pass up on the first recommendation, but now they had two. One with a well established reputation, the other eager to make his mark. They agreed on Robert Tweed. He offered a telephone conference before the hearing and to return to Homestead after the hearing to look at the site.

'You see?' said Max. 'Things *have* changed. The lawyers are moving into that new landscape of Lord Woolf and friends. This is not going to be a repeat of the fence-post saga. We don't have to do it all ourselves and Land Registry is paying the bills – as long as they're reasonable. Relax. Leave it to the experts.'

Cain was away the following week and left them in the hands of his young assistant, Sameer Shah, who set up the telephone conference. He also telephoned the Court to see if there might be time at the next hearing for their application to set aside or vary the injunction. He reported back that there may well be time but they'd have to check on the day. Things were definitely looking up. Robert Tweed (married, father of two – they'd checked his bio online) had a deeply reassuring voice. He was impressed with their witness evidence and thought they'd done quite a good job (not perfect) with their amateur claim and particulars – considering they were amateurs. He wasn't so sure about setting aside the injunction, and didn't appear to be an enthusiast for Alternative Dispute Resolution (ADR[6]), but he pointed out that Ogmore and Stoat were bullies and that bullies are best dealt with firmly. He could be a bully when necessary and given what he knew from his brief he thought this was just such a necessary occasion. In fact he'd quite enjoy it. They were not surprised their ambitious young Counsel was looking forward to the battle. Thanks to all their work he had a well-prepared case and some very impressive supporting evidence and his/their opponent was ripe for exposure. They arranged to meet him at the Court an hour before the hearing and when he assured them that there was nothing for them to do. 'I'm doing the work – that's why you've engaged me.' Lucy relaxed for the first time in weeks. Max was right, this was not, as she was beginning to fear, going to be a repeat of the fence-post saga.

A week later Lucy got a call from a police officer, a new one. Apparently Ogmore had kicked up a great fuss about their removal of the fence panels and gone to the highest level demanding that the police charge them with some crime. With her husband in prison and their firm sold off, she had decided in 1989 to move to their weekend cottage and look for work in the area, Mr Bulmer, the elderly, old-time solicitor who owned her firm and who had so unwisely taken her on, was well known in the nearby county town police headquarters as a duty solicitor. That's one who is listed to take cold calls from the station when some miscreant needed a lawyer. He'd been around for decades and had quite a good name at the station. Bulmer had had a word with the Superintendent on behalf of his Associate and the Superintendent had sent instructions down the line to the local station: investigate. Lucy was quite unaware of the string pulling until PC Windsmoor rang her.

The first thing he made clear was that they were perfectly entitled to remove the fence panels. Of course this was not new information, his colleague (the squatter expert) had said as much and they'd been acting on advice from him and their first solicitor, but PC Windsmoor was very pleased to be able to quote the legal precedent (*Chamberlain* v *Lindon* (1998) 1 WLR 1252[7]), and his report would go up to the Super' with the case name and number. 'No crime,' his report would say. But that was not all. PC Windsmoor was a thorough investigator, not only had he spoken with the gentleman who had sold Blackstone Cottage to the Ogmores in 1989, a Mr Severn, he had managed to trace the owners of the cottage right back to a Mr Loach who had bought the place in 1964, nine months after the first 1963 sale with the scribbled child's drawing plan. Apparently Mr Loach had bought the Black Hut as a ruin and turned it into Blackstone Cottage, a habitable weekend retreat and sold it on in 1970. PC Windsmoor had actually managed to speak to Mr Loach and was very keen to tell Lucy that although both Mr Severn and Mr Loach had rather hazy memories, they both were certain that hardly any land Homestead side of Blackstone Cottage belonged to them. Mr Severn was of the view that when he sold Blackstone Cottage to the Ogmores in 1989, 13 years earlier, his land Homestead side did not extend beyond the conifers. So his recollection matched Rick Stone's and Mr Loach's: the land Homestead side matched their Registered Title plan with the 'necklace' boundary to Blackstone Cottage.

If only they'd had this information a month earlier. It looked as though it was now too late as they'd more or less agreed Ogmore's 1963 deed plan in their letter to Land Registry, written before Joe Ogmore's physical assault.

'There's more,' he continued. 'Tony Severn (I went to school with him, by the way) said he was pretty miffed when he found he had much less land than he thought, less than the estate agent's particulars said. He's kept the property description and has given me a copy; it says half an acre here. Estate agents! He says he found out *after* he'd bought that it was just a small plot surrounded by your trees. He insists that he did not mislead the Ogmores as he had been misled. He is pretty certain that the electricity pole is on your land. That's the electricity pole not the telephone pole. The electricity pole is nearer her house isn't it? Look, I think I'd like to come round and see you before I put my report in.'

He came the following day. He confessed that neither previous owners of Blackstone Cottage were prepared to give evidence, but he really wanted the information he'd gleaned to be used in some way. He showed them copy of the estate agent's particulars Mr Severn had given him. 'Half an acre of mainly woodland,' it said. How did he find out it was less? PC Windsmoor couldn't say, but he warned Lucy and Max that his schoolmate, Tony, wanted nothing more to do with it. *She* had already been to see him twice and he was adamant he'd had enough of her; he wanted nothing more to do with the dispute. He insisted that *his* sales particulars did not mislead on the size of the plot sold to the Ogmores and it was considerably less than half an acre. He no longer had any copy of those particulars. Tantalising. If the agents at the time he bought had lied on the particulars why didn't he do something about it? Why hadn't he gone after whoever carried out the conveyance, the solicitor? PC Windsmoor couldn't say but could see it was unfortunate that his schoolmate had not kept a copy of the sales particulars given to the Ogmores, and that he was unwilling to be a witness.

Before he left he urged them to invest the £25 the Law Society charged and get a copy of their report on Joe Ogmore's striking off. The Officer having so pointedly suggested that he knew something he thought they should know, they made the investment and found in the report the list of offences: using his clients' funds as his own for a number of years and making numerous fictitious and 'improper' entries into accounts as well as breathtaking overcharging. One quoted example was a charge of £96,000 for work the Law Society priced at £8,500. As far as the Law Society was concerned his behaviour was 'at the very top of the scale of serious professional misconduct.'

Max and Lucy now decided to look into the matter of the electricity pole. It emerged that the owners of Homestead had been paid wayleave[8] for the pole until 1995. That year Mr Joseph Ogmore had informed the electricity company of the time (changed a couple of times since then) that the pole was on his land. The lady he informed did not question his claim and merely wrote to Rick Stone telling him that the wayleave would be paid to Ogmore in future! Lucy managed to contact Rick Stone. He told her that he knew nothing of this. He had always received the annual wayleave as had previous Homestead owners, and hadn't noticed the missing payment in his last three years of ownership. He'd been living and working in London at that time and the sum of money was just a couple of pounds a year and easily forgotten. He had quite enough trouble chasing up royalties he was owed which were an awful lot of pounds. Ogmore had certainly never told him about claiming the wayleave. If Rick Stone had been alerted to what was going on he would have acted to correct matters. More 'if only' hindsight for Max and Lucy.

It was becoming increasingly likely that Blackstone Cottage land ended where the conifers and the old fence ended, just where their surveyor, James Nunn, had placed a peg to mark the boundary point according to Homestead's registered Title plan. Bolstered by all this new evidence strengthening their case they looked forward to meeting their eager young barrister with his authoritative voice and a proclivity for bullying bullies.

SIX
September–October 2002

'The lies and nonsense that the law is stuffed with, forms so thick a mist, that a plain man can neither see through nor into it.'

Jeremy Bentham (1748–1832)

The man they met in the cramped interview room at the Court was not quite what they expected. For a start he was far younger, slimmer and shorter than his telephone voice suggested. No problem with young, slim and short, but there was something distracted about his manner. The file he held, their file, appeared to be falling apart. He was constantly shuffling papers. He kept looking over their shoulders rather than at them. When they reminded him that they'd been told by Cain's assistant, Sameer Shah, that there might be time to hear an application to revoke the injunction order he remained unenthusiastic but did eventually go to make enquiries. He was back almost immediately. 'No chance,' he said. 'No time at all.' Perhaps they should have gone with him; they were not convinced he'd tried very hard.

It was just gone 10 o'clock, they were due in court at 10.30, the first case of the day. Unlike on their previous visit, the Court was practically empty. 'Well, you will make it a priority?'

'If possible, but it's a bit complicated,' he said to the wall behind them. 'This is a directions hearing to plot out the times and directions for progressing your case. I'm going to see Counsel for Mrs Ogmore now to see if we can agree the programme but ... uh – I just want to check with you again, do you say that you were misled at the last hearing, that Mr Stoat didn't tell you that Ogmore had withdrawn all the documents from Land Registry, including her all important first conveyance with its altered plan, the one you wanted forensically tested?'

He was rummaging among his papers while he spoke and finally succeeded in locating a copy of the plan. 'You understood that the rectification land would be sorted by Land Registry before everything else? Do you think you were misled? I wonder …'

'Hold on a minute,' Max interrupted, 'as we have explained to Mr Cain on several occasions, we can't say he deliberately misled us as we don't know whether he knew she'd withdrawn all the papers. We don't know if she told him. We don't know how much he knows about what she's been up to. He did tell us that she is a friend of the family, and he seemed keen to disown Mr Ogmore, but how much he'd been told – well …'

Mr Tweed finally looked at Max. 'There's nothing in the Court Order about getting Land Registry to decide who owns what land. I'll have a word with Counsel.' Gathering up his disintegrating file he left for a second time.

Lucy was relieved they did not have to encounter Stoat again. It irked her that they'd been taken in so comprehensively at the first hearing, but she found it hard to believe that he had deliberately misled them. She had no difficulty believing his client would. Max was more concerned about the fact that the Court Order made no mention of Land Registry. The Registry's role was crucial. Without their determination on the 'rectification land' nothing else could be decided. Both Lucy and Max were confirmed in their low opinion of Judge Grey: how could he make an order without checking with them? The patronising lecture he started the hearing with didn't impress and then to confirm that injunction without even asking them to put their case and now to trump all that by forgetting the crucial part of what had been agreed.

'Why do you think Tweed's so reluctant to sort out the injunction …?' began Max just as Robert Tweed bustled into the room. He sat and showed them the Court Order they wanted changed.

'Can't be done.'

'What?'

'Can't be done, I'm afraid. You *consented* to the injunction continuing.'

'We did what?'

'Consented – agreed. You agreed to let the injunction stay.'

'Consented? Agreed? What? … Are you suggesting we agreed to let that woman have clear run of our land while we're …' They were both incredulous. 'The *Judge* ordered it.'

'No he didn't, at least not without your agreement.'

They were dumbstruck.

Could it be that in allowing her to keep her illegal fence up, in agreeing to let her access her shed, in agreeing to her using their land for bonfires they were actually agreeing to the injunction?

'But we didn't' Lucy bumbled, 'of course we didn't.'

'Well, whether you agreed or not, that is what you are deemed to have done. It says so here,' he showed them the Court Order.[1] 'See, "by Consent" I'm afraid that's it. Judges take very badly to anyone agreeing one day and then changing their minds. It's near impossible to get that sort of order overturned. Sorry!'

'Are you saying that you won't be able to remove that injunction?'

'Well no. Sorry. It's just too difficult.' He could see their confusion and dismay.

'Look I am sorry, I'll explain a bit more later, but I've got to sort out these directions with Counsel and we'll need to use this room, if you don't mind. You could wait in the courtroom. It's empty.'

They went through the two sets of double doors into the large, modern and empty courtroom trying again to make sense of it all. 'Stoat didn't say anything to the Judge about us agreeing to that Order did he?'

'I don't remember. I can't remember. The only thing I remember is he used the Hammer plan when talking about Ogmore's agreement to buy. I remember my sharp intake of breath amplified on the microphone when the Judge got round to looking at us … and told us we'd go to prison if we were to go on to our land. I remember the shock.'

'But it wasn't the Judge's idea. He's an innocent judge. Stoat must have said we agreed – consented. But why is there no mention of Land Registry or any of the other things we agreed in the Order? I'm pretty certain Stoat did mention all that 'willing buyer, willing seller' stuff. How come the Judge forgot all that?'

'The Order isn't signed by the Judge. It's signed by the Clerk.'

'But surely the Judge dictated it, how else could she have known what to write? What a mess! Looks like Judge Grey was only concerned with the injunction and look – it says here he read Ogmore's affidavit but there's absolutely no reference to our submissions. He didn't read them! All that hard work wasted!! Not such an innocent Judge perhaps.'

'Perhaps just an incompetent one. Do you think Stoat realised that? Do you think Stoat misled him? Do you think they're two of a kind, Stoat and Ogmore? Maybe Stoat *did* know she'd removed her deeds from Land Registry?'

'We should have insisted on speaking. On challenging the injunction. We should have made sure the Judge knew what we'd written for him. Were we stupid or were we tricked?'

'Both probably,' said Max.

The Court Usher came into the room looking for something and they apologised for holding things up explaining that the barristers were agreeing draft directions. The Usher told them not to worry, there was time and the Judge had things to do first, and left. They waited 10 more minutes. Then, through the two sets of double doors came the sound of raised voices. A shouting match loud enough to bring the Usher out again. It was not some battling litigants. It was their men now in the main hall shouting at each other in the public area.

'Stoat will bring on that heart attack any time soon,' said Max *sotto voce*. The Usher grimaced at the source of the noise, shook her head and left again. The doors flashed open and Robin Tweed burst in. He blustered over to them. 'Mr Stoat insists that you *agreed* to let his client keep her access to the land. He's *very* insistent.'

'Well, we did say she could access her shed and keep her fence up, and make bonfires on our land. But we didn't think this meant we agreed an injunction against *us* going there.'

Mr Tweed said, 'Well maybe you didn't appreciate how these offers were being interpreted by Mr Stoat and the Court. The Judge will have decided it's best to keep you all apart.' He swept out again, their file perilously close to being splayed around the courtroom.

'I still say he never suggested to us that he was going to tell the Judge that we agreed the injunction. Had he mentioned it we would never have agreed. Do you think Ogmore's attack was deliberate – to ensure a judge would want to keep us apart?'

'I still say I don't remember Stoat saying in court that we agreed – so either he didn't say it and the Judge inferred agreement, or he did say it but in such a way that we didn't pick it up. Either way it looks like we're stuck with it for now. I'm not sure I buy Tweed's "can't do" approach.'

'Well, why wouldn't he want to do something? What has he got to gain? Maybe he's right – overturning a court order labelled 'by Consent' *is* a near impossibility. Silly ass law as Dickens pointed out.'

'We just have to hope he's really working for us. Trouble is I can't forget another Dickens quote: "The business of the law is to make business for itself." So, let's hope Land Registry keep their promise and pay up.'

'But even if lawyer games don't cost us money,' said Lucy, 'they'll cost us hassle and we want that woman off our land as soon as possible. I just wish I still had my naive faith in judges. No evidence so far that things have improved over the past 20 years whatever Messrs Cain and Tweed say about the Woolf reforms.'

More minutes passed confirming their view that there would have been time for their attempt to be rid of the injunction had Robert Tweed been at all interested in trying. At the very least he could have established that they had been without a minder at the hearing when the Order was made, that they certainly did not agree it and that there was no evidence that they would.

Finally, the Usher came back to call the battling barristers into court. They seemed to have kissed and made up. They came in discussing cases, friends at last, at least professionally. Ogmore muttered something to the Clerk of the Court who replied quite clearly, 'Well, you haven't got a solicitor with you either.' Ogmore's reply: 'I *am* a solicitor,' afforded some amusement at the back of the Court.

The Judge who swept in this time was altogether different. She (the only lady Judge they were to encounter), surveyed her court and the cast of players with a cool eye. Stoat started with confidence by apologising for his opponent's failure to wear the correct garb (their Mr Tweed was wearing a respectable smart suite, no baggy trousers, no 17th-century wig, no 17th-century cravat). Ogmore's man had clearly planned this attempt to wrong-foot their man right at the start, but he'd misjudged his judge. She did not appear impressed with such game-playing. She held the draft directions the two men had drawn up, but she didn't want to talk about them, she wanted to talk about another matter. She had read Lucy and Max's letter to Judge Grey, and wanted to know why they hadn't been told that Ogmore had removed her papers from Land Registry, why this rather important fact was withheld when getting them to agree to buy the land *after* Land Registry had sorted out legal entitlement? She wanted to know what exactly had been agreed at the previous hearing. She wanted to know when Ogmore had written to the Registry and removed the papers.

Stoat and Ogmore were now the shocked parties. At first Stoat tried bluff and attempted a confident diversion expecting to confuse and throw her off track but it failed, she persisted and Stoat bumbled. He didn't understand your Honourable Ladyship … er … He hadn't realised … His client had overlooked … he couldn't say … your Honourable Ladyship … his client wasn't sure (much bobbing of heads between the two of them, much rifling through the very large pile of papers Ogmore had brought) … he thought, maybe, it was *after* … he thought, your Honourable Ladyship it was, it was *later* … he was so sorry but the letter to Land Registry couldn't be found … 'we don't have it with us today. As your Ladyship will understand the matter is in court so Land Registry no longer has a role to play.'

Circuit Judge Gloria Gold was having none of it. 'Show me the letter.'

Mr Stoat was so sorry your Honourable Ladyship, his solicitor (more sniggers from Max and Lucy) didn't appear to have the letter in her bundle but he was sure she could ...

The Honourable Ladyship turned to Mr Tweed. 'Perhaps you have the letter from Land Registry to your clients?' Mr Tweed was about to regret ... but his clients did, indeed, have the letter (as had he in fact, lost in the chaos of his file), which had been posted the day *before* the previous hearing, informing them that he'd already sent everything back to Ogmore at her request made a few days before that. Lucy tapped hard on Mr Tweed's back, gave him the letter and the Clerk passed it to the glorious golden Circuit Judge.

She turned an awesome face (she was a statuesque and rather beautiful lady) to Ogmore and Stoat. 'It is clear, Mr Stoat, that your client was fully aware that Land Registry was no longer involved and yet you proposed that before your client made an offer to the Defendants to buy land your client was occupying, Land Registry would determine who owned which parts of the land – the land you describe as 'rectification land' and yet ...' Stoat interrupted, 'I am sorry, Your Honourable Ladyship mentioned a letter from the Defendants; we have not seen this letter so we cannot know what the letter says,' he couldn't control his patience any longer, it showed.

Her Honourable Ladyship was also beginning to get impatient. She was on his tail and fully aware that no sale, no proper sale could take place until everyone knew where the agreed legitimate boundaries were. She was still waiting for answers. She was also getting impatient with her new unwelcome title. 'Mr Stoat, a mere "your Honour" will do.'[2] Mr Stoat's back registered Mr Stoat's humiliation and anger. Her Honour continued: 'You do not, then, have copy in that very large file of your client's, your client's solicitor's I suppose I should say, her recent letter to Land Registry?'

'Er – no your Lady – your Honour, it would appear not'.

Her Honour turned to Robert Tweed, 'Perhaps your clients will consent to forward to the Claimant's solicitors copy of their letter to His Honour Judge Grey.' Full agreement confirmed by Mr Tweed's clients.

Her Honour continued, 'I am going to revert this matter back to His Honour Judge Grey and Mr Tweed you may wish to consider your clients' position with regard to the injunction. You may wish to address the matter of the Consent Order.' Sighs of approval and relief from Mr Tweed's clients who were enjoying the show so far. 'I happen to agree,' she added, 'with the Defendants – these disputes are better settled by mediation or some form of ADR.' That's more like it. A proper judge. A modern judge. Their kind of judge.

Then the mood changed completely. Working as collaborators the Judge and the two barristers began dealing with the list of proposals for sorting out Homestead land: what should happen and when, the detailed timetable extending to Easter the following year, and having an all too familiar ring of 'experts' meeting and 'identifying issues' and lawyers 'exchanging' and 'serving' documents. And all the rigmarole that goes with the business of lawyering and judging. Lucy and Max exchanged weary looks and sighed in unison.

This was a civil dispute not a criminal matter. Ignore for the moment Ogmore's deceit and unpleasantness, the Court was concerned merely with who owned what land and where a boundary line should be drawn. Max and Lucy had already made it clear that they had no interest in fighting for the last blade of grass or even the last tree. Despite the aggression, the distortions, lies, delays and general unpleasantness and the growing evidence pointing to the possibility that the necklace boundary was correct, they had been prepared to agree the highly disputable 1963 plan. However, they were not prepared to hand over land stolen by adverse possession, that would have to be paid for by the thieves themselves, but they had already agreed to pay for it, so what was left? All that was left was for Land Registry to decide which Title was stronger and identify the 'rectification' boundaries on the stronger claim. Then the parties would have to decide on the price for any other Homestead land Lucy and Max were prepared to sell. Land Registry would do the first job and the willing buyers, willing sellers the second. Who needs lawyers, let alone judges to get their expensive hands on the business? Land Registry would pay Max and Lucy for the lost land which they could well afford to lose still leaving enough trees and shrubs and space between the two properties for them to have nothing more to do with these distinctly unpleasant neighours. After all, the Ogmores had managed to own Blackstone Cottage for a dozen years and have little to do with anyone in the village or even their nearest neighbours. Homestead was further away from Blackstone Cottage than Dunroamin' and other houses. Land Registry would be acting as arbitrator – at no cost either financial or emotional to Max and Lucy. That's how it should have been. That's how it would have been had the courts not intervened and taken control.

That's what the lawyers were up to now: controlling the litigation, setting their timetables, sorting out who does what when without even a glance in the direction of the Defendants, the paying customers. The Glorious Judge had her limitations after all. They all seemed to be enjoying themselves. Lucy and Max were not enjoying themselves. They were powerless. At the end they returned to their room to learn what had been decided for them, and Tweed went to the loo.

Max says it's a pity, he had been about to give Judge Gloria Gold full marks: she'd read the documents and may even have made a few enquiries before coming into court, and she didn't let Stoat pull the wool over her eyes. But she didn't see it through. She said she endorsed mediation, but she didn't test Stoat on why Ogmore rejected it. Could have scored 10 out of 10 but only got eight in the final assessment. Later another mark was lopped off for putting the dispute on the multi-track – the most expensive, lengthy and agonising of the three case management tracks.

Circuit Judge Grey got three from Max but zero from Lucy: far too keen to lecture, not keen enough to do his preparatory homework, he had landed them in the mess and let Stoat get away with dubious conduct so *nul points* and detention with 100 lines, 'I must read applications in full and I must hear both parties speak.' The first Judge, the one they thought was District Judge Dyer, they gave six as he was not to blame for being redundant and he did at least ask Ogmore whether she agreed to mediation, and made a note of her response.

They were interrupted by the return of Mr Tweed. Just as they were about to ask him why he hadn't taken the opportunities offered by Judge Gold to expose more Ogmore misbehaviour and try to get her to lift the injunction, he cut them short and held out an envelope. He'd written his instructions to himself on the back of an envelope!

'I had four objectives and all four were achieved.'

Before they could check those achievements Stoat suddenly appeared, full of friendly smiles. He needed to make a call. Could he borrow Mr Tweed's mobile? Mr Tweed seemed eager to oblige and handed it over immediately. Lucy wondered if this was wise. She had noted a curious thing: Mr Tweed's attitude towards Stoat had changed. He seemed over-polite, deferential. Robert Tweed, who had been so gung-ho before, now seemed subdued. He had said little at the hearing. Judge Gold had contributed more on their behalf. Nonetheless, he appeared to retain his eagerness for battle. He listed everything he thought important, and clearly thought they should consider important about the accumulating evidence against Ogmore's highly dubious claim based on her dubious deed plan.

Lucy agreed, of course they had a good case supporting their deed plan, but it wasn't conclusive. It was merely arguable and they did not want that sort of argument with that sort of opponent in Mr Tweed's sort of debating chamber. With Land Registry – yes, but not in the mayhem of court proceedings where litigation games and the wrong sort of judge too often determines the outcome. Robert Tweed persisted with the strength of their case. They pointed out the problems: Neither of the previous owners PC Windsmoor had traced was prepared to appear in court and swear to their recollections – in one case of 32 years. The electricity company did not keep archives of poles and ownership, and wrote to Rick Stone at the time Ogmore claimed ownership but he had not, apparently, objected because he had not replied. That, of course, was because he never saw the letter. As Max said, they could put up a good fight if they had to, if they wanted to, but it's all too complicated and potentially bothersome and possibly dangerous to their health both financial and mental and not worth the candle. They didn't want to and they didn't need to fight this out in court. They'll let Land Registry sort out the registration land and then let Ogmore buy enough land to keep her shed. Land Registry to compensate for costs and losses. The case would be taken out of court and handed back to Land Registry.

Robert Tweed pointed out that it was in court and informed them that there was no easy way to get it out unless Ogmore agreed.

They left for the promised site viewing at Homestead. Lucy suggested that she travelled with him to show the way. He did not seem at all keen but she prevailed. If they had to hand over control she wanted to know a bit more about the gentleman into whose hands control was being passed. She also wanted to make clear that they wanted their registered land back as soon as possible until boundaries had been settled. She knew that if they needed the help of the Court to undo the damage, they would need the skills and expertise of a barrister to get the help of the Court.

Lucy and Max were proving a bit of a disappointment to Robert Tweed. By the time they got to Homestead Robert Tweed was proving a bit of a disappointment to Lucy. She was perplexed by his response to her fence-post story of 20 years earlier and even more perplexed by his response or rather lack of it to her attempts to discuss the Woolf reforms. He seemed somewhat obsessed with Stoat: 'He's a bad lawyer.' She agreed – but his judgement was professional. Hers was moral.

Once back at Homestead he went up the road to meet Mrs Ogmore (Mr Ogmore apparently doing his usual vanishing trick), to look at Blackstone Cottage land and take lots of photographs which, when developed, served very little purpose and explained even less than the photographs that Lucy and Max had taken.

'Hopeless,' he said on his return.

'Hopeless?' they asked, 'What is hopeless?'

'Her claim. It's hopeless. She hasn't got a hope of persuading the Court that she owns the land she's after.'

'And presumably she won't persuade Land Registry either when they take back the investigation,' said Max, testing.

Mr Tweed straightened up. 'The matter is in court. It's the Court she has to persuade.'

They invited him to join them for a sandwich at a local inn. They resisted the urge to discuss the case over lunch and chatted about other matters. Back at the house he said he'd get the draft Defence and Counterclaim to them in 10 days. He expressed admiration for the view from Homestead and the beauty of the blue-sky day, and drove off in his cluttered old car.

Now things were back in the hands of Robert Cain. 'Things' began with a long, vitriolic letter from Ogmore who was obviously somewhat peeved by the encounter with Judge Gold. It showed in a series of unpleasant, arrogant, bullying letters predicated on the increasingly familiar distortions and lies. Not least the *our client* references to herself on Bulmer & Co. paper: 'your clients decided to take the law into their own hands and sawed down *our client's* [sic] fence post and removed five fence panels,' '... failure to comply with warnings given to your clients by the Police, left *our client* with no alternative but to apply for injunctive relief and thereby issue substantive proceedings in which we are now embroiled,' etc., etc.

It was hard work trying to keep calm through this heavy mud of malign twisted history. She accused Land Registry of withdrawing from the case on its own initiative, forgetting her letter (on her own notepaper) telling Mr Beige that he no longer had a role and demanding her papers back. She was very miffed indeed to find out that they had been offered indemnity by Land Registry: 'your clients seek to recover the cost of defending proceedings which they themselves precipitated'!!

Her lies and distortions certainly raised hackles, but as time went on were so ludicrously at variance with the known and recorded facts for anger to flip over into laughter. Lucy and Max were comforted by the knowledge that Cain was fully aware they were lies. It was all too clear that she wanted her claim in court. She had seized the first opportunity to get it there making sure their evidence couldn't be heard to thwart her plans.

Lucy and Max didn't learn until much later how hard she had tried to get it into court, how her attempts had been rebuffed until Stoat admitted her husband had been arrested and it was that attack that finally clinched it. The Court had a duty to keep fighting neighbours apart and although Joe Ogmore's attack had been a one-sided fight, it did the job. Lucy and Max didn't know what had been said at that *ex parte* hearing in the Royal Courts of Justice. They didn't even know that a hearing of major importance to them was taking place there. No one thought to tell them. They'd been told it was taking place 200 miles from London.

It was hard work, nevertheless, to cope with her perfected talent for accusing them of sins she had committed, 'We have no idea what has motivated your clients' disproportionate response and behaviour to this dispute'! They were supposed to be involved in the business of agreeing a price for the 'willing buyer, willing seller' deal. Problem was – the more dishonest and provocative her accusations and claims, the less willing the sellers became. To add to that, she was insisting on the Hammer plan with Stoat's marking of the extra land she wanted to buy, which was more than they were prepared to sell. They did not want this liar any nearer their home than necessary.

Then – a breakthrough. With his persistence, Robin Cain managed to corral her into agreeing 'reluctantly' to use an Ordnance Survey plan as a basis for any agreement. This was progress. At least they could dispense with the games she was playing with Hammer's plan.

A letter arrived from Land Registry disabusing every one of the stories Ogmore had been peddling: 'At the moment there is *no* application with the Registry for any rectification of Homestead's Title based on a superior claim to part of the land in that Title.' They now had official confirmation that near a year on from their first letter objecting to her land grab – and over three years from when she'd been caught taking down Homestead trees and been given copy of Homestead's Title plan – Ogmore still hadn't got the ball rolling on any claim. There had been no 'judicial process'. She really did not want anyone looking too closely at the facts. The Registrar's letter also made clear that if she wanted Land Registry to deal with it she still could, even though she'd got her way and persuaded the Court to take it on, thus contradicting her claim that as the matter was now in court Land Registry could no longer intervene. The letter enquired if she wanted to make an application and if she did on what grounds? It continued, 'Do *both* parties want us to try to facilitate an agreement at this stage?' One party did. The other did not – and she replied to that effect on her own home paper ('Your letter addressed to my solicitors has been passed to me'!) So the whole charade stayed in the hands of the Court … and Ogmore.

Lucy and Max never stopped nagging Robert Cain to persuade Ogmore to choose a non-litigious route to resolution without giving the misleading impression that they were weakening. Ogmore, meanwhile, was resisting any attempt to let Land Registry decide on the rectification land. She was also resisting – rather more cautiously as this was unknown territory for her – ADR. Cain had some admirable strengths, but he kept forgetting that his clients had indemnity for costs and so would keep referring to the threat of costs to persuade them to take his advice; however they did persuade *him* to repeat again and again that no sale could take place until they knew what land was being sold and that couldn't happen until who owned what had been settled by Land Registry.

Three weeks after Robin Tweed had promised to produce his work 'in 10 days' they were still chasing it. There was a deadline for the Defence and the delay was a worry. Eventually, two drafts arrived. Both full of errors. Errors of fact they could understand, he'd had little time to glean all the data. Spelling, punctuation and grammar were something else. As was lack of knowledge of the law. It appeared neither Tweed nor Cain knew Max and Lucy had every right in law to remove the trespassing fence. It had taken a mere police constable to find the relevant case (*Chamberlain* v *Lindon*[3]).The impression left by this work was that it had been written after a late night and a few too many beers. The muddle and confusion increased anxiety. They corrected what they could and sent it back. Cain warned that if they wanted to amend or set aside the injunction as soon as possible they'd better get the application in as soon as possible, as they would still have at least six weeks to wait before they'd get a slot in court. Already three weeks since the hearing before Her Honour and nothing to show for it. Cain nagged and two acceptable documents finally arrived but did not include Tweed's promise to make amendments or any reference to *Chamberlain* v *Lindon*. Cain wrote a letter for the Court drawing attention to the fact that Judge Gold had reverted the case back to Judge Grey.

Meanwhile Ogmore was still entertaining herself redesigning Homestead land. The provoking letters, the cynical charade on Bulmer-headed paper urged action. It was Friday. Lucy and Max proposed driving the 80 miles there and back to a new and higher grade court – a Civil Justice Centre – to which their case had now been allocated, to deliver the documents in person and get a date for the hearing before Judge Grey at the earliest. They had to act to curtail Ogmore's activities before she had altered the physical evidence completely.

They had no difficulty finding a parking space near the Civil Justice Centre in the new city and the Clerk said she would do her best to get them an early hearing before Judge Grey. She came back with a date for the following Thursday – less than a week. They were amazed. They had to check with Tweed and phoned the barrister's Chambers as instructed. The Clerk who answered first said that Mr Tweed was already booked that day but then said, 'He really wants to do this one. I'll see if he can move his other booking.'

He phoned back in minutes, 'Mr Tweed can do it'. They confirmed this with the Clerk and drove home congratulating themselves on a useful journey. They were on their way back to control.

The following Monday they got a call from Robin Cain. 'Sorry about this, Robert Tweed won't be able to make it after all. He couldn't alter his plans.'

As far as Lucy could see it was simply a matter of informing the Court and changing the date. To her surprise this proved to be another example of unthinking inflexibility in the Court service. They couldn't change the date. 'The Court won't change dates at such short notice just because a barrister can't make it,' Cain said, 'and you'd have to pay another £150 court fee. It doesn't matter anyway Mr Tweed has found a replacement, Mr Scroggs. He's more experienced and we've not been that impressed with Mr Tweed so far have we? Mr Scroggs comes highly recommended and could charge a much higher fee but will do it for what we've agreed. I think you may find this a better outcome.'

When Lucy expressed dismay and queried if this Mr Scroggs could get on top of his brief at such short notice. She was assured that, 'Barristers do it all the time. Take on cases at short notice. He's got Mr Tweed's file now and he'll be able to master it with ease by Thursday. I don't think you should worry about that.'

'Do you know Mr Scroggs? We don't. Will you be able to come with us?'

'No, I don't know him. Sorry, I shan't be able to get to your hearing; I shall be in Birmingham attending Robert Tweed's course on adverse possession. That's why he can't make it to your hearing.'

'But surely he must have known that when we telephoned his Clerk from Court for confirmation?'

'Well, yes. It may be a mistake by his Clerk. Or maybe he hoped to change the date of the seminar, but it wasn't possible at such short notice. Mr Scroggs will phone you Wednesday night when he gets to his hotel.'

When Lucy put the phone down and reported back to Max the thought occurred: surely you, Robin Cain, should also have known. We told you Friday early afternoon. You could have told us that you were attending a course with Tweed and sorted it out before we left the Court. But then a more disciplined mind less hungry for high profile success in what Robert Tweed rated as an easy win may be a better bet. Max and Lucy decided they would leave things as they were and go with Mr Scroggs.

The next morning, Tuesday, Mr Cain phoned again. He was forwarding a letter from Ogmore (Bulmer paper), but more important, the Court had contacted him to say that Judge Grey would not be able to hear the application on Thursday. It had been reallocated to a Judge Blacker.

'But I thought Judge Gold had said it had to be heard by Judge Grey. Shouldn't we remind them and get another date before Judge Grey?'

'No. I think that's unlikely to succeed,' said Mr C. 'The Court decides these allocations. We can't do very much about it. You'll have to stick with the date and the new judge I'm afraid. Besides Mr Scroggs has started work in preparation.'

This was beginning to look out of control again. They consoled themselves with the notion that a new judge might feel more free to overturn the injunction issued on the basis of false information. They hadn't been impressed with the low scoring Judge Grey. Besides, a more experienced barrister might be more focussed on untangling and then wrapping the business up efficiently without too much concern for getting his name in print.

The real blow came the following day. A near, knock-out blow. Cain had just received Ogmore's 'client's' Witness Statement. He was busy; he hadn't had time to look at it. Would they care to collect it and let him have their thoughts? As they had planned a walk to a pub lunch in the direction of his office with Claire and the grandchildren, of course they would.

Lucy went in to collect it while Claire, Max and the grandchildren did some shopping. She started to glance through it and immediately encountered the well rehearsed lies and distortions. These did not cause alarm. They were prepared and had collated a file to refute the familiar libels one by one. But then she came across a new one. Unfamiliar and potentially disastrous and much more shocking because it showed the lengths these opponents were prepared to go: The Ogmores had paid private detectives to spy on them. Private detectives had been snooping around and questioning neighbours in their previous communities.

Her Witness Statement made no reference to Max's past, although they later learnt someone had been snooping round his previous home and had sent packages to significant acquaintances including his ex-partner, but the significant acquaintances and ex-partner had refused to accept the packages so, presumably, nothing came of that investment (and, frustratingly, Max never found out what was in the packages).

Lucy, on the other hand, had the fence-post saga. Mr Doyle, now a widower, registered blind and succumbing to the damage of alcohol abuse, had been interviewed by their private detective. As had Charlene Payne, the difficult, noisy, hot-and-cold neighbour who'd moved into the semi next door just when the Doyles were hounding Lucy and Felix through the Court over one fence post. Neither of them had anything good to say about Lucy.

According to Ogmore's version, Felix and Lucy '*hounded*' their elderly neighbours through the courts over a period of 11 years, just for a few *feet* of land. Lucy says she was overcome with nausea. Ogmore's trick of accusing Max and Lucy of her own misdeeds had now gone too far. To add to the theft, the lies, the libel and slander, the assault, *she* was accusing *Lucy* of being a bad neighbour. In any other context this was a lie easily shrugged off, Lucy still had all the papers and files from the Doyle legal attack, but in this context it was sharply powerful and impossible to counter in the time available. Their evidence of bad conduct by the Ogmores was all in writing much of it supported by signed Witness Statements. There were no signed Statements from Doyle or Payne attached to Ogmore's Statement – only the words of Ogmore herself, that paragon of honest reporting.

It later transpired that the Ogmores, professional lawyers, had set private detectives on them as they wanted something to counter the blackened reputation of Joe Ogmore and the records of bullying and dishonesty by Hazel Ogmore. The spies had drawn a blank with Max. Nobody had come up to provide the evidence of bad character they sought. But Lucy, on the other hand, had had a court case which, according to Ogmore, she had pursued over a minuscule sliver of land for 11 years, hounding poor Mr and Mrs Doyle into submission. Bingo!! She was a bad neighbour and a litigation nut.

The Ogmores would have had a bit of a problem if they had ever attempted to make more of their private detective's work. Not only did Lucy hold all the records from the fence post case, but Mrs Doyle was dead and Mr Doyle was likely to be a bad and wayward witness, very unlikely to travel hundreds of miles up-country to appear in court. His first experience had proved rather unpleasant. If they did persuade him to turn up, Lucy had all the conclusive evidence that the Ogmore version of events was 'contrary to the facts'. Doyle had been bitter ever since the court case and Lucy had witnessed Charlene Payne attempting to damage other people's reputations. She, herself, had been taken in and believed the slanders, never suspecting herself to be a victim. Lucy had not seen Ms Payne as an intrinsically bad person just rather insecure, difficult and vacillating. Now she revised her view and regretted believing the convincing stories Charlene Payne had told about others.

Of course, there was no intention to get signed Statements. The intention was to raise an impression and to ensure it went unchallenged in any formal way – if at all. All Hazel Ogmore wanted was to leave her character assassination cold on the page of *her* Witness Statement.

Lucy couldn't stay for the pub lunch. She had to check things out. She phoned friends and neighbours in the road she'd left a year earlier. They were shocked. No one else appeared to have had a visit from the private detective. Whereas they could believe it of Doyle, the recluse who none of them knew well (but who some saw as a difficult curmudgeon), they were surprised that in all the years they'd never heard anything negative about either Felix or Lucy from the highly talkative Ms Payne. Lucy had to stop enquiring further, she could see how it would poison relationships in a friendly road in the same way that bitterness of divorcing couples can split friends and spoil friendships. She thought of rape victims who have to endure character assassination in court and knew, sickened as she was, people can suffer far worse. Some of her friends were angry on her behalf and insisted on writing Statements correcting what one of them described as 'totally slanderous lies'.

'So here we are,' thought Lucy, 'Ogmore has succeeded finally in blackening my reputation, thanks to Doyle and Payne, and the nastiness is contagious, spreading to neighbours in a friendly street of nice people.' Lucy still feels sick when she reflects on the damage Ogmore has managed to do. Years on, Lucy has been told that Charlene Payne, previously a very sociable lady, will not face Lucy's friends.

Max, family and friends were sympathetic and angry on Lucy's behalf. Ms Payne was dismissed as mindlessly indulging in loves and hates – but there was no escaping the fact that some of the mud would stick no matter how many supportive Statements were provided by supportive and sympathetic friends. The libel in the Witness Statement was a distraction and a very dirty trick to pull 24 hours before they were due in court but it was effective. In the event, it changed the whole course of events.

A week after the Court hearing which changed everything, a friend contacted Lucy to report that Ogmore did in fact phone Charlene Payne but was told to get off the phone, leave her alone, not to contact her again, and had the phone put down on her. Ms Payne had not expected to be exposed and did not like the consequences.

Still in shock but not yet in depression, Max and Lucy finally got to look at the letter from Ogmore to Cain. They had little interest in its lengthy excuses for why she'd acted as she had – excuses based as usual on a tangle of distortion which would take forever to tidy into something resembling the truth. Neither of them could concentrate on it, but they did see that less than 24 hours before the Court hearing she had written that she agreed to some form of ADR. 'Too late, Mrs Ogmore, too late,' said Max.

Malcolm Scroggs' call came late in the evening. He'd settled into his hotel and had a few queries about the case. He checked that they had applied to lift the injunction and for an Order that Ogmore make her case for any claim she wanted on their registered land with Land Registry. Yes, he had the plans and yes, he had copy of all the correspondence. He knew that Ogmore had offered to buy land over and above land she was claiming was legally hers by right of her dubious 1963 plan. They stressed first things first. They wanted their right of access back and she would have to negotiate access to her shed if she needed it until ownership was settled. This should goad her into setting in train the case she should have activated with Land Registry three years earlier. He said the purpose of the hearing was to get the injunction set aside, and they confirmed that Judge Gold had suggested Mr Tweed make the application. They agreed to meet at the Court the next morning at 09.15.

The following morning they set off early allowing extra time just in case. They needed it. Traffic was slow on the motorway and chock-a-block in the city. Nevertheless, they arrived on time near the courthouse – the Civil Justice Centre – and made straight for the parking spaces they'd identified the previous week. There were no spaces there or anywhere nearby. As they found themselves driving past the Court a third time and 15 minutes late, Max proposed that Lucy jump out with the briefcase and pacify Mr Scroggs. He would find somewhere to park and join them as soon as possible.

Lucy went through the lengthy security system, up in the lift and saw a man who was clearly their new Defender. This gentleman was unflustered, suave and cool. Well preserved, late forties, good tan, black hair with blond silver streaks somewhat bizarrely parted and plastered down each side of his forehead, and wearing equally bizarre red-rimmed glasses – and a tight flash of a smile which did not extend to his eyes. Lucy's delay was unfortunate but not a disaster he assured her. First he must find a conference room. Would she mind sitting in the lobby meanwhile? Normally he would expect their solicitor to attend, but he did understand that Mr …er … Cain was attending one of Mr Tweed's courses.

They were already running late by 20 minutes and there was no sign of Max. Lucy sat and waited in the bustling lobby observing the comings and goings of court personnel, lawyers and anxious, tense and sometimes angry litigants. Then she noticed two men approaching: Mr Scroggs and Mr Stoat.

They were sharing a joke. Stoat's face froze on seeing her. Her face did something similar. Mr Scroggs smoothed over and asked her to sit in the room he'd found at the end of the corridor. He just had a few things to discuss with Counsel. So, from his reaction Lucy could see Stoat was still smarting from the humiliations before Mrs Justice Gold and clearly resented Lucy and Max for his uncomfortable experience (but not his instructing solicitor and her doppelgänger client). However, he did seem to be getting on better with their new man than with Robert Tweed. Was this a good thing – or a bad thing?

SEVEN
October 2002

'I don't want to know what the law is; I want to know who the judge is.'

Roy M. Cohn, New York Times, *April 1988*

Malcolm Scroggs opened the file and pages fell out – he hadn't managed to tidy up after Mr Tweed. Lucy assured him Max would arrive soon once the traffic jams allowed him to find a parking space. It was now 09.40. They had 50 minutes before the hearing. If Mr Scroggs was as competent as his pre-publicity claimed and had indeed mastered the file in the time available – as well as discussed the case with Robert Tweed, Lucy reckoned they should be able to achieve their objective of removing the injunction.

The objective began to slip away right from the start. Mr Scroggs had grim news. He announced he had done some phoning around the night before to colleagues in the area, the court circuit.[1] He said that they had told him that this Judge Blacker has a reputation for inflexibility and this had been confirmed for him at a meeting with Stoat and the Judge just before Lucy arrived. In his view the Judge was going to reject the application, he was certainly going to be difficult to persuade. Scroggs was sure Lucy and Max had already been warned that many judges are against setting aside Consent Orders. 'If he doesn't grant it, you may have to pay the other side's costs for today,' he added. Obviously yet another lawyer unaware that the couple was indemnified for costs, and hoping to pressure them with the cost threat. The whole purpose of the rushed hearing was to get rid of that so-called 'Consent' Order so they could access their land and stop Ogmore 'improving' it. If that can't be achieved the whole day was a waste of time – and money, if not theirs – somebody's.

A new judge, the wrong judge, a new court, with impossible/impassable traffic, a new Defender, with an oddly cold, distant manner, private detective mayhem, tangled poisonous snakes of lies and deceit and now this one hope of regaining control from the squatters fading and all the lawyers keep trying to frighten Lucy and Max with costs. Lucy wondered why they were doing that. Did they know something she didn't know? Should she take the threat seriously? Besides, what had this inflexible new judge been told? Did he know that Lucy and Max had been misled? Did he know that they had never seen or signed any agreement to any 'Consent' Order? Circuit Judge Gold knew so had Judge Blacker conferred with her? How could 'the best justice system in the world' make such a mess of everything? Lucy knew that they needed this new man to be convinced and confident. Would he fight their cause? Would he use his vaunted knowledge and experience to their advantage? They knew nothing of him and the brief telephone conversation with him the night before had given them little guidance as to who he was. Could they trust his judgement – indeed could they trust *him*? They had no choice, they had to.

'The Judge, Judge Grey, was misled,' Lucy began. 'We were misled. We had agreed to let Ogmore get to her shed and to light her bonfires on our land. At least that's what we thought we had agreed. That and only that. When the Judge threatened us with prison if we put one foot on our land, we began to suspect something else was going on. Now we think that Judge Grey knew nothing of what the squatters had been up to. He couldn't have read the papers. He didn't know that Joe Ogmore was arrested because he attacked us, not, as Mr Stoat claimed, because there was a fight. There wasn't a fight. There was an attack. The police sergeant saw the evidence and arrested Ogmore who had not a scratch on him. Can you explain why we should be excluded from our land and the attacker given free rein?'

'Well, the Judge most likely thought the important thing was to keep both parties apart and you don't need to access that part of your land. If you'd agreed to let her get to her shed and light bonfires on your land she'd need to have access. You must not forget Ogmore has only been charged. He hasn't been found guilty. Yet.'

Max still hadn't made it. There wasn't much they could do until he arrived. He needed to listen to all this. Malcolm Scroggs changed tack. 'What about her offer to buy the land?'

'What land? Until we know what land belongs to who how can we talk about buying and selling land? We need to know what we are selling.'

'Land Registry has agreed her application for the rectification land, hasn't it? So, she owns that plot, the one on her conveyance plan?'

Lucy sighed, he *hadn't* read the file. He obviously hadn't read the Statement from the Registrar setting out the situation making clear that one year on and innumerable letters on, Ogmore still hasn't made an application for the 'rectification' land. Land Registry certainly had not agreed her non-existent application. Lucy, now fearing the return of the debilitating depression she felt when she read about the work of the private detective, wearily explained what obviously needed to be explained, adding that Ogmore strongly objected to the Registrar granting them indemnity. Evidence, in both Max and Lucy's view that Ogmore and Stoat were hoping to bully with costs. Mr Scroggs started rummaging through the collapsing file. Lucy found copies of the letter and Statement from Mr Brown, the Senior Land Registrar. Perhaps this would make him reconsider the situation, but, what else did he not know?

Mr Scroggs was clearly not the untidy sort. He found the disorder in the file irritating. He read the Statement as if for the first time and said finally, 'Uh huh, I see. Well, nevertheless would you be prepared to sell the land she's still trying to claim as adverse possession? I think she offered two thousand, which she thinks is the going rate.'

'Well, the going rate for what? Ten square yards? Half an acre? First, we have to sort out whether or not her dodgy deed plan prevails. We didn't believe it could if properly investigated but we *were* prepared to let that through un-investigated before all this, before she engineered her land grab out of Land Registry's hands and into court. Before the assault. Before the work of the private detective.'

'Engineered?'

'Pretending to be shocked and horrified because we took the fence panels down. Our first solicitor's proposal is endorsed by the police officer who found the precedent. She's been told we acted perfectly legitimately. It's highly likely she knew anyway, but wanted an excuse to get this into court. Then the attack, the assault. Max's neck is still very painful two months on. Looks like he is a genuine case of whiplash. The constant irritation of lies and distortions. We have to challenge them all the time in case someone, some decision-maker, believes them, and now this nauseating business of the private detective. These are awful people and we don't want them any nearer than absolutely necessary.'

'But you do want an end to this?' Well, at least he understands that. Perhaps he doesn't have Tweed's professional ambitions. Perhaps he will find a way to "put an end" to all this. 'How about 5,000?'

'No.'

'10,000?' How can he talk about price without knowing how much land?

'No. We really do not want those people any nearer us.'

At last Max arrived full of apologies. First he'd got lost in the traffic. Then he couldn't find his way back from the car park to the courthouse, then he couldn't find them in the courthouse. It was 10 o'clock. They had 30 minutes. Lucy gave him the latest news and Scroggs' warning about the new Judge, Judge Blacker. Max agreed they did not want to sell any land to the squatters.

'Well,' said Scroggs, 'you're likely to win on the adverse possession claim but lose on the rectification.'

Max ran through all the arguments for their legitimate ownership of all the land in their Title, but Lucy just wanted the whole demeaning, unpleasant business over and done with and Max could see that and so he stopped and let Malcolm Scroggs take over.

'We've got about 15 minutes before we go into court. How about I propose to the other side we'll drop this application. It's all rather more complex than you think and its doomed anyway I fear. We'll let them keep the rectification land and they'll have to drop the adverse possession claim. I could sort that out today. What do you think?'

Max was about to reply when Lucy interrupted.

'So that would be an end to it? No more court visits?'

'Yes, an end to it today apart from some tidying up between your Mr Cain and Mrs Ogmore's solicitor.' That brought the first laugh of the day, 'Hazel Ogmore *is* her solicitor.' Mr Scroggs flashed one of his cold smiles.

Neither of them considered this much of a deal but if he was right, if the so-called 'Consent' Order could not be revoked and if fighting over the rectification land would just drag out their dealings with 'these crooks', who knows what other dirty tricks they had up their sleeves; it was possibly a deal worth making. That is what Lucy thought, anyway. Max was still angered by the private detective damage, the lying trickery made him want to fight on and expose the chicanery they had had to deal with for the past year, but he, too, hated to think he would have to have further dealings with these people.

With hardly a word of discussion they agreed, conscious of the time slipping away and based on the facts presented to them, particularly Scroggs' assessment of the Judge and the near impossibility of successfully removing the injunction, they agreed to his proposal. He left to talk to Ogmore's Counsel, to talk to Mr Keith Stoat.

While he was out of the room they exchanged views on their new man. Neither was confident but at least he appeared to share their desire for a speedy end to the saga. They could trust him on that it seemed. Tweed could have come up with a similar suggestion at that hearing before Circuit Judge Gloria

Gold. Why didn't he? Inexperience perhaps or perhaps a desire to get more mileage out of his contract? After all, even before the matter was dragged into court, they had already begun to think that despite all the accumulated evidence against it, it was hardly worth the candle to fight the Ogmores' 1963 plan. They would be compensated for the small loss of land and they would still have at least three acres to manage. They thought it sensible of Scroggs to research the Judge: that is one important advantage an experienced lawyer has over a litigant in person. Know who you are dealing with – the nature and prejudices of the person who has to be persuaded. It seemed clear to them that Judge Gloria Gold had been an unpleasant surprise for Stoat and Ogmore. Perhaps Stoat hadn't done his homework.

'He's a bit odd, Scroggs,' said Max. 'He doesn't smile. He's difficult to bond with and that hair parted in the middle and Brylcreemed down over his forehead, and those red frames.'

'He does smile – a sharp flash of teeth. Eyes cold. I was a bit disappointed when he showed he didn't know we'd already made the offer to Land Registry to let the rectification claim go unchallenged and he didn't seem to know that Ogmore had never lodged a claim. He seemed to think Land Registry had given that 1963 plan the OK and allowed Ogmore's claim for rectification.'

Neither of their Defenders seemed at all concerned about the tricky pretext Ogmore had used for getting her land claim into court and out of the hands of Land Registry. No *court* had countenanced Ogmore's attempt to justify her injunction on the facts she originally presented. Max and Lucy had every right in law to remove the trespassing fence having tried for nine months to get the squatters to remove it. Only when the report of the attack reached a Judge's ear did Ogmore and Stoat get what they wanted. It was the physical assault that swung it.

This was confirmed a year later when Lucy finally managed to get copy of the documents revealing the course of events. Ogmore got her injunction and all that followed, from that attack, it may well have been her idea, she certainly said something to her lumbering husband as she crossed him on the way back to her house 'to call the Police' and whatever she said made him grab the trowel and throw himself at Max and start hitting.

She must have covered miles in the region to get a court to issue that temporary injunction. Without it her land grab stayed with Mr Beige who was proving such a disappointment to her. On day three she decided to go for broke and Stoat left his London chambers for the walk to the Royal Courts of Justice where he told the High Court Judge about Joe Ogmore's stay at Her Majesty's pleasure, but insisted the months inside had nothing to do with fighting. He then went on to talk of Ogmore's latest arrest. He described the attack as an 'argy bargy', leaving the venerable High Court Judge to assume that two sets of warring neighbours had come to blows. The High Court Judge was very cross with both parties and Mr Stoat shared his head-shaking disapproval. He was also delighted because no High Court Judge is going to deny an application for an injunction that keeps battling parties apart and this High Court Judge was not going to break with tradition even if he hadn't heard Max and Lucy's record of events.

Over a year after the attack Max and Lucy wrote to the High Court Judge who had granted the temporary injunction *ex parte*[2] to ask what had led to him to grant it. They wanted a transcript of the proceedings. The High Court Judge couldn't remember the case and at first nobody could find either the file or any trace of the Order, but Lucy had a date to go on and a possible name – Keith Stoat, and eventually they found the tape. The High Court Judge was sufficiently concerned to have the tape transcribed at the Court's expense. The transcript is very poor, names are misspelt and for some reason Stoat becomes Raynor, and quite a lot is recorded as 'inaudible'. Stoat had tried to claim that Max and Lucy threatened to demolish the beloved shed in two days' time without further notice. The Judge spotted that Julian Pilling's letter didn't actually threaten that, but did *not* appear to grasp that the demolition was not imminent so the *ex parte* injunction was not needed: Ogmore had days to reply to Mr Pilling, ask for time and negotiate on the trespass.

The High Court Judge was of the opinion that this was 'an ideal case for mediation'. If Max and Lucy been there they would have so agreed. Keith Stoat was there and did agree with him: 'Absolutely,' he said, adding, 'we thought Land Registry would be providing one but somebody jumped the gun.' 'Absolutely' indeed! This from the side that rejected mediation at every stage including when Judge Dyer raised it. 'Jumped the gun' indeed! Who jumped the gun? Could it be Mrs Hazel –solicitor and Litigant-in-Person – Ogmore, who dragged out her illegal stay on their land for as long as she could, ignoring all requests to leave and then exploded into action without warning or negotiation, rushing from court to court to get an injunction moving the game on to her playing field? Stoat and Ogmore had certainly perfected the art of damaging the opponent by dishonest innuendo. An excellent tool for any aspiring litigator with limited scruples: accuse the opponent of your crimes. Tit for tat taints both sides.

'This is terrible,' the transcript records from Keith Stoat and he was not referring to himself. The High Court Judge agreed, 'It's no way for neighbours to live. The costs will be simply enormous, if they … the parties were here I'd shout at them – but they're not.' Well, one party was there being very ably represented. The other party did not even know the proceedings were taking place. The High Court Judge did insist on certain safeguards, which neither Max nor Lucy (through ignorance), nor Mr Cain (through lethargy) took advantage of and so it was that a week after the scene at the Royal Courts of Justice, Judge Grey fixed the temporary injunction and played his important role in this drama – working title '*Squatters' Delight*: if it can go wrong, it will go wrong'.

Eventually Malcolm Scroggs came back into the room some five minutes or so after their due time in court. He was holding the infamous Hammer plan. No longer cool and languorous, he urged them to consider what he was about to suggest. 'They agree the proposal *if* you'll agree to let the chalet stay.'

'Oh not that plan still,' said Max, 'We thought we'd got rid of that.'

Mr Scroggs ignored him, didn't hear him perhaps, but hurried on, 'As you can see some of it is built over the boundary line but we're not talking much – say five, six feet.' He stabbed his finger at the drawing of the shed. 'I don't think she'll agree otherwise. She seems quite prepared to go the whole hog.' So, Max thought, that is why he has the Hammer plan, he hasn't seen the site. He simply doesn't know where things are. He doesn't even know what things there are. He doesn't know anything about the land he's negotiating over, on our behalf. However, Max thought, what real objection would we have to her keeping her shed-chalet on our land? Only a desire to make her suffer a bit.

In the car travelling to court Max, concerned at Lucy's silence on the journey and aware that her anger arising from Ogmore's private detective work had turned into depression, told her that in his view the problem was Ogmore's unreasonable obsession with the shed-chalet. He thought that she was prepared to gamble on getting away with the high risk games she was playing to protect her ego by at least keeping her beloved chalet where it was. She just had to win at least on that. Max had developed his amateur psychological theory by surmising that her self-esteem was more important than anything else. She'd lost a lot when Joe got caught and struck off, his professional career ruined and her career stunted, so she had to shore it up any way she could. She seemed detached from reality and totally lacking in self-awareness. She showed not a shred of embarrassment when referring to herself as her solicitor, or when shamelessly lying. Robin Cain had reported that two other lawyers who had had dealings with her professionally declared her mad without any prompting or collusion. Lucy felt that made her more rather than less dangerous. They had already seen how far she was prepared to go.

Now, in that stuffy little room at the Civil Justice Centre, Max and Lucy exchanged looks and contemplated Mr Scroggs' proposal. They were both thinking the same thing. This would get her out of their lives and behind a high fence. Lucy could not envisage her demolishing that shed and she would have to if they insisted on no extension to the roadside boundary. Without an extension the downhill boundary would cut through her trespassing chalet.

'So, if we agree you think you can tie things up in the next week or so?'

'I can tie most of it up today if you want.'

'The sooner the better but we shall need some sort of guidance on where the boundaries are to go. As Mr Tweed may have told you, we can't get access to some of our boundaries with Blackstone Cottage because of the terrain.'

'Well, we'll ensure the agreement we draw up stipulates that the two surveyors meet and peg out the boundaries.'

'Sounds better.' Max looked at Lucy, 'Well?' Malcolm Scroggs looked at Lucy. Lucy paused, unsure. Then said, 'OK'. A simple word. A troublemaking word. She thought she and Max were saying OK to a sensible if unsatisfying agreement. A grown-up agreement, a generous agreement, free of vengeance and retribution. They were giving the woman what she did not deserve and had no justified claim to, but it was just a small extra bit of land and they would be compensated for any loss. She thought that despite his scrappy knowledge of the dispute, Scroggs would understand and appreciate their generosity.

'I've not mentioned the other trespass, the one in the other corner of her plot where she admits she's trespassing,' he said as he rushed from the room.

Alone, Max and Lucy first questioned whether they had done the sensible thing, and having decided they had, congratulated themselves on their sensible behaviour. They even speculated on Ogmore's surprise that her wish could be granted so easily. They'd shown her that *they* were not obsessive. They'd shown the Court that they were not obsessive – possibly a serious challenge to court prejudices. No more vicious games for Ogmore. No more money-making for the lawyers. No more patronising lectures from judges. They were free to get on with the life they'd been planning. Land Registry would pay legal costs as well as compensate them for the land they'd given up. What sensible people they were!

Scroggs rushed back into the room. Would they be prepared to let her keep the other bit of land her path trespassed on? Max and Lucy didn't pause to think. They knew the intransigent Judge was waiting. They said yes and smiled.

The Judge, Judge Blacker finally arrived in court some 35 minutes after the allocated time. This was a large courtroom and the Judge seemed very distant in all senses. Lucy and Max had been directed to sit some rows behind their man. They could not hope to communicate with him; they just had to hope he was now master of his brief. He was certainly assured and confident, and Lucy found herself wishing he'd had the case from the start. The Judge seemed a little less austere than the image they'd gleaned of him from their barrister. He knew the area where they lived and declared it sad that neighbours should fall out in such a beautiful part of the country. He knew the area enough to know that the terrain was difficult to map and wanted to be assured that surveyors would agree the boundary lines. Their man was happy to confirm that. Smiles all round.

Max and Lucy do not have a transcript of that hearing. The Judge seemed to think that everything had been wrapped up rather well and was tidying the files (which, both Max and Lucy feared he had not studied), preparing to leave when Keith Stoat intervened. He wanted to establish that when 'Mr Ogmore tried to escort the Defendants off the land, and a fight ensued, he truly believed all the land belonged to him and his wife, Mrs Ogmore.' Max and Lucy woke up at that and protested, 'No, not true,' expecting some appropriate reaction from their Defender. Their Defender said nothing and ignored their protests.

They returned to the meeting room with him where he attempted to calm them by saying that Stoat's intervention had no significance. In which case why did he make it? Max wondered. There were clearly gaps in Scroggs' knowledge, gaps of quite important information; besides, he'd spent more time talking to Stoat than he had to them. It could well be that Stoat, and possibly Ogmore wearing her solicitor hat, had planted several lies and distortions in him. Lucy gave a full report of the attack and went back over Hazel Ogmore's irritating, unscrupulous conduct from the time she was caught tree-felling three years earlier. Scroggs said that the conduct was particularly bad because they were both lawyers and Hazel Ogmore was exploiting her position as a solicitor. Well, Lucy and Max thought, *that* was the right reaction. He then asked if Stoat had misled them. He said that he'd been told by Robert Tweed – who had been told by Robin Cain – that they had been led to believe that Land Registry was going to be left to settle the rectification land first and then Ogmore would negotiate to buy more land if she wanted.

They agreed that's what they had thought was the arrangement but when they got home they found a letter telling them that Ogmore had demanded her deeds back and sacked Land Registry.

'But did Keith Stoat mislead you?' Scroggs insisted.

Max sighed, 'Well, of course we were misled, but whether he did it knowingly, deliberately we can't possibly know, as we told Robin Cain *and* Mr Tweed, it's possible that Ogmore didn't quite get round to telling him what she'd been up to. We had to wait quite a long time, an hour or so, while they had a very long conversation before we all went in to see Judge Grey and found ourselves lumbered with this so-called agreement we'd never agreed. We found Stoat very difficult to deal with. Far too emotional. We think Robert Tweed found him a problem too.' They waited for Scroggs' response. What did he think of his opponent?

Malcolm Scroggs pondered. 'I find him … insufficiently detached. Odd – and rather unwise in my view.'

'We don't understand why the Judge thought we'd agreed to the injunction remaining in force. Why he didn't ask us about it? He didn't ask us anything. He didn't even invite us to speak. What a crazy system – locking us into an agreement without a scrap of evidence we'd agreed it. Is this the reformed civil justice? Doesn't seem much improved. I've had first-hand experience of what went before. That certainly needed scrapping.'

'Well, things are much improved.'

Urged on by Max, Lucy gave a full account of the fence-post case. She was certain that Scroggs had been given Ogmore's version of it.

They'd been back from the courtroom for about 20 minutes and Scroggs suddenly seemed to remember why they were there. He wanted their agreement to allow the rectangular plot on the 1963 plan with the additional land needed to accommodate the trespasses by part of the shed-chalet by the road and the path in the opposite corner of Blackstone Cottage. Yes, they had agreed that. He assured them that Ogmore would not have consented to anything that day if they'd insisted that she remove her shed. They were not impressed with that attempt to bring pressure. As they saw it, Ogmore was in far too weak a position for that threat to be real, but they let it go for the greater good of getting her out of their lives. They got Scroggs' assurance that the surveyors would meet to peg out the plot. The precise details would be decided by the parties on the ground at the site meeting, and then translated on to the selected OS map, the one agreed even by Ogmore. Finally Land Registry would rectify the register, recording what was agreed and described on that OS plan.

Max thought that was the end of the day's work and a glance at his watch galvanised him. The expensive parking ticket was about to run out and he'd have to move to another parking space were the session to continue. Also, he wasn't too sure how to get back to the car. He started packing papers back into his briefcase. Suddenly Scroggs made for the door. Would they agree to let him sign an agreement on their behalf? Both Max and Lucy were thrown by this. They hadn't really thought, but both assumed that something would be drafted, and then forwarded to them and to Ogmore and when they'd had a chance to look at it and agree it they could summon the surveyors and get the whole murky business out of the way.

'Well, no,' said Mr Scroggs, 'we need to get something in writing today while we're all here. I'm off to Somerset to visit a sick relative and I won't be back in Birmingham until sometime next week. Mr Stoat will be in London. We know what we've agreed don't we? Might as well get it done today.'

Max and Lucy were on the point of leaving. Lucy was just a little perplexed, but decided that if it was going to be drafted that day she had better stay to see the draft. Max said he'd leave it to her. He has always maintained that he thought what Scroggs was about to do was a preliminary step, a draft agreement; the important work was to be done at the site meeting. That was more or less what Lucy thought, but she decided to wait while Max went car hunting. Scroggs was still at the door and Max was putting on his coat when he reminded Scroggs about using the OS plan they had finally persuaded Ogmore to use.

Malcolm Scroggs left the room. Max found the scrap of paper on which he'd scribbled the name of the square where the car was parked and also left. Lucy waited. As she waited, she reflected that the moral high ground was all well and good, but a bit of justice would have been acceptable. She thought of the embarrassment the Ogmores had caused her and her innocent friends from her old home town. She thought of Max still needing treatment for the back injuries he'd suffered from Joe Ogmore's attack. She thought of the hours and hours of work, the travelling, the drafting and re-drafting of court documents, of letters to and from solicitors and Land Registry, their unpleasant dealings with the Swales as they slowly became aware of their complicity and irresponsibility, the work to get evidence and Witnesses Statements in an area where they hardly knew anybody, the phone calls and emails, the police interviews, the hanging around courtrooms and police stations. The stress created by a growing awareness of the unfit-for-purpose, updated, but still out-of-date civil justice system. The constant interruption to their renovation work in the house and on the land, the curtailment of their deserved freedom to pursue legitimate, interesting and worthwhile ambitions for their retirement. The time-wasting, the lies, the libels, the anger and indignation that had to be hidden from her angry and indignant family and friends. And the squatters, the thieves, the aggressors, the liars, the libellers escaping scot-free with an enlarged garden – free of charge. Not an impressive performance from the best legal system in the world.

Scroggs returned. No sign of Max. Lucy was staring out of the window at the traffic below. Scroggs sat. They waited. 'This isn't really such a fair agreement,' she said.

According to Lucy, Scroggs shifted in his chair and shrugged. Lucy explained, 'Knowing how Ogmore distorts things, it would be good to make clear she has no right to the extra patches of land. It's highly likely she doesn't have any right to any extra land beyond *our* registered plan. Perhaps if they'd had to pay for those two patches: the shed and the path land, say a token £100 to acknowledge they know their adverse possession claim was rubbish?' Scroggs shrugged again.

There'd been no mention of payment until then, so, Lucy thought, perhaps it's just too late. She should have thought about it from the start. Scroggs should have thought about it. He's the expert litigator. The arguments for getting it over and done with as soon as possible still held, but this was all so hurried and there was so little time to think things through. It's not as though this compromise had ever been considered before. At the previous hearing they could insist that no agreement would be made without referring to Robin Cain. Mr Scroggs was here and now and wanted action here and now.

Lucy decided to change tack and find out more about this man whom she had not bonded with (not that she thought that so important: bonding can cloud judgement). She asked about the sick relative he said he wanted to visit in Somerset. It would take him some time to get there. It was an aunt of his, diagnosed with a brain tumour.

'Your husband died from a brain tumour, I believe.'

Lucy felt sick at the thought that these people had been discussing her private life. Gossiping about Felix, her late, much-loved husband. Further evidence that these people had been prying into her private life and gossiping about it. She asked what type of brain tumour had been diagnosed, adding that not all are the same, not all are fatal. It depends what type, and where it is, and how soon it's diagnosed. He nodded. He was not going to be forthcoming and she decided against trying to engage with him any further.

'Look, I don't know how long Max is going to be and you obviously have to get off. What do you have to do next?'

'Well, I'd just like you to read this draft agreement.' He'd held it in his hand all along, this draft, and now handed the three sheets of paper on which were scribbled in handwriting she found difficult and then impossible to read – some agreement. Why had he not shown it to her immediately? Had he been waiting for Max? She couldn't read it and gave it back to him to read to her. She made hurried notes.

C's (Ogmores) and D's (them) agreed terms. Ds give Cs permission for next 14 days to remove fence lying north of boundary line. All interim injunctions and undertakings discharged. Boundaries to Blackstone Cottage as shown on plan. HMLR amend Title plan accordingly. No order to costs. Full and final settlement.

'Okay?' said Scroggs.

Lucy read back what she'd written and checked with him. 'Okay?' He nodded and left. She hadn't asked any questions and Scroggs hadn't offered any explanations. Lucy had switched her mind off just at the very moment when she most needed to be focussed. She hadn't registered that there was no reference to surveyors. She hadn't registered that the draft had been scribbled by Stoat. She hadn't registered the importance of the fact that before she'd handed the scrappy paper back she'd glimpsed the Hammer plan attached.

Lucy says in her defence that she was very, very tired and that it had not crossed her mind that she had a part to play at that stage, because Max was not there. He had not seen whatever Messrs Scroggs and Stoat had scribbled on those sheets of paper. Scroggs had even proposed dealing with the matter without any further reference to Max and Lucy. It had been Lucy's decision to stay. This was clearly just an early draft for them to to mull over together in less fraught circumstances and come up with amendments – like the many amendments to Cain's draft letters and Tweed's draft Defence and other work.

Still no sign of Max. Scroggs returned. The room was required so they moved to the lobby. Once there Lucy could see no reason to hold Malcolm Scroggs any longer. She assumed he was waiting out of politeness to say goodbye to Max. He needed to get some lunch before he went on to visit his aunt. He agreed to leave. They shook hands and Lucy asked him to convey their best wishes to his colleague, Robert Tweed. There was no flash of shark-smile in reply. Lucy feared that Mr Tweed was in some disfavour and not merely due to the disorganised file.

Lucy went down to the entrance lobby of the Civil Justice Centre and sat noting the comings and goings of court users. Litigants and solicitors and barristers. The latter two groups looked very cheery, in contrast to the former. She also noted the security cameras recording this cast of players in the law game.

Max returned at just gone one o'clock. In great haste. He'd parked on double-yellow lines right outside the Court. Not the wisest location for law-breaking.

The traffic was just as bad leaving the city and the motorway an unnerving racetrack, so it was only on leaving it for the more peaceful dual carriageway that Max asked about the draft Scroggs had shown Lucy. She rummaged in her bag and found her notes which she read out to him. The conversation then went something like this:

Max asked, 'What plan?'

'Um?'

'What plan? You just read out "boundaries as shown on plan" – what plan?'

'I don't know. Presumably the plan the surveyors draw up after their survey ... When we agree it.'

'Uh huh.'

'They'd attached the Hammer plan that Scroggs ...'

According to Lucy, Max jammed the brakes so hard they practically swung the full 180 degrees to face in the opposite direction. She was thankful they were now off the motorway and on to the deserted dual carriageway.

'Are you saying they attached the Hammer plan to the agreement? Oh! Lucy! Why didn't you stop them?'

'I don't know what your problem is, Max. It's a draft. They know they've got to draw up the plan to send to Land Registry on the OS plan. I wasn't asked for my opinion. Scroggs was going to draw it up without either of us seeing it. He wouldn't have suggested that if ... What on Earth are you fussed about? You nearly killed us both. Thank Heavens the road was empty.'

Max pulled into a service station. 'Why don't you get us some sandwiches and water? We're both hungry and tired. I'll look at your notes.'

When Lucy got back into the car, Max pointed out that there was no reference to surveyors in the agreement, that she hadn't been given a photocopy of the scribbled draft and that there was no reference according to her notes to the only boundary with any proper identity: Blackstone Cottage's boundary with Dunroamin'; the one and only boundary that could be said to have any fixed point. In fact the only fixed point on the whole Blackstone Cottage plot apart from the house itself.

Lucy pointed out that the Judge had insisted on the surveyors and Malcolm Scroggs seemed to take it for granted they would do the mapping out. She was sorry, she hadn't thought to ask for a photocopy but it was unreadable anyway and Scroggs hadn't proposed giving one to her. He was the paid professional.

It was his job to think of that. She did agree, however, that the all important carport boundary should be identified as the key reference point as there would be no other way to survey the Blackstone Cottage plot without starting from there. She confidently assured Max all that would be sorted out the following week when the surveyors met.

Max says that they drove home each in their own thoughts, both of them apprehensive. Had they let themselves once again be bounced into a bad agreement? Lucy says she worried for a while but by the time they reached home she was convinced Scroggs was unlikely to do anything as stupid as fix them with Hammer's plan and if he'd made a mistake he'd sort it out. He'd have to. Max had other thoughts.

EIGHT
November 2002–January 2003

'It would be wrong to condemn all solicitors as I have obviously not met all 56,000* in England and Wales.'

James Pickles, Judge for Yourself, *1992*[1]

Despite all the setbacks Lucy was confident that confusions and problems would be resolved on the ground when the mischievous Hammer plan had been binned and the surveyors set to work on the actual site working with the agreed OS plans. The day after the hearing, Friday, they faxed a letter to Cain making clear that although Scroggs had used the Hammer plan because he knew nothing of the site, they wanted the agreed OS plan to be used in any agreement. No response and no law work for the professionals at weekends so they had to wait until the following Monday. Mrs Hazel Ogmore, solicitor at Bulmers Solicitors acting for Mrs Hazel Ogmore citizen and litigant, also wrote to him forwarding her transcription of the scribbled, handwritten document Lucy had glimpsed at court. She attached her Hammer plan. Her transcribed Order referred solely to that plan. It made no reference to surveyors. It made no reference to an OS plan. She had decided to make an alteration because Counsel had made an error. Counsel had made quite a few errors, but not the error she decided on. She'd confused her points of the compass and her alteration made the agreement, already bad enough, a nonsense. Her unilateral decision meant more confusion and more time-wasting – and more costs.

There was no response on Monday from Cain until Lucy finally made contact at 4.30, 30 minutes before Cross, etc. & Co. closed their office to outsiders. Cain informed her that he'd spoken to Scroggs and been advised that they would have to stick with the Hammer plan for the survey. Cain reported that Scroggs' view was that the scribbled notes Lucy had seen had been lodged at court and were now an order – set in stone!

Max and Lucy were incredulous. They were held to the wording of an 'agreement' Lucy had only glimpsed and Max hadn't even seen? Max expressed his displeasure with heat. Lucy tried to find something positive: 'They'll have to abandon the Hammer plan and send the OS plan to Land Registry. We still get to decide how the new boundaries configure.'

Max remained less than happy. 'Why,' he wanted to know, 'had Scroggs allowed that plan to be used. It can only mean trouble. There was enough in the file making clear to him it should never be used and Ogmore had even agreed to use the OS plan. Besides, a glance at it was enough to see it was useless.'

'If it's useless then there's nothing to fear,' Lucy countered, 'it'll be binned.'

'Not just useless,' said Max, totally unpersuaded, 'mischievous, dangerous.'

That evening Lucy got a call from their surveyor, James Nunn. He was off on holiday and would not be back until the 18th. So the survey would have to be delayed. If the agreement *was* an order, Ogmore would have to remove her compost box and about 30 feet of encroaching fence on the roadside before the survey – because the Order stated 'within 14 days'. In which case how would anyone know precisely how much fence to remove? If it was an order how could they establish that they'd *gifted* the two extra parcels of their land? More to the point how were the surveyors to know what shape and size exactly the extra bits of land were? If Ogmore continued to get away with things like this they could see that *she* would decide what land they were giving her and they'd have little say in the matter.

Another more anxious letter to Cain. 'We have some concern that what was agreed last Thursday will morph into something we did not agree … We have agreed only that the shed and path can stay, and no more than that … *We* decide the boundaries created by the encroachment of the shed and path … we cannot be harried into giving land we do not wish to give and did not agree to give … Malcolm Scroggs used the Hammer plan merely to discuss the proposals as he hadn't seen the site … LR pointed out that it is not accurate … The fence must be removed to the Blackstone Cottage side of the telephone pole which remains on our land … .' Lucy apologised for the repetition but wanted to make clear that *they* would decide what they were giving, 'and are willing to return to court if she forces us to.' Lucy's sixth sense had returned. She sensed trouble.

They didn't receive the faxed copy of Ogmore's transcript until the following day. Max replied pointing out Ogmore's confusion with points of the compass and repeating the contents of Lucy's letter but more trenchantly. Cain faxed the draft of a letter to send FAO Mrs H. Ogmore at Bulmers, Solicitors, acting for client Mrs H. Ogmore. Max tweaked it a bit as did Lucy when she returned from business in London that night.

The following day Max made more calls to Cain who finally emailed back saying that if his understanding was correct, the Court had already made the Order in the terms agreed by Counsel and their ability to alter it was very limited, but, in his view their position did not appear to be inconsistent with the terms. He suggested they awaited Ogmore's reply to his letter and in the meantime leave the typed version of the Consent Order unsigned. So, what did it mean if it wasn't signed? Max wrote again asking Cain to verify with Scroggs that the Consent Order can be tweaked – by both sides – 'since it is in the interests of both parties, and of the Court itself, that it properly reflect the parties' intention and neither of us had proper sight of the draft document last week – I (Max) had no sight of it at all.' He ended by stressing that they wanted the agreed OS plan used from now on.

Ogmore wrote confirming that the surveyors would meet on the 19th November, 'her client' would remove the fence and the compost box by the 14th, but until the demarcation had taken place she could not be precise about how much fence or how much compost bin to remove. No mention of telephone pole and the implication that some of the compost box was not trespassing!

Monday morning, 11th November, Cain called to ask if they agreed the draft letter he'd forwarded to them as he'd like to send it to Ogmore. They assumed it had already gone. Lucy had phoned just after five the previous Thursday and a temp had taken her instruction to send it. The temp didn't get round to passing it on to Cain who 'was not in his office' (i.e. had gone home). The message disappeared the following day, Friday. Cain had produced four versions of his letter with hardly any changes after version two. It could have gone a week earlier.

The following Wednesday morning, 13th November, Lucy and Max heard noises up on the road near the shed. They went to investigate. Ogmore had decided to get her compost box and fence panels moved without alerting anyone or abiding by the agreement to get permission to go on to Homestead land. Hardly a misdemeanour by her standards. What peeved more was that the fence had not been taken back far enough. No reply from Ogmore to Cain's letter.

Two days later, Friday 15th, they were leaving on their way to Oxford for a book launch when the postman arrived earlier than usual. Lucy opened a letter from Cain with two enclosures. One was another draft letter to Ogmore for their approval. The other was copy of a letter from a clerk at the Court dated 11th November. 'The Judge, His Honour Judge Blacker, has asked that

I write to both parties regarding the Consent Order filed on the above case. His Honour has pointed out that the dotted red lines encloses three sides of the property, whereas only two sides are variously described in that Consent Order submitted. *Please prepare and send to the Court a definitive Consent Order to which both parties are agreed.*'

They had to read it three times before the implications began to sink in. She grabbed her mobile and to her surprise got through to Cain. 'So, it's not carved in stone. We can alter it, improve it.' Pause on the other end. 'Well,' he said eventually, 'It's a bit more complex than that. I've been on the phone with Ogmore and Scroggs. Ogmore is very angry, she accuses us of trying to reopen the terms of the Consent Order and Scroggs confirms my view that the Court actually made the Order on the date of the hearing.'

Pause on Lucy's end. 'But it is the Judge, the Court, who seems to want things sorted "Please prepare and send to the Court a definitive Consent Order to – which – both – parties – are – agreed'!! We're not agreed to the Order Scroggs and Stoat – and no doubt Ogmore – agreed. This surely sets us free to get things corrected before the surveyors meet.' Another pause. 'I've sent you a letter, have you had time to read it?' Mobile connection died.

So, the Judge, the very same Judge that Scroggs had warned them against, a warning they had taken seriously enough to abandon the application they had gone to court for and to agree the trespassing shed and paths could stay, this 'intransigent' Judge on his own initiative had spotted an obvious error in this second misnamed 'Consent' Agreement and was asking for another agreement which *both* parties agreed. Max wanted to know why Cain had not faxed the letters to them the day before when they had a bit of time. Cain knew they were occupied all weekend. It was pure chance that their notorious postal service had delivered the post two hours earlier than usual so they could catch it before they left. It was getting perilously close to the day for the surveyors' meeting. They had time to look at his draft letter to Ogmore on the journey and tried to phone to suggest he wait to send it until after they'd talked it over with him on Monday. They couldn't get through. Later they learned that he'd already faxed it to Ogmore. What a contrast to the constant redrafting and delays with the previous letter. And how unfortunate – for Max and Lucy.

They existed that weekend in a bubble of convivial relaxation with guests blissfully unaware of what had been taking place. But then how could they know? No one was going to tell them what was going on. Certainly not their antagonists, but what about the lawyers charged with the task of looking after their best interests? Why didn't they keep them in the loop, keep them informed, take their instructions? They were able to piece together those events a year or so later after they finally managed to wrest their file from the avaricious grasp of Cross & Cross & Co. It had been quite a tussle.

From the papers they eventually recovered they could deduce that Robin Cain had found their adversary very unpleasant, but this did not explain why he was so pusillanimous in his response to the Judge's letter. For there is no doubt that he and Scroggs could and should have saved them from what was to follow. From notes in the file, Cain appeared to have firmly resisted Ogmore's attempts to bully him initially, but over the following weeks vacillated between firmness and feebleness, and appeared convinced there was little he could do to rid them of the Hammer plan or even 'send the Judge an agreement to which both parties are agreed.' He appeared to have a very shaky grasp of land surveying in general and the battleground of this contest in particular.

He also showed no understanding of the law on Consent Orders. This story would have been so different if Robin Cain had acquainted himself with Lord Woolf's new landscape of civil justice: this monumental makeover had taken place just three years earlier. Unfortunately, as already said, it would only work to benefit clients of the civil justice service if the professionals read it and applied it. The professionals in this case either hadn't read the reformed rules or simply did not want to apply them. It may be said that Robin Cain was a general practitioner who had other cases to contend with. He couldn't be expected to give their case his attention twenty-four/seven or even nine to five. His and their misfortune was that Ogmore could and was more than willing to – for her very own client.

But then what about the two barristers: Scroggs and Tweed? They must have been ignorant of the rules on consent agreements and unaware that they could and should have had the first revoked and the second rewritten. How else to explain their failure to act? It was a long time later that the sad thought occurred to Max and Lucy: their troubles stemmed not just from incompetence but possibly, just possibly, collusion with the enemy.

Stoat, however, must have congratulated himself on his successful sleight of hand substituting the Hammer plan for the agreed OS plan, not to mention getting an agreement signed by Scroggs which failed to mention that his client had been gifted Homestead land or any mention of the OS plan. Whether Stoat knew the rules on Consent Orders no one can say. He may have known but hoped to get away with pulling the wool over the eyes of others. He had, after all, tried to argue that Max and Lucy had no right to take down Ogmore's trespassing fence and it is hard to believe he was unaware of the precedent establishing that they had every right. Most lawyers know that. He was a barrister experienced in property disputes, could it be true that he knew less of the relevant law than the jobbing small town lawyer and the police constable who had told them, correctly, of their rights? Is it possible that he *innocently* foisted two 'Consent Orders' on the Court and Max and Lucy, totally unaware neither was by *legitimate* consent and one was actually invalid?

What they learnt long after the event, far too long after to make good use of the information, was that Ogmore had been more than a little upset by Cain's letter which had insisted that the OS plan should be used to send to Land Registry. She had faxed him to say that there was no point in the surveyors meeting unless there was agreement as to the plan to be used. She wanted confirmation 'before close of business today', that the surveyors would only use Hammer's plan. Her letter spewed out irrelevant complaints indicating a less than calm soul. She followed that fax with another the next day saying more or less the same thing and threatening to call off the survey. But it was the letter from the Judge that sent her over the top. She received the letter on Thursday 14th November. As did Cain.

First a call from her to Stoat, leading to a call from Stoat to Scroggs, leading to a call from Scroggs to Cain, leading to a call from Cain to Ogmore. Nobody called Max or Lucy. They had been at home that Thursday. They could have taken the call. They could have given advice. They could have given instructions. The Judge wanted them to 'send a definitive consent order to which both parties are agreed'. If the Order had had to go back to court because Ogmore insisted on the Hammer plan and they refused to agree, they would have drawn attention to her letter of a month earlier stating her agreement to use the OS plan. They would have drawn attention to the weaknesses in the Hammer plan. They might even have slipped in some facts about the dubious 1963 plan and the highly dubious Ogmore conduct. The Judge would then have had to decide. They were beginning to have doubts about the image of Circuit Judge Blacker sold to them by their Mr Scroggs. As it turned out, neither the Judge nor they were given the chance to decide anything. Ogmore was in charge.

Cain wrote up a telephone attendance note that day, Thursday 14th November. They found it in the file they finally wrested from his firm. According to his note, he told Ogmore that the Court had raised a query and if the Consent Order did not accurately reflect what the parties had agreed, it was his view that it could be amended with the consent of the Parties and with the consent of the Court. The note recorded the unsurprising fact that Ogmore disagreed. She said that the Order had been made and that was that. The note continued: 'She said that there was no problem with the Consent Order as indicated by the Court because she had three boundaries to her property' (she had four, of course, but let that go) 'but there were only two which impacted on Homestead.' In reality the third Dunroamin' boundary was crucial – as was to be confirmed several years later, and, moreover, Homestead did share a stretch of that boundary with Blackstone Cottage. Cain's attendance note reveals all: he had agreed with Ogmore that the third boundary – the only fixed boundary of any use, was irrelevant. He hadn't bothered to check with his clients.

Everyone except Ogmore and her gang would have benefitted greatly had Cain grasped the basics of surveying, nothing complex, most people could have coped. Once again justice thwarted by an inability to understand plans. Mr Cain and the fence post Judge had problems in common, problems from which they did not suffer the consequences. Judge Blacker, on the other hand, had been quite right to raise his query. It may well have been that the Judge understood a lot more about surveying. Maybe he had noted that there was nothing on the Hammer plan to indicate any other fixed point for the surveyors to work from. Mr Cain's foolish agreement was compounded by failing to ever let Max and Lucy know so that they could correct his misunderstanding. His note continued, 'Mrs Ogmore was, however, rather "excited" about the question of the Order. She did not agree that the Order could be altered in any way.' His note continued: 'I said that although I appreciated that the Hammer plan had been attached to the Order, it was not accurate and it would be necessary to use the OS plan when submitting the boundary to Land Registry. Mrs Ogmore did not agree. I said that therefore we did not have an agreement. She asked what I was going to do about it bearing in mind the Order had been made. I said that if the Order was incapable of implementation, the parties would have to go back to the Court or agree something different. She said this was "rubbish" and I told her she should not speak to me in this way and that I was not intending to continue this conversation.' He then put the phone down on her.

Mr Cain described this as a heated exchange when Max made contact with him. His verbal report was more dramatic. 'She shouted at me. She would not allow me to speak. I found her impossible.' He did write a controlled letter to her that day. Then he signed off on their case. Just when they most needed him. 'Pusillanimous man!' said Max. What the file revealed was that Ogmore had faxed four letters to Cain that day. The first sent at 10.47 informed him that she would be away until the day of the survey and that the Hammer plan must be used. The second sent an hour later, after a flurry of calls to and between barristers, demanded confirmation that the Hammer plan would be used. The third informed Cain that the *two* barristers were agreed: the Judge does not understand the Order and both sides must write to the Court stating that the third boundary is irrelevant; the Hammer plan must be used; the agreement can then, if so wished, be translated on to the OS and an agreed version sent to Land Registry. The fourth was sent at 18.55 long after Cain had gone home.

Max and Lucy knew nothing of this and in their uninformed state they were in a quandary. They wanted the survey over and done with. They wanted a boundary fence up. They did not want Ogmore to have any more land than they'd verbally agreed to gift in court. The Judge's letter suggested that they could dispense with the Hammer plan for the survey and get everything back on track.

The following Tuesday, 19th November, the day of the survey, Mr Nunn, sympathetic though he was, did not want to ignore Cain's and Scroggs' advice. They had said that jettisoning the Hammer plan was not possible. The only possibility was that Max and Lucy could try to insist that the surveyors transpose the boundaries they were about to identify on the land, on to the OS plan and that the OS plan be sent to Land Registry and to the Judge. He also reported that Ogmore was complaining forcefully that it was a disgrace that he, James Nunn, did not have a copy of the Consent Order with him.

Ignoring lawyer's advice seemed a dumb thing to do. Mr Cain was the expensive professional, over £200 per hour expensive, he was supposedly working for his clients and he was confident in his advice. So, Lucy and Max left the two surveyors to do their work, using the Hammer plan.

An hour or so later James Nunn reappeared. They'd mapped out two boundaries and had come up with a proposal he would like them to look at on site. It was not explained to them at the time, but a year later they learned that the two surveyors had agreed that they would start from a peg planted by Royston Hammer a year earlier somewhere in the undergrowth on the southern riverside boundary at the Dunroamin' end. So these two 'experts' started the survey from *no* independently fixed or even mutually-agreed survey point! Max and Lucy never found out why they ignored the only discernible boundary available, the line of the carport wall. No checks were made to verify whether the peg was still where it had originally been planted, let alone whether it had been planted correctly in the first place.

Although 'The Proposal' was based on the Hammer plan, Max and Lucy believed that when the plotting was transposed to the OS plan they could ensure that the shed boundary had a kink in it to accommodate all the trespass by the chalet before returning to the boundary line described on the 1963 (dubious but allowed) conveyance plan. This plan gifted a bit more land than they had previously envisaged, but without a kink it would gift far more and they were not prepared to gift Ogmore far more. This was something their barrister should have thought to discuss with them at court before he signed anything 'on their behalf'. Lucy admits she was peeved that they were forced into this position, but thought that if their legal advisers were correct, and at that time they had to assume they were, she and Max had little choice. This was the best they could hope for. So, they let James Nunn know that they agreed his proposal so they would give her a bit more land by the trespassing path near Dunroamin' as long as the shed boundary had a kink in it. Lucy says she even shook hands with Royston Hammer to seal the agreement (she insists she *was* wearing gloves).

Neither Lucy nor Max appreciated the significance of the fact that no Ogmore was in sight let alone shaking anyone's hand, even though they were both in the house. Just as the Doyles had stayed inside when the Judge came to inspect the fence post. Of course, both Lucy and Max took it for granted that the two professional surveyors had carried out their work professionally and mapped out the boundary lines starting from the line of the carport wall. They knew nothing of the secret peg. Nobody had told them otherwise, and they didn't double-check the paid experts.

Between them Nunn and Hammer agreed that Hammer would draw up the plan to send to Land Registry and the Court. Apparently he was about to go on holiday and hoped to get his plan to Cain, *for agreement*, before he left. The following day they received copies of two letters from Cain and an invoice for over £11,500 including the barristers' fees. The firm had been working for them for two and a half months. There were no bill ledgers to explain the sums. Judging by the difficulties both had encountered trying to make contact with their protector they were not by any means his only clients. They certainly did not engage his attention for a full lawyerly working week. A quick review of the file confirmed overcharging. Most unwise. They needed to work with Mr Cain, they needed to trust him. That bill reduced their already teetering trust and they questioned what he'd managed to achieve for his fees, bearing in mind that they were now in a far weaker position than when he took the case on. They noted the account had been drawn-up on the day of the survey. Alienation was setting in.

His letter included a draft letter for the Court which did nothing to restore confidence. He had either ignored or failed to understand what he had been told. He reported that he'd seen a draft of a letter Ogmore intended as her reply to the Court. He didn't copy it to Max or Lucy. In any event they could not agree the draft that *he* intended to send: It 'confirmed' that the carport boundary was irrelevant! He asked that the Consent Order drafted by Counsel be sealed.

Was Cain losing his grip? Max called and emailed immediately instructing him to send nothing. Fortunately he caught Cain in time. The letter was not sent.

Throughout these weeks of turmoil and confusion Lucy and Max were entertaining different house guests and dealing with more building work. After the last guest left, they returned to the land battle. They emailed their surveyor, James Nunn, to ask if he had heard anything from Hammer or Ogmore. If not, perhaps he should draw the proposed boundaries on the OS plan and send it to Ogmore, Hammer and the Court. He emailed back that he'd heard nothing from either, but suggested they wait until Hammer returned in a week's time, 'and to be frank, I cannot see me preparing a plan for submission to the Court within that timescale.'

Cain wrote a holding letter to the Court and another to Ogmore. No response from either. Days passed. Max and Lucy were off to Brussels the following week. If nothing could be done before they left, nothing could be done until after 9th December, by which time Ogmore could have got up to all sorts of tricks, so they made time to interpret the surveyors' proposals on to the agreed OS plan and sent it to Cain to forward to the Court. The following day, the last solicitor working day of the week, but 10 days after the survey and nearly a month after the disaster at court, Mr Cain came back on board. He agreed with their suggestion, but first wanted Nunn's approval of their plan; if he approved it, Cain would forward it to the Court with a covering letter. The plan got James Nunn's approval so it was all down to Robin Cain.

By now they were accustomed to setting aside time and reserves of patience when attempting to make contact with their mentor, and by midday when the silence from Cross & Cross & Co. was becoming an irritating brake on their other arrangements, they emailed instructions to get the plan, explanation and covering letter out that day to be at the Court the following Monday, but so diminished was their trust in their mentor/guardian they asked to see a draft of his letter beforehand. This was important as this was their response to the Judge's request for 'an agreement to which both parties are agreed.' They added that copies of Ogmore's 1963 plan and the letter from Land Registry stating the Hammer plan was inadequate, should also be attached.

Malcolm Scroggs, they said, 'may have to write to the Court to explain that, whilst he had our authority to sign an agreement on our behalf, he had no such authority to sign and attach the (Hammer) plan. The only authority he had was to state our agreement to cede enough land to accommodate the shed and path according to our specific say-so with respect to the precise boundaries. Signing the plan', their email continued, 'was a disastrous error for which he must make amends. Please confirm that you will ask him to set the record straight. It is vital that we use the window of opportunity presented by the Court's letter to get this across and as soon as possible.' At the time they considered this merely a statement in writing of what they had established in several telephone conversations. Several years later that email was to prove quite useful as telephone conversations fade into the ether.

Mr Cain's covering letter to the Court confirmed that the surveyors' proposals were agreed by his side, but that the Ogmores had not yet indicated whether the proposed boundary was agreed and their 'expert' was away until 3rd December. His letter concluded with the hope that the parties would soon be able to confirm that the OS plan with the dog-leg boundary by the shed, was the plan that should now be attached to the Consent Order – as 'Land Registry would require an OS plan when registering the new boundaries.'

Max and Lucy left for Belgium believing naively that at last they had wrested control back from the squatters. One thing was now clear to them: they should not rely on anyone, only on themselves. Before leaving they advised both Cain and James Nunn that nothing further should be done with the Ogmores or the Court until they returned. They assumed that Mr Cain was back on board working hard for them.

A year or so later after they recovered their file they realised that their Mr Cain had been rather anxiously working for himself – to protect himself from possible trouble from his clients, and from his professional body. Whether through carelessness or laziness, or overwork or for whatever reason, Mr Robin Cain had taken his eye off the ball and delayed just at the very time when their case most needed his undivided attention. That was why he was now so insistent that his letter and enclosures were sent to the Court as soon as possible.

He had kept his clients in the dark. They didn't know, but he did, that Ogmore had forwarded her response to the Court *before the survey*, without waiting for his agreement. She had sent him a draft by fax at 7pm on 14th November long after he had gone home, which stated that *the third boundary was irrelevant* and that '**both parties agreed the Consent Order** *drafted by both Counsels.*' She '*respectfully*' asked the Court to seal it.[2] He had not responded to her draft. It was only a draft after all. He only learned later that she had sent it to the Court unaltered. That lie to the Court which was to cause all that followed went unchallenged. She had lied to Cain as well. In a letter sent the day after the survey she had told him that she had replied to the Court saying that *he would be writing separately*. She wrote no such thing. This was a lie to him which compounded her lie to the Court. She knew and Cain knew both parties were not agreed. Cain had failed to pass Max's instruction to Scroggs, so no effort had been made by anybody working for Max and Lucy to put the record straight with the Court.

Cain also failed to explain to them that the Order was not an Order until sealed by the Judge.[3] The Judge had not sealed it so their advisors' insistence that they would have to use the Hammer plan for the survey was just plain wrong. *They* could have done the insisting. With a determined, on the ball, committed Defender who knew his job, had the basics of land surveying and took the time to apply a little common sense, they could have saved themselves the years of litigation games and stress to come.

Ironically his telephone attendance note for that day records Lucy's advice to him, 'Stoat is trying to suggest that there was an agreement ratified by the Court, but [Lucy and Max] think that the agreement was merely submitted to the Court and was not an endorsement of what was agreed.' In other words, they thought the 'agreement' was not fixed. Why else would the Judge have asked them to send another agreement 'to which both parties are agreed'? Far from being dumb to ignore the advice of their solicitor, it was dumb of them to heed it. They were correct. The (non-) agreement had not been sealed.

While they were enjoying their *moules et frites* in the Grand Place, Cain was panicking, or despairing, or possibly just sighing over a letter from the Court. A letter containing a version of Ogmore's transcribed Order – *sealed* by His Honour Judge Blacker! It had crossed with Cain's letter and plan. Cain had delayed too long and he was now trying to 'make amends'. He phoned the Court and learned that Ogmore had been badgering the Court for days to seal the Order, the Judge had not seen Cain's letter and plan, only Ogmore's letter saying both parties agreed the draft she had sent him – so he sealed the Order!

Two years later, at the same Civil Justice Centre where the dirty deed had been done, Max and Lucy finally managed to unravel the mystery that had nagged at them. Why did the Judge seal Ogmore's version of the Consent Order without waiting for their reply to his letter? The answer was all there in the Court file: Ogmore had told Cain one thing and the Court something quite different. She had lied to both.

Cain could see the need for urgency but not the need for panic (Cain did not seem to do panic – a slight pinking and fluster was more his style). It seemed perfectly reasonable to send his version of the surveyors' proposal transposed to the OS plan a little late as he believed Ogmore when she told him that she had told the Court that he would be sending his own reply later. Despite all he knew about the lady, Cain believed her since lying to the Court is generally considered to be a Very Bad Thing. Solicitors can get struck off for such conduct.

Having gone for a high risk strategy she gambled on Cain and the Court falling for her lies and relying on the usual tardiness of lawyers and Court officers. She then rammed home her campaign. The Court internal memos revealed that from 20th November Mrs H. Ogmore bombarded the Court with demands that the Clerks inform the Judge that he could/should seal the Order. And the clerks eventually complied. The Judge sealed the Consent Order.

Who could blame the Clerks? Who could blame the Judge? The solicitor acting for the Complainant had told them in writing unequivocally that 'the parties are agreed' and they had heard nothing to the contrary from the Defendants' solicitor.

Cain did phone and write to the Court to try to retrieve the situation. Max and Lucy, of course, knew nothing. They were enjoying the good company of Belgian friends with yet more moules et frites and certain carefully selected wines. They only discovered that the Order had been sealed four days after their return, not from their well-paid Defender but from Land Registry. The Registry copied them their letter to Ogmore thanking her for forwarding the sealed Order. She had sent it immediately she had got her hands on it. The Registry was preparing a draft filed plan to send to both sides for approval. Max and Lucy would have known nothing of Ogmore's busy time had Land Registry's letter not been copied to them. Cain got quite a lengthy call from Max. James Nunn then got quite a lengthy call from Cain. Nobody had heard a thing from Hammer, or Ogmore, both lying doggo.

Max wrote a full-blooded reply to Land Registry enclosing their interpretation of the surveyors' proposals set out on the OS plan and asking for a copy of the plan Ogmore had sent to them. He also wrote an acerbic report on recent events and expressed his dismay that Bulmer & Co., without a moment's consultation with them or their representatives, should have taken such premature action on the sealed Order even before they had been notified that the Order had been sealed. He called for a further Land Registry survey to peg out the properties including Dunroamin', as the boundaries for all three properties interrelated and needed clarification. He concluded with, 'We now look to Land Registry to play the appropriate managerial role in bringing this matter to a conclusion; and we are perfectly agreeable to having the entire affair adjudicated by Land Registry's solicitor.' They were to learn in the following years just how amusing

Max's letter must have been to lawyers and Registrars alike, demonstrating, as it did, their total failure to grasp the role of Land Registry.

Max sent Cross & Cross & Co. a cheque for £4,000, making clear it did not include payments for either Scroggs or Tweed. It was quite soft in tone. Far softer than the tones that could be heard inside Homestead as they reviewed their position and compared it with the position they had been in before lawyers and courts started playing litigation games. His letter concluded, 'I am sure that such innocent mistakes are commonplace and that there is a straightforward procedure for correcting them. Malcolm Scroggs needs merely to write to the Court to explain the error. Will you please ensure that this is done?'

Such naivety will have brought forth more guffaws from lawyers, 'needs *merely* to write to the Court to explain the error'. Lawyers in general and barristers in particular do not admit to errors, they do not do humble. It's quite possible that they considered Max's demands impertinent. Other people make mistakes. Mistakes should be attributed to clients.

And bills must be paid by them. They got a reply from Cross & Cross in the form of a threat to issue County Court proceedings if they didn't pay up in full. They did not feel threatened. They felt angry. Lucy phoned pointing out that there were several problems for Cain to resolve. Christmas was approaching and she had innumerable other commitments and could do without the stress caused by Scroggs' errors and Ogmore's chicanery (although she did not know the level of chicanery at the time). They had heard nothing for three weeks, no response to their enquiries and no report on any action taken to 'put things right'. She wanted a copy of Cain's letter to the Court and a copy of the Court's reply. If the Court hadn't replied what had Cain done about it?

Max had written twice to Land Registry giving his record of events and enclosing their interpretation of the surveyors' work on the OS plan. He warned that even though he hadn't seen the plan Ogmore had sent to the Registry, he feared that there might well be more argument, 'despite the fact that we sought to put an end to a dispute, not of our making, by gifting land.'

Christmas guests were invited and builders, electricians *and* plumbers needed cajoling to complete more of their work to make the house habitable before they arrived. That was quite stressful enough without dealing with the mess created by the lawyers. Whether they had the time or not, another letter to Cain was required before the Christmas break to state that the payment should not be construed to imply that they were satisfied with Scroggs' work; they wanted to know what has been done 'to set the record straight'. They would not pay for two people from the same chambers to review the same brief because one could not honour his undertaking to attend on the day. They repeated that they still had not seen a sealed copy of the Consent Order. 'We don't understand how the Order can be said to be in its final form when Judge Blacker's request that the parties agree an Order has yet to be complied with so, please write to Bulmer & Co objecting in your own lawyerly words, to Ogmore's arrogance in sending to the Court and to Land Registry the Order we have not agreed and do not agree.'

Someone or something nudged Mr Nunn to contact them. He still hadn't heard a word from Hammer and was dismayed to learn that Ogmore had sent a plan to Land Registry which he hadn't seen. He was very confused, he said.

Land Registry's 'rectified' plan arrived on Christmas Eve and got dumped in the in-tray until Christmas was over. Christmas was a houseful of pleasure except Lucy's computer got sick and she lost key documents and emails. At a lull in the general fun she managed a brief note to Land Registry. 'Your draft plan has errors; we cannot agree it in its present form.' And after Christmas Max wrote to Cain with questions and instructions, all of which seemed perfectly reasonable at the time bearing in mind that they hadn't a clue what had been going on: (1) what is the status of the (draft) Consent Order? (2) Ogmore yet to remove all trespasses; (3) Scroggs to write to the Court explaining his mistakes – requesting they be put right (!!); (4) a record that the 'slivers' of land given to Ogmore were gifts not rights; (5) an up-to-date statement of account which removes any attempt to bill us for two barristers duplicating the work. His letter ended with the apocryphal, 'Thank you for your assistance in concluding matters.' They laugh at that today.

Cain finally replied to their several letters on his return to the office after Christmas, and finally sent a copy of the sealed Order – which they had already managed to get from Land Registry and which he had had for over a month. He knew that it was exactly the same as the unsealed versions.

Cain's letter tweaked reality here and there Ogmore style, for example suggesting that he had written his initial reply to the Court soon after receipt of the Judge's request, whereas he'd written his brief note two weeks later and only then after he had been prodded. More tellingly he tweaked the Judge's letter suggesting the Judge saw a discrepancy in the barristers' work which in Cain's view was not a discrepancy. The Judge had not mentioned a discrepancy; he had noted an omission and asked for 'an agreement to which both parties are agreed'.

Cain lamented the fact that the Judge had sealed the Order without seeing either of his letters. He reported that when he phoned the Court to ask why he eventually got a call informing him that the Judge, having now considered his letters, had directed, 'No further directions until OS plan is received.' What OS plan? Did Judge Blacker mean the one they had sent, or what? Cain surmised that the Judge may be open to substituting 'an' OS plan for the Hammer plan, but then doused the hope in cold water saying that all would depend on Ogmore agreeing. Was it likely that Ogmore would agree? She knew that her gamble with that *ex parte* injunction gambit was about to succeed and she'd done brilliantly, getting a hearty chunk of Homestead land without having to pay a penny for it. She now held the upper hand and from what was known of the lady with or without her husband's help, her *chutzpah* was likely to be in overdrive.

Whereas Cain tentatively acknowledged that Scroggs and Tweed had caused more problems than they solved, he didn't take the view there was much he or his clients could do about it. Any claim for negligence would be 'very difficult, as Malcolm Scroggs is likely to say that he considered he had authority to sign the Consent Order *and* the plan and that *he had explained both to you*!'

'Is Cain saying that Scroggs is likely to lie?' asked Max 'when did Scroggs explain anything to us? When did he show us what he planned to sign and when did he show me what he *had* signed? Why hasn't he admitted he made a mistake? Why hasn't he sorted things out at court? He's made the mess, he should clear it up.'

'Cain doesn't *know* he's likely to lie.'

'We don't *know* what Cain and Scroggs have said to each other. Scroggs seems to have conveniently forgotten that I reminded him to use the OS plan. Page after page of his file, which he assured us he had read, made that patently clear, he could not have missed it. Cain knows that. We just don't know what Cain believes and we don't know if they've done anything for us in the past two months. All this 'if Ogmore agrees','I advise a stealthy approach' and 'we should avoid confronting Ogmore as she seems incapable of adopting a rational approach', all this stuff, this giving in to bullies, liars, thieves and cheats is so spineless. Ogmore *is* irrational and at the end of the day if we go back to court, and I think we should, the Judge, any judge – how many have we had so far, four? – *any* judge will see that.' Max had not lived through the fence post saga so he could believe what he said. Lucy had and was not so sure, there seemed to be something about the judging business that made it difficult for these near deities to see what is blindingly obvious to mere mortals.

Cain could not complete his letter without due stress on money, 'I really do need to ask you to let me have the balance due pursuant to my firm's account before further costs are incurred.'

Not until they do the job they're paid to do. Not until they undo the mess they've created Max and Lucy decided, so they replied asking again for copies of correspondence with the Court and letting Cain know that they had themselves written to the Court after Christmas. They had heard nothing from anyone apart from Land Registry. They did not add that they had decided *they* could do no worse than their lawyers and *they* were cost free. Cain was alarmed, 'We must ensure that any correspondence I write to the Court is consistent with yours – and vice versa. Hopefully Land Registry will make a site visit and this will resolve matters in your favour. I have still not received the Court letter (about waiting for the OS plan).' Cain never did receive that letter. It was not in the file Max and Lucy retrieved from Cross & Cross & Co two years later.

They called for a meeting. Cain informed them that the meeting 'will, of course, increase the costs further. I need to be put in funds beforehand. Please respond to this particular point prior to our meeting.' They decided to play this like lawyers, not quite getting round to replying until the day of the meeting, and replied to Cain's second 'urgent' email very politely asking for their 'position on costs' with 'We do not yet have a position on costs, we hope to be clearer after we have talked to you.' They gambled correctly that Cain would not cancel at that stage.

According to Cain's near illegible notes found in the file, the meeting lasted two hours. They made it clear they would not pay for his time there. He accepted that, Lucy suspects because they were moving into assertive mode, all deference gone; now they were clients expecting good service. They started by asking to see the promised reply from the Court, then, what action had Scroggs taken with the Court to remedy his error, and has he apologised for making the error in the first place, and finally, 'How do we get out of the mess we're now in?'

Robin Cain's answers were all in the negative: nothing from the Court, nothing from Scroggs, nothing much to be done in the circumstances, but hope that Land Registry comes up with something acceptable to them that he could send to the Court. He mainly wanted to talk about Scroggs and Tweed. He seemed to think that they were wholly responsible for 'the mess'. He was quite pleased to tell them their rights should they wish to lodge a complaint, against the barristers.

For most of the time between the fateful day in court right up until a week before that meeting with Cain, Max and Lucy had been pinning their hopes on Ogmore calling it a day, banking her underserved gains and agreeing some plan which reflected the surveyors' proposals. For two months or so she had said nothing to suggest that she rejected those proposals. In fact she'd said nothing at all on anything and even she must have been more than pleased with the outcome. She'd done so very well, achieved far more than she had any realistic hope of achieving before the day in court, 'Before Scroggs' valiant work on her behalf so radically changed the game,' as Max put it. Up until that day Max and Lucy had every reason to believe that once a judge heard what she'd been up to and the lack of supporting evidence for her claim, the most likely outcome would be a court order that she remove her shed and pay their costs. Instead she had escaped costs, even her own, kept her shed and acquired extra parcels of land without paying a penny.

She now informed Land Registry that she agreed their draft plan and that there was no agreement at the surveyors' meeting; 'the only agreement is embodied in the Consent Order and Land Registry has been directed [sic] to amend the file plan in accordance with the plan referred to and annexed to the Court Order, initialled by both Counsels.'

Two whole *months* after the surveyors' meeting, Mrs Hazel Ogmore of Bulmer & Co. who, like her client had become un-contactable, had returned to the known world zombie-like to inform the Registry she awaited confirmation that the Court Order will be complied with – *as directed*. So, Hazel Ogmore was not going to bank her profit, call it a day and be satisfied with her ill-gotten gains, she wanted yet more, proclaiming she always had a right to whatever she had appropriated. Max had thought it was all about her obsession with her shed, but they had let her keep her shed in place. It wasn't that. It was some other deeper, nastier obsession in a lady who lived with her ex-con husband in the house next door. Lucy wanted a fence between them, soon, but where would that fence go?

On the last day of January 2003 Max and Lucy wrote to Cain setting out complaints against Tweed and Scroggs, but not a complaint against him. A necessary compromise as they needed Cain on-side at least for a while, and, besides, they thought he might still redeem himself. Nothing had been resolved. The boundary was still in dispute.

NINE
February 2003–August 2003

> 'Establishing the exact position of the legal boundaries at the time of registration can be expensive and may lead to unnecessary disputes.'
>
> *Land Registry advice on the Land Registration Act 2002*[1]

Their letter to Robin Cain was to feature prominently in the battles to come. The first was a battle to ensure Cross & Cross & Co. profited as little as possible from the debacle the firm had helped to create. Four-and-half thousand pounds was demanded over and above what the firm had already been paid. Even though Land Registry (Stamp Duty payers) was offering to foot the bill, Max and Lucy were not inclined to hand over another penny, and certainly not to either of the barristers. Cain agreed not to pay Counsels' fees but ignored their request for a copy of the letter from the Court suggesting that the Judge was prepared to wait until Land Registry had come up with a plan. They never did see such a letter and, although much later they did get to see a note on the Court file to that effect, they never found evidence that the Court had ever relayed the information to Cain by letter, or that Robin Cain had chased a reply.

It was a week later that the game changed their way, just a bit. Land Registry wrote to both Max and Lucy and to Bulmer & Co/Ogmore saying that, 'If the parties cannot agree the effect of the Consent Order they will have to return to court,' and although the Registrar refused to send a surveyor out he did suggest that the correspondence could be used in court. Here was an opening.

A few days later, without warning, the Ogmores' gardener started putting stakes in the area of the battle line and planted a few baby conifers next to them. It looked to Max that stakes and baby trees described a line that dog-legged around the shed. Seized with optimism he wrote to their adversaries saying that if the gardener was correct, 'At last!' there is agreement and no need to return to court. Land Registry can just interpret the line of the trees on the correct OS plan 'and the matter is settled.' He delivered the letter by hand to the house along the road.

The following day Bulmer & Co. wrote back in full battle cry: 'Your letter to our client [sic] has been passed to us for reply.' Apparently it was 'our client', not Lucy and Max, who had proposed the site meeting with surveyors where 'proposals had been made', but (in bold print) '**No agreement was reached. Our client's surveyor advised her that you wished to have 24 hours to consider the matter and our client also wished to consider the proposal.** Nothing further was heard from either your solicitors or surveyor about the matter.' The lies were coming thick and fast and how much time and effort would it take to rebut them? Was it worth the effort? The letter on Bulmer paper informed them that the gardener didn't know what he was doing and that, 'We [sic] have advised our client [sic] that it is essential that the Court Order be complied with in order to conclude the litigation between the parties ... We [sic] are instructed by our client [sic] that once this has been finalised, she [sic] is willing to consider any proposed variations suggested by you.' Copied to Cross & Cross & Co. and to Land Registry. The trees and stakes were removed.

It was around this time that Robin Cain finally admitted to the two barristers that he had been specifically instructed not to pay their fees. Both barristers pointed out that any complaint would have to be lodged within three months and it was over that time since Scroggs had signed the disastrous (non-) Consent Agreement. Cain replied that Max and Lucy were trying to resolve things without pursuing a complaint, that's why they delayed.

Meanwhile James Nunn was trying his best to sort out the new confusions created by Land Registry's attempt to interpret the Hammer plan on to an OS plan. The eight inch wide wall of the Ogmore's carport was five feet on the LR interpretation, and the telephone pole was plotted in the wrong place.

Max and Lucy replied to their tormentor addressing the letter to her elusive husband as well. They ignored the attempt to legitimise Ogmore in her role of independent lawyer acting for a genuine client and posted the letter through Blackstone Cottage's front door. They corrected the distortions in the letter and made three proposals for settling the matter: (1.) agree the boundaries described in their letter; (2.) refer the matter to a mediator and (3.) return to court. They also reminded the squatters that there was still a section of the roadside fence to remove. They copied their letter to Cain.

The reply on Bulmer paper dismissed their proposals: the Consent Order rules supreme. However, there was an intriguing addition: 'your solicitors wrote to the Court confirming the terms of the Order.' Of course, they knew Ogmore for a liar, but not for one so foolhardy as to lie about this. Had Cain written to the Court confirming the Consent Order? Even Ogmore would realise they would follow that allegation up and if it were a lie they would shout loud about it. Ogmore had even copied her letter to Cain.

Silence from Cain. Did that signify guilt? They had believed that they had prevented him from sending his foolish reply to the Judge. Cain had told them he didn't send it, that he had sent his holding letter instead, but the silence whispered guilt. They wrote two more letters. One to the squatters posted through their letterbox recording events and correcting Ogmore lies, and one to Cain copying their Ogmore letter and politely severing the contract. They had had enough. If Ogmore's allegation had substance, they were not working with Cain again. Had they known what they later found out they would have severed relations earlier on other grounds, but in fact Cain had not 'written to the Court confirming the terms of the Order.' They found that out much later when they were given access to the court file, but the damage was done. From now on they were acting as litigants in person and notified the Court and Cain accordingly.

Cain wrote a polite reply gently warning them of the 'misunderstandings' that can arise with regard to procedures and Court Orders, continuing, 'it may well be that the Court will adopt a more lenient approach towards you as litigants in person.' Then again, as this story records, it may not. He also flagged up Counsels' fees … *and* his costs.

The blunt reply from his ex-clients was that they would not underwrite any payments by Cross & Cross & Co. to the barristers, as the firm had selected and instructed both of them, and the hasty, under-researched and ill-thought-out so-called 'agreement' that was the outcome of the barristers' representation had caused nothing but trouble for the ex-clients, and for Land Registry.

Evidence of the collateral damage from Scroggs' signature on the Hammer plan was mounting by the day. An increasingly confused James Nunn was trying to grapple with Land Registry's attempt to interpret the plan and relate it to the known world that was Blackstone Cottage and surrounding properties. His letters with queries received replies which raised more queries. Eventually, in March 2003 the Registrar sent a letter showing *his* exasperation, 'It is of course unfortunate that the parties decided to annex the Hammer plan to the Consent Order instead of using an extract from the Ordnance Survey. That decision means that we have to interpret the plan before we can give effect to the terms of the Order.' The Registrar, Mr Brown, who had taken over from Mr Beige, repeated the suggestion that '"the parties" return to court for a plan based on an Ordnance Survey plan.'

Lucy and Max had no enthusiasm for courts of any kind, but could see no alternative in the light of Ogmore's intransigence and the existence of Scroggs' signature on both the so-called Consent Order and the attached Hammer plan. First they wanted their file back from Cross & Cross & Co. Cross & Cross & Co. had no intention of handing over their file without payment. *Impasse.* Lucy and Max decided they could do without the file for the moment. They had quite enough of a paper mountain of their own to be going on with, and they disliked blackmail.

They decided to call Ogmore's bluff. They knew she was working on her own under the name of Bulmer & Co. and so they decided that the next missive would be sent to her boss, Mr C. V. Bulmer, LLB of C. V. Bulmer & Co. Their next missive was a draft new Consent Order based on a plan drawn by James Nunn, which was a new version of the Ordnance Survey plan on which he had described the rectangular 1963 version of the Blackstone Cottage plot, with the addition of two small tranches of land to accommodate Ogmore's trespassing shed and path, two concessions Max and Lucy had agreed so unwisely and so unnecessarily to give to the squatters free, gratis and for nothing on the advice of Malcolm Scroggs.

Mr C. V. Bulmer's reply, which certainly wasn't signed by him, was arrogantly dismissive and full of inconsistencies and distortions. It bore all the hallmarks of Ogmore. It repeated the assertion that Cain had written to the Court agreeing the terms of the Consent Order. He/she forwarded copies of this letter purporting to have been written by C. V. Bulmer to James Nunn and to the Court stating that Max and Lucy were a nuisance and lying about what had happened at court and what had happened since: 'Land Registry has never suggested that there were problems transcribing the Hammer plan to the Ordnance Survey plan.' Max and Lucy were either unwilling or unable to accept that the matter had been concluded on the day at court and were obstructing and preventing Land Registry from carrying out their duty. The letter to James Nunn, purporting to be from Mr Bulmer, had a postscript in Hazel Ogmore's hand.

In an attempt to resolve matters and emboldened by the repeated advice of the Registrar to agree a plan based on the Ordnance Survey plan, the two litigants in person mimicked draft consent orders they had seen and came up with a document that seemed clear and sensible to them, but which would have been thrown out with contumely by any judge had it ever seen a courtroom. It never did see a courtroom, but it did get as far as the Court. They sent it to Ogmore and copied it to the Court.

Their draft consent agreement and Ogmore's reply were both placed before Circuit Judge Blacker. Lucy found this out when able to inspect the court file. Access to the file came far too late to be much use, but it did explain a mystery: there she found a note written by the Judge in response to Ogmore's letter and also to Lucy and Max's draft agreement. Of course, Ogmore's was written on official Bulmer notepaper. Solicitors' headed notepaper far outranks Litigants in Person's notepaper and the Judge must have given it far more credibility. He ordered a hearing so he could issue an order in respect of the hearing on 31st October 2002 – he couldn't remember if he had made one or not. So obviously he couldn't remember that he had sealed it. Lucy and Max were surprised to receive a court notice of a hearing for 13th June. They hadn't asked for a hearing but, prompted by the advice from the Land Registrar, were beginning to think that despite all their misgivings they would have to return to court. Nevertheless, this out of the blue court notice was a surprise. The following months were full of surprises, mostly nasty surprises caused by a lethal concoction of the Court, Ogmore and Land Registry.

It is clear from the file that Lucy and Max also managed to contribute their bit to the confusions, mainly because they had little understanding of the rigidity and illogicality of the court system and Land Registry's rules. They continued to copy the Court with their letters to Ogmore/Bulmer thereby compounding the chaotic mess. Max had lost patience with Land Registry. He slammed them for refusing to survey the land to see how their rectification proposal would apply in the real world. He felt they were exacerbating the trouble.

Lucy meanwhile had turned her ire on the barristers, in particular Scroggs. If he'd made sure he understood what they had agreed before he signed anything, all would have been over and done with months before. True Homestead will be smaller, a tenth of an acre would have been shaved off their three-and-a-half acres, and Blackstone Cottage would be bigger, 50% bigger, but if that first Consent Order could not be set aside – and Scroggs, Tweed and Cain insisted Consent Orders rarely could, then they'd take the compensation proffered by Land Registry as a reward for a bit of land they could afford to lose. However, neither Lucy nor Max was prepared to give the Ogmores even more land. They'd given away quite enough to people who would never appear on their list of charities. If the Ogmores had behaved in a friendly, polite and civilised way, and if they had offered to pay for land they had no right to, if they hadn't lied and cheated and bullied and harassed, if they hadn't slandered and libelled and defamed, if Joe Ogmore hadn't attacked them and engineered their land grab out of the hands of Land Registry and into court, ... *if* ... *if.* If only Scroggs had used his skills and knowledge for his *clients'* benefit.

The immediate problem as Max and Lucy saw it was the proposed plan from Land Registry could only be applied on the ground by either adding yet more of Homestead to Blackstone Cottage or driving a fence straight through the shed. Max may lose his patience with Land Registry and Lucy turn her anger on the lawyers paid to represent *them*, but they were not placing the real culprits in the firing line: Stoat, Hammer and the Ogmores.

Neither Max nor Lucy knew why they had been given a date and time for a hearing in June, but they decided to go along with it. They wrote to the Court Manager (Heaven knows why they thought that was a good idea) setting out what they wanted: a new order declaring and fixing the boundaries between Homestead and Blackstone Cottage. Ogmore let them know any application to the Court would be contested on the basis it was vexatious and an abuse of process and what's more she would claim costs on an indemnity basis. She repeated her assertion that Cain had written to the Court confirming the terms of the Consent Order. 'Perhaps your redress lies with your legal representatives.' Now, there's impressive cheek!

Cain *had* to answer – was this true? Lucy imagined Mr Robin Cain turning pink and flustered when he found that he had been either rumbled or libelled, either was possible. Deep lobster pink she suspected. The tone of his immediate reply (an immediate reply from him was quite a surprise) suggested deep purple-red. He did not (underlined) write to the Court specifically agreeing the terms of the Order. What was the significance of that 'specifically'? He set out the events following 31st October day by day and included his report of the exchange with Ogmore when the Judge's hand grenade was thrown into the trenches. Apparently Ogmore was incandescent, her plans were going perfectly and now this threatened everything. She need not have challenged her blood pressure, she was to recover all the lost ground because Cain, true to style, had delayed and the Court Office, also true to style, had delayed and Ogmore, very true to style, did not delay for one moment. Had certain people known about Ogmore's lies, Mr C. V. Bulmer would have been in trouble and Mrs Hazel Ogmore, Solicitor of the Supreme Court, would have been severely reprimanded – possibly struck off like her husband, but, of course, no one did know until much later. The damage was compounded by Cain's lethargy and she got away with it.

The pincer attack on Land Registry by hard man Max and soft man Nunn finally produced clear and useful confirmation from Mr Brown, that Hammer's plan was a problem. Land Registry could not give effect to the Court Order if the parties couldn't agree, so, he repeated that in his view, 'the parties will have to invite the Court to make a new order which incorporates a plan based upon the Ordnance Survey and which delineates the legal boundary.' Yes, the Registry will continue to pay their costs.

Mrs Hazel Ogmore began showing new signs of flickering incandescence. First there was Cain's denial that he'd replied to the Judge to say the Consent Order was agreed, implying that she was lying! And now Land Registry wanted a new non-Hammer plan. She phoned Robin Cain to persuade him to her line of thinking; even though she was well aware he no longer acted for Max and Lucy. Cain let his ex-clients know that not only had he refused the call, but that she would not get anything from him of any use to her. Her plan to deal with Land Registry was a little more complicated and would take more time.

Meanwhile, she had to deal with the landowners next door who were planning to return to court for a new order and had given notice that if she didn't agree to either a mediated resolution or a new non-Hammer plan by 31st March they would make their court application as urged by Land Registry.

The Ogmores decided that boldness was called for – as usual. It had worked in the past getting the whole business out of the hands of the Registry and into her natural habitat with her people speaking her language and playing her games. All brave and forthright stuff. The Ogmores decided to try boldness again.

Max had a meeting at Homestead with a structural engineer for an ambitious building project. As they stood in the open air considering the engineering challenge they could hear the hammering. Both men went up the road to investigate and discovered Joe Ogmore directing his gardener to drive large stakes into Homestead ground. It was 1st April, the day after the deadline Max and Lucy had given for a response to their three options. Max, with his witness nearby, told him to stop. Joe Ogmore remained bold and nodded to his man to continue. Max pointed out that this was provocation and he had been bound over to keep the peace. Just a slight waver at that, but he remained bold…-ish. Max said he was calling the Police, and he and his witness returned to Homestead and phoned the Police.

When they returned to the scene of the provocation armed with a camera, Joe Ogmore had been replaced by his brass helmeted wife standing legs apart, firmly planted on Homestead land, hands on hips and bold as her hair.

Max told her that he would decide where the stakes will go. Ogmore the

Bold replied, 'You'll tell *me* what to do? With the trouble you're in.' Words not said looking at Max, but at her hired-hand. What imaginative variation on the truth had she been telling him? Hadn't he said something like that to Max and Lucy when he drove past them the previous year as they were removing the trespassing fence panels? 'Oh! ho! You'll be in trouble,' he had said.

A policeman called fairly quickly and went to see the bold land grabbers. He returned and advised Max and Lucy to have their surveyor mark out the boundary by the shed according to the Ogmores' 1963 conveyance plan. The boundary on that plan would slice five feet off the back of the shed. Max wrote unequivocally, some would say *boldly*, to the Ogmores setting out the events and reminding them who was in trouble. He copied the letter to the Court and to Land Registry.

This triggered a flurry of letters from Ogmore to Max, the Court and Land Registry ignoring most of the content of Max's letter but giving her (and her husband's?) view of the state of play.

Max and Lucy started an application to the Court for possession of property. It reads quite well even though in litigant-in-person language (a cross between normal English and abnormal lawyerspeak). They also asked James Nunn to mark the end of the roadside fence near the shed according to the Blackstone Cottage 1963 conveyance plan which he duly did.

This was wasted effort. The bold Ogmores had been on to the Court and regained control. Max was telephoned by the Court Manager and informed that the Judge, presumably having sorted himself out rather too late in the day for Max and Lucy, had decided that, after all, the final order stood. The Consent Order was back in full force and if they wanted to have it amended or revoked they would have to make a proper application on notice. Max checked out what that may mean and the news was bad: Consent Orders are very rarely revoked or amended without the full consent of both parties, so if Max and Lucy did decide to go that way it would mean full-blown proceedings in the High Court, Queen's Bench Division with most likely Scroggs as well as Stoat and the Ogmores as opponents. Their words against Max and Lucy's. More paperwork, more irritation, more lost time.

Ogmore rushed into a yet greater flurry of correspondence to the Court and Mr Brown at Land Registry. The latter replied to her with the least equivocal statement yet: 'In the absence of agreement, or some further judicial determination, we cannot give effect to the Order.' He did not copy his letter to Lucy and Max. Had they known of its existence they would have thought it very helpful. His reply to James Nunn was not helpful. James had been trying to get the Registry to agree to a site meeting to see how the problems could be resolved on the ground, but Mr Brown made clear he would only come if all parties agreed. 'Some hope,' said Max.

Lucy wrote a long letter to the Court Manager and included drafts of what she intended to send when they did make a formal application. She stressed that they were drafts and she merely wanted practical help in filling in forms – the correct terms, who to send the forms to, how to arrange a hearing on site (she did not want a repeat of the fence-post saga and 11 court visits before any judge looked at the problem on the ground), and she wanted an indication of when and where the hearing would be held. She thought that was what the new consumer-friendly court service did. She was mistaken.

Mistaken or not, the planned application for a judge-determined boundary was made redundant by Ogmore's and Stoat's next bold move. They issued a pre-action protocol letter to Land Registry for judicial review challenging the Registry's decision not to rectify Homestead's boundary according to their 'Consent' Order. The *coup de grâce* was the statement, 'By *consenting* to the use of the plan forming part of the Order, both Claimant and Defendant accepted that it was capable of interpretation.' So, Scroggs' use of the plan he had been specifically instructed not to use meant the couple accepted that that very plan was capable of interpretation. Moreover, the pre-action letter declared, 'no one, least of all the Defendants, had put an alternative interpretation forward.' The fact that the Defendants and their surveyor had put forward two possible interpretations on the necessary OS plan, and Hammer and Nunn had come up with another at the site meeting, seemed to have slipped the Judicial Review Claimants' collective mind. They gave the Registry until 1st June 2003 to respond. Cool move by the squatters and their mentor. Lucy and Max would have to abandon their application and all the work they had put into preparation was wasted, and now there was real pressure on the Registry. The one thing bodies like Land Registry will avoid at all costs is a full-blown judicial review.

Lucy and Max were miffed. They were even more miffed when they saw attached to the squatters' application a General Form of Judgment or Order from Judge Blacker dated 8th April. It had been sent to Bulmers (Ogmore) but not to them. It stated that, 'the Order of 28th November 2002 does stand as the final Order in this case.' They had been busy planning their application in ignorance of the state of play. Unlike them the Registry *had* received a copy of the Judge's *final* Order but had still sent their letter to Ogmore saying they declined to give effect to the Consent Order.

Two things reverberated in the minds of Lucy and Max. One they had known all along, Scroggs should never have attached the signed Hammer plan to the Order, the other they had long suspected, Cain and Scroggs had had weeks to do something about that stupid mistake, all the days until 28 November, a full four weeks after Scroggs' disastrous decision. Despite all their clients' entreaties, they had done nothing. They had said nothing could be done as it was a done deal on 31st October. It clearly had not been a done deal on that day.

The Court's cranking processes were well behind the action. Max and Lucy received a date and venue for their now abandoned hearing, a day in early July. Ogmore had already notified the Court of the threatened Judicial Review, but internal mail failed to deliver on time.

Now Max and Lucy had to get up to speed on judicial reviews. They learnt that such action was supposed to be used where there is no right of appeal or where avenues of appeal have been exhausted. Land Registry offers an appeals procedure. Ogmore/Stoat had not tried it. No avenues had been tried let alone exhausted. Max and Lucy had not been sent a copy of the letter Land Registry had sent to Ogmore declining to to 'give effect to the Consent Order'. How could they hope for a truth and justice service if nobody kept them informed?

How can they hope for anything resembling such a service when papers sent in draft form to the Court Manager for client advice and guidance are placed before a judge, the very Judge Blacker who is managing the case, and who, no doubt with a modicum of impatience, now instructs the Court Manager to inform these litigants in person that as everything is in draft form there is no substantive application to list for hearing so it cannot be listed!! 'Oh my God!' said Max. 'Help!' said Lucy, 'are we trapped in some farce? How do we get out into the real world?' They did have a date for their 'proper' application – 8th July.

Phone calls with Mr Brown, District Land Registrar, led them to the Agency Case Review Team at Land Registry Headquarters in London. Mr Brown couldn't face a judicial review, he wasn't expected to. Everything is kicked upstairs when things get tough.

The lady in London who picked up the phone and the case, a Mrs Ruby Cohen, first proposed that they write to Judge Blacker directly asking him to stay the Order until he determined on their application to him due to be heard in a month (a blink of the eye in court timescales). They duly wrote to the Judge, a letter mixing humble respect and implied criticism. They reminded him of his request of 11th November 2002 and pointed out that 'At no time did we or our solicitors write confirming the terms of the Order as presently drafted.' They wanted to know how the Order was sealed on 28th November 2002 without their confirmation and how it came to be re-affirmed on 8th April 2003. They respectfully requested a stay on the Order pending a determination of the boundaries by the Judge himself.

Meanwhile they continued their efforts to get Ogmore to hand over copies of her instructions to Hammer and any report from him explaining how he'd come up with his plan. They tried Ogmore's boss, Mr C. V. Bulmer, would he help? His final reply? 'Correspondence between our client/this firm and our client's expert is privileged.' They could have got a court order to make Ogmore hand over the papers, but they didn't know this and, anyway, they strongly suspected that no such documents existed, and yet it was that plan causing all the problems for Land Registry, for the Court and for them. They tried a rather wordy almost conciliatory letter direct to the Ogmores at Blackstone Cottage.

> 'You wanted some of our land. We offered you some of our land free of charge. You wanted to avoid costs. We offered to release you from our well-founded claim to costs. We are asking for disclosure of the information we and the Court need to progress this matter and will reciprocate with any information you want from us.'

However, they ended with: 'You will be well aware by now that we regard the courts as the least efficient arenas for settling matters reasonably where genuine grievance is felt by both parties.' Why conclude with that when they were forwarding a copy to the Judge they needed on their side? Why antagonise the Judge by suggesting he's not the right person for the job?

'We thought that judges were sensible grown-ups and would agree with us,' says Lucy. 'We forgot what unchallenged power does to people, even people who start out as sensible.'

They were deep into discussions on the structural challenges of their new building project with their engineer and team of builders when they got the call from a court clerk. The Judge would not grant a stay. Clearly he was not sympathetic. He wasn't going to stay the Consent Order, nor was he going to manage the case as Max and Lucy thought a manager should. His response did reveal something of his mindset. His points score had been bouncing up and down, but now took a serious dive.

Two days later Mrs Cohen telephoned to tell them that Land Registry could, after all, 'give effect to the Order and must do so in the absence of a stay from the Court or a different order.' The nature of the game suddenly changed with these two unexpected phone calls. Land Registry's plotters and planners in London had had to come up with a resolution to avoid a judicial review. The work for the draughtsmen had proved difficult, but they now had one interpretation of the Hammer plan which they could apply to an OS plan. Mrs Cohen would send copies to both parties.

Meanwhile Ogmore/Stoat/Bulmer sent Stoat's redundant skeleton argument[2] for 8th July. Essentially it rested on their claim that the terms of the Consent Order were agreed by *both* parties in the compromise agreement made and the *law* was clear that all other matters were 'buried beneath the surface of the compromise. The Court will not permit them to be raised afresh in the context of a new action … *Extrinsic evidence of what may or may not have been in the minds of the parties at the time of their agreement is not admissible.* A judgment or order by consent is binding until set aside. Fresh proceedings must be commenced if it is sought to set aside a final judgment or order by consent.'

The argument continued, 'It does not matter that Ds [Max and Lucy] secretly [sic] believed, *which is improbable* [Lucy's italics] that the Consent Order meant something other than that which appears on the face of it.' Stoat suggested that the most obvious grounds for applying to set aside the Order would be a mistake, 'but there is no allegation of mutual mistake here or any suggestion that C (Ogmore) induced any mistake or knew that a mistake had been made by Ds.' So, was Scroggs *not* induced to sign and attach the Hammer plan? Scroggs may or may not have made a mistake, either way Ogmore knew that a mistake had been made. They had believed for many months that Scroggs had been trapped into error because he was ill-prepared and had failed to spot the trap. Now they feared that as he had misled them to think that the Order was a done deal, when in fact he could and should have acted on the Judge's letter before it was sealed, Scroggs had not been entirely committed to their cause: he had not acted 'in their best interests'. They just couldn't understand why not.

Lucy and Max conceded that Stoat was probably correct in asserting that fresh proceedings were necessary if they wanted to set aside the Consent Order. The trouble was that all the advice they had had on setting aside the Order was not to try: (1.) it should have been done immediately, within a week; (2.) courts don't grant it; and (3.) it costs a lot of money. They had hoped that their approach would avoid such a difficult challenge, but their approach depended on Land Registry map-makers support and now that support had been removed: the Registry could after all 'give effect to the Order'.

Lucy and Max phoned the Court urgently. Naively they imagined they could discuss with the staff at the 'Civil Justice Centre' how best to proceed correctly. They had failed to find that advice elsewhere and even if it meant checking with the Judge the correct procedure, they could see no reason not to. As they saw it, post-Woolf reforms, it was the duty of the Judge to manage the case and their query was a query about managing their application. They wanted to know if they should first apply to set aside the Consent Order, then in a separate action, apply to have a declaration of the boundary. 'If you advise this is, indeed, the correct procedure we shall amend our application accordingly.' These Litigants in Person simply had no understanding of how the adversarial legal system worked. If parties can be advised on the procedure a Judge considers to be correct, a lot of the fun is removed from the game, the gamble is far less exciting and ordinary people could get to play it. Besides it is not the Judge's role to 'enter the arena'. He is above all that. He or she is not a *manager*! Judges' decisions on the correct procedure come later, after money and emotion has been spent.

To compound their errors, they added – 'We believe fervently that most disputes can and should be resolved in less formal and confrontational ways.' Again that unwise suggestion that the Judge was not the right person for the job!

'As I said,' protests Lucy, 'we thought that judges were sensible grown-ups and would agree with us. We thought they knew what a mess they'd made in the Family Courts and were changing for the better.'

No lawyer would be surprised by the next letter from the Court confirming the telephone message of the Judge's refusal to stay the Consent Order. The Court Manager reported him as stating that, 'It is not the function of the Court, still less that of a judge to advise one party to a dispute how to proceed.' There's a distinction between helping litigants by setting out the *correct procedure* and being partisan by suggesting the *best strategy* to one side in a dispute. They were not asking the Judge for help, they were asking the court service for procedural advice. If the Consent Order needed to be sorted out before anything else, the hearing on 8th July was a waste of time and money.

Max, meanwhile, was attempting to persuade Mrs Cohen to delay filing her new registration until after 8th July. She would not do so. Max kept asking why not. She kept saying the Registrar had to file it: the Registrar could find himself in prison if he refused to comply with a court order. Max kept asking why and when and who had discretion as to the date for registration. She said it was at Land Registry's discretion. Max wanted to know why if Land Registry was not time-constrained they had to file the registration before the hearing. 'Because you haven't obtained a stay.' There then followed an increasingly acrimonious circularity of argument with endless repetition. Max was exasperated. He decided he would complain to the Head Registrar. Mrs Cohen, who had also lost her cool, riposted 'You go and do what you like,' and put the phone down on him.

Max made his complaint and then they studied the new plan with its tracing paper overlays. As far as they could see it shifted the boundary between the Ackroyds' Dunroamin' and Blackstone Cottage five feet towards Blackstone Cottage. Either that or they had made the carport wall over five feet thick when in fact it was less than a foot. It looked as though the new plan would affect Dunroamin's Title.

Lucy thought they ought to let the Ackroyds know. They had a good social relationship with them; after all, it was they who first provided all the early information about what the Ogmores had been up to before they bought Homestead. The Ackroyds, too, had felt threatened by the conduct of their mutual next-door neighbour and both couples had conspired and gossiped together. Max and Lucy had made a point of keeping Dick and Alice in the loop, as when they invited them to meet Land Registry's surveyor the previous summer to watch his work. But then in October of that year Ogmore had sent a copy of an agreement between her and the Ackroyds which the Ackroyds had signed without mentioning anything to either Max or Lucy. This had upset Lucy; understandably, she wanted to know why the Ackroyds had ignored them on a matter of central concern to them. As neither Max nor Lucy fully understood what was going on, as they didn't see the significance of the agreement and as they had other compelling matters to consider, they decided not to make a fuss. They didn't want to open up a new battle front with another set of neighbours if there was nothing to be gained.

Prompted by a confused James Nunn, Lucy wrote a letter to Mrs Cohen of some technical complexity setting out the confusions caused by the new Land Registry draft plan. As nothing in the text of Mrs Cohen's response to the pre-action letter explained the mysterious five foot gap between Ogmore's carport wall and the Dunroamin' boundary, she had to ask for an explanation. The explanation came back: the wall was not five feet thick, there was a strip five feet wide and 55 feet long of *unregistered land* that the owners of Blackstone Cottage and Dunroamin' had together agreed should belong to Dunroamin'. The boundary then dog-legged back five feet towards Dunroamin' at the end of the strip to return to the original boundary between Homestead and Dunroamin' that had existed from when both houses (Homestead and Dunroamin') were built in the early years of the 20th century.

Anyone, Max and Lucy in particular, who bothered to check all the conveyance plans after 1963 when Blackstone Cottage was 'born', would have seen that Blackstone Cottage and Dunroamin' abutted each other. There was no strip. Blackstone Cottage had always been five feet nearer Dunroamin' and five feet further from Homestead. Until, that is, the secret agreement between Ogmore and the Ackroyds.

Mrs Cohen decided that the strip of land Ogmore had generously handed to the Ackroyds was not owned by anybody. The agency decided that to make everything fit (Homestead's conveyance, Dunroamin's conveyance, Blackstone Cottage's conveyance and the Consent Order and the agreement between Ogmore and the Ackroyds), they would declare that the strip was an unregistered ditch between Blackstone Cottage and Dunroamin'. Blackstone Cottage was unregistered, Dunroamin' was registered and neither showed any sign of an unloved strip on their various conveyances but, if the owners of Blackstone Cottage and Dunroamin' had done a deal giving Dunroamin' a strip of land belonging to Blackstone Cottage that was alright with the Registry even if it did result in a rather odd plan. It also very conveniently shunted Blackstone Cottage's roadside boundary five feet nearer Homestead.

A five foot shift back to its pre-deal place would result in Blackstone Cottage's roadside boundary shunting back Dunroamin' way so the downhill shed boundary would cut straight through the shed even on the Consent Order plan! No argument. By getting the Ackroyds to formally (as well as willingly), agree that the strip belonged to them she successfully engineered the boundary back towards Homestead and she had only lost an insignificant slice of land in the deal. So, that agreement was a cool move by Ogmore and/or her advisors. But they had been planning it all for years, and they were lawyers.

Max and Lucy responded to the Ogmores' proposal that they withdraw their application by suggesting instead that both parties agree to apply to the Court for an adjournment to a later date so that they and their advisors could review the situation in the light of their newly-rectified Title. Ogmore agreed to a two-week adjournment.

Meanwhile they asked James Nunn to measure Blackstone Cottage's roadside boundary yet again and mark where he found the end of Blackstone Cottage's roadside boundary to be according to the hot-off-the-press new plan sent by the Registry. He couldn't be precise from the plan but he did assure his clients that according to their new rectified Title plan the roadside boundary above the shed was at an angle between 90–92° with the road – and cut through the shed! The new Title plan avoided awkward details: no shed, no compost box, no paths and no poles of any type. The only detail was Blackstone Cottage land – the house and its carport.

Armed with the new Title plan, and confirmation from their surveyor that the downhill boundary by the back of the shed was at a right angle with the roadside fence, Lucy and Max decided there was no need to continue the very risky application they had embarked on. They could sort out where they should put up a barrier to the squatters by applying the plan to the site. They withdrew their application. They then wrote to the Ogmores asking them to apply the new plan to the site so that they could see for themselves that the shed and other items still encroached on Homestead land.

Needless to say, the Ogmores did not agree but contacted their new friend Mrs Cohen again asking her to confirm that the shed was within Blackstone Cottage's curtilage. They wanted the items on their tricksy Consent Order plan to be the key factors, not the boundaries. Their letter contained a threat: if the shed is not within the curtilage of Blackstone Cottage, Land Registry has not implemented the Consent Order. They wanted a statement from Mrs Cohen declaring that the shed, etc. was within Blackstone Cottage territory.

Mrs Cohen wrote an ambiguous, you might say lawyerly, reply; 'whilst we are only concerned with the external boundaries and their measurements, and not what is within them … if the shed is shown within the curtilage of Blackstone Cottage on the plan attached to the Consent Order, it should be in a similar position on the ground and Title plan (even though it might not be shown thereon).' The word 'should' denied the Ogmores the clarity they needed.

They forwarded copy of Mrs Cohen's letter. Maybe they hadn't noticed its ambiguity or maybe they hoped Max and Lucy hadn't. According to C. V. Bulmer & Co. Mrs Cohen's letter *confirmed* the shed and all the extras were within Blackstone Cottage territory and the matter was concluded, 'finality has been achieved.'

Unfortunately, Mr Brown and Mrs Cohen between them hadn't done Max and Lucy any favours either (quite apart from the sloppy work over the five foot non-ditch). Max had again tried to get Mr Brown to send a surveyor to establish once and for all the measurement of the roadside boundary according to this brand new, filed Title plan. Mr Brown replied that the Registry couldn't measure the boundary for them or tell the parties where on the ground the legal boundaries lie. Mr Brown was not going to help sort out where Lucy's fence should go.

Lucy was worried that a fence erected in what later might be deemed the wrong place could lead to confrontation. With reluctance they decided they would have to buy some legal advice, but they were not going to hand everything over to another batch of Messrs Cain, Tweed and Scroggs. They would buy an hour or so of some lawyer's time to advise on the next best course of action. They still had a lingering hope that there was some lawyer out there who would give good, useful advice, but they would decide what to do and take responsibility for their actions. By now they'd heard recommendations from friends of a couple of local firms within easy driving distance. They decided to give the nearest a go.

Mrs Cynthia Buxton was a forceful-looking woman and seemed quick to grasp the essentials of the case. She agreed that the best course of action was a possession order, but insisted that they ask James Nunn to check out the roadside boundary finally and for good according to their new Title plan before they took any action. She agreed that their action was not to re-litigate the Consent Order, but to accept the Hammer plan, the boundaries on the plan and the measurements on the plan, and if the items on the plan didn't fit on the ground because they were incorrectly located on the plan, so be it. Neither the wording of the Order nor Land Registry's interpretation of the Order referred to the items. Stoat had missed that little trick when he persuaded Malcolm Scroggs to sign the Hammer plan.

She advised that Land Registry's interpretation of the Hammer plan was most likely accurate and that the features on it (that's the shed, etc.) were least likely to be relevant. If Mr Nunn's final measurement confirmed all the evidence so far, and it was clear to him that the shed straddled the boundary line, a possession claim was the simplest, and possibly cheapest, solution. Lucy and Max are agreed even now that her letter following the interview they had with her in the summer of 2003 has proved over time to be the most sensible. She told them that if the Ogmores played difficult and it did have to go back to a court, the most probable action the judge would take would be to order a single joint expert to measure everything on the ground and determine the boundary. She told them that to make doubly sure they should themselves apply for an independent land survey.

She advised not only on their squatter claim but also on Joe Ogmore's attack and the claim they should consider against him for personal injury, and also on their claims against Land Registry, and against the Swales for their lie about disputes on the Seller's Property Information Form, and against their conveyancing solicitor, the one who had slowly nursed their purchase of

Homestead but had failed to follow up on their query about disputes. Her advice, at a mere £200 plus VAT, has stood the test of time. She even advised on their draft pre-action protocol letter agreeing most of it, but expressing concern that they had included a claim against Joe Ogmore for his assault. They unwisely failed to make the amendment she suggested. She did remind them that her advice could only be very limited since they were acting as litigants in person, as they were fully entitled to do and that she could not take responsibility for the conduct of the litigation or its outcome. They fully accepted that, 'We acknowledge that as long as you are not formally instructed by us, the decisions we shall take are our responsibility and ours alone.'

They took her first bit of advice and invited James Nunn back again for yet another survey. Without access to Blackstone Cottage land the exercise was rather limited, but he could at least scale the roadside boundary from both Hammer and Land Registry plans and project a boundary downhill in the shed area. This once and for all survey was as thorough as he could make it: first, a tape measure (de-luxe quality), then a wheel and finally a laser. They all confirmed the same thing: a section of fence and a section of the shed trespassed according to both Hammer plan and their rectified registration plan.

They sent their pre-action letter to the Ogmores and waited for an acknowledgement. Despite their prompt 10 days later, no response of any kind was forthcoming after three weeks, so they lodged their claim at court and were given a date in early September, just before they were about to leave for a six-week working holiday on French canals. They followed Mrs Buxton's advice and proposed an independent, jointly appointed surveyor.

They finally got a response, on Bulmer paper. Ogmore did not want an independent surveyor: 'It would not be appropriate particularly as we intend to make an application shortly to strike out the claim.' Ogmore had a conditional fee arrangement with Mr C. V. Bulmer which would mean that if she succeeded in getting their claim struck out or rejected she would be able to hike her costs up considerably.

Stoat's Defence relied on the consent agreement saying that Max and Lucy were trying to re-litigate matters that had been already settled and that it had been the *intention* of *both* parties to apply the Hammer plan! If the Land Registry's newly-filed plan did not reflect *the intention of both parties* as shown on the 'agreed' (Hammer) plan, the rectified Title plan is wrong. He denied everything else on their claim.

Max and Lucy went back to bother Mrs Buxton again. Her view remained that they were not trying to set aside the Consent Order by the back door, but that the items on the Hammer plan were wrongly mapped and anyway are not mentioned in the Order, and that what takes precedence are the measurements and the boundary lines. She speculated on what a judge might do: he might agree that the lines and measurements are the key factors or he might say the features are, but she held to her opinion that the latter choice would be difficult to sustain. Besides, why were the Ogmores so resistant to an independent survey which would sort everything out for good?

They noted that the judge listed for their hearing was the same District Judge Dyer, the first Judge they had met a year earlier, who had read their brief Statement describing the uncongenial antics of the Ogmores, had noted Hazel's refusal to consider mediation and had generally disapproved of her. They felt heartened by that.

TEN
September 2003–November 2003

'Lawyers are the only persons in whom ignorance of the law is not punished.'

Jeremy Bentham, philosopher, jurist, political scientist, 1748–1832

They shouldn't have done. The man they encountered in the small room where the hearing took place was not the same short, smiley-faced man they had encountered a year previously. This man was taller, late forties, with an air of boyish overconfidence to be found in certain more irritating teenagers. Max and Lucy exchanged looks in bewilderment. Same name, different face. An altogether different man. This District Judge Dyer reserved his smiles for Ogmore, there without husband, who acknowledged him with a serious nod of her head. She had tried this role of dignified victim of disgraceful conduct by her neighbours on her first encounter with the first (not) Judge Dyer, but then the facts were weighed against her, it didn't work, she just looked rather ludicrous. Now she had her Hammer plan with Scroggs' signature on it, she had Circuit Judge Blacker's signature on the sealed Order, she had Mrs Cohen's filed 'rectified' Title plan to Homestead with Blackstone Cottage's boundaries marked in red. Now Ogmore could give full play to her suppressed outrage. Was it feigned? A strategically adopted act to advance the cause, or genuine? In which case Max and Lucy had a very dangerous opponent dislocated from reality, obsessive and, if the new Judge Dyer was any guide, convincing.

'Well, Mr Goodchild and Mrs Graham,' he started, 'I have looked at all the papers for this application,' this was less than 30 pages in total as neither side had started on disclosure, 'and it seems to me that you have a problem.' Max and Lucy were going to hear that phrase again and after this first time they would know that if they heard it, they did, indeed, have a problem, quite probably a problem with the Judge. This was the first time they heard it and they took the words to mean that it was a problem they could sort out, believing they could explain and resolve any problem in the more relaxed atmosphere of a hearing in a small room in front of a District Judge (the 21st-century equivalent of a Registrar). This new version of District Judge Dyer then gave his interpretation of their claim. This took up more than half the time allocated for the hearing and, more alarming, was drawn mainly from Ogmore's Witness Statement. He made particular reference to Mrs Cohen's ambiguous letter which he appeared to think was an unambiguous endorsement of Ogmore's defence. He asked Max and Lucy if this was a correct record; they replied that although certain statements were correct the record was incomplete, partial and therefore incorrect. District Judge Dyer did not ask what was incorrect and refused to allow Max to read his prepared Statement. He did ask them to persuade him of their case so Max began to repeat what was in their application and in a brief Witness Statement he had written. These papers were there in front of new Judge Dyer together with their letter proposing a single expert survey.

The Judge then did ask questions, but not of Mrs Ogmore. He wanted to know why they had not sought to set aside the Consent Order and if the Swales had admitted there was an unresolved dispute, but in response to their replies Dyer said these were not matters he could deal with. So what was the point of the questions?

Max tried to re-establish the purpose of the hearing expecting to persuade this Judge to order an independent survey: 'Despite the best efforts of Land Registry nobody knows where the boundary between Homestead and Blackstone Cottage is on the ground, so no fence between the properties can be erected. A survey by a single, jointly appointed expert can solve that problem. Our assertion that there is continued encroachment by the Defendants (the Ogmores) can be tested and the Court may then act accordingly.' This all seemed fair and reasonable to Max and Lucy, and others. It seems just as fair and reasonable to them now, but for some reason, it did not seem fair and reasonable to this new, *real* District Judge Dyer. He did not want to direct that an independent, single surveyor take the newly-filed Title plan and the Hammer plan and survey Blackstone Cottage and its boundaries with Homestead. He rejected the idea. He ordered Max and Lucy to draw on the Hammer plan where they thought the shed, etc., etc., etc., was in reality on the ground. He then called a halt to the proceedings without any further discussion. Time was up!

In view of their imminent departure for six weeks, Lucy was relieved they did not have to find an independent expert and then have to argue with the Ogmores over the choice before they went away. She didn't see much of a challenge in measuring from a given point the distances to each corner of the shed then gauging from the overall measurements of the structure where to place the result on the Hammer plan. Max, on the other hand, was far less sanguine. What on Earth, he wanted to know, was the point of such an exercise? It wouldn't have any authority, it would be too easy for the Ogmores and their mentor, Stoat, to dismiss and they'd have to start again. Besides, he didn't take to this new District Judge Dyer. The man claimed he'd read the papers so why was he so friendly and indulgent to Ogmore when he'd been told what she'd been up to? Why didn't he ask *her* to explain *herself*? And why did he seem to be unaware of so much in the Statements they had sent? Lucy had her misgivings about that too, but was still certain that once this Judge Dyer *Mark II* was made better aware of the history and the purpose of the claim his attitude would change.

She thought it worth a try to remind Hazel Ogmore of her vulnerability to the truth about her past misdeeds. If they could settle the boundary question 'outside court' they could save a whole lot of time, money and stress. As they were leaving the Court she approached Hazel Ogmore to suggest that she agreed to the independent survey, pointing out that if court action continued, the history of her actions, the actions of a solicitor of the Supreme Court, as Hazel Ogmore liked to remind everybody, were bound to be revealed in court. Lucy was confident of the strength of their argument, she was convinced that even Stoat would see that they were not attempting to circumvent the Consent Order; they were working from the Order, but simply trying to overcome the mess the Hammer plan was making. Lucy admits she didn't fancy meeting this new version of District Judge Dyer again. She remembered the two Registrars from the fence post scandal and feared that even youngish judges were not romping joyously in Lord Woolf's new civil justice landscape. Lucy pointed out to Hazel Ogmore that her conduct over the land was a matter of record. Lucy was convinced Ogmore would not want that to come out in court.

As she approached her opponent, the woman shied back slightly as if she expected to be physically attacked. Lucy remembered how Hazel Ogmore, the arch bully, had attempted to portray Max and her as bullies. Now Lucy had to work out again whether this was an act or if the woman was slightly deranged and actually did fear her. She later reflected it was more likely the former. She had heard how in divorce cases some not entirely scrupulous lawyers might encourage their female clients to show fear when approached by their divorcing husbands. It helps in custody and maintenance blackmail battles. But there were no witnesses to this show except a rather bemused Max. Ogmore refused to speak to either of them.

That same day, however, she wrote to them on Bulmer headed paper. She had driven straight back to Blackstone Cottage so she must have kept a stack of Bulmer headed paper and envelopes at home. Her letter accused Lucy of threatening her, 'whilst still within the Court precincts'.

Lucy replied wondering if Mrs Ogmore was confused by the stress of the events in court and misheard. Lucy only wanted to point out they could agree things without returning to court, but if they did return Hazel and Joe Ogmore's conduct over recent years with regard to Homestead land would have to be revealed in court.

'Yes', said Max. 'I'd call that a threat.'

'It's a statement of fact. They've got away with hiding the facts so far because no judge has stayed with the case long enough to hear them. Perhaps they have some plan that they think will let them get away with it again. I was trying to encourage her to have a re-think.'

'Doesn't look like you've succeeded.' It certainly didn't. The reply came in full pomposity (Bulmer paper) '"Our client" did not mishear, 'and note that under Civil Procedure Rules 6.5.3 and 6.4(2) any further documents which you serve directly on our clients will be returned to you unopened as such service is not deemed to be valid service.'

Max blamed Land Registry's craven response to bullying by judicial review for the new mess created: a Title plan that simply failed to establish where the new boundaries fall on the ground because of the contradictions between boundary lines and objects – the shed, the paths, etc. Mrs Cohen eventually replied that whereas she regretted the difficulties Max was having with the Ogmores, Land Registry had no formal role in the dispute and as the plan shows only General Boundaries, it is 'not for us to say where the boundary on the ground should be.' The Registry was relying on the General Boundary Rules. If they had accepted Max's invitation to see how their plan worked on the ground, 'the difficulties' could have been avoided, by Max and Lucy, but then perhaps Land Registry would have had to face difficulties of their own. The lack of precision in the General Boundaries Rules is a useful get-out card … for the Registry.

When Max and Lucy started carrying out the District Judge's instruction to draw on the Hammer plan where they thought the shed, etc. was, they were accosted by a far more visual and confident Joe Ogmore attempting to intimidate them. What did they think they were doing on his land? They pointed out they were carrying out the Order of the Court. The following day they received the threat (on Bulmer paper) of another injunction if they went on Blackstone Cottage land again, so they just waited for the Ogmores to leave their house and finished their measuring. They then translated their findings on to the infamous plan.

Both Max and Lucy were sure that Mr C. V. Bulmer had little idea what his associate was up to. Mr Nelson, the Bailiff, and the police officers who knew something of her had little time for Ogmore but said that Bulmer was an OK man, a duty solicitor for minor criminal cases and often seen in the county town nick bailing out some miscreant or encouraging said miscreant to help the Police with their enquiries. A few days before their departure for six weeks, irritated by the time-wasting Order from District Judge Dyer and now frustrated by the Ogmores' bullying and irrationality, they decided to write to him directly asking him to transfer the case to someone else in his firm. They made it clear that they found his Associate Solicitor, Mrs Ogmore, impossible to deal with, 'As the solicitor acting in the case, Mrs Ogmore has free rein to conduct matters in an irresponsible manner and indulge any notion at no cost to herself … we can no longer deal with her.'

With the memory of Cain's report from those of his colleagues who had encountered Ogmore professionally and who had independently and immediately declared her 'mad', Max and Lucy decided to go whole hog and let Mr C. V. Bulmer know that they could not be expected to progress 'this matter' if they were required to deal with a person they were convinced was 'incapable of reason, and determined to abuse the legal system in their vexatious actions'. They felt sure that by now C. V. Bulmer would have had enough knowledge of the lady to suspect the description was accurate and this letter would give him an excuse to take the case on himself.

The request itself might not have been totally hopeless, but perhaps the letter went a little bit too far. They had never met Mr Bulmer and were relying on gossip about him. By that time they had had two years' experience of Hazel Ogmore and they really should have wondered how she would have managed to get away with things so far if she were not a talented spin-mistress.

They forwarded to both Bulmers and the Court their version of the Hammer plan showing where the shed was according to Nunn's survey, together with a description of their technique and report on their findings, which was more than anyone had got from Mr Hammer, apart from, possibly, the Ogmores.

Alarm bells rang when they received a court notice for a date at the end of the year for the next hearing. This was a hearing of any application the Ogmores might choose to make. There was no mention of their application and no date for a hearing of it. Their application was with the Court. The Ogmores hadn't actually made any application, but were clearly being urged to do so by District Judge Dyer Mark II.

One final act before they left was to send a few requests of their own for further and better particulars: (1.) where does it say in the Consent Order that the shed and base, etc. were to be entirely on Ogmore land?; (2.) give names and contact details of the tree surgeons caught felling Homestead trees under orders from Ogmore; (3.) give names and contact details of the landscaper who carried out work on Homestead land under orders from Ogmore and (4.) please explain why you believe the roadside boundary to Blackstone Cottage should be extended beyond the length on your original conveyance.

Not exactly elephant traps for Stoat and his clients but potential for a bit of fun thought Max and Lucy. They forgot that their prim, self-satisfied Mr Dyer Mark II had demonstrated a vacuum of mirth. They left on the long planned, six-week investigation.

2003 was the year of *La Canicule*, the year of the sustained heatwave that killed crops, cattle and people throughout France, so working from a boat on the cooling waterways had an extra appeal. While Max was working Lucy was reading and writing up her record of the Ogmore war. Among the pile of books she had taken with her was a large, unattractive brick of a book titled *Civil Litigation* (11th edition, 2003) by O'Hare and Browne.[1] She had baulked at dishing out over £50 on such a boring book but, bearing in mind the time she expected to have over the six weeks, and the battle they were destined to return to, Lucy made a last-minute investment decision. She would write up her report and reflections on her encounters with the civil justice system. Her choice of reading material caused much ribald comment from guest sailors enjoying their airport tomes, but when she finally forced herself to open it Lucy saw that Messrs O'Hare and Browne had provided more than a doorstopper and that the contents of this and similar books might provide an essential, rather than nice-to-have, assistance in their court battles. Thanks to that book they felt a little more confident in how they would approach Stoat's threatened strike-out of their applications. Clearly the book was not enough in itself; it had little to say about litigants in person for example. It did, however, open up the possibility of accessing the mindset and language of the foreign land and language of legal professionals.

And it contained a bombshell. It stated unequivocally that Orders cannot be entered on the record as Consent Orders if any of the parties is a litigant in person and has not signed it. Max and Lucy were litigants in person when Stoat pulled his first trick and got the first Order described as a Consent Order. This was right at the start of court shenanigans and effectively barred Max and Lucy from their own land while giving the Ogmores free roaming rights. This was the Order Tweed and Scroggs had insisted could not be challenged, removed, altered because it was described as a Consent Order. This Order was invalid. This invalid Order had led to the disaster of the second ostensibly 'valid' Order and started the whole mad nonsense in which they now found themselves trapped.

On their return to Homestead, having worked their way through the Himalaya of correspondence stacked for attention, they realised that Bulmer & Co. had not responded to their request for further and better information sent six weeks earlier. A schoolmarmy letter to Mr C. V. from Lucy asked for the courtesy of a reply and also acknowledgement of their earlier response to 'his' request for further and better particulars that they had managed to send before they left. (This was their amended version of the Hammer plan illustrating the trespass-by-shed.) She also expressed regret at Mr C. V. Bulmer's 'unfortunate' reply to their request that someone, anyone, took over from Ogmore. His response had been, 'I have no plans to change any arrangements in my civil litigation department.' He could out-do Hazel Ogmore in self-aggrandisement. Apart from himself and Hazel there was only one other lawyer in the firm at that time, a new recruit both to his firm and the increasingly overcrowded legal profession.

The response that finally came to their requests for further information was a dismissal of their queries: he/she was not going to answer them, followed by the long signalled application to strike out their claim. The Ogmores' argument had hardly changed: either the claim was an abuse of process because 'all of these matters have been *or should have been* litigated in previous proceedings,' or because 'the Claimants have no real prospects of succeeding and there was no compelling reason why the case should go to trial.' The Court form was signed by Ogmore, obviously still in full control.

Mrs Buxton had given sensible advice on litigation generally and their legal tussle in particular. She had pointed out correctly that the land in dispute was very small and could have little effect on the value of their house or amenity. This they knew well. That was why they let the squatter get away with her dubious 1963 plan and in addition keep the two extra strips of land, gifts made despite their deep dislike and contempt for her and despite all the evidence they had accumulated confirming the necklace boundary to Blackstone Cottage land. The problem was they wanted a fence up, at least on the boundary nearest them, the one by the shed, but where was it to go?

Mrs Buxton had also been concerned about the money litigation had cost them so far and warned them about the potential financial loss they could incur if the fight continued. Again, a sensible warning, but again they already knew all that and, unlike the fence-post saga of 20 years earlier, they had various routes to recompense, in fact they were already embarked on recouping losses from Land Registry, the Swales, their conveyancing solicitors and, especially their barristers, Mr Robert Tweed and Mr Malcolm Scroggs. They were now emboldened in their pursuit of those two gentlemen thanks to the investment Lucy had made in the work of Mr O'Hare and Mr Browne.

They could, of course, give in yet again and let the Ogmores have for free another extra wedge of land, thus letting the land thieves and their man, Stoat, get away with unethical conduct – yet again. Who had told *the Ogmores* that the legal fight was not worth it? Certainly not their free-of-fees solicitor, Mrs Ogmore, and her family friend, barrister Mr Keith Stoat. Giving in yet again would be feeble, cowardly. It was also bad citizenship. They had given in unnecessarily, not only because they had been misled by their lawyers, but also in the mistaken belief that it was the sensible thing to do, and to avoid further entanglement in a deeply unpleasant fight. Further concessions would not be sensible; giving in again would be … wimpish.

Something else, not only the avoidance of shame or a desire for a just outcome, drove Lucy on: curiosity drove her on. To have one boundary battle in court may be considered a misfortune, to have two opens up an interesting opportunity for research, the sort of research Lucy enjoyed. She says her father always encouraged curiosity in his children: to ask why, how, when, where and who and to search for answers wherever. Her mother would add, 'And how can we make things better?' The success of the Ogmore land theft plan so far had already revealed quite a lot about our poorly functioning civil justice service. Could it redeem itself? And were there lawyers out there more trustworthy than the ones they had encountered so far? Were there judges with good judgement who had fully absorbed the Woolf reforms and recognised their responsibility to seek out truth and dispense proportionate justice? This next stage, the final one they thought, should provide answers. In any event it would provide rich material for research.

ELEVEN
November 2003–July 2004

'If this is justice, I'm a banana.'

Ian Hislop

Lucy's diary for the months of November and December 2003 shows that the antics of the Ogmores were only one of the challenges they had to deal with. As well as commitments to friends, family, business and charity work, and also their pursuit of claims to recover losses arising from the Ogmore war, they came back to the major building work programme and *dust*! Not the best time of the year to knock down walls. On certain days it was a fine judgement which was the most irritating: disappearing builders, electricians and other artisans, or a non-functioning civil justice system and a pair of rogue lawyers. Lucy says it was no contest, the workmen were skilled, wanted to do a good job and enjoyed a joke (as well as innumerable cups of tea – with biscuits). There was nothing to compensate for the conduct of the Ogmores et al.

Hazel Ogmore's Statement[1] in support of their application rehearsed the now familiar themes: everything has been litigated and everything had been agreed; the Hammer plan prevailed and the telephone pole 'fixed' the end of her roadside boundary. She also added a few extra ingredients just to annoy and/or confuse. She suggested that the new fence along the road had been erected in 2000. An Ogmore untruth. When Lucy and Max had walked up the road past Blackstone Cottage in early May 2001 there had been no new fence, and Lucy had noticed Blackstone Cottage's terrace. She would not have been able to see it if the fence had been in the way. Max and Lucy had four or five Witness Statements from neighbours making clear that the new fence had been erected in the summer of 2001. Ogmore finished her 'true testimony' by respectfully submitting that the claim be struck out as abuse of process and unreasonable with no real prospect of succeeding so it should be summarily disposed of. She asked for costs on the indemnity basis.

Max and Lucy had less than two weeks to respond as the Court (Judge Dyer) set Sunday 30th November for their reply. Courts don't open on Sundays. Mrs Buxton was away so they asked for an extension and got an extra five days. They decided they would have to buy some more Cynthia Buxton time and she gave them a couple of hours. Her advice remained the same, Max and Lucy would have to show the Judge that they are not trying to re-litigate the claim 'settled by consent' the previous year, and they must make that clear right from the start. 'The District Judge has a lot of paper to read in a fairly limited time. What helps him is to have a clear idea of the matters in dispute right at the beginning.' She advised them to write a Statement of what they intended to say, 'it is easier to take in an argument from a written submission, although you will be expected to go through your argument verbally to some extent.'

Max's Witness Statement opened as Mrs Buxton had suggested and then went on to record that Ogmore had lain doggo for two months ignoring every attempt to get her response to the surveyors' proposal. Lucy had found this worrying echo of the opposition's action in the fence post saga somewhat disturbing. Was she being haunted by that case? Besides, wasn't such conduct deemed unacceptable under the new rules?

Max's first principal point was that nothing in the wording of the Order made reference to the features on the Hammer plan apart from the boundaries. He pointed out that as the features had been incorrectly plotted, Land Registry would have had difficulties interpreting the Hammer plan on to the correct OS plan if the Order had specifically referred to them. As Ogmore had refused to provide copy of any instructions or reports, he could not explain the anomalies. As for the telephone pole, there is no reference to it in the wording either and she should explain why she thinks it significant. Besides, the pole had been moved further on to Homestead land by BT in October 2003 while Max and Lucy were in France. It was no longer in position to fix any boundary.

He exhibited Mrs Cohen's letter which Ogmore was relying on and pointed out the ambiguity about the word 'should' with regard to the position on the ground of the features. He reported Mr Nunn's survey of the roadside boundary which had identified continuing trespass, and the Ogmores' denial of trespass and insistence that the matter was closed. He went on to report on Ogmore's conduct, and that she had rejected mediation.

'They have not shown a proper concern for the overriding

objectives of the Access to Justice Act nor have they shown a proper concern to assist the Court to deal with matters justly.

'The Defendants are continuing to be obstructive and would be content to prevent us from erecting a barrier between our properties indefinitely. We attempted for over a year to persuade the Defendants to assist in determining the boundary on the ground. We believe this present application by them is another attempt to prevent a fair and just resolution which would allow us to erect a barrier and hopefully enjoy our property without the fear of future attempts by the Defendants to appropriate our land.'

On costs he asked that the Court to apply the Civil Procedure Rules concerning the conduct of the parties and referred to the rule stating 'management' should 'ensure that the parties are on an equal footing.' He filtered Woolf-speak into his Statement to prick the conscience of their adversaries which he suspected included District Judge Dyer.

Messrs O'Hare and Browne had helped to inform their response to the strike-out application. Addressing each of their opponents' arguments they asserted that there were clearly reasonable grounds for bringing the Claim: the position of the shed and so on had been surveyed several times and each time trespass had been found on their land, but the Ogmores will not accept that they are trespassing. The compelling reason why the case should be disposed of at trial was the need for a resolution of the question where on the ground Max and Lucy should erect their fence. 'Unless and until the Court makes a determination on the Claim, there will be continuing dispute as to the correct position on the ground of the western boundary. If the Court would order an independent survey and pegging of the boundaries according to the two plans, we would know where to put our fence.'

A week later Max and Lucy received Bulmer's reply to their request, sent three months earlier, for further and better particulars. It did not give further and better particulars. A week after that they received a bundle of documents – 74 pages of documents and Stoat's skeleton argument. This substantial pile arrived just two working days before the hearing listed for 29th December. It started by admitting that most things were agreed and that, 'neither party is seeking to undo the Consent Order or to rectify it in any way. All there is now is a straightforward issue of interpretation of the plan.' He meant the Hammer plan. He then foolishly went into detail, suggesting, for example, that there was a stone wall all the way down the 50 foot boundary between Dunroamin' and Blackstone Cottage land. ('Would that there had been,' says Max, 'all this could have been avoided.') Stoat also suggested that certain yew trees gave the line of the riverside boundary. ('A wandering drunken line,' says Max, 'as the OS surveyor reported. Even Ogmore doesn't claim them on her land.') He stated that there was only one measurement on the Hammer plan (there were three). He compounded that error by stating that the lack of a measurement for the shed boundary was a 'deliberate decision made by Counsel'! He must have been blind to the measurement clearly written for all to see. This was hardly a forgivable error, he didn't have to visit the site to check, merely to look at the plan he was relying on. He stated that '*in fact* there are no dimensions on the plan that forms part of the Court Order', and concluded triumphantly that 'given the plan' it was 'a matter of *fact*' that the shed, etc. were on Blackstone Cottage land! 'A fine sophisticated lawyer's argument,' said Max.

Stoat concluded with a judicial quote on the case he was citing as the precedent and on which he relied: the case of Henderson v Henderson (1843).[2] He did not provide copy of that case until 10 minutes before they were due to appear before the Judge, just as he had done with the American Cyanamid[3] precedent on their first encounter with him in 2002, when they were also acting as Litigants in Person.

Christmas was predictably busy and made more so by building work and *dust*! They were given refuge by Lucy's family over the festive period and had just a few hours on their return to Homestead to prepare for the hearing on 29th December.

The hearing began badly and got steadily worse. By the end Max was vindicated in his deprecation of District Judge Alfred Dyer. Lucy had originally thought his assessment too premature and damning; she had clung to a hope that the logic of their case would be irresistible to any moderately competent judge. However, competent or not, this Judge made clear from the start where his sympathies lay, she could read it from the disposition of his smiley face and his grim face.

When Lucy started to remind him of their proposal for an independent survey, 'So that we can all understand what we are talking about,' the Judge asked her to be quiet as he must listen to Mr Stoat. Lucy knew the applicant should speak first and Ogmore was the applicant. She hoped the session would not be too formal, 'This is a civil justice *service* ...' She got no further, 'Mrs Graham I'll listen to what you have to say later. I must listen to Mr Stoat first.'

He listened to Mr Stoat for quite a time and then he listened to Max for a shorter time. Mr Stoat had spent much of his allocation reading extracts from various judgments, in particular those that established and supported the *Henderson* v *Henderson* precedent. The rule in *Henderson* v *Henderson* is well known. It requires litigating parties to bring their whole case before the Court so all aspects of it may be finally decided once and for all, subject, of course, to any appeal. Except in very special circumstances, the parties cannot return to the Court to advance arguments, claims or defences which they could have put forward for decision on the first occasion but failed to raise: a rule of public policy based on the desirability, in the general interest, that litigation should not drag on for ever and that a defendant should not be oppressed by successive suits when one would do.

The rule is directed at 'abuse of process' so a new claim against the same party on the same matter will be struck out unless the circumstances have changed and compelling new evidence has come to light, for example, new injuries in an accident case, or if there has been some kind of fraud or mistake. In most cases before most judges, Ogmore's lie to Judge Blacker, *had it been known at the time*, would likely have rescued Max and Lucy from *Henderson* v *Henderson*, but it wasn't revealed until months later and, besides, District Judge Alfred Dyer was not like most judges. The general rule is that you should bring forward all the relevant facts the first time. The cases where *Henderson* v *Henderson* has not been followed appear to be where the second claim is quite a bit different from the first. One of the main reasons for the rule is to prevent the risk that different courts faced with different actions by the same parties, dealing with the same subject matter and raising the same issues, will come to different conclusions. This would be unfair to the parties, particularly to an initially successful party who fails in the subsequent proceeding, and (Heaven forfend) it would bring the administration of justice into disrepute. It is a rule which all lawyers know, all barristers know, but it is not one that all litigants know. If they did they would be very wary indeed of barristers who turn up on the day, not having mastered their brief, offering to sign *on their behalf* agreements they had never seen or agreed.

Blissfully unaware of the potency of the mix of this precedent and the wrong sort of Judge, Max simply repeated the arguments in their Statements: all parties were agreed that he and Lucy were not trying to set aside or skirt around the Consent Order; that, in the light of the Ogmores' opposition, they wanted the Court's help by ordering an independent survey to determine the position of the boundaries between Homestead and Blackstone Cottage on the ground so they could erect a fence without further dispute. So this Claim was quite a bit different from previous claims. The new evidence was Land Registry's difficulties and their inconclusive attempt to interpret the Hammer plan, and the compelling reason for hearing their Claim was the need to identify the relevant boundary on the ground in order to erect a fence. Simple. Sensible.

But they were not in a Centre for Simple and Sensible, they were in a Centre for Civil Justice sitting in the room of a judge who did not appear to be keen on simple or strong on sensible. At that stage they believed Scroggs had just made a mistake and that they were unfairly held responsible for it. Scroggs had been asked to put things right and, by all accounts, had refused. They could not understand why. Somehow they had to persuade this Judge that they were merely trying to put right a mistake made by their Counsel and in the most direct and least expensive way, but it was beginning to look like they were classified, by this Judge, in the vengeful, vexatious category. Worse, it was beginning to look like this Judge believed it was his duty to protect the unfortunate Ogmores from these vengeful, vexatious neighbours.

In allowing Ogmore to throw out Max and Lucy's application, Judge Dyer read a quote from the Rule Book, the *Civil Court Practice* book for 2003,[4] to the effect that the Defendants (the Ogmores) had to show that the Claimants (Max and Lucy) had no *real* prospect of succeeding, defining 'real' as the opposite of 'fanciful'. He added the bemusing stipulation the Court should not carry out a mini-trial in order to establish whether the prospect was real or fanciful. This test of real versus fanciful requires the Judge to undertake an exercise of judgement. It is a discretionary power, but an exercise of that power based on a judgement not of probability but of the absence of reality.

As far as District Judge Dyer was concerned it all boiled down to the fact that the Hammer plan showed the shed on Blackstone Cottage and that the boundaries drawn on Land Registry's plan were only general boundaries. He focussed on one part of Max and Lucy's Claim: Land Registry's interpretation of the Hammer plan and ignored the other part: the shed was plotted incorrectly on the Hammer plan. He went on to say that the shed and fence were there at the time the 'Consent Agreement' was made and *everything should have been sorted before it was signed*. They couldn't argue with that. Max had been saying as much from the moment he realised what Scroggs had got them into. Judge Dyer quoted Mrs Cohen's letter which was in both bundles and interpreted her ambiguous '*should*' as Ogmore wished. As argument had been restricted to whether or not to throw out their application, Max could not see an opportunity to unpick Cohen's letter when he presented his case.

Judge Dyer stressed that it was not in his jurisdiction as a mere District Judge to make any observation about the circumstances that led to Scroggs signing the agreement – that was for a higher grade of judge. Judge Dyer appeared to believe that there had been detailed and lengthy discussions throughout the previous court action and that *both* parties had tried every method available to settle matters in detail beforehand!

A reading of his words in the transcript of that hearing shows some serious confusion in his understanding of the case before him, but absolute clarity as to his Decision: 'I am satisfied in this case that Mr and Mrs Ogmore have established the absence of a realistic prospect of success in showing that they are trespassers. Furthermore, I can see no other compelling reason why the case should be disposed of at trial.' The compelling reason was where should and could Max and Lucy put up their fence to protect their land from further encroachment. The compelling reason was that nobody knew for certain where the boundary was on the ground and therefore nobody could say if the Ogmores were trespassing or not. If the Ogmores knew for certain *they* could have put up a fence – if they wanted to. They hadn't done so.

Stoat moved immediately. He wanted a summary assessment on costs there and then. He wanted to show correspondence demonstrating how 'very reasonably at all times the Ogmores have conducted themselves and generously in the face of grotesque provocation … .'

This was just too much for Lucy. She had constrained herself during the previous session but this lie forced an objection. Judge Dyer compounded her indignation by his condescension, 'Please Mrs Graham, I appreciate your disappointment.' 'I'm shocked,' she corrected him.

Stoat continued, 'Costs follow the event and in this case I would wish to point out that at all times the Defendants have been extremely straightforward and helpful to the Claimants if only they would read what is being written and what is being said, and that they have acted reasonably throughout this matter.' Lucy managed to control her anger. Stoat intended to negate their argument of vexatious conduct by his clients by getting his retaliation in first. He had no evidence to support his gross distortion of the facts. They had evidence of Ogmore's conduct, but were diverted by the Judge from showing it there and then.

The transcript of Max's response reads quite well considering he must have been reeling, not just from Dyer's decision but far more from Stoat's extraordinary assertions. Lucy scribbled 'mediation' on a note for him and immediately he mentioned the word Dyer became interested. Max's mention of the *Railtrack*[5] case sparked further interest and Stoat became concerned. He began by implying that he knew a lot about mediation in general and the *Railtrack* case in particular, but he couldn't actually come up with any information on either and he then went that little bit too far: 'the correspondence will let us see whether it was a real offer of mediation or a smokescreen … .'

Max muttered 'scoundrel' under his breath and Stoat exploded. Judge Dyer had not heard the description, but was all too aware of Stoat's fury. Max fumbled a denial at first but then apologised. He still regrets that apology. He should not have allowed himself to be bullied into making it. He should have explained why the word described Stoat's conduct accurately. Stoat then read out a letter from Ogmore (without contextual background) presented as though every word was a precise statement of fact, and then added a few more readings from other Ogmore letters also out of context which repeated again and again Ogmore's 'advice': that the Consent Order was final, that both parties had agreed it, that Cain had written to the Court agreeing it, that Land Registry had no problem with the Hammer plan and nor did the surveyors. The sealed Consent Order was the final deciding factor and the Hammer plan presented no problems. Max and Lucy were attempting to 'completely undo *all the efforts* which were made on 31st October.' There was no question now Stoat and Ogmore shared identical talents for the Big Lie.

Max did not have an opportunity to come back with rebuttals and his list of Ogmore misdemeanours because Judge Dyer was still hunting for a report on the *Railtrack* case. Stoat suggested that if the Claimants were relying on it they should have brought a copy. Lucy replied that they did not expect to be discussing costs, at this hearing. They had done some work in preparation for an adverse costs decision but not for today; besides, there were further relevant cases on mediation.

Judge Dyer was still hunting for the *Railtrack* case and told Stoat that he had not conceded on the *principle* of costs (let alone the *quantum*) and that he would put off that decision until a later date. Stoat persisted in his attempts to get a decision there and then, but the Judge was not minded to do so and Stoat gave in.

That left the matter of an appeal. Max and Lucy had done limited work on appeals and knew nothing of the correct procedure. Dyer A. outlined the procedures and they decided to appeal immediately to him. An unwise decision. Perhaps they should have waited and appealed to a Circuit judge but as there was only a tight window of 14 days to make such an appeal and that included the New Year holidays, they would have had no time to do the necessary homework and get advice, so perhaps the outcome would have been the same. District Judge Dyer rejected the appeal.

Well, a lot of time, a lot of work, a lot of aggravation, a lot of appalling lies, and a lot of money and we still don't know where exactly to put our fence. So much for our civil justice service, "the best in the world"? What must the rest be like?' Max felt vindicated in his assessment of District Judge Alfred Dyer, but it was a Pyrrhic victory and his disgust at what they had witnessed was overwhelming. Dyer had been given the background story and the case they had put for allowing the independent survey was well argued.

'I think he's not very bright,' said Lucy, 'at least not in the way we, the public, need our judges to be. He may be great on precedents, but Woolf et al. set out the overriding objectives of the Rules and he ignored them. You made clear why we were there, but he couldn't see the role he needed to play. No one else could play it and if judges claim to offer a civil justice service they should provide it. Who else can? Neither he nor Stoat came up with any justification for refusing an independent survey – apart from Scroggs' signature on that non-Consent agreement. Seems to me he just couldn't get past the *Henderson* v *Henderson* stuff and see the wood for the trees. Lacks common sense. Lacks good judgement. He certainly hasn't thought of the implications. Does he even understand that there is a difference between Hammer's drawing and the real world? Frankly, I can't stand the echoes of the fence post saga. It's spooky. That was about the Court making a mess of where a fence post should go, now it looks like the Court is making a mess of where our fence should go.'

'Well,' said Max, 'if it's down to Scroggs' signature on that Consent document then we double our efforts to make sure Scroggs pays. We'd better get something in writing from Dyer to make clear why he threw out our Claim. I'll write to him asap.'

He wrote immediately the next day indifferent to whether such action was *correct procedure* or not. He started by drawing attention to the cost of transcribing the lengthy hearing which would be unnecessary if the Judge would confirm two important points in their recollections of what had been said. 'We do apologise for the inconvenience but we believe it better to write now while memories are still fresh'.

First he recalled Dyer questioning them at both hearings on why they had failed to seek a variation of the Consent Order and their explanation: Counsel failed to act. Then he summarised from their notes their recollection that Dyer had ruled that the Consent Order plan overruled the LR plan and that items on the plan overruled the boundaries so that the measurements, scaling and angles on both plans had no significance.

He concluded with: it would appear that in order to establish clarity and, above all, to avoid further disputes, both the HMLR plan of 2nd July 2003 and the overriding Consent Order plan will need to be amended to ensure that they do not conflict with your ruling and with the facts on the ground, and to make clear that the fence and shed are contained within the boundaries of Blackstone Cottage. This will involve adding an extra parcel of our land to Blackstone Cotttage land on both plans. He also asked for the return of Lucy's interpretation of the surveyors' proposed solution on to the selected OS plan[6] which she had sent to Cain, Nunn, Ogmore and the Court. Max had given a copy to Judge Dyer during the hearing but discovered on their return it was their only clean copy and they wanted it back.

No one will be surprised that this impertinent display of *lèse majesté* drew no response. Some will certainly be surprised that Max tried again three weeks later asking for clarification and help. This time a response: 'The Judge is not prepared to respond in the manner proposed.' The brief note did not say in what manner he might be prepared to respond, if at all. No *civil* justice *service* there.

Ogmore-Bulmer started the New Year off with a Part 36 offer.[7] Stoat had said that his clients were *not* claiming costs on an indemnity basis. Now they were. They wanted over £8,500 and threatened a claim for interest at 10% over base rate, amounting to some 14% in those heady days for savers, and a claim on the indemnity basis, hiking the claim up by possibly 100% if the offer wasn't accepted within 21 days. But the Judge had stated that he had not even conceded they would get costs in principle, let alone the amount of costs he would allow. If his one-track mind was now focussed on the role of mediation he might not allow any costs at all. Max and Lucy decided it would be unwise to accept the offer, so they didn't.

Both parties exchanged their lists of authorities on mediation. Max wrote to Mr Brown at Land Registry to enquire whether the Ogmores had ever proposed or agreed to mediation. He also wrote to the Court to ask for a copy of the note by the first Not-Judge-Dyer who had written down Ogmores' rejection of their mediation proposal. Land Registry had no record of Ogmore advocating or agreeing to mediation.

Max reluctantly agreed with Lucy that they would have to get help, expensive lawyer help, if they were to stand any hope of getting through to this inflexible if not dense, District Judge and get the necessary homework done before the hearing in late February. They decided that this time they would go for quality, an expert on mediation. By 2004 the internet was beginning to be useful. They found two rating agencies for lawyers: Chambers and Partners and Legal 500. Chambers was the most appropriate for clients like them and they selected two from the eight recommended lawyers expert in mediation in their region. They interviewed both by phone and selected Guy Castor. He sounded forthright and fun telling them that his rate per hour was £220 plus VAT, but he would reduce it to £200 plus VAT (so £235 per hour) for this 'interesting' case. He sounded just the man they wanted, and, after all, Chambers and Partners choose their recommendations carefully.

Lucy and Max saw no implication in his failure to make the promised call to discuss the package of papers they had sent him the following day. However, although he charmed them with his apologies, wit and easy confident manner, this was not quite enough to prevent them reminding him that he had agreed to reduce his hourly rate. His standard contract letter lacked the necessary amendment. They arranged to see him the following week, somewhat relieved that the Court had postponed the hearing by two months to April.

Meanwhile Ogmore & Co. were getting exercised about mediation. They demanded copies of the four cases Max and Lucy had identified as relevant to their case, with the help of the internet and O'Hare and Browne. District Judge Dyer wanted copies of two of their cited cases. Both these adversaries also wanted copies of the full transcript of the *ex parte*[8] hearing at the Royal Courts of Justice which had started the whole court saga off when Stoat had given his gloss on Ogmore's attack, and just failed to mention the several mediation offers that had been made to his client and rejected by her. 'Well, at least Dyer's showing interest,' said Lucy, 'perhaps he's hoping for a seminar on mediation in April.'

Max's 97-year old father had been rushed to hospital and plans were frozen as they both hurried to his bedside on the other side of the country. He rallied and they returned home but, a week later, news came that he had died. The court shenanigans were ignored. Max was the only child and he had grief and a funeral to contend with.

The next two weeks were frenetic and sad. Ninety-seven is a good age and his father had had a good, interesting life, working right up to the age of 85, as a solicitor. But bereavement overwhelms the positive initially until time and perspective mends. Lucy booked a few days in Paris to ameliorate the sharper edges. A valuable break that achieved some of the objective.

They came back to the usual dust and disappearing builders, and silence from Castor. Should they cut loose from him? They couldn't. It was the usual trap: they had invested too much time and work in him to start again and if

Chambers and Partners[9] recommended him he may still come up trumps. He had until mid-April now, an extra two months to prepare. He had already started on a campaign to make Land Registry own up to their responsibility for some of the mess they had contributed to. Despite his letter, the Registrar refused to acknowledge any responsibility relying on the get-out-of-gaol-free 'General Boundaries Rule'. Max urged Castor to try personal contact with Mr Brown to seek clarification of his position and to let it be known gently that they had done quite a bit of work to save the Registry money: gifting land to the squatters – 'to bring an early end to matters' (!); acting as litigants in person; refusing to pay the two barristers and lodging a complaint with the Bar Council; consistently urging mediation.

If Max and Lucy had concerns about Castor, they felt more positive about his secretary who was, in effect, a paralegal hoping to qualify as a solicitor. She was a woman they found good to do business with. Throughout the coming months she showed herself both resourceful and pleasant, and on more than one occasion, an effective apologist for her boss.

They agreed with Castor that they should chase Land Registry on the 'margin of error' allowed with the General Boundary Rules and point out that in this case it was some five feet not the acceptable nine inches cited by the Registry. Lucy suggested that he, Castor, should write to the Ogmores saying that they would agree that the shed could be deemed to be entirely on Blackstone Cottage land, but that this would require an amendment to their Title plan and Land Registry would agree to this if the Ogmores also agreed. Guy Castor proposed that Lucy write the letter so she did.

Max and Lucy wanted to know how they could persuade this particular Judge to do something useful to resolve the enigma created by his rejection of their application. At the very least they would have thought there would be some mechanism in the *Civil Procedure Rules* (CPRs)[10] to get him to first state and second clarify his ruling. Their reading of those Rules suggested that he could and should have resolved the essential matter of where they put their fence at the hearing, but he seemed so taken with *Henderson* v *Henderson* (and Stoat?) that he failed to identify the valuable role he could and should have played. Judge Dyer refused her request to release copies of any of his handwritten notes. He didn't give a reason. Lucy had been given copies of the handwritten notes from all the previous judges without demur.

She wrote to their new expert champion with an update on that and on other claims they were pursuing against their vendors and their conveyancing solicitors. He was more focussed on their Claim against Land Registry and suggested, that as this was not his area of expertise, they should consider getting Counsel's opinion. They disliked that idea, but decided to have another attempt to get the Ogmores to agree to ask the Registry to amend to their Title plan so that it accorded with Judge Dyer's ruling – effectively handing yet more of their land to the squatters. They had already made this sensible offer in a *without prejudice*[11] letter a week earlier, but true to form Ogmore had rejected it. In the light of the latest letter from Mr Brown they tried again: 'As we are merely requesting your agreement to amend our filed plan to remove a further parcel of our land so that it is recorded as part of your property, we find it difficult to understand why you are so reluctant to agree. The proposal is entirely to your benefit and we do not believe there would be any cost to you … We would be most grateful if you would reconsider this matter and assist both parties, the Court and Land Registry, in a final and sensible resolution (that) removes the conflict between the present Title plan, the Court ruling and the verifiable facts.'

The only reply they got was Stoat's skeleton argument[12] on costs and a substantial bundle of documents. The most interesting item in the bundle was a copy of the letter Mr Royston Hammer had written to his client one week after the site meeting in November 2002. It had taken well over a year and several requests, but finally they could see the response from Mr Hammer, architect (not land surveyor) to the proposals they had agreed at that site meeting. He had attached a version of his trouble-making plan amended as had been agreed. His plan gave the Ogmores a long sliver of extra land on the riverside boundary and shaped the boundary in a dog-leg around the shed exactly as Lucy had drawn on the OS plan which she had sent to Ogmore, Cain, Nunn – and the Court (aka Circuit Judge Blacker) in response to Judge Blacker's letter. This amended version of Royston Hammer's plan was what he recommended his client to agree. If she did not agree why did she not let the Court, Land Registry and her opponents know immediately? Could it be that her Counsel pointed out that she needed to delay in order to prevent a timely request from her opponents to amend, and set aside the Not-Agreed Consent Agreement? Timing was of the essence and the Court would frown on a belated application, most likely reject it, so, from her point of view, *delaying* was of the essence. First, she must get it sealed. Lucy had found in the Court records evidence that Hazel Ogmore had telephoned the Court several times first asking, then demanding that the 'agreement' be sealed[13] by Judge Blacker. One month after Mr Royston Hammer had sent her the compromise plan, the Judge, ignorant of Hammer's letter and her games, duly obliged.

The letter accompanying Hammer's amended plan explained the techniques used to measure Blackstone Cottage land: starting somewhere in the dense undergrowth in the far riverside corner of the Blackstone plot, not at the correct fixed point where the carport met the road. Why did James Nunn agree to that? Lucy, still recording everything for her research and eventual report, wondered what could be done to ensure that important documents like Hammer's letter were revealed in a timely manner, or revealed at all. What sanctions would be sufficient to force the Ogmores and Stoats to behave?

Lucy sent a copy to James Nunn who replied that he had never seen the letter before and although there were aspects on the plan/measurements which were not agreed, the letter did outline the compromise they had agreed on site. He also repeated that he had tried and failed over months to contact Hammer to learn whether Ogmore agreed it. He then reported on his two recent surveys which both confirmed that the boundary line, which was the cause of the current litigation, ran through the chalet and that Ogmore's fence ran a further five feet beyond the roadside boundary described on Hammer's plan, even allowing the generous transfer of a five foot 'ditch' from Blackstone Cottage land to Dunroamin'.

Stoat's skeleton argument started with: 'the only argument the Claimants (Max and Lucy) have is their *alleged* offers of ADR, but the Consent Order was a form of ADR and ever since it was *agreed* they have been seeking to resile from it.' He seemed to have forgotten his previous skeleton argument which stated that neither party was attempting to resile from the Consent agreement, a point he had actually made to the Judge in court. The argument continued with two pages listing 20 or so items purporting to support that position and including such gems as: 'Ds (the Ogmores) have never refused ADR in this action.' Was Stoat unaware that they had refused to agree to an independent survey to settle the matter in 'this action'? Then there were the statements that Cs (Max and Lucy) have acted unpleasantly 'invariably referring to D in pejorative terms in *all* correspondence,' therefore, 'mediation had no real prospect of getting anywhere.' He cited one example – the fact that Lucy had written to the Law Society asking for their position on solicitors acting unsupervised in their own case and describing the dangers that can arise. That was the worst he could find presumably and the 'pejorative' was only to be found in her brief record of Ogmore's actions. There then followed 43 citations from correspondence making up the bundle of 137 pages. The commentary created an interesting record of the history from the day the 'agreement' was signed to his clients' application to strike out. Quite apart from an expected partiality – that, after all, is his job, Stoat showed once again his tenuous grasp of the facts; repeating Ogmore's lie that Cain had written to the Court confirming the terms of the Consent Order. He glossed over letters from 'C' (which he no doubt suspected would be in C's bundle of documents anyway) describing them as 'Long and not germane to anything much.' Thus freeing Mr Dyer from any necessity to read them. Two such letters contained proposals on some form of ADR. It would take forever to unpick the story and reveal the facts.

Lucy had taken a day out of her demanding schedule to drive to the Civil Justice Centre to inspect the file and in the end the journey proved most useful. It was on that inspection that she acquired copies of key documents which were later to reveal that Circuit Judge Blacker did not deserve the opprobrium they had heaped on him. It took some time for the penny to drop, but when she studied a copy of Ogmore's reply to the Judge's request for an agreed agreement, and took time a few weeks later to look more closely at the items retrieved from the Cross & Cross file from the same period, she realised how the Judge and Robin Cain had been misled by Mrs Hazel Ogmore, Solicitor of the Supreme Court. This was perfect evidence of Ogmore's bad conduct should they need to argue about costs.

Guy Castor had at last set a date to honour his promise to visit and see the site. Lucy volunteered to go through Stoat's work in time for his visit in order to identify some examples of what was a distorted truth and *possibly* disprovable, and what was an evident lie. She would show the evidence of duplicity she had discovered at court so he could incorporate some of the more salient points in the Witness Statement he was drafting for her. Only trouble was the date for this visit was just three solicitor days before the hearing. Both Max and Lucy had become impatient with their guardian's delays and excuses. He had not used the extra two months to any good effect for them and even his excellent secretary/paralegal was showing signs of deep embarrassment at the constant prevarications and broken promises. He forgot his promise not to charge them for the visit. By the time he arrived (an hour and a half late) Lucy was exhausted with the preparatory work but had a large dossier ready and he was impressed (and shocked) with the evidence she had accumulated of Ogmore's conduct. Lucy provided lunch. He had two days to prepare their case, draft Lucy's Witness Statement and select and collate the documents. Neither Lucy nor Max had confidence he would provide the quality work Chambers and Partners had led them to expect. They just hoped he would supply some work in time. He faxed through a draft Witness Statement on the Sunday evening just 18 hours before they were due in court. There were some essential corrections needed. For example his draft suggested that Ogmore had actually lodged a Claim with

Land Registry before the litigation began. Castor had ignored Mr Beige's very pertinent report which had clearly stated that no such Claim had ever been made. He had forgotten all the evidence Lucy had provided on Ogmore's agreement to use an OS plan, corroborated by Lucy's correspondence with Ordnance Survey for permission to use the selected and agreed plan.

Nevertheless, he did include a large section on the evidence of Ogmore's duplicity with regard to her letter to the Judge.

Castor's 'Claimants' ADR Submission' had obviously been taken from the computer file for some other case(s) with no tailoring to Max and Lucy's. Apart from their case number there was no reference to the case itself. However, District Judge Dyer would get his tutorial on ADR with particular emphasis on mediation.

Once again Max and Lucy were obliged to drop all plans to find time to deal with this much belated and essential paperwork. On the morning of the hearing they faxed back the signed final page of Lucy's Witness Statement, and Max's signed agreement. They were due to meet up with him an hour and a half beforehand at a large, rather grand hotel in the countryside en route to the Court. This time it was they who were late. They had allowed plenty of time to get there, but although they had seen the hotel many times over the years, they were quite unaware that its entrance was not off the motorway. It was hidden away among houses off a minor road. Worse, by the time they had realised this after several false goes, they were trapped on the motorway with no exit for 10 miles, 20 miles there and back, and mobile connection was impossible for most of it. The thundering HGVs and the heavy rain added somewhat to the growing anxiety.

By the time they met up with Guy Castor they were less than cool and he was around the same temperature. Lucy stifled any comment on the cause for the emergency meeting and they ordered sandwiches and did their best. The discussions did little to reduce the heat as all three became aware of how many gaps there were in Castor's grasp of the case he was about to present to a less-than-impressive Judge in 40 minutes' time, and that included the time necessary to get to the Court. He kindly let Max pay for his lunch. Max was not feeling so kind.

The journey was frustrated by traffic so by the time they finally struggled into court, after an in-car seminar, he went immediately to hand the documents, which should have been sent at least a week earlier, to Ogmore and Stoat. When Max and Lucy next saw him he was bristling from the lathering he had received from Ogmore, 'What a nasty person she is,' he said,' I see what you've had to put up with.' Lucy reminded him that Stoat always delayed delivery of documents, sometimes right up until they were actually sitting in court. He did not seem consoled. He was more concerned that the Judge had not received the papers.

District Judge Dyer ruled that such late submissions were not admissible. He was prepared to hear oral argument, however, and look at evidence. If their previous encounter with Dyer had started badly and steadily got worse, this one started worse still. Mr Dyer was stolidly unconcerned with the pile of evidence provided showing just how bad Ogmore's conduct was. That is to say he was totally unconcerned about the 22 listed misdemeanours Castor had in evidence against her of which he selected some 10 or so and showed evidence to support his allegations. Although costs in a case usually follow the event and the losing party pays the winning party's costs, the Woolf reforms say that this is a starting point from which the Court can readily depart. The rules say that, in deciding what order to make (if any) about costs, the Court must have regard to all the circumstances including the conduct of all parties and list examples, not exhaustive, of what may be taken into consideration including any action *before* as well as during the proceedings, in particular the extent to which the parties followed any relevant pre-action protocol. Ogmore (and Stoat) had ignored Max and Lucy's attempts at pre-action protocols just as they had ignored much of the content of their letters, 'presumably our pre-protocol letter is deemed not germane to anything much,' Max opined. Stoat asserted that Max and Lucy had lodged their Claim immediately Land Registry produced the rectified plan, without warning. Was he really unaware of the several proposals they had made for settling matters without going to court? Was he unaware of their formal pre-protocol letter, their reminders and Ogmore's total lack of response? Did he know nothing about the extra boundary checks and their invitation to Ogmore to do likewise? What of their proposal of an independent survey? The familiar question arose: how much had his client told him? Was he misled? Was he careless and failed to do his homework? Or was he deliberately misleading the Judge?

District Judge Dyer cannot be excused blame. He ignored all the evidence of offers to mediate, all the evidence of the Registry's rejection of the inadequate Hammer plan (although just one look at the plan should have been enough), all the evidence of the land theft, all the evidence of distorting the truth and telling downright lies, all the evidence of escalating the dispute and bringing it into court precipitously and under false pretences, ignored the lies in the application for a judicial review, ignored above all the detailed evidence of Ogmore's lie to Judge Blacker and lie to Cain and then lying low until she got her sealed Order.

He awarded costs in full, but at the standard rate. He is the only judge who had been shown the accumulated evidence of Ogmore's disgraceful conduct. He can make no plea of ignorance in mitigation.

By ordering the costs hearing and then ignoring all the evidence on conduct this District Judge had added considerable extra costs to a matter he could have handed to an independent surveyor right at the start. An independent surveyor would have made a far better fist of resolving the key issue, the only issue: where should the fence go, at a tenth of the cost. Max and Lucy decided this Judge was (and still is) a liability to litigants and the civil justice system. They have not changed their minds over the years. He doesn't rate a score out of 10. He rates dismissal.

They were divided in their opinion of Guy Castor's performance. Lucy was sitting next to him and exhausted by the stress of the morning and the previous few days (she was still waiting for the kitchen work to complete), she was grateful that they had somebody else who did seem to be on their side, doing battle. She did not see how he could have done any better with that particular Judge. Max was sitting at the back of the room and able to watch the behaviour of all the players. He was unimpressed by Castor who he thought lacked energy and clear direction. 'He let far too many things go. We had warned him about Dyer, we'd told him he would have to be clear and forceful. Dyer is the sort to be impressed more by style than content. Stoat had style, Castor was relying on content, and Dyer seemed incapable of fully understanding what he was being told. Stoat understood though. You should have seen his reaction when Guy read out the items revealing Ogmore's lies to Judge Blacker. He looked angry with his client. She started frantically whispering to him and I'm not sure he was really calmed by whatever distortion of the truth she fed him.'

Outside the courthouse Guy Castor tried soothing words for his clients and promised to write to them the following day. Unwisely, he tried the 'don't let it get to you … in a few days you'll be able to put it all behind you' approach, as if it was some minor family quarrel. This is an approach which is unlikely to work at such a time with most people and certainly not with Max and Lucy. Lucy was well into her report on the failures of the civil justice system. Max was well into recovering all financial losses. Neither had any intention of 'putting it all behind them'.

Castor did actually manage an email the following day and a thoughtful letter the day after. He drew attention to the fact that Ogmore had not achieved costs on an indemnity basis and standard costs usually result with anything between 10 and 40% less than claimed. He was relieved that they had decided on two 'sensible' objectives: (1.) to achieve an 'uncontroversial' boundary marked on the ground and (2.) to recover all costs expended so far. 'What else should be our objectives?' wondered Max who was still unhappy with Castor's unimpressive performance and, unlike Lucy, not persuaded that he could not have done better.

Castor was not very optimistic they would get proper compensation from Land Registry and recommended they get Counsel's opinion on that and various other options he outlined. He had just the man in mind. His clients were underwhelmed by the proposal, they were already returning to thoughts of dispensing with professional representation except on a Mrs Buxton-type contract.

He did acknowledge his agreement to reduce his hourly rate, but not his original offer to visit the site free of charge (the journey alone cost over £500). 'Shall we counter charge for the two lunches we provided?' was Lucy's ungrateful response. He then warned that all future charges would be at his normal rate. One of the options he proposed was to appeal Dyer's original decision to summarily dismiss their trespass/independent surveyor application. They would have to move quickly as they were out of time. As it would involve the Court of Appeal and more stressful, expensive court games, it was an option easy to dismiss.

Guy Castor was full of huge sympathy. Nevertheless, he insisted that they 'had failed to give [themselves] the best chance by not instructing competent lawyers' (so, how do we identify 'competent lawyers' … in advance?) and … 'because of the complexities of the Civil Litigation system and the myriad of rules that apply' (and who made the rules?), he 'really did urge [them] to take Counsel's opinion.' Quite apart from this vote of no confidence in himself, Max and Lucy felt the need to point out that it was the incompetence of Counsel that had landed them in this predicament, albeit incompetence amplified by the Judges, the Court, Land Registry, other lawyers and the perfidy of Ogmore and her team: the Ogmore Gang.

The Court Order they received the following week confirmed the ruling on costs at the standard basis, but revealed that the cost issue would go on for at least another three months and that Dyer had no intention of letting the case out of his hands. In his delegation of work role Guy persuaded them to engage a cost draughtsman, unsurprisingly he had just the man in mind.

Mr Knapp was a slim, dapper man in his early sixties with an easy manner and a quick smile. They had been in touch with him by phone to agree some of the gambits in his strategy, but met him for the first time in the Court lobby. He was a non-practising solicitor who discovered his accountancy talents in the course of his earlier trade at about the time he decided he disliked adversarial unpleasantness. He had been a law costs consultant ever since. As far as the couple could judge, he was good at his job and managed to reduce the Ogmores claim by 25% and managed to reduce Stoat's fee by 30%, despite what he described as 'a generally hostile Judge'. However, once his own fee and other incidentals were taken into account this still amounted to a considerable sum that the couple would now have to reclaim from various individuals, which did not include Stoat, Ogmore or District Judge Dyer.

Max and Lucy attended the first half of the hearing and watched Mr Alfred Dyer carefully. He didn't give the Ogmores' costs expert everything he wanted, it was true, but then, according to Mr Knapp, everything he wanted was too much according to all the rules. Lucy was interested in the process to see if this cost hearing post-Woolf was going to be very different from the same exercise she had experienced with the fence post saga pre-Woolf. Felix and Lucy had been confused and confounded by the decisions of that irascible Registrar 20 years earlier, but, then, so had the Doyles' solicitor, Mr Gee. This Judge also changed his mind (or possibly forgot his earlier ruling) and allowed the Ogmores a 'success' fee[14] – adding an extra 33% to some of the costs he allowed. Mr Knapp objected and insisted later he was correct, but the Judge was unreasonably obdurate. Why Mr Dyer was able to overrule his own Order neither Max nor Lucy ever understood. Even Max with a calculator in his brain could not follow what was going on, but at least two of the three men in front of them seemed to understand the strange rules and rituals and in the end Mr Knapp appeared to have saved them more than his fee so, as far as they could tell, he was worth it. But perhaps that was only because the original demand was way over reasonable and they were contending with a hostile Judge, and that hostile Judge was District Judge Alfred Dyer. With another Judge … who knows? But then they believed that any other judge would have allowed them their independent survey avoiding a costs hearing altogether.

Knapp, like Castor, thought District Judge Dyer's rulings bizarre, but then went on to express his dislike of the law business in general. Max suggested he would have been happier in a less adversarial sector of the dispute resolution trade – ADR[15] for example. He agreed ADR was a cleaner business and hoped that it would take over most civil disputes in the future, 'But it will see my job disappear so, not until I retire if you don't mind!'

Max and Lucy went for lunch during the more detailed negotiations reflecting that if they had been fully exposed to the full costs of all court dealings with the squatters they would be in despair at that moment. They did have something else to reflect on, however, which did not cause despair but did cause deep anxiety and anger.

Contrary to normal procedures, Lionel Knapp had shown them copy of Hazel Ogmore's checklist for risk assessment, the essential part of her Conditional Fee Agreement (CFA or no win, no fee)[16] with her boss. This is usually filled in with careful judgement by the solicitor in the firm acting for the litigant, but, of course, this solicitor was the litigant and careful weighing of the likelihood of success was down to Hazel Ogmore's careful judgement.

She wanted an increase in costs of 100% and for that she needed to suggest the prospects for success were just fifty-fifty. There, in her familiar scrawl, were her responses to some of the pro-forma questions. Next to the query 'Knowledge of the opponents', she had written: 'Untruthful, liars, manipulative, selective in what they disclose.' Under the heading 'The Success Fee reflects the following:' she had written, 'the Claimants are totally unpredictable and regarded as loose canons; evidence of fact is likely to be an issue; "your" [sic] opponent has in previous proceedings demonstrated a lack of veracity and have shown a willingness to mislead the Court.' Lucy says she still finds all that takes her breath away. She knows that Stoat saw some judges on his own and if these were the words whispered in their ears no wonder they were hostile. It explains why Ogmore had been so successful in persuading her boss, Mr C. V. Bulmer, to reject all their attempts to see him

If Max and Lucy were in any doubt about the initial source of District Judge Dyer's hostility, a few electric minutes in that cost hearing dispelled them. Lionel Knapp read Hazel Ogmore's words out and asked Alfred Dyer for confirmation that he did not believe them. Alfred Dyer changed the subject. Lionel Knapp read some more and repeated his request. Lucy says that Alfred Dyer looked at them both and changed the subject again. Mr Knapp managed to say he was very surprised as he and his clients' solicitor found this to be most untrue and ... but Ogmore's cost expert spoke over him on a general point about Conditional Fee Agreements, and that was that. A little later under close questioning by Lionel Knapp, Ogmore's expert admitted that Mr C. V. Bulmer, Head of the small law firm, was 'not familiar with the regulations for conditional fee arrangements and left such matters to his Associate, Mrs Ogmore'!

Throughout the years of fury and frustration in their dealings with the Ogmores, Lucy had been nagged by curiosity about their nature – what drove them to behave as they did? Originally she had agreed with Max it had something to do with the shame of Joe Ogmore's imprisonment, compounded by Hazel's need to prevent exposure of her inexcusable annexing of their land. They both displayed high and totally unreal opinions of themselves. For quite some time Max and Lucy believed that explained her obsession with retaining the chalet in place, but they had let her keep the chalet in place (for all the world to see) and the lies and libels kept on coming. She certainly had an extraordinary ability to lie very convincingly, transferring her particular character deficits on to Max and Lucy. It was not until Lucy heard readings from a book by psychotherapist Stephen Grosz – *The Examined Life*[17] – did she find an acceptable explanation. He tells the story of a father in a prestigious position who disowned his Jewish daughter when she married Patrick, a blond, blue-eyed Catholic. For 16 years the daughter and her growing family were shunned by her parents. To her great sadness and distress she had no contact from either her father or her mother and she could not understand why; her father was not a strict Jew. Then one day her mother made contact. She was divorcing her husband. He had been having an affair with his secretary for over 20 years. His secretary was called Kathy and she was a blond, blue-eyed Catholic. The father had transferred all his guilt and shame at the deceit and betrayal on to a son-in-law he did not know. 'I'm not bad, he's bad. I'm not bad, you're bad.' The daughter described this as, 'The bigger the front, the bigger the back.' Stephen Grosz explains that in psychiatry such transference of shame is described as 'splitting', but he prefers her description: 'splitting' suggests two separate parts whereas her description acknowledges that this blind and cruel transfer of guilt and shame takes place in the same individual and the whole individual is threatened by any attempt to reveal the true guilty party.

Most of the time in the following months of 2004 allocated to the land theft, were taken up with recovering costs and apologies from various miscreants, but in December Lucy decided to try to unravel the mystery of C. V. Bulmer's role. She wrote to Ogmore quoting her words on her CFA form about Max and herself, asking her to provide all the evidence on which the Statements were based. She copied the letter to Clive Vernon Bulmer and in her accompanying letter asked if he would corroborate the assertion that he was not familiar with CFA regulations and left such matters to his Associate (as stated by Ogmore's cost expert). She referred to her earlier attempt to persuade Mr Bulmer to take an active interest in the matter and check what his Associate was up to, adding that she was dismayed that he had not considered taking an independent view. She repeated her offer to meet. The reply came 10 days later. It was relatively emollient: Clive Bulmer agreed that the language on the form was 'unusually colourful,' and that, 'it is not always ideal when one's colleague is also a party to proceedings.' He went on to point out that in neighbour disputes 'feelings can run high' and this 'can lead to uncharacteristic behaviour'. He then returned to more predictable language ... 'the way our legal system works there can only be a winner and a loser. What would be the point of meeting? We are solicitors and we do not feel there is, any longer, a legal issue to address.' The letter was signed by him and might have been dictated by him but for two rather important facts: Ogmore was no longer listed as a member of the firm, she had been replaced by a Mr R. S. Jonas and RSJ not CVB appeared in the letter's reference; and a week later Lucy was amazed to receive another letter – also signed by Mr C. V. Bulmer but without RSJ in the reference.

'I write to you following a letter from my firm dated 14th December. The previous letter was sent without my knowledge and approval and contains incorrect and misleading information ... my firm has no instructions to enter into any further communications with you.'

The first letter was signed in biro and the indentations showed it to be a genuine signature not a stamp. The second was signed in ink which the spit test also proved to be genuine.

Not only did Mr C. V. Bulmer not know anything about CFAs or what his Associate was up to. He didn't even know what he was up to.

TWELVE
August 2004–December 2006

'Some third person decides your fate: this is the whole essence of bureaucracy.'

Alejandra Kollontai, La Oposición Obrera

As the Court had spectacularly failed to help define the boundary line on the ground, Max and Lucy had to find another way to sort out where their (de)fence should be erected. The first objective after the costs hearing was to persuade Land Registry to amend Homestead's Title plan so that it did not conflict with Dyer's ruling, but the first problem with that was Dyer's refusal to clarify the reasons for his decision. Then Lucy referred to her bible (O'Hare and Browne version) and discovered that Alfred Dyer, or Fred as they called him in their more forgiving moments, should have written, signed and sent a form[1] stating his reasons for refusing them right to appeal. It took calls to the Court and a lengthy letter to Fred to finally extract the completed form – some nine months after it should have been sent. It said, 'The Clmts' case was that they could rely upon a plan produced by HMLR rather than the one signed by their Csl incorporated into a Consent Order – no real prospect of success upon the basis of the evidence and submissions. *Henderson* v *Henderson* applies.' They had not been relying on the Registry's plan; they had argued on the basis of both plans. The Court Officer suggested that this was a 'further' copy, but Lucy pointed out that she had inspected the court file the previous March and more recently had asked the same officer to check the file for it and neither of them had seen it. If it wasn't newly minted, Fred must have been hiding it somewhere.

After Alfred Dyer had dismissed their application for an independent survey, Mr Brown at the District Office had changed his mind and agreed that the Registry carry out the survey – as long as Ogmore agreed. For once she did agree, but only if Max and Lucy paid for her 'surveyor' to attend. Max and Lucy could see no reason to pay for a survey on 'the Queen's highway' (Ogmore's roadside boundary) and their own land, but offered to do so *after* the survey *if* the Registry's report proved there was no trespass. Ogmore insisted on the money up front regardless of the outcome. *Impasse* again.

Why Mr Brown considered it reasonable to insist he couldn't honour his agreement to survey 'the Queen's highway' and a 60 foot line on Homestead's land *without* the squatters' agreement Max no longer cared, and when he learnt that Blackstone Cottage had been registered and that this had happened without any reference to the owners of the properties on either side despite all that had happened, he decided he had had enough of Mr Brown.

Guy Castor proposed that they get a court order for the survey they needed and ask the Registry to write to the Court agreeing the proposal without a hearing. Unfortunately, Mrs Cohen elected to write to the Court. Her lengthy letter was full of her fictitious account of the events of the previous three years: she asserted that Ogmore had *established* her paramount title to the land she occupied following her 'application to the Court for a declaration of the boundary'! Where did she get that idea? Lucy and Max had suspected that Ruby Cohen's failure to check the history, deciding instead to accept what she'd been told on the phone by Hazel Ogmore, had driven her actions all along. Lucy phoned her the following day to try to point out the errors. As before, she found herself interrupted before she could even finish a sentence. Mrs Cohen insisted her letter was correct, that she did know the facts and that Max and Lucy would have to argue the matter in court. Lucy managed to resist the provocation. She stressed in her opinion that matters are best resolved by discussion and not by confrontation. She then wrote to the Head of the Team asking for a meeting so that their complaints might be discussed openly and that so they might establish at least some agreed ascertainable facts.

The Man in Charge (MiC) wrote many weeks later after reviewing the file. He offered to pay the reasonable costs of both parties' surveyors to attend a further survey which would be carried out by the Registry. At last! Progress. Ogmore couldn't find an excuse to avoid it this time. They withdrew their application to the Court, which had been put on hold, so there was no charge. MiC wanted an explanation for Dyer's various decisions. As he already had the long-delayed form giving Fred's refusal to allow an appeal, they couldn't do more: they could not explain his decisions, only report them.

Initially, the couple found the Man in Charge more civil and accommodating than his lower orders. He remained civil throughout, but this only partially compensated for standard HMLR rule-bound obstinacy. He invited them to see him in London, but when they got to his office they learnt that he had been summoned to the High Court (as witness, not accused) and the meeting they had hoped would resolve so many misunderstandings never took place. They did identify Mrs Cohen. It was not difficult as she was the one person in the large open office displaying serious hostility.

Max started the New Year with a four-page letter to MiC setting out their complaints about the performance of this public service made wealthy by the increasingly buoyant housing market. He ended with two options: (1.) the *quango* could refund them in full for their losses and re-rectify their title to reflect Fred's ruling so they could then erect a fence to protect their property; alternatively (2.) as their lawyers had repeatedly advised them to appeal Fred's ruling, indemnify them for the costs of Counsel's advice and if advised to appeal further indemnify them for the costs of the appeal. The reply took a month to arrive. MiC rejected both options (politely) – without giving reasons. Yet another *impasse*. He did suggest they put the fence where they thought it should go. Land Registry was obviously happy to leave their clients to fight amongst themselves. Max was abroad so Lucy replied: 'There appears to be incomprehension on both sides and your letter does not really advance our understanding of your position as it makes assertions without evidence and argument. We are dealing with ascertainable fact, not mere opinion.' This slightly nicer cop approach was no more successful than Max's nasty cop. MiC was too busy to meet. This final refusal to talk raised the query: was he really inadvertently detained in court on the day they went to London to see him? This time her reply was more pointed: 'It is not for the *client* of the civil court service or HM Land Registry's service to pay to remedy problems created by the under-researched and ill-thought out decisions of representatives of these public services. You suggest we put a barrier where we think it should go. We do not know where it should go – that's why we want a survey! On the basis of *our* surveyor's reports we believe it should go through the chalet.' She ended with the now familiar proposal of a proper mediated resolution of this tiresome business and wanted to know if the new LR rules, introduced in 2002, included a mediation service which she recommended in preference to expensive and unreliable lawyer-controlled litigation.

She then made a very special request. She referred to Mrs Cohen's imaginative story that Hazel Ogmore brought everything into court with an application for a court declaration of the position of the boundaries. 'We have never seen that application and know nothing of it. We would be grateful if you could forward copy.' Her disingenuousness paid off. MiC changed his mind and proposed a meeting. He had made all his false assumptions on inferences he had drawn from the Consent Order and information from Mrs Cohen. He had checked nothing. He was sorry if he had got it wrong. Had Mrs Cohen checked anything? Was she sorry if she had got it wrong? Apologies for the delays and time-wasting would have been accepted, had they been offered in full. Telephone calls ensued. Lucy proposed that if the Ogmores wanted to attend the projected site survey they should do so, but need not be bound by its results. If the survey finds that the rectified plan is wrong, let them have the extra square footage of land necessary to encompass the shed and re-rectify the plan to ensure they are no longer trespassing. If the Ogmores demur then leave their plan as is and let Max and Lucy have a new plan so that they can legally erect a barrier around the chalet and put an end to the whole silly business. Then HMLR can pay for all the trouble HMLR, Mrs Cohen in particular, has created. Different words, of course, same import.

Problem sorted? That would be too easy. Can't have the boundary going round the shed, says MiC, because it would not be a straight line would it? The boundary on the Consent Order plan is a straight line isn't it? Lucy's weary sigh could have been heard in the next village. If the shed crosses a straight line boundary, and the line must be kept straight then it has to be angled further on to Homestead land to encompass the shed. Ogmore would be getting considerably more that a few square feet of Homestead property and the riverside boundary would have to shunt even further towards Homestead? Lucy gave up on him and just went ahead with arranging the survey with the newly-appointed surveyor and with the Ackroyds at Dunroamin' who she still thought should be informed, particularly as the surveyor may need to access their land. The survey was finally set for the last day in March 2005, over two years and several hundred letters, faxes, emails and telephone calls after Max and Lucy first tried to persuade Land Registry to help sort out the problem they had played a big part in creating.

Two Land Registry surveyors turned up. So did James Nunn looking rather disconcertingly nervous much to Lucy and Max's alarm, as though he was not confident that his innumerable reports on the roadside boundary were about to be confirmed. Ogmore was at home, but refused access to her land or any cooperation. She did not give a reason.

The two surveyors reported that the shed transgressed. James Nunn was clearly relieved. However, it did not transgress anywhere near as much as his surveying had recorded and there was a moment of shock for him and Max and Lucy when the surveyors went several feet beyond the mark he had made to indicate the end of Blackstone Cottage's roadside boundary: Ogmore's fence was only nine inches longer than the Consent Order measurement, within the General Boundary Rules. James Nunn had got it seriously wrong. Only when the surveyors projected a boundary line downhill past the chalet did they agree that the chalet quite clearly crossed that line by several feet, but – and a big BUT it was – they could not confirm this as Ogmore had refused access to her land and they needed access to complete the job and provide finality. James Nunn wrote a report recording that both LR surveyors concluded that the chalet was trespassing over Homestead's downhill boundary – on the basis of the evidence available.

Nothing was forthcoming from MiC or Mrs Cohen or the two surveyors for a month. Yet another letter to MiC. Lucy reported the surveyors' statement that the HMLR plan did not encompass the chalet, 'which continues to encroach according to your plan but not according to the Judge's ruling. We are not prepared to offer any further parcels of land to the encroachers and any proposals you make should bear this in mind.' It was well into May and still the much-promised report had not arrived. Yet another letter from Lucy: 'Surely this matter, which has been in your hands since early 2004 and in Land Registry's in-tray since late 2001, is not so complex that further delay is justifiable.' They did not get the surveyors' report for another two weeks. MiC wanted to see it and think about it before forwarding it. Whatever he saw and thought resulted in an inconclusive report which made no mention of the clear and repeated statements by the surveyors that the downhill boundary cut through the chalet. Instead the report emphasised that without Ogmore agreeing access to Blackstone Cottage land they could not reliably locate the chalet. So, nothing was achieved. The boundary line on the ground remained unknown.

A lengthy, time-consuming letter from Lucy recorded that both surveyors had stated that the chalet trespassed, and then recorded the history of Ogmore's conduct. She repeated that neither she nor Max was prepared to give the thieves and attackers any more of their land.

Land Registry rules governing customer care required a reply within five days. No reply within five or even 15 days. When he finally wrote, MiC ignored the contents of her letter, said the LR plan was correct and he could not help further. The next and final stage would be a complaint to the Independent Complaints Reviewer.

Lucy had heard of the ICR and reports were not encouraging. Max was fairly certain it was not worth the work, but Lucy was now fully hooked on her research and had already begun her report; this would be another opportunity to investigate first-hand, and with *locus*, how the system works (or 'screws you up' as Max put it). She drafted a complaint as succinctly as she could and sent it in early July and received a response immediately. The Senior Investigations Officer, Colin Priest, began very well. He pointed out the role of the ICR and talked over her complaint in several telephone conversations; she was surprised and impressed with his work. He wrote to apologise for the delay in completing his initial investigation which was due to staff changes and shortages. She was sad when six weeks later Colin Priest wrote to apologise again for the delay due to the backlog of work and to report that he was leaving the Independent Complaints Reviewer (ICR)[2] and her case was to be handed to a colleague. It was early February 2006.

Stanislav Kerociewk, the new Investigations Officer, did not show any evidence of his predecessors' assiduousness and concern. In fact, he hardly showed anything at all until 13 months after she had lodged her complaint when he forwarded his response signed by the Independent Complaints Reviewer herself who, of course, would have no idea whether the report was accurate or balanced or fair. It was 20 pages long and would have required her to second review the evidence Mr Kerociewk listed. He started with sloppy errors of fact, including easily verifiable dates, and then gathered pace with irritating errors of judgement and very partial selection of evidence: There was no reference to Mr Brown's initial refusal to produce a rectified plan and his instruction that they all return to court for a new order. He glossed over the mess created by the Registry's failure to identify the five foot 'unclaimed' ditch at the right time. Needless to say, he completely ignored all record of Ogmore's conduct. He did refer to correspondence and telephone calls between her and Mrs Cohen just before the 'rectified' plan was issued thus confirming Lucy's long-held suspicions that their expansionist neighbour had whispered slanders in Ruby's ear at a key decision time. There were paragraphs referring to Max's ongoing negotiations for compensation which were not in Lucy's complaint, but which she now suspected had some influence on Mr K.'s attitude to a complaint he had not investigated. He completely ignored their application to the Court/DJ Dyer/Fred to order an independent survey because HMLR had refused to do so.

He pointed the finger at Scroggs and Cain: not HMRL's fault that the wrong plan was attached to the Court Order, 'they' should have gone back to court for the right one. He couldn't understand why Lucy and Max withdrew their application to the Court for a new order following the issue of Cohen's new plan. 'I'd have thought it was fairly obvious: we started the application because HMLR advised us to, but then the Registry pulled the carpet and floor from under us by producing the trouble-making plan we now have. We couldn't hope to persuade any judge, let alone Judge Blacker, that a new order and survey were necessary.' The final straw was his decision that Ruby Cohen's ill-informed letter to the Court represented a 'fair appraisal' of the situation. He made no mention of Lucy's complaint about Cohen's antagonistic manner. Lucy realised too late that she should have asked if the telephone calls with the lady had been recorded 'for training purposes', and if so, requested a transcript.

Mr K. emphasised throughout his report the challenge of surveying their steep terrain, the General Boundary Rules and the limited powers of HMLR as well as his own limited authority to investigate matters 'in the round'. He clearly considered actions and inactions by their lawyers to be at the base of all the problems and not failures by HMLR. These limitations and errors by others allowed him to dismiss most of Lucy's complaints because, 'boundary issues are extremely complex and subject to a number of interpretations'! He upheld two of the eight complaints he chose to identify: delays and the abandoned meeting with MiC, but apologies and compensation had wiped the slate clean. A poorly-researched and poorly-drafted report was hardly worth further effort and Lucy was glad she had not spent too much time on it in relation to other challenges, but she did indulge in a piece of sophistry before she filed all the papers away. She acknowledged his/her 'considered final opinion' and suggested that, notwithstanding the current constraints on investigators, he may have noted during his considerations certain underlying weaknesses in HMLR's service which might be addressed to improve it, in the public interest, and serve to promote a better understanding by the Registry of their duty of care to their clients when *guaranteeing* Title. She did get a reply. It was neither surprising, nor disappointing, nor impressive.

The ICR statistics for Land Registry complaints hardly encouraged optimism. In the year 2005-2006 fewer than 15% of complaints were upheld fully or partially. Lucy did not enquire whether the two complaints out of her eight which were upheld meant her case was 'partially' upheld or whether it came in among the 86% rejected. As for the independence of the Independent Complaints Reviewer: both Mr Priest and Mr K. came to their role *from* Land Registry and Mr Priest left to return there – promoted.

THIRTEEN
2003–2006: the Attack

'"What is truth?" said jesting Pilat, and would not stay for an answer.'

Francis Bacon Essays, Works V1: Of Truth

The ICR[1] complaint was something of a sideshow, mainly for Lucy's research. Their principal focus was on recovering costs which Max was tracking on a 'not a penny more, not a penny less' basis. Lucy helped but felt it was best left to him on a 'horses for courses' basis. She turned her attention to a more pressing concern for her.

Joe Ogmore's physical assault on them had left a nagging fear. What was Joe Ogmore's mental state? He had attacked them on land he had to know was not his. He appeared unfit. There was just one of him with his wiggly-ended trowel and there were two of them with a garden fork and a pair of secateurs. He ran, or lumbered at them. He didn't try to talk to them, he just chanted over and over again, 'Get off our land, get off our land.' Later events made it look like the attack was a deliberate strategy to get an injunction which would take the land ownership dispute into court and out of the hands of Land Registry, and Lucy did clearly remember seeing Hazel Ogmore say something to him as she crossed him on her way back to the house to 'telephone the Police'. It did seem that whatever she said caused him to change from a walk to a lumber and grab the trowel. On the other hand, he seemed highly excited. Max said his eyes were bulging and he was sweating profusely. Could he have been in his right mind when he attacked? Or was he just maliciously attempting to start an affray to give a judge good cause to issue an injunction? If it was all feigned why was he so careless for his own safety? He couldn't have known Max would not retaliate, but he might have learnt from his private detective of Max's very special training in attack and defence and he could have observed that Max was certainly a fitter man than he. Both Ogmores seem to display irrationality. The extraordinary skill at lying could be interpreted as just a skill to be put to bad use in enlarging their property without paying. On the other hand it could suggest a detachment from reality overwhelming sensible judgement. From time to time, not constantly, Lucy feared that this man could attack again. He had spent time in prison, he could know of people who could cause harm for a fee. There was no question, but both Ogmores had allocated the role of enemy to Max and Lucy. What if the enmity, the obsession and a detachment from reality combined to make a real and present danger?

Thanks to the stalemate the Court, lawyers and Land Registry had helped to establish, there was little hope of erecting an incontestable and effective barrier between the two properties, one which would protect them and yet not be construed as establishing a boundary. To avoid further contest it would have to be well on to Homestead land and not open to any challenge. Lucy felt vulnerable. Not all the time, she could usually talk herself out of it, telling herself she was overdramatising and should recover her inner cool, but from time to time she wondered if she was dismissing a rational fear.

Sergeant Edwards had kept in touch with them over the months after the attack. The crime photographer, a black leather-clad, dour man, captured the bruises on Max's inner arms caused by the trowel when Max put his hands up to protect his head, and the cuts and bruises around his right thumb where Ogmore had tried to wrestle the secateurs from him. The five or six short deep cuts on Max's scalp were originally the worst of Max's wounds and the best of the evidence. Unfortunately, from an evidence point of view, Max's impressive recovery system had dried up several of the cuts and the photos did not reflect the full extent of the damage. If Lucy had followed her brother's advice to get photographic evidence immediately they would have had a gory record of a bloodied Max. She had been too shaken to consider it and those were pre-smartphone days. The crime photographer's work did not capture the damage to Max's neck and spine by the thud on to the compost when Ogmore pushed him which exacerbated an existing neck problem. Years later Max's neck and shoulders are still constricted and painful. He still needs sessions with his osteopath.

Four days after being charged, Joe Ogmore had appeared before the magistrates. The Crown Prosecution Service had suggested that the case should be committed to the Crown Court. Ogmore's defence lawyer (C. V. Bulmer?) had agreed so the case was eventually set down for a hearing in March 2003. A lot had happened by the time it did come to court. Max and Lucy were embroiled in trying to extract themselves from the mess created by lawyers, Land Registry and courts, and were only vaguely aware of the criminal case until, a month before they were due to attend as witnesses, Sergeant Edwards asked them to meet him at the County Police Station to go through their Witness Statements and bring evidence they had to rebut any assertions Joe Ogmore's defence might chose to make. The CPS did not know the details of the defence, which could be withheld until the Court appearance. So Max and Lucy went armed with everything they thought could be useful: plans, Witness Statements, letters from the Swales and Rick Stone and the Ogmores' letter offering to buy the land they claimed to believe they owned. Also Mr Beige's succinct summary stating that no Claim for adverse possession or even rectification had ever been filed. Suspecting that the Defence barrister would work on blackening their characters just as Hazel Ogmore had done, they added the character Witness Statements of support from friends.

Lucy appreciated the help and good sense of the lady from Victim Support. Although Max hated the very idea of being a victim he was glad to know there was support for their witness roles in court from the Criminal Justice Support Unit. This was a first for both of them. All either of them knew about the Criminal Court Service was gleaned from TV dramas, not always a reliable source of information. They just hoped the Criminal Courts were more efficient than the Civil Courts. No doubt because it was better financed and more high-profile, they were able to find more help on the internet about appearing as witnesses.

They were rather unnerved by the lack of CPS preparedness revealed at the meeting with Sergeant Edwards, but he seemed confident telling them that his interview with Ogmore on the night of the attack had given him plenty of ammunition for the CPS barrister. They did not get to see the transcript of that interview until much later and when they did they could see a great armoury for the representative of the Crown to use. Ogmore's claims included: 'we did not know we didn't own all the land we thought we owned until these new neighbours accused us of trespassing; we have always used all the land we thought we owned and therefore have possessory Title; we have been dealing with our claim with Land Registry; the new neighbours jumped the gun while our application to Land Registry was being processed and threatened to pull down the shed; my wife called the Police and the officer told these neighbours to stop removing any more of the fence, but they went back after he left and pulled down even more.'

All these assertions could easily be proven lies with the evidence available to the CPS. His record of the actual attack, on the other hand, would not be so easy to challenge, there were no independent witnesses. With that it would be a case of he said, she said, he lies, she lies. All the 'evidence' was in the Witness Statements. Nearly all. There were also the police photographs of damage to Max, and the complete lack of damage to the accused. Ogmore denied he had any implement. He decided to swap the weapons of choice giving Max the fork and Lucy the secateurs, no doubt to support his claim that Max had started the 'affray' by prodding him with the fork. He admitted that he had not sustained any injuries and he was not aware that the fork had actually touched him. The transcript then went on to record an interesting display of police interview techniques.

Up until then, Sergeant Edwards had let Ogmore have the floor only prodding him with gentle questions. Then the tempo speeded up TV drama style. PS Edwards cornered him using his own words. As when Ogmore claimed that he had merely pushed Lucy's shoulder because she was lunging at him with the secateurs. PS Edwards challenged the physical logic. If he, unarmed, was being threatened in such a way with a potentially dangerous weapon why would he go towards the threat? If she was holding secateurs and lunging at him she would be over an arm's length away, 'How come you then went into range of her secateurs in order to push her? You haven't got particularly long arms and how do you explain the reddening around her ear and jaw line?' Ogmore said that Lucy, like Max, must have got all her injuries pushing through the bushes to come on to his land. 'But these were not scratches,' said the Sergeant, 'the injuries were all in one place; swelling and redness commensurate with being hit or punched.' Joe Ogmore could not explain that any more than he could explain Max's injuries apart from, 'They must have got their injuries pushing through the bushes.' He absolutely denied that he had anything in his hands. He certainly did not attack Max holding a trowel. Sergeant Edwards always seemed concerned that although he had looked carefully he could not find the trowel with the wiggle at the end. They had assured him it was unlikely he would. It was far too easy to hide in the undergrowth and both Ogmores were lawyers (she a personal injury specialist); they would know they had to deny and lose the weapon. Nearly two years later Lucy found that trowel – by the shed on Ogmore land, she was trespassing at the time. Max took a photograph of it in situ. 'Not conclusive proof to convince a court of its existence,' says Lucy, 'but satisfying all the same. Strange they didn't get rid of it altogether as we had assumed.' Lucy still has the photograph.

With or without the trowel, PS Edwards from Tyneside had quite enough from the interview and physical evidence to bang Joe Ogmore up overnight and charge him the next morning. His solicitor, the one and only C. V. Bulmer, had then got him released on bail until trial in March 2003.

The Crown Court was an hour and a half drive away. As they entered the vast Victorian lobby, they observed among the milling crowd a thin, young-looking man with a blond quiff hunched over papers on a desk in front of him. He looked like a sixth-former taking an exam. He was wearing barrister gear and when he looked up and caught Lucy's eye he knew that his clients had arrived and she knew that this was the CPS's man (or boy). The case was much delayed. It would not be heard until after lunch. They could see the Ogmore team huddled round a table crowded with papers and coffee cups. A different barrister for this crime, no Mr Stoat in sight, instead a very smooth and distinguished looking gentleman accompanied by his junior. They all seemed quite assured when Max and Lucy first looked their way, but as the hours went by they seemed to lose some of that confidence. One possible cause was the loss of a key witness. Police Constable Northcote was the cheery policeman who knew something about squatters' rights, and when summoned by the Ogmores to arrest Max and Lucy (for removing two fence panels) had a better idea and suggested to Max and Lucy that they may like to take down all the remaining panels which were unequivocally on Homestead's land, warning them to leave the skeleton posts behind and not to damage them. Ogmore asserted that PC Northcote had advised Max and Lucy not to touch the fence, and they had ignored his warning. Now Joe Ogmore's smooth and distinguished (looking) barrister had finally, in the Crown Court lobby an hour *after* the case was originally listed for hearing, read PC Northcote's Witness Statement and realised why the Constable had wondered over to the Prosecution table and was engaged in friendly chatter with Max and Lucy. His Statement recorded what he had actually said and done and fully contradicted Joe Ogmore. Mr Smooth Barrister told Mr Northcote to go home, he would not be needed. Steve Northcote left reluctantly; he really wanted to watch the trial. The Defence Team was diminishing. Apart from the Ogmores and Mr Bulmer, there was just one other; an intense, academic-looking gentleman who the Prosecution Team decided was Joe Ogmore's expert witness. This gentleman apparently believed Max's injuries were caused by his fall on to the dry compost.

Max, Lucy and Police Sergeant Edwards found that idea amusing; they had seen the injuries and they had seen the compost box. Boy Barrister did not understand the joke, he had seen neither. From other things he said, it was becoming disturbingly likely that he had not done his homework. All he had seen were the expert's report, the Witness Statements and the photographs of the damage taken 44 hours after the attack, together with the various Statements by Max's doctor and osteopath also made some time later. Max's unusually good repair system worked against him for once. The blood had stopped dribbling even before PS Edwards had arrived on the scene; by the time the photos were taken much of the bruising had faded. The doctor's record described the short, deep cuts to Max's head as above his right ear whereas the photos showed most of them, correctly, on the top of his head. None of the photos was dramatic. Boy Barrister made a couple of phone calls to the Area Senior Crown Prosecutor but did not explain why.

When, eventually, the tannoy called *Regina* versus *Ogmore* both sides were a little weary. Joe Ogmore trudged into court with the Prosecution and Defence teams. Lucy, Max, the doctor and Police Sergeant Edwards had to wait with the lady from the Criminal Justice Support Unit (CJSU). She had thoughtfully taken Max and Lucy to look at the courtroom so they would have some idea what to expect. Hazel Ogmore waited on her own.

Some time later both teams returned. The Judge had decided that if the Prosecution or Defence wanted to continue they would have to do so some months into the future. The current trial which had been expected to end the previous day was still ongoing and he would have to swear in a new jury. Then Boy Barrister reported that the Judge, having looked at the papers, expressed misgivings about the trial continuing saying jury trials are always difficult when dealing with neighbour-on-neighbour attacks. Max suspected that Boy Barrister was nervous about his upcoming court performance. He went to make another call to the Area Senior Crown Prosecutor and returned to announce that the CPS agreed to a ruling without trial for Ogmore to be bound over to keep the peace. Lucy was relieved to avoid a possible attack by Mr Smooth Barrister in open court; she'd been wondering if she would perform as well as Mrs Britton had 20 years earlier in the fence-post saga, but this still left her concern about Ogmore's mental stability. 'Could the Judge order that Joe Ogmore has to have counselling sessions? He lives just too close for comfort.' Both Boy and the woman from the CJSU regretted that it was simply not a possibility. The two teams and Joe Ogmore went back to see the Judge, and 20 minutes later the Prosecution returned to the table to report that Ogmore had been bound over, adding that should have some effect on his future behaviour. Lucy remained fairly relieved but Max was not. Boy Barrister did not want to discuss things in the lobby so they were invited into a court antechamber. Once inside they were vigorously assured by all that their version of events was uncontrovertibly true and believed and that Ogmore was lying, but they were also told that juries were very unpredictable and might be impressed by the expert's opinion.

At that Lucy ran to a chair – one with arms:

> 'This is the compost bin OK? It's slightly higher off the ground than the real compost bin but the sides are about the same height. Now show me how Max could have got those five or six short deep cuts, not scratches, on the top of his head falling backwards on to the compost.'

There was a moment of realisation on Boy Barrister's face. His fresh, young skin turned very pink. He could see it was impossible. *Now* he could see, *after* he had accepted Joe Ogmore's agreement to be bound over. As a result of not doing his homework, of not asking the right questions, of not talking about the case with the only witnesses to the attack, the victims, he had let both Joe Ogmore and his expert witness off the hook. He had not done enough homework, enough prep. He had failed the exam and he had failed the victims of criminal assault.

The expert witness's report was nine pages long. The first six were entirely taken with his CV: his academic qualifications; his scientific and other academic publications; his memberships of committees, working parties and societies. Under 'outside interests' he listed just one: detective fiction. The next two pages were taken up with listing the evidence. On page nine, the last page, in the final two paragraphs he dismissed Max's injuries as trivial and came up with his theory on how the damage was done. Max thought it interesting that a man with such self-regard, who had never seen him, would have the self-assurance to pronounce in a court of law before judge and jury on secondhand evidence. He could have been taken apart by any reasonably well-prepared barrister but in 2003 expert witnesses still had a lot of credibility, which they sold at a good price.

Max did not share Lucy's view of the outcome and two weeks later they received a letter confirming Max was right. Hazel Ogmore, masquerading as her boss, C. V. Bulmer, wrote to tell them triumphantly that her husband had been 'found' not guilty of either ABH or common assault, that his agreement to be bound over was neither an admission of guilt nor a conviction, that the criminal prosecutions set in motion by their 'untruthful allegations' were fully refuted by Mr Ogmore's 'distinguished forensic pathologist' who had concluded that Max's injuries were sustained when he fell into the compost bin. Max moved from discontent with the CPS, Boy Barrister and the Criminal Justice Service –

to fury with them all. Attached to her letter was a copy of the Court Statement. It did indeed say 'Not Guilty'. How on Earth could this be? Was the thug now not only getting away with being merely bound over but actually claiming that he was *found* innocent of both charges, and that Max and Lucy had been lying?!

In cold anger Lucy wrote the same day to the Area Senior Crown Prosecutor enclosing a copy of Ogmore's letter and asking what action they should take to set the record straight. The Senior Prosecutor chose to reply to selective parts of both letters. It was true there was insufficient time to hear the case that day and it would have had to be listed for two months hence. The CPS did not agree the expert's report and let Bulmer & Co. know this, warning the Defence that the expert would be challenged at trial. As there was no trial there was no finding of fact as to the allegations in the case. When Joe Ogmore agreed to be bound over the Judge ordered a not guilty verdict. So! A Judge, who knew even less of the facts than Boy Barrister, had let Ogmore off with a 'Not Guilty' verdict. The Senior Prosecutor's letter went on to claim that Boy Barrister had been their man at all stages of the criminal charges 'so he was very familiar with the case', but paperwork showed that another barrister had represented the CPS at the Magistrates Court. It was not surprising that Boy B was feverishly trying to gen up for his role in court when they first saw him on the day of the trial. Not surprising that he was pleased to avoid the task altogether with the arrangement agreed by Prosecution and Defence. Once again Max and Lucy had been let down by two barristers from the same Chambers failing to master the file.

It was later, over two years later that a further attempt to explain the system was offered by the Head of the Crown Court Team. He confirmed the previous account; the Judge could not hear the case that day, but he then tried to explain how the Not Guilty 'verdict' came about: 'In the case of a bind over, this is always done by the prosecution offering no evidence on the original criminal charges and the Court then entering a formal verdict of Not Guilty in respect of that charge. A formal verdict is not a verdict decided upon by a jury. A bind over is not a criminal conviction and it is correct to say that as there was no trial, there was no finding of fact by the Court as to the allegations in this case.' Not an explanation that consoled either Max or Lucy. It seemed to them that some other wording could be found that made clear that no trial had taken place and that there had been no finding of fact either way. If Lucy and Max had been alerted to the possibility that Ogmore would be able to boast that he was 'found' not guilty – and then add insult to injury with his claim that the expert's evidence had triumphed and that Max and Lucy had lied, they would have … what could they have done? They were only 'witnesses', and victims. The Criminal Justice System decides the rules.

Just after the non-trial they had been contacted by the helpful lady at Witness Support urging them to claim criminal injuries compensation from the Criminal Injuries Compensation Authority (CICA). They had not thought of this, but she was most insistent and they began the process some weeks later making a claim with the Glasgow-based agency for Max's injuries. It took quite a time and involved more medical evidence, but they finally reached an agreed sum and so several months later Max received the first payment into their 'costs recovery' account.

There was one consolation offered by Boy Barrister. As there had been no trial, they still had the option of making a claim in the civil courts. For most of the year they were fully embroiled in dealing with the consequences of previous experiences in the civil courts so this suggestion was ignored, or kicked into the future. But with litigation as with life, the future has limits.

Most civil cases should be brought within six years of the Claimant realising they had suffered loss. For personal injury cases that limit is reduced to three years, so by July 2005 Max and Lucy had to make a decision whether to go back to court or live with the injustice and, in Lucy's case, apprehension. They both agreed they did not want to put themselves at the mercy of the Courts again, but they did want an acknowledgement of the evidence that had been withheld from the Criminal Court proceedings. They wanted a stop on the Ogmores' claim that Joe Ogmore was not guilty and that Max and Lucy had lied. Lucy was more concerned to see just how much of a threat Joe Ogmore might be. They knew that what they wanted for that, in fact for everything, was mediation, but how to get Joe Ogmore to agree? During the four years of Max and Lucy's dealings with their land-grabbing neighbours, mediation as a form of ADR had become mainstream. Many litigators even in the backwoods where they lived knew of it and most were not happy about what they saw as a threat to their livelihoods. ADR = Alarming Drop in Revenue was the not-so-funny joke among certain of the legal business fraternity.

In 2004 as a precaution, just in case, Max and Lucy had persuaded the two police officers mainly involved, PS Edwards and PC Windsmoor, to write reports of what they knew, and also got PC Northcote to agree that they could use his Statement which had been prepared for the Defence in the criminal case but which, in the event, would only have been useful for the Prosecution. They also obtained the transcript of PS Edwards' interview with Ogmore. Obtaining other evidence proved more troublesome. They found themselves in the ironic situation whereby Ogmore, the Defendant, had all the papers from the criminal case, but they could not access the papers from the Prosecution, and the Police could not disclose evidence from their file to anyone except for police purposes. The Force Solicitor who imparted this information was most apologetic, but regretted that the situation was inherent in the procedures. Max observed that justice was hamstrung by situations inherent in the procedures.

In July 2005 they finally came up with what they thought would be a fairly painless way of achieving their objectives. They would make a claim in the Small Claims Court and then propose mediation. Ogmore could ignore the mediation proposal, but would have to respond to the Small Claim and hopefully the judge would agree to recommend mediation – they could not be so unlucky as to encounter another version of District Judge Dyer. They started with a brief letter to Joe Ogmore asking for an apology and £500 for distribution to a charity of their choice. They received a reply immediately in inappropriate large print: Joe Ogmore was very sorry that the events of three years ago were still a cause of upset. He reminded them that the prosecution had been withdrawn and the Crown had paid his costs. He wished them well for the future and trusted everyone could move on. Max and Lucy did not find themselves keen to move on, being patronised by a thug and a liar may have had something to do with it. They checked with the Court about the rules for Small Claims and just managed to get the Claim into the nearest court in the county town before the deadline. They asked for an apology and £1,000 in token compensation. Ogmore/Bulmer contested the Claim. Bulmers now had an additional Assistant Solicitor bringing the firm up to three in number. An Associate who had joined the firm a year or so previously had become a Partner and it was she who was fronting this action. Hazel Ogmore had been a Law Society Panel Solicitor for personal injury before she retired and presumably still had some expertise in the area. They were not surprised to find that the new Partner, Tracey Wormelow, wrote in a style identical to Mrs Hazel Ogmore. Ms Wormelow wanted a large quantity of documents including all medical reports. Lucy replied that she was happy to oblige, but asked for the Civil Procedure Rules (CPR)[2] stating that medical reports were required at the time of issuing the Claim. She enclosed a copy of their completed Allocation Questionnaire where Ms Wormelow could see a request for a stay of one month to attempt to settle the Claim either by informal discussion or by ADR. As all correspondence would now go straight to Bulmer without passing through Ogmore hands, Lucy hoped to persuade the, as yet unknown, Tracey Wormelow, to meet up so that a few truths could penetrate the miasma of untruths created by the Ogmores, now aided and abetted by Keith Stoat. He was back.

Max and Lucy were cheered by Ms Wormelow's response. Her client agreed to one month's stay to enable mediation to take place. Lucy tried again to persuade her to meet up and clarify matters and hopefully save expense, but her attempts failed. Bulmer & Co. appeared unwilling as ever to talk face to face. Were they fearful, if so of what? Or were they instructed?

Now there was the task of finding a mediator in the region. It seemed fortuitous that the search coincided with a national campaign to promote mediation and the county town Court put them in touch with a brand-new service in the town itself. The same town where Bulmer & Co.'s office was located. Having first checked the nascent website of 'BetweenOurselves', Lucy had a pleasant chat with the coordinator, Elaine Boyd, about two mediations: this one with Joe Ogmore and another with the Swales, who had also agreed to attempt a mediated resolution of the Claim against them (for stating falsely on the Seller's Property Information Form that they had not been notified of any disputes). Both contracts seemed to be progressing although there were two momentary glitches with each: the Swale contract looked for a while as though the Swales themselves would not attend but planned to leave everything to their solicitor; however, Mrs Boyd finally assured them that both Swales would be there. With the Ogmore contract, Max and Lucy did not want the lawyer mindset mediating, they wanted to test whether or not Joe Ogmore was a serious physical threat as Lucy half feared. The expertise they wanted from the mediator was to be found more in the psychiatric field than the legal. Lucy had explained this to Mrs Boyd on first contact so she was a little dismayed to read in the first letter from her, 'You have asked us to provide a mediator with a legal background.' Lucy telephoned to correct the misunderstanding.

The civil tone in Mrs Wormelow's last letter disappeared in her next. She had changed back to her Hazel Ogmore impersonation. It was as intimidating and demanding as any from the genuine model. Lucy noticed that the signature was the same as on most pre-Ms Wormelow letters, so, who wrote it? Despite the provocation, a week later Lucy managed to secure agreement on a mediator.

The Court, however, intervened to ensure that nothing was ever so simple. Stoat had submitted a response on Joe Ogmore's behalf to the Claim Lucy and Max thought they had lodged in the Small Claims Court. *Henderson* v *Henderson* was once again in play. A District Judge in the county town Court ordered that their Claim be struck out. The Rules allow that when a claim is struck out on a Judge's own initiative without a hearing, the Claimant can challenge the Order as long as they do so within seven days. A mediation process is not precluded by any court decision; nevertheless, they felt it wise to challenge the Order.

Their Statement pointed out that: (1.) mediation had been agreed as had the mediator; (2.) the subject of the Claim had not been the cause in any previous action; (3.) the case had never been heard let alone adjudicated before any judge or jury and (4.) striking out a claim without due investigation where the substance of the Claim has never been addressed in any form of dispute resolution procedure at any time, does not resolve a civil dispute between neighbours. They acknowledged that they had failed to number their paragraphs according to the rules so their Claim did not 'conform to certain rules or practice directions.' They denied that their Particulars of Claim[3] were 'prolix and contained irrelevant averments', but welcomed further explanations of the accusations. They warned that certain (Ogmore-style) Statements in the Defence would be strongly challenged.

On costs they pointed out that although the Claim had not been allocated to a track, it had been lodged in the Small Claims Court and met the requirements of that track, and the Defendant, himself a lawyer as was his wife, did not need representation by his wife's old firm or the services of Counsel, particularly as his wife had been placed on the Law Society's Personal Injury Panel; the costs were being raised artificially high and disproportionate to the Claim; the parties were not on an equal footing. Max's Witness Statement replayed the complex history as succinctly as possible for a judge who came to the case ignorant of the back-story.

The hearing took place some seven weeks later, and thus Max and Lucy met Judge number seven: District Judge Andrew Carmine. No sign of Ms Wormelow, Mr Bulmer, Scoundrel Stoat or either Ogmore. Nor of any Defence documents. As Claimants they should have received the Defence at least a week earlier, but nothing arrived. Lucy knew it had been delivered to the Court. She herself had witnessed the delivery by Joe Ogmore in person on the very day when the mediation with the Swales was taking place in the self-same courthouse. She had been in the Court office when he walked in and handed the package over.

So, it was just Max and Lucy and District Judge Carmine at the hearing. The transcript does generate some sympathy for the beleaguered Judge. The Claimants were grasping in the dark for the essence of the Judge's enquiries. Not knowing what the Defence documents said, they could not follow the line of questioning. However, Judge Carmine managed to make some sense of it all, with limited help from the Claimants. Lucy was unaware of Stoat's precise reason for invoking *Henderson* v *Henderson* and was confused – and confusing. She failed to understand at first that his argument hinged on the DIY Defence and counterclaim they had hurriedly written for the first hearing with District Judge Not Dyer. Only when she realised that was she able to point out that they had cited *Mrs* Ogmore in the documents, not *Mr* Ogmore. Tweed's version, which was clearly identified as the substitute for theirs, made no mention of Joe Ogmore nor any reference to the attack, and it was his version which was the one in play when Scroggs signed the (non-) Consent agreement.

Aware they had not seen the Defence papers, Judge Carmine began by reading from the Ogmore/ Wormelow/ Bulmer/ Stoat letter which reiterated the all too familiar argument for striking out their Claim, referring not just to the 'Consent Agreement' but also to the work of Judge Dyer, 'Although these (latter) proceedings were specifically on the land dispute,' the Judge read out, 'an alleged assault was also *pleaded*.' Interesting word, 'pleaded'. In ordinary English 'to plead' is 'to ask for something'; 'to beg', 'to implore'; it does not mean 'to mention', 'to refer to' or 'inform'. It would appear that in litigation English merely to mention a fact means to plead. Litigation games-players have fun with such abuse of the English language.

The Judge accepted that Max and Lucy were not trying to re-open the land issue and that what they wanted was an apology, which he could not order 'and damages for an assault, which, if proved, in the normal course of events would be a perfectly ordinary straightforward claim.'

Once Judge Carmine had established that they were not time barred (by one day!), he reinstated their Claim saying that he had struck it out for the wrong reason. He allowed three months for mediation and a further three months if needed. If the mediation failed they could reinstate the proceedings.

Max was still irritated by the latest Ogmore trick of failing to copy them with the Defence papers. Judge Carmine could see this was unfair and he was not pleased that he had been misled about the Consent agreement. However, he warned them that they might still fall foul of *Henderson* v *Henderson*. They might still be challenged on the basis that Joe Ogmore should have been included in the earlier proceedings. He did not elaborate and they did not think to ask him to explain. There may still be a proper reason for striking it out. They wished each other a merry Christmas and a happy New Year.

Just into the New Year, 2006, Bulmers sent a letter indicating their discontent with Judge Carmine's decision. They claimed to have sent Max and Lucy copies of the Defence pack and demanded copies of documents, mainly medical reports, from Max and Lucy. That was followed by a 'Without Prejudice' letter offering to settle for £500. The letter referred to Max's pre-existing condition and that the offer was 'made on the basis of no admission as to liability, but solely to bring to an end the protracted disputes'. This presented a quandary for Max and Lucy: the whole point of the Claim was not money but acknowledgement of the facts and to test the mental stability of their neighbours. To accept the offer would not advance either objective. To accept would achieve nothing, besides; Max and Lucy had learnt to be very wary of any 'Without Prejudice' negotiations with these people.

Lucy's reply to the first letter pointed out that the documentation demanded was not required when lodging an application in the Small Claims Court, but she sent some 40 photocopied pages anyway. To the second letter she replied that both Max and she would normally rely on 'Without Prejudice' negotiations, but the unfortunate experiences they had had when dealing with Bulmer & Co. clients had led them to ask that all negotiations be in open correspondence. They were beginning to think that on balance it might be wise to accept an open offer, give up on truth and justice and just hope Lucy's fears about Joe Ogmore were misconceived.

Then BetweenOurselves pulled out of the mediation. The mediation they had organised with the Swales had failed. The Swales had gone to the mediation venue but refused to meet and talk to Max and Lucy sending their solicitor instead. He was not the mediating type. Nothing had been achieved except that Max and Lucy learned first-hand some of the impediments to successful mediation: the pressure to mediate is often filtered to potential users through litigators who have other objectives; and a mediation requires a skilled, committed and, ideally, talented mediator. On their feedback form they had carefully avoided any criticism of the ex-solicitor mediator, and restricted themselves to general observations about the process and incidental concerns like the physical space – the two, tiny, cramped rooms offered by the Court certainly did not help. Elaine Boyd had telephoned on receiving their feedback and as far as Lucy was concerned they had had a good, long, wide-ranging talk about the challenges and benefits of ADR, so this withdrawal came as a bolt from the blue particularly as it came in the short, final paragraph of an otherwise long, friendly letter recalling most of what Lucy had said and mostly agreeing with her. However, both Max and Lucy reckoned that they had learned enough about mediation and about the Swales and their solicitor to ensure the £250 was not a complete waste of money, and the preparatory work and the day *not* mediating a complete waste of time. Naively, Lucy had assumed that Elaine Boyd was committed to mediation, but slowly she became aware that Mrs Boyd was a businesswoman who saw in BetweenOurselves a way to cope with a potential threat to her main career – as solicitor.

Now they had to try to find another mediator. A combination of central government encouragement and training courses combined with some nervousness in the legal profession about future trends for their business had generated a mushrooming of mediation services. Most law firms had renamed their litigation departments 'Dispute Resolution'. Max and Lucy decided to opt for experience this time and selected a nationally known mediation organisation with an office in the region. The Court (Judge Carmine) agreed to an extension of a further three months so Lucy made contact with Open Talk UK. Initially things went well, but then through the grapevine Lucy heard Open Talk was on the point of losing government funding and staff were leaving. Nevertheless, a mediator was identified and in March Open Talk wrote to Ms Wormelow to arrange to talk with her by phone. Despite several attempts over a period of two months Ms Wormelow could not be persuaded to respond until in early May 2006 she replied to Open Talk to report that Joe Ogmore saw no merit in a further stay of proceedings for mediation. He had withdrawn agreement. She reported that her client had made an offer while waiting for the mediation to take place and the offer had been refused. She said that BetweenOurselves withdrew because they considered that the contract had been compromised and strongly implied that Max and Lucy were to blame. She did not copy her letter to Lucy and Max. If Lucy's contact at Open Talk had not forwarded her letter they would have known nothing about it.

Lucy wrote immediately to Elaine Boyd for an explanation of Wormelow's assertion that BetweenOurselves considered it had been compromised, and then to Tracey Wormelow reminding her the offer had not been rejected, but that Max and Lucy invited her to repeat it in open correspondence. She had misrepresented the facts. Elaine Boyd replied immediately by return: 'At no time did I or any other member of BetweenOurselves convey to Mr Ogmore or any representative of Mr Ogmore that "the mediator … had been compromised"'. So, Max and Lucy learnt a bit more about Joe Ogmore and it was not encouraging: like wife, like husband – they are a team. But what of Ms Tracey Wormelow?

Having rescinded his agreement to mediate, Joe Ogmore's next step was to get the Judge to rescind the Order extending the time for mediation and reinstate the case. He did not copy this correspondence to Max and Lucy who found out from a chance call to the Court a couple of weeks later. The Court forwarded copies of the correspondence which revealed several weeks earlier, on receipt of Ogmore's application, Judge Carmine had decided he needed a hearing for the application and a date in June had been set. Nobody had told Max and Lucy who found this failure by the Court compounding dubious conduct by Ogmore rather alarming, particularly as their worries about the Ogmores had increased following an incident in their woodland.

Walking along the wide lower path in their small wood one day in mid-April, Lucy was shocked to see that three large trees had been felled on Homestead land. Max joined her to inspect the evidence. As they clambered with difficulty over the steep terrain someone started throwing stones down at them. Evidence of Ogmores above. They called their local tree feller and a friend and neighbour from the Forestry Commission. It was agreed that the trees had been felled in the recent past, most likely when Max and Lucy were away. The tree feller tagged the remaining trees in the area and Max took photographs. The felling had cleared the view directly below Blackstone Cottage as the trees had been close to Blackstone's riverside boundary. For the first time Blackstone Cottage was fully visible from the path below. Max wrote in protest, it was all they could do without yet another court case, and nothing would put the tall trees back. Joe and Hazel replied true to type: they knew nothing about any tree-felling or stone throwing. They denied everything. They then added that they were pleased to observe Mr Goodchild had 'recovered sufficiently to traverse such precipitous and steep terrain'. Selective observation, they could see Max through the trees and bushes, but failed to notice that three trees had been cut down just on the other side of their boundary – revealing a better view of the river below.

What small remaining doubts Max and Lucy had about who was running the show at Bulmers were dispelled by subsequent letters on Bulmer paper. Not just the tone but the vocabulary was familiar. An attempt to patronise on the subject of 'without prejudice' negotiations caused amusement and an attempt to get more of Max and Lucy's medical records was easily rebuffed. The man in charge at the CPS had already told them that the Service had not provided the other side with any medical records which were not relevant. Max and Lucy had sent everything relevant and were disinclined to be bullied or intimidated by pompous letters from the Ogmores, who now objected strongly to receiving their tree-felling letter by hand delivery: only the Royal Mail can post a letter through the Ogmore's letterbox. Ms Wormelow informed them that she was instructed that in future she would only deal with correspondence relating to the court case.

Max wrote to the Court stating that they agreed the Defendant's application to set aside the Order granting an extension for mediation, and requested that the application be dealt with by correspondence rather than the arranged hearing. 'Clearly, if one party to mediation withdraws agreement, as they are fully entitled to do, no mediation can take place.' But then just three working days before the scheduled hearing, Ms Wormelow sent them a copy of a letter she had sent to the Court asking that the hearing be used instead as a directions hearing to allocate the case to a track.[4] Ogmore, for obvious reasons, wanted the case on the Fast Track; Lucy and Max for equally obvious reasons wanted the Small Claims track, they wanted a degree of control with a Small Claim. They had decided that if the Claim were moved to a judge-controlled track they would withdraw the Claim altogether. A hurried letter to the Court said they regretted they could not agree Bulmer's request and asked that for track allocation be decided at a later date which would allow them more time to prepare (letter copied to Ms Wormelow in the same post). Lucy phoned the Court twice to have confirmation that Judge Carmine had seen their request and asked for a warning if their attendance was required the following Monday. They had a meeting that day which they would cancel if absolutely necessary. They put their faith in Judge Carmine's sense of fair play.

A week later that they received Judge Carmine's next order. He reinstated his original striking out. He ordered costs to Joe Ogmore. Why had nobody warned them the hearing was going to take place and what on Earth had been said at the hearing to have brought this about? They asked to review the Court file – and to listen to the Court tapes. The second request was denied, they would have to order a transcript. As they had no idea how long the hearing was, they had no idea what a transcription would cost. The first request was also denied; they would have to identify what documents they wanted and refer to him for approval! How to identify documents they may not have seen and might not know existed was somewhat challenging. The Judge set a date in early September for a further hearing to review the matter. He also referred to yet another letter from Wormelow to the Court which had not been copied to Max and Lucy.

These vacillating rulings and Bulmer's transparency failures should have surprised Max and Lucy, but they were seasoned campaigners by now so, with Lucy's full approval Max wrote to the Court saying that they wanted to know what had been said at the hearing they missed so they could prepare for the review – it would assist everybody if they were better informed. He explained that they had been given permission to hear the tape for a past hearing which would have been invaluable had they known its contents at the right time. They asked what had caused the Judge to revert to his original Order? No reply. Max wrote a reminder. Still no reply. They heard nothing. The review hearing was imminent. Once again they were unprepared for a hearing due to lack of important information. What was the point of disadvantaging them in this way? What would be lost by ensuring that they were adequately informed?

The disadvantage was compounded on the day by a painful sore throat Lucy had picked up. They arrived at the small courthouse to find just two other people – a rather dishevelled man and a rather plump lady bursting from a shabby black suit. Neither was Joe Ogmore. The dishevelled man was summoned and went in alone, so the fat lady had to be Ms Tracey Wormelow. She refused to acknowledge them. Soon there were raised voices from the Judge's room and a bell rang with increasing panic. Then the dishevelled man threw open the door and stormed out banging the door behind him. The Court Usher finally responded to the bell but the dishevelled man had gone. 'I fear the honourable Judge will not be in the best of moods,' whispered Lucy.

She was right about that. The Judge was not a calm man. He announced that he was striking out their Claim because the matter had already been litigated. He had only reinstated the proceedings because there was an agreement to resolve differences by ADR. This had failed 'for some reason' so he duly struck the Claim out again. The assault 'formed the basis of the pleadings[5] in proceedings which were compromised, so the matter was resolved.'

Lucy agreed to be spokesperson despite her sore throat. A heated Judge and an annoyed Max might be a combustible mix. She began by pointing out that Joe Ogmore was not cited in their earlier Claim and that they had not 'pleaded' the attack. Judge Carmine did pause a bit on that, but then turned to Tracey Wormelow. 'Do you accept that this is not a matter that has been resolved by the Consent Order?' Ms Wormelow did not. He continued, 'You say it squarely falls within *Henderson* v *Henderson*?' She did, 'Absolutely, absolutely.'

Lucy tried again. 'We contend this is not a case of *Henderson* v *Henderson*. We did not make any agreement with Mr Ogmore. He did not turn up at any hearing. He did not provide a Witness Statement. He was not involved. The CPS was pursuing him on the assault.' She then made the serious error of saying what she really thought, 'I can understand that it would be convenient to dispose of this matter in this way but I do consider that the …' She got no further and from that moment on they had lost. District Judge Carmine was hot in his objection to the implied criticism ending with another request to Ms Wormelow to agree that the matter *should* have been litigated at the earlier stage. She absolutely agreed – yes.

If there had ever been any flexibility in Judge Carmine it had now disappeared. Lucy was on the point of reminding him that at their first hearing he had said that he had struck out their Claim 'for the wrong reason', but here he was striking it out again for the very same reason. Registering his sensitivity to criticism she stopped herself. She changed tack. She began an argument based on the new Civil Procedure Rules, on the need for a level playing field, proportionality, saving expense, etc. That got nowhere, the Judge was unmoved, he reiterated his judgment and added, 'And you pay the Defendant's costs.' He did seem prepared to bear in mind their Small Claim with regard to proportionality and costs.

Lucy's next tack was to focus on Joe Ogmore's games, starting with mediation, first agreeing and then withdrawing without explanation other than he didn't see the point, and the constant delays. She drew a blank there and was on the point of listing all the occasions when Bulmers had failed to forward correspondence and documents and the lack of transparent negotiation, when she was struck by this Judge's argumentative style and his partiality. This Judge liked an argument, was he an ex-barrister or a barrister *manqué*? He was clearly beginning to enjoy himself, now putting words into Joe Ogmore's mouth, arguing Joe Ogmore's case, Tracey Wormelow failing to do so.

Lucy abandoned argument and changed to talk of the inexplicable or at least the unexplained withdrawal of service by BetweenOurselves. Ms Wormelow couldn't explain it, Max and Lucy couldn't explain it ... 'But we suspect there may be a connection with the fact that they are a local firm of solicitors.' At this Ms Wormelow woke up, 'That should have no bearing on their role as mediators. We were absolutely surprised ... .' The Judge decided that was the most obvious explanation: a local firm would not want to get involved in a mediation involving a local solicitor. 'Perfectly understandable. But not Mr Ogmore's fault.' This was true and Lucy lost her train of thought. Later she drew attention to Ogmore's assertion that BetweenOurselves pulled out because they were compromised, and the mediator's swift rebuttal of the lie, but the Judge was not interested. He did not see anything wrong in Ogmore's disingenuous accusation. He thought that the 'without prejudice' offer to settle had been made at that point and Lucy's attempt to correct his misunderstanding and then elaborate on what had actually happened was curtailed by Judge Carmine now in full flow as Joseph Ogmore's Counsel: 'The only reason that I rescinded that strike-out order was because Mr Ogmore said, "I am quite happy to go down the mediation route." He could quite happily have said then, because I had made no bones about it I thought the case was an abuse of process, "That's the end of it." So to say he has been unreasonable when he gratuitously said, "Reinstate the proceedings so they can be resolved by mediation", is a bit of a big step to take, is it not?' The Judge had completely forgotten his own explanation that he had reinstated their Claim because he had struck it out for 'the wrong reason'. And Ogmore had never asked the Judge to reinstate the proceedings for mediation.

Max and Lucy were momentarily dumbstruck. Not so Judge Andrew Carmine now comfortably in Joe Ogmore's shoes. He would not be stopped. Lucy managed an exclaimed, 'Mr Carmine!' hoping to check him but on he went just pausing for breath at, 'I am quite convinced there has *not* been unreasonable conduct' (by Joe Ogmore) when Lucy managed, 'Well, I am amazed. I am amazed.' He told her she would have to stay amazed and pay all costs. He advised them to get advice from a solicitor or, even better, a costs draftsman. Lucy was genuinely amazed but recovered enough to enquire about the tapes for the hearing. His riposte was smart, 'You are entitled to get a transcript and you can have that with my blessing.'

Max passed Lucy a scribbled note: 'Scroggs' and Lucy remembered they wanted further confirmation from a judge, even this Judge, that Tweed and Scroggs had been negligent. Judge Carmine was not prepared to help, 'If you think they might be, go and get some legal advice about it.' Lucy indulged her irritation by letting Judge Carmine know that, 'The barrister had been found guilty of negligence anyway.' Which was true as will be revealed later. Judge Carmine said he was only concerned with their Claim for an apology and compensation for an assault. 'Which you have not considered on the evidence,' Lucy reminded him. And that was that.

So, Joseph Ogmore, Hazel Ogmore and those at Bulmer & Co. could now report that the Claim had been thrown out. They could even add, 'As abuse of process,' and few would know the truth. The form giving the reason for rejecting their application to appeal was missing from the General Form of Judgment, a repeat of Judge Dyer's failure three years earlier. This time they knew what was missing and asked for it. They had decided that there was good reason to test the appeal process beyond District Judge rejection level. The form eventually arrived with the predictable *Henderson* v *Henderson* explanation 'No real prospect of success on appeal'. They got their application in just on time. What followed were three weeks of work compiling and drafting documents: the Appellant's notice; the skeleton argument; the Witness Statements and all the attachments.

The appeal was transferred to the large Gothic courthouse 50 miles away where the CPS's charge against Ogmore had failed to be heard. Yet another Judge, His Honour Judge Pelt, judge eight, entered the arena. He wanted transcripts of the last hearing with copies sent to the Court and the Defendant. They decided to get transcripts of all three hearings before Judge Carmine.

Above all they wanted the transcript for the hearing they did not attend: the one the Court had failed to warn them was going ahead without them, the one no one had warned them would result in throwing out their Claim a second time.

They were not to know for some time, if ever. They were told that another of Judge Carmine's decisions was being appealed and as the tape for that hearing was on the same tape as theirs and was with transcribers, they would have to wait, but this should not cause a long delay. However, it did. The transcripts for their first and last meetings with the Judge arrived within a week of placing the order. The one they really wanted took two nudges and four weeks to reach them even though the transcriber managed to turn it out within one day of receiving the tape. When it arrived they were no more the wiser. They had expected a transcript of some length, after all Ms Wormelow would have had to persuade the Judge to rescind a second order and he would not want to look vacillating. Whereas the other two transcripts were fairly long: 68 folios (approximately 4,900 words) and 91 folios (approximately 6,550 words) this one was just one folio, 72 words and it told them nothing. The Judge was aware of their letter saying they agreed the Defendant's request and asking that any decision on track allocation be determined at another time, but was he aware that they had asked to be alerted if that hearing were to take place so that they could change arrangements to attend? The brief discussion amounted to no more than a review of Judge Carmine's various orders followed by an immediate decision to revoke the two Orders staying the proceedings for mediation and reinstating the Order to strike out – and order costs to Joe Ogmore. The Judge admitted that he might be 'dis-remembering', but he believed he had originally reinstated the Claim merely for mediation, so the original strike-out could be reinstated for the original reason: abuse of process. He should have been sent copy of the transcript for the first hearing with his words,'I struck it out for the wrong reason' highlighted.

Over the years since reading that transcript Max and Lucy remained mystified. Why had it taken so long to get to them? Why was so little said and why was there no consideration of their letters and requests? It was not until much later when Lucy started to review the Joe Ogmore Claim for her records that she spotted an even greater mystery that heightened her suspicions that something was wrong with that transcript: they had been billed for one folio (72 words) and that was about the size of the transcript sent to them, but the cover page by the transcriber stated that the size of the transcript was seven folios and 504 words. Lucy did try to investigate this anomaly but much too late, the transcription service only kept records for three years. No one could come up

with an explanation and, despite their suspicions, nor could Max and Lucy. All they could do was curse themselves for not attending the hearing.

In late November 2006 they received notification from the High Court of a 20-minute hearing of their appeal application adding only they should attend. Then two weeks later after sending two transcripts, an amendment to that order: 'If the Claimants' application is successful, the appeal hearing will follow immediately thereafter so *both* parties should thereafter attend the hearing at the time and place proscribed.' Max wondered if this amendment was a result of his memorandum attached to the copy of the transcript they had forwarded to the Court. The memorandum had listed five reasons for their appeal and drew attention to the part in the transcript of the first hearing where the Judge said that he had struck out their Claim 'for the wrong reason', and the part in the transcript of the third hearing revealing that he had thrown it out again for the same reason, which, apparently, had turned from the 'wrong reason' to the 'right reason'.

Wormelow objected that they had too little time to prepare. So, two weeks is not long enough for the professionals to prepare for a hearing but our litigants in person had been expected to cope with less than four days. Bulmers asked the High Court Judge to rescind the second Order and reinstate the first so if the appeal were allowed to go ahead it could be listed for a later date convenient to both parties. Needless to say, she did not copy her letter to Max and Lucy who would have been quite relieved to hear they might have more time for their appeal were they to be granted permission to make it. Christmas was coming.

The next Court Order informed them that the hearing on 15th December was postponed to a date yet to be arranged. Unfortunately, His Honour Judge Pelt did not agree Ms Wormelow's proposal that the permission to appeal hearing take place on the 15th with just Max and Lucy, and the appeal itself, if permitted, at a later date. A sensible proposal from her, but, perhaps, not one convenient to the Judge.

Then it was a case of arranging a date. The Court Session ended on 31st March 2007 and the Judge's Clerk was tasked with finding an agreed date before then. The Ogmores would not be available throughout the month of January but Max and Lucy would. However, *they* would not be available from early February until mid-March. A date was finally fixed for 30th March 2007.

FOURTEEN
2007

'Legalese is a poor tool for getting things done in today's world and a fine way of obscuring simple matters to the wonderment of the laity.'
Martin Cutts, Research Director, Plain Language Commission

January and February were Ogmore- and Bulmer-free. First, the Ogmores were away so, of course, Bulmers had no instructions, then Max and Lucy were away. The initial Bulmer-Ogmore contract was a rare one: it is not often that the client will be her own (schizoid) solicitor. This new Bulmer-Ogmore contract was also rare in that when Ms Wormelow wrote that her firm was instructed by her clients to say this or that, or to do this or that, she was stating the truth. Usually, lawyers publicly assert that they are following their clients' instructions when in fact it is the other way round.

In the event the appeal was only sparked into life two weeks before the hearing. Max and Lucy had anticipated what Stoat et al. would argue and had prepared their case during January. They had two folders of documents ready before they left for their tour, together with their brief 'Grounds for Appeal' and skeleton argument.

Their main argument, and they believed the clincher, addressed Stoat's all too familiar *Henderson* v *Henderson* gambit. This time it could not be applied because the Consent agreement was an agreement on Robert Tweed's *substitute* Defence which made no mention of the attack. Theirs, which had referred to it, was no longer 'on the table'.

They realised they would be on difficult terrain criticising a judge to a judge, but that's what appeals are, they could not avoid it, so they recorded the handling of their Small Claims application: Carmine's vacillations and contradictions. They described how Joe Ogmore scuppered the mediation by withdrawing agreement without notification, negotiation or clearly stated cause. Then how they had been misled by both court and the opposition about the hearing they missed: they were told they would be alerted if they needed to attend, but were not alerted and had no warning the original striking-out order would be revisited and reinstated, they had assumed for a different reason so they were in the dark at the final hearing until they realised that their Claim had been struck out on exactly the same basis as first time.

They also argued that there was insufficient time to prepare for the award of costs, that insufficient weight was given to the conduct of the parties and that they had lodged a Small Claim.

The files they prepared were heavy with supporting documents: photographs, CICA forms, Witness Statements, CPS correspondence and the five transcripts – three from Carmine's hearings, one from the Royal Courts of Justice hearing and one from Dyer's striking-out hearing. They had collated everything they could anticipate they'd need for one court chance to present their case, over 300 pages. All paginated and referenced and collated in three editions: one for the judge, one for Ogmore/Bulmer/Stoat (the Ogmore Gang) and one for themselves. Many days of work.

So they did not take kindly to Ms Wormelow when, just one week before the hearing but some three months after notification of the appeal, they received information that their opponents had applied to the Court yet again to strike out their application to appeal, and a Witness Statement by Joe Ogmore which introduced a new element to the argument. Now he (or Stoat) argued that as they had referred to the attack when asking Disaster Dyer to order an independent survey, they should have made it an issue in *that* application. Joe then gave his interpretation of Lord Bingham on *Henderson* v *Henderson*: the principle applies not only to matters that are in issue in proceedings but also those *which should have been in issue* in proceedings.

Joe went on to allege that Max and Lucy were seeking to go behind his 'not guilty verdict' in the CPS case. He followed that with, 'Counsel for the Crown had expressed his opinion that, in the light of the forensic report, and *other evidence,* the Prosecution could not proceed.' Counsel for the Crown (Boy Barrister) had said no such thing to them and the CPS Chief had offered another explanation, besides – what other evidence? The expert's report would be rubbished again, this time in court, if the Court would allow the appeal, but what 'other evidence' was there? Once again, no clarity, no transparency. Could it be true? Could Counsel for the Crown (Boy Barrister) have actually expressed that opinion to the Judge? They had not been allowed into the hearing so they could not possibly know. Joe Ogmore had his wife's talent for lying, but would he lie to the Court – like her? There was no way they could get a definitive refutation from any authority on these assertions in the time available. Four years had passed since the hearing, would Boy Barrister, now four years older and presumably four years wiser, be any help at such short notice? If he had these reservations why did he so emphatically insist that he believed Max and Lucy, and not Ogmore, even before Lucy's dramatic demonstration of the so-called expert's nonsense? There was nothing to be done in the time; they would just have to do the best they could on the day.

All their work now had to be revisited in the light of this very late submission and new versions had to be written, printed, collated and inserted and then delivered to the Court. Nothing for it, they would have to drive the 90 miles there and back and deliver by hand. As well as several urgent calls to the Court they also had to contend with a flurry of unfriendly emails ostensibly from Ms Wormelow referring to Practice Directions and threatening costs for any delays. They could not rise to every provocation there just wasn't time. Provocations were best ignored, besides which Lucy had been looking more closely at Lord Bingham's speech and could see argument both ways. She optimistically saw a way of turning the Ogmore Gang's citation their way, so they both retained some confidence.

Then, on arrival at court on 30th March 2007, they were handed yet another late submission by Stoat. They should have anticipated this trick; they knew the man of old. At least this time it was not a thick law report thrown at them in court. This was Stoat's Defendant's skeleton argument. As their case hearing was delayed for over an hour they had some time to read it. Experience had taught them not to be distracted by obvious errors of fact: Stoat constantly referred to DJ Dyer when he meant DJ Carmine; he asserted that both Homestead *and* Blackstone Cottage had large gardens; he got his dates wrong; he declared that their application before Judge Dyer was for possession when in fact it had been for an independent survey and removal of any identified trespass; he was predictably highly selective in his account of the history. He accused them of hoping to reopen the issue of land ownership.

One new argument rang alarm bells: Tweed had stated clearly that his Defence and Particulars of Claim replaced Max and Lucy's hastily written version, but Stoat asserted that as there was no order *permitting* Tweed's substitute, the original was still on the table: 'still extant whatever the later document might have asserted to the contrary.' This could knock on the head Max and Lucy's principle argument: the Consent Order arose from the Claims and Defence 'on the table' at that hearing in October 2002 which made no mention of the attack. 'Tweed and Scroggs between them may well have scuppered us – again,' said Max. As for the Court rule insisting on permission to substitute one edition for another, they didn't know whether or not Glorious Judge Gold gave permission, they didn't know if Tweed asked for it, they didn't even know if it was a rule.

'I think she *told* him to produce a substitute,' said Lucy, 'Cool move by Stoat handing this to us 30 minutes before we go in front of a judge and 45 miles from home where the documents are.' Back at home was Judge Gold's Order stating that Tweed *must* file a Defence. Although the word 'substitute' was missing, as he was ordered to produce a Defence and given the option of producing a counter-claim, surely permission had been given! But they did not have a copy of the Order with them and it did not occur to them to insist that Stoat show it to them before they went into court.

They knew nothing of this new Judge except that the friendly Senior Court Clerk had warned them that he could be irascible and had urged them to ensure all the documents were in order and clearly numbered. They had been clearly numbered until the late arrival of Ogmore's submissions and, of course, there was nothing in the files to address this latest, wet-off-the-printer attack from Stoat.

Lucy agreed again that she would do the talking, but was thwarted from the start. As the opposition now had a striking-out application before the Court, the Honourable Judge decided that Stoat should introduce the case. He then swept out of the courtroom in search of the Appellants' two files. He'd forgotten to bring their hard work with him. When he returned he became confused about where documents were and as he wanted Stoat to assist and not Lucy what followed could be read as a comedy script, but Lucy and Max had lost their sense of humour. Lucy, dismayed that Stoat was going to set the scene, felt obliged to interrupt and point out that they had only just seen his version of 'the history' and they disagreed with it. The Judge insisted that he would hear the background from Stoat and all Lucy could do was sigh deeply and let Stoat get on with it. Although, as Stoat tied himself and the Judge up in knots jumping from 2002 to 2005 and back and mixing all previous cases up, she did intervene once or twice to correct a year or a page number. She then realised that the Judge had the latest paginated version delivered just days earlier and Stoat had brought the previous version compiled before Ogmore's belated submissions. The pagination was different in each version! It *was* a comedy!

Lucy finally got her turn. The comedy dialogue continued, but this time both Judge and Lucy were working from the same pagination. As she feared, the Judge had had the scene set by Stoat and now she would have try to unset it. It took a few pages of comedy banter before she got some idea of what was in the Judge's head.

When he said, 'As far as I know (your original) Claim was never withdrawn,' she was able to respond: 'Well, I would have thought the words "This is in substitution for both Particulars of Claim between Defendants and the Claimants numbered XZ 123 is precisely that, sir. Page 23. That is exactly what is said.'

The Judge asked Stoat what he had to say to that and repeated the quote. Stoat was flustered momentarily. 'There was no *Order* permitting a substitution. A substitute pleading does not exist,' he protested. Here was the advantage of last-minute argument. Lucy had no hope of checking it out. She started to respond, but Stoat was still unsettled and interrupted, 'Sorry, the Judge is asking me a question at the moment, Mrs Graham. His Honour is asking me a question at the moment! No application was made to amend the Particulars of Claim.' Of course, Golden Judge Gold had ordered Tweed to amend the Defence and Counterclaim, but did this amount to permission to take their DIY version off the table? What a fiddly, silly nonsense! But it looked possible that it would scupper their Appeal. Here was another word for her foreign language (legal) dictionary. 'Substitute' could be added to 'consent', 'plead' and 'abuse'. In legalese, Tweed's 'substitute' document was not a substitute; in legalese you can be deemed to consent to something you would never consent to; in legalese you can be deemed to have pleaded something you had not asked the Court to consider: in legalese you can be accused of abusing the Court when absolutely no abuse had been committed – at least by you. Trick words sounding familiar but meaning something dangerously different. Lucy did not think to insist that Stoat provide evidence of the Order Circuit Judge Gold *did* make.

The only thing to salvage from all this was ammunition for their Claim against Scroggs, a battle which was becoming more heated and challenging. She had failed to persuade Carmine to help in that campaign, maybe this disconcerting Judge would oblige.

> Lucy: 'So, in fact this Defence and Part 20 Claim is *not* in substitution for …'
> Judge Pelt: 'Well, it says it is but it isn't. No. It can't be, you see, because you can't just do that I am afraid.'
> Lucy: 'So it is an error on the part of the lawyer?'
> Judge Pelt: 'Yes, I am afraid so. You can't just substitute. You can't simply say, "I am bringing an action to an end", you have got to get leave to do that …'

Lucy: 'So he should have done that.'
Judge Pelt: '… or the agreement of the other side.'
Lucy: 'He should have done that.'
Judge Pelt: 'He should have done that yes.'
Bingo!

Lucy then tried argument based on her understanding of the New Litigation Landscape where 'intention' is important and a 'just outcome'is important. It was not their intention to 'plead' the attack; they had not asked for damages for the attack, they had asked that Hazel Ogmore prevent any possible future attack.

Judge Pelt then gave his Judgment. Considering the amount of confusion he had displayed during the proceedings Lucy thought he was making quite a good fist of it at first. Nevertheless, having relied on Stoat to set the scene he did, of course, get quite a few facts wrong, and, of course, he left out all the facts Lucy and Max thought important. Mr Stoat had not thought them important so the Judge never heard them. But it was when His Honour Judge Pelt said he had not seen their very first Defence (the one Lucy thought had been withdrawn) that her admiration faded. Not only had he seen it, only a minute earlier he'd been quoting from it and it was that quote which had lost them their appeal. He had decided that that reference in their first Defence was indeed a 'cause of action' (more for the legal dictionary), as it was still on the table at the time of the Consent Order. Yet another impatient Judge, this one clearly anxious for his lunch (he had already mentioned stopping for lunch), he would not stomach further interruption. They would never be granted the time to put their version and correct the image of litigation-nuts Stoat had so predictably projected.

Then it was a question of costs. Lucy's argument: costs had escalated unnecessarily and in any event their Claim was lodged in the Small Claims Court where costs are a minor issue. The Judge asked her to tell him who was to blame other than them, for costs escalating unnecessarily. She decided against pointing the finger at the case managers, District Judge Carmine and HH Judge Pelt. 'Often litigation proceeds in a way which is nobody's fault but which somebody has to pay for, unfortunately,' he said. Managers who let costs get out of control can be sacked, but litigation is managed by judges and they don't tend to get sacked, or even lose any money. Lucy wanted to point out that they were hardly to blame, they'd lodged a Small Claim, stuck with mediation, worked to find an alternative mediator, provided papers on time to everybody, kept everyone informed, but HH Judge Pelt was focussed on Carmine's earlier warning that they, 'may still fall foul of *Henderson* v *Henderson*.' But not for the *same* reason, surely? Why had he said it didn't apply in December and then say it did six months later?

She managed quite well in resisting pressure from an impatient, hungry Judge from then on, but when he ignored her argument that if the mediation had failed and/or the case had not been allocated to the Small Claims Track, they would not have pursued it, she knew the gentleman sitting above her did not consider litigants had the freedom to make such decisions. Besides he was fixed on *his* decision and wanted to get to his lunch so she stopped, only saying, 'We have no interest in being reduced to penury by litigation as others have been. We have an interest in resolving a matter of grave concern to us because we have heard Mr Ogmore is claiming that (1.) he had been found 'not guilty' in the criminal case and (2.) we had lied. Neither is true. He was not *found* not guilty – there was no trial, and we certainly did not lie. We would have been content to agree things in private with Mr Ogmore through mediation or through a Small Claim.' She should have added, 'We do not know the man and we do not understand him, we only know he attacked us.' That might have given HH Judge Pelt food for thought if not his belly.

One small thing to His Honour's credit: in his summary at the end he did come very close to conceding his management of the appeal had added costs. But not close enough. Stoat then announced that he would not be charging for his services which drew commendation from the Judge. After the hungry Judge had swept from his dais and out of their lives, Lucy quietly thanked Stoat for his offer. The cold look of contempt she got in return confirmed to her that the offer had little to do with her or Max. It was obvious that Stoat had now fully grasped who might well find himself asked to pay his bill. Was Stoat beginning to regret his major role in the mess Scroggs found himself?

Ogmore/Bulmer costs Claim dragged on for the rest of the year. Max let Bulmers know right from the start they were claiming them back in full from Scroggs' insurers who would want to check them first. This was to put the brake on any imaginative accounting by whoever was drawing up the bill. Although neither Max nor Lucy thought that Ms Tracey Wormelow was that sort of imaginative lawyer, they were equally sure Joe Ogmore was. Lucy, on the other hand, was pursuing her report and took the opportunity to ask Ms Wormelow which of the two letters signed by Mr C. V. Bulmer in 2004 were genuinely from him. This was a wild card attempt to find out whether Mr Bulmer had signed a letter without reading it or whether his signature had been very impressively forged – she was still on the trail of the altered Blackstone Cottage conveyance plan and Joe Ogmore's proven proclivity for altering documents. Her attempt was predictably rebuffed by the enemy. Wormelow's Statement attached to the Bulmer Claim was so replete with errors of fact that Lucy took the opportunity to correct them, hoping that her efforts would give the lady pause for thought. It was well over a year later that Lucy realised that Tracey Wormelow needed more than a pause to get her thinking.

Max and Lucy paid up weeks before any court order arrived and turned their attention to recovery of outstanding losses from others. That, however, was not the end of the matter. Bulmers cashed the payment, but then activated two 'default costs certificates' which added an extra £250 to the bill. As the bill had been paid a few weeks earlier, Max assumed the two orders that arrived were typical results of court delays and they went into the file for Lucy's report. Some four months later letters began to arrive demanding not just the £250 but also £320 interest, followed up by the threat of bailiffs. Although these sums could just be added to their various claims against Malcolm Scroggs and others, as with the Land Registry indemnity cover, Max and Lucy were not prepared to just pass the costs on. They wanted explanations. Bulmer & Co. claimed they had sent a letter in July explaining these add-ons, a month after the firm had cashed Max's cheque. No such letter was seen by Max or Lucy. The copy they finally received from the Court Clerk raised questions. Why had the Court sent 'default payment' demands after payment had been made? Why hadn't any legitimate interest charge been added to the original Claim at the time? Now both Max and Lucy suspected that not Ms Wormelow but Mr Ogmore in full bullying mode was managing matters. If they wanted to challenge what they suspected were dubious claims they were told they would have to return to Judge Carmine for help – and pay a court fee for it. A fairly resistible proposal. They asked for an explanation from both the Court and Bulmers of these additional demands. They asked for copy of any order justifying them. All they got was a copy of the original Order. Could they spend more time on this? Was it worth it? Recovery was moving along and on the 'not a penny more, not a penny less basis', they were moving into the black, so they paid some to keep the bailiffs away, fully aware they were being bullied and fairly convinced the money was not owed, but the only way to sort it out was to invest both trust and money in the civil court system. Money they had, enough to pay what was demanded, trust in the Court of District Judge Carmine they did not have. They left it at that and for several months so did Ms Wormelow. A full year later, many months after they had forgotten all about it, Ms Wormelow rose from the dead and restarted demanding money with menaces, but by that time recovery was coming to an end and it looked as though they were likely to be getting a few pennies more, so both Lucy and Max agreed they would pay a bit more and Lucy would record this second attempt to extract money well after time. The first time Bulmers had tried this trick, Mr Castor's excellent paralegal assistant had seen Bulmer's Gang off with the weapon of some Civil Procedure Rule, but they had no such valiant defender this time and the sum of money was simply not worth the fight. Lucy suspects that Wormelow's ploy was not unique to her and therefore worth an entry in her report, but not worth testing the good judgement of District Judge Carmine.

Lucy was encountering difficulties trying to review the assault case file at the small local County Court. Access to the files at the first two courts had been fairly easy and had delivered invaluable results, but just as the tape of the hearing they missed eluded them for months, the same was happening with Lucy's review of the file. The helpful High Court Clerk could not find it and was sure it had been returned to the County Court. The County Court admitted they held 'some of the file', but was sure that the rest was still with the High Court. Several weeks later she was informed that both parts were now with the County Court, but that Judge Carmine wanted to check it first before releasing it for viewing. 'Somehow I don't think this is going to be such an interesting and valuable exercise as it has been in the past,' said Lucy. She was right. Apart from the two folders they had prepared for the appeal, it was quite a slim file and contained nothing of interest.

FIFTEEN
2007–September 2008

'Professional people have no cares
Whatever happens they get theirs.'

Ogden Nash

Most of the time they had available for the squatter problem was now spent on recovering costs, but such a mess had been made by HM Land Registry (HMLR) and the legal service-providers, not just the lawyers and judges but court personnel too, they still did not know where exactly to put up their fence. Six years on from first discovering they had a squatter problem, they still did not have an unequivocal, authoritative marking on the ground of any of the boundaries between themselves and the squatters, the most important being the one nearest them running down behind the shed. Ogmore bonfires were still smoking their trees and Ogmore rubbish was still littering their land, but the spraying and clearing seemed to have stopped. Or so they thought.

In October 2007 they came back after a few days away to find a short stretch of reed fence beyond the paving at the side of the shed on what appeared to be their land. It looked like the Ogmores were adding another strip of Homestead to Blackstone Cottage. James Nunn was certain that unless the boundary had a kink permitting it to skirt round the shed and its path, it had to cut through the shed. He had reminded them the two HMLR surveyors agreed with him. All three were confident that if the straight line boundary on the Hammer and HMLR plans was applied to the site the shed was trespassing.

The Man in Charge at HMLR had proposed they put a fence where they believed it should be. As Judge Dyer had frustrated their attempt to get an independent survey they were not certain where it should be. An option could have been to angle the line way into Homestead territory, but unsurprisingly

Max and Lucy were reluctant to give Ogmore yet more of their land. They considered they could do nothing. The problem of the boundary remained unresolved – until now. Could this bold, unilateral action by Ogmore remove the *impasse*?

A builder and his mates who were working at Homestead offered to put up a fence where Lucy and Max thought it should be. 'After all they've put up their fence where they think it should be and have done everything to prevent you getting a proper survey.' Max was already thinking along those lines. He decided against a proper fence, but asked them to mark a line with metal posts connected by wire. They put the first post in at the end of Ogmore's roadside fence some nine inches Homestead way from where the Land Registry surveyors had marked the end of the boundary, and then one more post down hill before taking the line around the shed outside the path and reed fence at the back of it for four more posts, and finally four more in line with the first two posts to continue down hill for a total of about 30 feet, half the length of that boundary. Lucy photographed the men at work and took several photos of the reed fence and the area around.

Ms Wormelow's letter in protest not only demanded that they replace the posts in a straight line but also accused them of destroying six mature rose bushes and a courgette plant. Lucy's photographs were a good idea: no roses, no courgettes in sight, nothing but weeds and grass under muddy boots. The letter threatened yet another injunction. However, the following day a second letter arrived. An emollient letter, a sensible letter proposing that an independent expert determine and plot the boundaries, costs shared equally. More than four years on from Max and Lucy's original proposal the Ogmores agreed at last to an independent survey. Deep sighs of relief to be heard in Homestead. Lucy admitted she had been wrong to oppose the metal posts idea, Max's strategy had worked. All would have been very well but for the penultimate paragraph of Ms Wormelow's letter. Apparently the reed fence was erected to protect the privacy of the Ogmore's garden 'subsequent to your enlarging the hole you had cut through the trees and the construction of a pathway up to their boundary.' This was the ancient path just below the road that Rick Stone had used, as had Max and Lucy – most memorably on the day of the attack. They had been walking it ever since they moved into Homestead. No tree cutting or construction required.

Lucy was determined that the lady fronting for Hazel Ogmore should be clearer about certain facts. She wrote welcoming the proposal but describing at length the history of their dealings with her clients and attaching the HMLR plan with added data: the roadside measurement and the two angles on the shed-side boundary. As the Ogmores had finally agreed an independent survey, Lucy proposed they invite Land Registry back to carry out the work they had offered and attempted to do in March 2005 as this would be 'at no further cost to either party'.

Lucy was surprised when the proposal was rejected. She could not understand why the Ogmores would object. Why pay when the survey was offered for free? Wormelow's reply returned them to the familiar territory of confusions and distortions: the owners of Blackstone Cottage had *always received the wayleave for the electricity pole* declared Wormelow/Ogmore, confusing the electricity pole for the telephone pole. Plenty of evidence in Ms Wormelow's long letter that sections had been drafted by her clients and she was prepared to risk her reputation endorsing them. She had attached a version of the Hammer plan recently amended by Royston Hammer himself. The letter concluded with the demand that they agree to a Royal Institution of Chartered Surveyors (RICS) survey. If not, her clients would erect a fence 'in line with the Consent Order' and 'will seek an injunction restraining you from interfering with the erection of that fence, or with it once it is in place.' So, how would 'her clients' know where to put it 'in line with the Consent Order'? They had clearly got this first attempt wrong. Mr Hammer had told them to move their reed fence nearer the shed, so Max and Lucy were correct – it had been trespassing.

Max and Lucy replied briefly asking for copies of Hammer's instructions for his original December 2001 and recent November 2007 plans. They also asked for any evidence that the wayleave had 'always' been paid to the owners of Blackstone Cottage. They were being mischievous; they already had dockets of the wayleave payments made to previous Homestead owners. They also asked for any evidence of Ogmore ownership of Homestead land beyond the rectangle drawn on Blackstone Cottage's 1963 conveyance. Lucy wanted confirmation that no such evidence existed and that the adverse possession gambit in 2002 had been a hoax.

Bulmer's reply expressed surprise that Max and Lucy still had not learnt about privileged documents 'having had the issue of legal privilege pointed out to (them) over a period of five years and *four* sets of legal proceedings.' With the aid of Messrs O'Hare and Browne,[1] Lucy rebutted yet another attempt to patronise: 'We are well aware that privilege can be waived in the interests of transparency and the proper conduct of litigation which in this country should be conducted with "cards face up on the table". Litigation is not supposed to be a war or a game and we regret to observe from our dealings with your firm that you are too often tempted to regard it as either one or the other or both.'

On a matter more germane to the survey, she asked if they were no longer confident in Land Registry's interpretation of the Hammer plan as they omitted any reference to it following Mr Hammer's recent re-survey of the site. They pointed out that registered Title plans are required by law to be drawn on the relevant and most recent OS plan. Lucy rejected the claim that the original Hammer plan was 'definitive' as it had generally been dismissed as inaccurate, but said that they would agree the plan Hammer had amended back in November 2002 after his meeting with James Nunn, together with the four posts they had placed on Homestead land around the shed to allow Ogmore easy access to the shed for maintenance.

Answer came there none, so a fortnight later she wrote again asking for a reply. They received a holding reply; Ms Wormelow was taking her clients' instruction, 'and will revert to you'. Max and Lucy decided that if the Ogmores remained intransigent they would have to pay their bit for a RICS land surveyor. It seemed an unnecessary cost in the circumstances and Lucy could not fathom why they objected to Land Registry surveyors doing the work, but if it finally led to a fence it was a price worth paying.

December 23rd, Max was out last-minute shopping and Lucy was in, having washed her hair, busy with last-minute preparations for the family invasion the following day. There was a knock at the door and through the hall window Lucy saw a familiar shape, Mr Nelson the apologetic bailiff. She had been advised not to let bailiffs in – even apologetic ones, besides her hair was in curlers and she was behind with Christmas preparations. From the other side of the door Mr Nelson was even more apologetic, saying he was obliged to go through the motions but would call back at a more convenient time. They arranged a date after Christmas leaving Lucy to ponder on what the latest Ogmore trick was.

It was the old familiar injunction trick of getting things into court without the necessary preliminaries – like sending Wormelow's promised reply or a formal pre-action protocol. She welcomed Mr Nelson with a cup of tea and he was as fulsomely apologetic as ever. He really, really wanted to assure her that he fully sympathised. He'd read all the papers and being local he knew something of their adversary. He knew they had had to put up with a great deal of very bad behaviour but … he really really would advise that Max and Lucy brought everything to a close now. 'How?' asked Lucy pointing to the latest Stoat/ Ogmore attack. Mr Nelson sighed. He shook his head. He pondered. 'Well, I suppose give them what they want.'

'We haven't read this latest batch. We don't know what they want over and above what we have already given and what we are prepared to agree anyway. If this is the usual mishmash of allegation, distortion, confusion, time- and money-wasting lawyer games, we'll have to find ourselves a good reliable lawyer to look after things while we are away on one of Max's projects, and we have not met a good reliable lawyer so far. Do you know of anyone locally?' Mr Nelson did and left her with the name of a firm and a recommended man.

All lawyering had stopped for the festive season. No office would be open again until 2nd January so Max and Lucy delivered a letter copied by email to ask the recommended man for help. They also scrambled together some papers with all relevant plans and two background reports ready for a meeting once the law business opened up again. But for the second time they were counting on a firm which did not do litigation. However, the recommended man *could* recommend a man who did at a firm based over 20 miles away in the same town as the County Court. 'Saves on travelling costs, and he is recommended as a bit of a Rottweiler who enjoys a fight,' reported Max. 'Well I hope he can get up to speed fairly quickly; this injunction hearing is in two weeks' time. We'll have to see them today.'

Later that day they fought their way through the traffic in that sad, dowdy, post-industrial town and arrived in the busy, cramped reception of Ethan Ganz LLP, Solicitors, and met Hannah Katz, the recommended man's Assistant. A lot of black, glossy hair, red lipstick and very high heels, Hannah was a busy young lady managing to juggle departing clients with an animated conversation on her mobile and rushed enquiries to one of the four receptionists while flicking hair out of her eyes. A big, film star smile with outstretched hand to Max, a more restrained welcome for Lucy and great effusive apologies to both – they would have to talk in the reception area as all the rooms were taken, 'It is rather short notice, I'm sure you will agree.' They did and handed over the pack they had prepared emphasising the need for whoever was dealing with the case to read the two background reports so that they were better prepared to deal with the Claim and the Claimants. In that brief discussion Ms Katz warned them with a flick of her hair that the Consent Order plan overruled Land Registry's plan if they conflicted, and it was now too late to set aside the misnamed Consent Order.

'So, if there is conflict and we have been misled, maybe we should challenge Land Registry, again for getting it wrong, again?'

'Yes, you may well have a claim there. I'll talk it over with Mr Rottman when he returns.'

'Not Mr Ganz?' Apparently all that remained in that town of Mr Ganz was his name; his person was in one of his properties in Italy or Florida or Barbados. They would meet up with Senior Partner Wolf Rottman next week.

The Senior Partner was a large presence, physically and vocally; perfect casting for a Rottweiler lawyer. He confirmed that he would attend the hearing on the injunction application the following week and after looking at the plans said he would instruct a surveyor to make overlays showing how the land had changed (hands). He estimated his firm's costs at about £3,000 and Max asked that no other costs, like the surveyor, be incurred without their say-so. The Rottweiler confirmed what they knew anyway, it was too late to set aside the Consent Order. It was agreed that Hannah should do most of the work but that he would represent them in court and be in overall control of the case. After hand-crushing handshakes to both he left them with Hannah to study the plans with much hair-flicking, and report more on the conduct of the Ogmores.

Max quite liked Hannah who appeared sharp and enthusiastic. Lucy had a few misgivings which she kept to herself, but was pleased to learn that Ms Katz was a paralegal as they had had good experiences of the two paralegals they had encountered. Fresh with their law degrees and yet uncontaminated by the prevailing culture of the law business, they seemed to be what was wanted: polite, efficient, informed – or else eager to access required information, and focussed on customer needs. The following day Hannah wrote asking for a couple of documents she had identified as possibly significant, and Lucy forwarded more documents and reiterated instructions agreed at the meeting: a RICS surveyor to survey all boundaries. They no longer wanted an HMLR survey as the agency might be in the firing line if their rectified Title plan were found to conflict with the overriding, albeit faulty, Consent Order plan. If so, HMLR would have to re-rectify Homestead's Title plan *and* compensate them for losses arising from their mistake.

Late the very next day a letter from Ms Wormelow was hand-delivered (without permitted access to Homestead) with the proposal that the parties return to the original independent survey idea. There was no mention of the threatened injunction. If she had 'reverted' as promised with this proposal rather than an unannounced injunction application taking the matter into court, what was to follow would have been avoided. But it was in court with expensive time-wasting court procedures and costly lawyers so Max and Lucy now had Defence Statements, Witness Statements, further hearings, lists of documents, emails, letters, telephone calls, meetings all just to get an independent survey. Expensive, unnecessary add-ons. Court action could and should have been avoided altogether. Ms Wormelow had ignored the Woolf reforms requiring the correct pre-action procedures. It was doubtful she had heard of Lord Woolf.

They had to wait until the following Monday to contact Hannah who had a very long list of questions for Max and Lucy, many arising from allegations by the Ogmores. Lucy dealt with them easily, but was dismayed to hear that without their say-so Hannah had already engaged a local firm to make plans overlays. She told Hannah to cancel the redundant instruction and ensure that the precious HMLR plans and overlays they had given her were recovered asap as they were the only ones they had. Lucy was mildly concerned by the tone and content of a letter Hannah had sent the previous Friday. Apparently the paralegal wanted 'sight of all relevant correspondence'. Lucy doubted that the girl had any idea of what her request involved. Was she expecting Lucy and Max to find, collate, copy and forward some several thousand items in the next few days? If so she would be disappointed. From experience of other lawyers, Max and Lucy had some idea of what would happen and it would not include a careful perusal of all relevant documents; clearly Ethan Ganz LLP were simply covering themselves and placing the onus on their clients. Lucy offered to send all she could find on their rejected proposals for an independent survey. Lucy was of the opinion that in the light of their conduct the Ogmores should pay all costs of their now unnecessary, inappropriate, injunction-triggered court action.

She wondered why Ms Katz was so eager to attend the listed hearing; the opposition suggested merely writing to the Court agreeing directions. Dates would have to be changed because Max and Lucy would be out of the country, but nothing else. The opposition was not even insisting on a Defence. A Defence would call for a Reply 'if so advised' and neither would be necessary unless conflict arose after the survey. Hannah then informed Lucy the £600 they had paid on account was already used up – in less than a week. They would have to send more. This paralegal had absorbed the law business culture early in her career.

The contract they finally received was out of date. The very up-to-date invoice was slightly more transparent than usual so they thought they should be able to keep track of costs. Ethan Ganz LLP, replied to Bulmer & Partner agreeing the draft Directions with some changes. One change that should have been made in Max and Lucy's view was the deletion of orders to produce a Defence. Defences and Replies to Defences were redundant at least until after the survey. They may not be necessary in the end if both sides agree the survey result – and Lucy gets to put her fence up. Everything should have been focussed on a cost-saving survey. Even with their absence for six weeks and the amended dates all should be concluded by the end of May they thought.

Ms Katz told them that she did not attend the Court and she did not bill for attendance, but the Court Order stated that she did. Moreover, the Order omitted the 'if so advised' from the direction on Defence. There were some 10 directions from the Deputy District Judge (who Max and Lucy never saw or heard so he has no name – apart from Judge Nine), ending with several ensuring the mire would get thicker and dirtier. Ms Katz forwarded it to them with demands for more money. They replied detailing the agreed fees and reminding the firm that the initial estimate of between £2,500 and £3,500 had included the costs of the injunction hearing which did not take place. They then brought the contract up to date stating what they wanted from Ethan Ganz: (1.) engage an agreed RICS surveyor; (2.) ensure the instructions to the surveyor best protected their interests and (3.) prepare any obligatory Witness Statements. They paid the bill and amended the obsolete contract as per their letter. They questioned the need to lodge a Defence.

Hannah Katz didn't like that, nor did Wolf Rottman. The two-page letter in reply adopted an adversarial approach, and repeatedly referred to the unpredictability of litigation: EG LLP could not possibly say how much it would all cost. So why give the estimate? Moreover, Ms Katz was, 'under a duty to advise you that if you fail to file a Defence you run the risk of judgment against you. You must comply with the Court's directions.' In fact what Ms Katz should have done before taking the Defence any further was to check whether Ms Wormelow would agree to amend the Directions. After all she had not insisted on a Defence in her version. Lucy's misgivings were strengthened, but Max suggested that Ms Katz's inexperience was showing and she was picking up bad habits from the Rottweiler and applying them inappropriately; besides, they were leaving in a week and had other urgent matters to attend to, they could not start again, they were stuck with Ethan Ganz so they would have to let Ms Hannah Katz get on with it.

Of course, she couldn't get on with it, she simply did not know enough. A week before their departure they conference-called Ms Katz and gave her many of the points they would like to be in their Defence mostly refuting the allegations in the Claim: they had not refused an independent survey, they had been urging one for years; no rose bushes or courgettes had been seen let alone damaged and they had photos to prove it. Ms Katz asked them to draft a Defence that she would then remodel to the Court's requirements. Max pointed out that with his draft the work would only take about an hour and should not cost her estimated £400. That was not well received and led on to a discussion of EG's invoicing policy. Lucy put it bluntly: costs were rising for no apparent reason, but they had signed a contract and were leaving soon for a six week tour, they were stuck with Ethan Ganz. The longer the conversation went on the more Lucy became aware of the expensive minutes passing and just as they were approaching another six-minute billing[2] addition, she brought the conversation to a close. She had never actually fallen out with any of the disappointing lawyers they had engaged over the previous six years. She came near to doing so in that conversation.

Wolf Rottman phoned later to try to undo the damage. He offered a more relaxed invoicing system and acknowledged that they would not be in a position to deal with anything while they were away. They suggested that the firm should try to keep in touch by email, but warned that in view of their itinerary they couldn't guarantee it would always be possible.

They then made time to draft a Defence as requested. Lucy and Max suspected that following Hammer's latest visit to the site and the repositioning of the section of reed fence, the Ogmores might fear they would be found to be wrong. Max and Lucy's draft pointed out that their wire and post marker fence was in response to the Ogmores' unilateral action with the reed fence erected without notification or agreement, but as the required independent survey had not taken place, they could not say one way or another if the line of their fence aligned accurately with the boundary described on their Title plan. They rejected any claim that the Consent Order plan and the latest amended version of it were accurate and pointed out that the Ogmores had refused to aid transparency and clarity by providing copies of their surveyor's instructions and reports. They dismissed the nonsense about the rose bushes and courgettes – their photos clearly exposed another Ogmore lie.

Ms Katz emailed her first draft Defence just one day before the Court ordered deadline. It was not impressive. Lucy was mildly alarmed by Hannah's ignorance of the background and more than a little miffed that all the effort she had put into the two reports she had given her had been ignored. She decided to amplify their draft Defence, not least to ensure that the paralegal would have a clearer idea of the facts while they were away. In effect she wrote a Witness Statement from which Ms Katz could extract appropriate bits.

A new, amplified version duly arrived by email. Apart from some insignificant and correctable errors it seemed just about acceptable. Later that day Hannah emailed again with a sensible proposal: she would ask Wormelow to agree to stay the matter until after they had the expert's report. Max and Lucy enthusiastically agreed. Ms Wormelow's clients did not and Max and Lucy cursed the nameless Deputy District Judge Eight for overindulging in needless, untimely Directions.

Rottman reiterated that his firm was in charge of managing the case *on their behalf* and Hannah confirmed that she did not believe they would have a pre-trial review while they were away so, as far as Max and Lucy were concerned, there would now be a ceasefire until they returned in late March.

Unfortunately the Ogmores did not do ceasefires, particularly while the enemy was on leave. The Monday after their departure Hannah Katz received an angry letter from Bulmers: 'Your clients who have denied destroying roses and courgettes have, in the last week, cut through a leylandii shrub which had been growing on our clients' land for at least three years ... Photographs have been taken.' Hannah Katz wrote a letter (not an email) on 12th February when Max and Lucy were in Quito, Ecuador, requiring an early response to these allegations with further instructions on the previously agreed changes to dates! She compounded this irrational deed by adding, 'I am under a duty to advise you that any such conduct can be detrimental to your case. Accordingly, I advise that you do not embark upon such course of conduct until this matter is resolved in the Courts.' Fortunate that Max and Lucy knew nothing of this, they could enjoy a fascinating journey in blissful ignorance. Perhaps, not fortunate – had they seen that letter they could have sacked Hannah sooner and the next mess-up might have been avoided. But then again it might not, Wolf Rottman was untested, would he have avoided what was to come?

They were able to access emails in Quito but it was time consuming. The internet connection in the hotel was unreliable and very busy so they found an internet café. Max had several business and research matters to monitor and initially Lucy also checked her in-box, but whereas Max continued checking for a while, Lucy realised she had better things to do. After Quito they went to the Galapagos, from there to the wineries in Mendoza, then back to Santiago, Chile to go on to Easter Island. Max made a couple of attempts at email while in Santiago, but Lucy did not bother. 29th February was the last day of their stay on Easter Island. They booked a table for 8pm at the most recommended restaurant and went for an early evening walk. As they passed a crowded and noisy internet café, Lucy caught the novelty of emailing friends from Easter Island and Max thought it a good idea to send some research reports back. They were each allocated a short connection window.

As Lucy came to the end of her in-box (and her allocated time) she came across a series of increasingly desperate emails from Hannah Katz who claimed to have written to her on 12th February – but there was nothing from her until the 20th, followed by two more on 25th and 27th February. The content of all three was incomprehensible and only the short ones delivered in full. As far as they could discern the paralegal wanted them to sign a Defence document *and return it by 4pm on 22nd February*!! It was now 29th February. She had not copied the emails to Max. If she had ever had any good manners and client-care awareness those qualities had clearly evaporated. She appeared to hold Lucy and Max responsible for failing to respond as ordered! Lucy had to buy another window to access all three emails, but the technology did not extend to opening the attachments and the queue for print-outs extended to the following day, by which time they would have left the Island. Apparently Ms Katz had lied to Ogmore/Bulmer (a reverse from the norm) and informed them that this (new?) Defence was with her clients for agreement and signing.

Unable to access the attachments and to think in the noise and heat, Lucy believed that Ogmore was just asking for more information. She emailed back saying that Ms Katz was aware they were away and she had authority to sign documents on their behalf, and they must trust their lawyer 'will always act in our best interest'. She then reminded their lawyer that if clarification was demanded, Ogmore had refused to clarify anything. Max's email was more pertinent. Adopting Katz's style he wrote, 'We are regretfully obliged to state that we shall hold you responsible for any procedural failures ... please do not assume that we are going to compromise our commitments and the confidence you required us to invest in your firm by vetting our email every day on matters over which you, but not we, have control.'

When they returned to Santiago for their flight to New Zealand, Lucy checked emails again as Max was busy with amended travel plans. She managed to access Katz's first email in full but not open the attachment so she still hadn't grasped what was going on. She mistakenly inferred that Hannah Katz had not received the signed Defence and papers they had posted weeks earlier, before they left. Surely everyone realised that they had engaged lawyers to act for them when away. They tried contact again in Christchurch, but the email bounced so only when they were staying with friends in Sydney did they get to open the attachment and finally grasp something of what had been going on. Apparently, the Defence was deemed deficient by Wormelow, or Ogmore, or Stoat and an amended version had been drawn up by Ms Katz which she had attached to her email of 20th February. They were incredulous. Had she really expected them to download, study, agree, print, sign, and return a legal document in 48 hours? Max replied forthrightly, 'Was it not clear to everyone, courts included, that we would be away?' Of course, it was clear to Bulmers which is why they were harassing so vigorously, but it was not clear to the Court because the Court had never been informed. 'We cannot make informed decisions,' he continued, 'without access to papers nor take any action until after Easter (23rd March). We return on 20th March.'

In the interim Ogmore/Bulmer were enjoying themselves. Katz had sent her amended Defence and Bulmers would not accept it unless they (or their clients) agreed to pay costs arising, otherwise another court order was threatened and sure enough a draft order and a Witness Statement by Ogmore (Mrs) arrived within a day.

A grown-up professional law firm would have bitten the bullet and accepted responsibility, but not Ethan Ganz, LLP. Young Ms Katz decided to shift the blame from herself to her clients. Her next letter, sent by post and therefore not seen by them until their return, would make even the most avaricious, unethical lawyer blush. She informed them that her Defence document was written according to their 'strict instructions' (a fledgling Ogmore, it would appear) then, 'I am duty bound to advise you that if *you* (our italics) failed to amend the Defence … (it) would be detrimental to your case. Accordingly *you must* pay the costs incurred. … You would be liable to pay our costs … together with the Claimants' costs. This would be in addition to the costs awarded in respect of (their Response).' She ended with a delightful touch: 'To assist you and to ensure that we retain a positive working relationship I have made provisions to waive the costs incurred in drafting the original Defence in the sum of £220.50. I trust that you appreciate this gesture.' Oh dear! Ms Katz failed to understand her clients … any clients. No client would appreciate such gall. Moreover, the original estimate for the first Defence was £400, so what was going to be £400 *into* the EG account was now only £220.50 out. *And all arising from her and Rottman's failure to draft an adequate Defence.*

Ms Katz then went away for three weeks. She didn't tell her clients and she didn't tell Bulmers who wrote refusing her request to stay their putative claim for seven days and promptly seized the moment to add costs and mayhem by lodging it. Meanwhile the case had been moved to the same Civil Justice Centre with parking problems where Scroggs (and Stoat and, possibly, Judge Blacker) had triggered six years of Ogmore trouble. HM Court Service sent track allocation questionnaires – demanding £200 on filing, together with notice of a telephone hearing on Bulmer's Claim for costs listed for 25th April.

Max and Lucy had a valuable time in Australia and managed a couple of days in Hong Kong and returned to a family Easter. They went through the usual mountain of correspondence and saw for the first time their lawyer's ill-judged letters – but not much else from her. Nothing to explain the need for the amended Defence and nothing after 7th March. They had no difficulty dismissing her imprudent letters. They were seasoned campaigners and impervious to lawyer intimidation, particularly of the Hannah Katz variety. They wrote two letters to her on 25th March: one reminding her of the warnings they had given about the Ogmores and Bulmers, then making clear their position as EG clients, then asking for all missing correspondence and ending by pointing out that she had written and signed the Defence – they had merely complied with her request for help. The second letter reminded her to forward the missing papers, and for the fifth time, requested that she return the Land Registry plans and overlays she had failed to return for two months. They then went on to give their second genuine client instruction: write to Bulmers saying, 'As neither party can know the correct position on the ground of the boundaries until the independent surveyor has identified them, we propose removing our provisional wire and stake fence to await the outcome of the survey when we will at last be able to erect a proper fence. We consider that your clients were most unwise to erect the section of reed fence without attempting to achieve agreement as to its position on the ground and suggest that they also remove that section of fence to leave the area clear for the proposed survey – and remove mutual irritants.' Both letters were emailed and copied in the post and followed up the next day with calls and another email to Ms Katz on the selection of the independent surveyor.

Ms Katz finally emailed that she was a very busy lady and would not be able to take their calls, only emails. She attached a letter of 'advice'. They had already decided to sack Ms Katz, but her attempt at 'advice' would have clinched it if they hadn't. She could 'not accept' that they were not informed that an amended Defence was required and the reasons for it. She had emailed them three times and they had emailed her that she had authority to act in their best interests on their behalf which was deemed as their approval. As they had neither seen nor 'approved' anything, 'approval' was added to their Dictionary of Legalese. She would have been 'professionally embarrassed', she continued, if she had asked the Court to stay action for six weeks while they were away, as 'the Court has to deal with matters in a cost effective and timely manner.' Not very cost effective and timely to fail to inform the Court of one side's absence – even Dyer seemed to have had no difficulty with their six-week absence in his case.

The Defence, Ms Katz declared, must make clear why the matter is being litigated. It was blindingly obvious from the file that it was only being litigated because the Ogmores insisted on litigation and the Court system indulged them. They could see no value in litigation. Could she tell them how, as Defendants, they could avoid it? She then 'advised' that they agree to pay all the costs arising from (her) inadequate Defence. 'If you choose to ignore this advise [sic] I am duty bound to advise you that you will ... incur the costs of Bulmers' application and Ethan Ganz's work as well.' Max felt 'duty bound' to reply in kind, but Lucy persuaded him to hold fire until they had spoken to Wolf Rottman who called them on the 31st just as they were drawing up a list of Ms Katz's inadequacies (and, by implication, her firm's failures). An emollient Mr Rottman did not appear to want to lose clients. Max gently toned down his email, but they still wanted his paralegal off the case.

That same day solicitors for both sides sent in their completed allocation questionnaires. Ms Wormelow's handwriting had dramatically changed – it was now identical to her client's. She, like Hannah Katz, wanted a fast-track case – no money in small claims and no court would accept multi-track for this neighbour dispute. She declared that 'her clients' had already spent £6,852 and estimated a final cost of between £15,000 and £20,000. Ms Katz estimated that her clients had already spent £2,200 and that the final bill would be around £9,000. Unlike Ms Wormelow's clients, Ms Katz's clients would not see that form until some years later. As it was all to do with them (their money, their land, their stress, their time) they would have been interested.

Ms Katz did not find pleasure in their list of her failures despite the gentler tone of delivery. Her next letter was as rebarbative as ever: she did not reply to Bulmers' letter announcing the activation of Ogmore's latest Claim, 'as you *failed* to provide instructions on the issue of costs occasioned by the Amended Defence', 'despite being advised in my letter of 6th March, on the consequences of not agreeing (to pay Bulmers) you have *failed* to provide instructions.' The letter was peppered with, 'I cannot accept ...', 'I fail to see ...', 'I am duty bound to advise ...', 'it is not this firm's policy to notify clients ...' of absence – for three weeks when the opposition was filing a claim for costs and no other member of the firm covered the case. This was a first for Max and Lucy – every firm they had known, adequate to bad, had notified and covered for absent lawyers. But Ms Katz asserted that Wolf Rottman *had* covered for her, in which case why did *he* not deal with the enemy action? Where's the evidence he covered and why did he not mention it when he phoned? He certainly never ever billed for any cover.

This time Max did not hold back. 'These abusive comments would more appropriately be directed at our opponents, rather than us, the clients, who are entitled to both first-rate representation and courtesy – neither of which elementary skills Ms Katz has yet learnt to deploy ... We are not prepared to spend more time responding to Ms Katz's correspondence. We did not engage solicitors at considerable cost either to do the work ourselves, be required to remedy negligent work, or to tolerate this provocative and totally inappropriate conduct. We do not know what Ms Katz intends by this attitude. We do know we want no further dealings with her.' The letter was emailed to Rottman that day.

The next day Max followed up with a five-page letter. It is still on file. It is calmer: reasoned, detailed, controlled, but still damning of Ms Katz, reiterating that they did not want her working on their case and why. He asked for a senior member of the firm to take over. This was a 'client instruction', their third. The second of a week earlier (proposing to Ms Wormelow that the fences be removed prior to the survey), had yet to be followed. Max's lengthy letter brought a prompt email from Wolf Rottman. He would be available for the case and needed to talk urgently about representation. He claimed to have no record of their request that Ms Katz be replaced. They wondered how many other letters he had failed to read properly, or at all.

At their meeting 48 hours later they found him urbane and pleasant. He agreed that either he or another senior member of his firm would take over the case and deal with the telephone hearing on Ogmore's Claim for costs arising from the rejected Defence. On his paralegal he said very little. He listened. He did not defend but nor did he apologise. He did say that in his opinion the original Defence was adequate which confirmed Lucy's suspicions, which she still holds, that the whole business was another cost-raising gambit by the Ogmore Gang. They had repeatedly warned Ethan Ganz, LLP to be alert to the antics of the Gang and to call their bluff whenever confronted with some dubious prank. Lucy now reinforced the warning with illustrations from the history of their dealings with the squatters, pointing out that Mr Cain and Guy Castor's paralegal had resisted Ogmore bullying quickly and effectively.

Lucy and Max were confident they could make a strong case for negligence by Ethan Ganz: Either the Defence was negligent or the firm's supine response to Bulmer bullying was. Either way, Ethan Ganz was responsible and Ethan Ganz, LLP would have to pay 'all costs arising'. Lucy and Max said this at the meeting; it was already in Max's letters and emails if Rottman would just make time to read them – properly. It drew no response from Mr Rottman. The only costs he mentioned, apart from his own, were those claimed by Ogmore (£1,325.64) for the rejected Defence which his Cost Draftsman described as exaggerated. Max and Lucy were relaxed about that, whatever the final amount someone else would have to find the money.

Max handed Rottman the CVs of three RICS surveyors and as one was also listed by Bulmers they agreed to select Jason Higgins of Millett and Hunt Ltd. They left Wolf Rottman with four points they wanted him to make forcefully at the telephone hearing two weeks hence: (1.) the Ogmores had repeatedly frustrated their attempts to settle the boundary; (2.) they had rejected their court application (to Dyer) for an independent survey in 2003; (3.) they had refused access to the surveyors from Land Registry in 2005 thus aborting that attempt and (4.) they had leaped to litigation without the correct pre-action protocol and without carrying out the promise to 'revert'. Max wrote a few days later reiterating these points and forwarding a cheque for EG's latest bill which he warned they would pay for now but intended to review later. He also asked if there was a reply to their first instruction – to write to Bulmers proposing removal of fences.

Nine days after that meeting, nine days after they had sacked Ms Hannah Katz, the same Ms Katz wrote an attendance notice of that meeting. A meeting she did not attend. They knew nothing of this note or, indeed, any notes until they finally made a formal complaint about Ethan Ganz's representation over a year later. Ms Katz's version differed somewhat from Max and Lucy's recollection. According to Ms Katz, Wolf Rottman (WR) 'pacified the clients' and 'confirmed that HK had not done anything wrong ... HK attempted to contact the clients on numerous occasions to no avail ... HK could not progress matters without client instructions.' Had WR attempted to say any of that at the meeting Max and Lucy attended, they would have been able to put him right, and if he had failed to respond correctly they could have sacked Ethan Ganz LLP, but he had been in a 'dispute resolution' mode and eager to avoid any areas of conflict. Hannah K's 'attendance' note continued her revisionist history by reporting that WR confirmed that all costs would have to be paid by the clients. The meeting would have lasted a lot longer and been considerably less amicable had WR indeed 'confirmed' that. HK went on to report that, 'The clients were happy and content with the (projected £2,000) costs arising.' Perhaps 'happy' is another word for the Legalese dictionary. In fact, both Max and Lucy were indifferent: in their view clients do not pay costs arising from professional negligence.

Unaware of HK's imaginative note, Max wrote again to Wolf Rottman offering to assist, if need be, in preparation for the telephone hearing on 25th April as any accompanying papers would have to be filed five days beforehand. He rehearsed yet again the need for a robust response from EG LLP, this time emphasising the need to make the Court aware of their opponents' unreasonable demands on the rejected Defence as well as their unreasonable action in taking the matter into court when the principle of an independent survey had never been rejected, and they had not sent a pre-action protocol letter. He then asked yet again if they had had a reply from Bulmers on the fence removal proposal. Of course, there had been no reply because HK had not made the proposal.

Wolf Rottman copied to them his 'Without Prejudice' letter to Bulmers. At last a good letter from Ethan Ganz, Solicitors. He robustly denied any damage to any plants – these, 'are false accusations'. The first Defence was 'straightforward for a straightforward matter'. 'Costs should be managed proportionately to a straightforward boundary dispute … we are endeavouring to avoid such spiralling costs and feel sure the Court is equally concerned.' He proposed that any costs should be costs in the case, but they would consider a modest contribution towards the costs of Ogmore's original reply on an 'entirely without prejudice basis'. Cheered by Rottman's letter, Max and Lucy relaxed. A competent lawyer was in charge, they no longer had to deal with insider damage, now they were only fighting on one front. But a day later they learnt that Wolf Rottman had handed the matter to his colleague, Aubrey Smythe, a fellow Senior Partner and a Deputy District Judge, as the Rottweiler had other commitments that day. His clients were disappointed that once again their investment was not buying what they needed; they were also surprised he had not mentioned other commitments before. Now they would have to brief another lawyer. Nevertheless, a Deputy District Judge should know the cast of players at the County Court and once up-to-speed should be able to do a reasonable job.

Meanwhile Ms Wormelow was busy with applications, Witness Statements, draft Orders and Bulmer bullying: 'With respect, we suggest you read the Particulars of Claim in this action as removal of the posts and wire will destroy the primary evidence which was the basis of these proceedings … (your clients) were given the opportunity to remove the fence and agree to mediation by a member of RICS, *which they declined*.' The hollow nonsense of this 'primary evidence' excuse could be blown away if the matter were to come to trial simply by referring to Wormelow's failure to produce her promised reply to their letter and her failure to follow the pre-action protocols. When they finally received copy of her letter this familiar twisting of the facts annoyed and worried them. In the early years of dealing with the Ogmores they had been convinced that solid evidence would easily expose the many lies as merely risible, but experience suggested that, inexplicably, they were serving the Ogmores well.

According to EG's billing ledger this three-page reforming of facts was received on 29th April (after the telephone hearing), but it was faxed to EG on 21st April, so it was possible that Aubrey Smythe had read it. Had he seen through the tactics and lies? Had he done his homework? Or, ignorant of the facts, had he been persuaded by the breathtakingly pompous, self-righteous style employed by Wormelow/Ogmore? As Max and Lucy did not actually see the letter until later, they were not aware of the potential danger. They were relying on their email to Wolf Rottman encouraging a robust attack on the Ogmore Gang. The day before the hearing they followed that up with another, again to Mr Rottman, as they had heard nothing from Mr Smythe: 'Please make clear that we do not understand why the Court is involved in a matter where there is no contention – all both parties want is an independent survey and the surveyor has been identified ... this could have been achieved years ago had they responded positively to our various attempts to persuade them to agree a boundary without resort to litigation.'

Late that day they did receive a call from the unknown Mr Smythe. He ran through the points from Rottman's letter to Bulmer, then, when Lucy tried to get him to emphasise the points in their latest email (suspecting he had not seen either of their latest emails), he questioned whether this would be possible in a 15-minute telephone hearing. Lucy wondered if anything would be possible in a 15-minute telephone hearing. He asked if she wanted to him to try to extend the hearing to make those points and Lucy laughed and said, 'If our experience is anything to go by, what we want is not important, our lawyers decide.' This elicited an embarrassed giggle similar to the giggle from Mr Beige when Max asked him why the Registry did not check with neighbours before registering a property for the first time.

The billing ledger for the day of the hearing records Mr Smythe spending 30 minutes preparing for the hearing and 18 minutes' 'advocacy'. If all that was required was to argue the points in Max's last two emails together with the points in Rottman's last letter to Bulmer – and to argue them clearly and forcefully – half an hour preparation for a 15-minute hearing could just possibly do – assuming that he was already well briefed by his colleague. But this was an Ogmore hearing and as things rolled out later it became clear that clarity and forcefulness were not in Mr Smythe's armoury, nor were salient facts. There are two versions of Mr Smythe's 'telephone (attendance) note' on file. The one sent to Max and Lucy at their request reported that prior to the hearing, their Defender had tried to get Ms Wormelow to agree a timetable but she had refused. Max and Lucy could have told him she would refuse anything she was not alerted to in advance as she, unlike solicitors at Ethan Ganz, really did take advice from her clients and would be lost on her own. Smythe had asked for the costs of the amendments to be costs in the case but, as he had only a flimsy hold on the facts and could not argue anything, the Judge (a different judge – Judge Ten) did not agree. However, since there was no time to consider cost quantum, another hearing was set. That's two hearings, with two sets of costs to add to the costs generated by a negligently drafted defence. Wormelow had another take on the 15 minutes which she hurriedly recorded into a letter to him that same day. Apparently, Mr Smythe was not ready in time and kept the Judge waiting. Furthermore, in reply to the cost application and to Directions Bulmers had sent – but which had not been seen by him – their Defender had stated, 'There is little I can say.' Ms Wormelow's letter then proposed that the quantum of their Claim could be agreed without another hearing. She made a few additions which brought the claim up to £2,000.

The following Monday Lucy picked up a call from Wolf Rottman. He was reporting back on behalf of his colleague. In the course of the conversation, when Lucy was reinforcing the warnings they had given about who was really running the show for Bulmers and the cost escalating traps their opponents might indulge in, he said that he had noted that Lucy and Max were truthful in their reports. It was only after the call that Lucy thought of the implication of that odd statement: he may have actually believed the Ogmore Gang's various mis-Statements and lies, despite the file of evidence refuting them. He really needed to read the file.

The call was followed a week later by a package of correspondence from EG which contained Aubrey Smythe's attendance note – but not the full attendance note. Max and Lucy did not discover for another two and a half years that the note sent to them had been doctored. The final paragraph had been removed from their version. The full version voiced Mr Smythe's serious concerns about Hannah Katz who, he complained, had acted incorrectly and without authority, 'It seems to me she needs some training in relation to who should sign documents and what a Statement of Truth means.'

Rottman's draft letter for Bulmer seemed competent, slicing away at Bulmer's inflated costs claim and drawing attention to Wormelow's rather poor maths. He strongly refuted Ogmore's accusation that plants had been damaged and that the proposal to remove the posts was a ploy to remove 'primary evidence'. Nevertheless, he proposed that Max and Lucy did nothing about their posts until after the survey. Despite serious misgivings, they decided that on balance it would be sensible to take the senior Partner's advice and leave the posts in place. They took strong exception to another part of the draft purporting to respond to Bulmers' libellous accusations against them; 'We cannot comment on your previous dealings with our clients, but we are grateful for the background information you have provided.'

'How about *our* information?' said Lucy. 'About time he read the two reports I gave Ms Katz and responds with the standard, "your comments are noted".' The letter did later contest some accusations stressing that his clients had been forced to incur litigation costs because of the unreasonable conduct of the Claimants.

A problem with their new champion mystified them at the time. All their emails to him bounced. They had drawn his attention to this, suggesting that he get his IT technician to look into it, and in the meantime the only way they could use 21st-century communication was to email via 'enquiries' which was delaying and irritating. Nearly two years later, on reviewing the full file, they realised why, and also why billing guides were no longer attached to the firm's invoices. From May to July 2008 the invoices simply listed the number of emails, letters, phone calls, etc. with no details – and no names. They thought this was Mr Rottman's way of doing things. When they discovered how wrong they were they also understood why those emails bounced.

Rottman called a few days later to tell them that the Court had sent notification of the date for the second costs hearing – three days after receiving the notice. Aubrey Smythe was not going to make it; he was hearing cases as a Deputy District Judge that day. Neither was Ms Wormelow, she was on holiday. Max and Lucy had been told by their expensive advisors that no allowance would be made by the Court for their absence – apparently Ms Katz would have been embarrassed even to mention it, but Bulmers saw no problem in asking the Court to find another date to convenience them. When Wolf Rottman phoned Max and Lucy to explain that he intended to ask the Court to put back the second hearing, he laid heavy emphasis on the 'exceptional circumstances'. Lucy and Max knew there were no exceptional circumstances but that Rottman had to justify his firm's failure to notify the Court of *their* absence from the country – and accept responsibility for the consequences. Max took the rare opportunity offered by this call to voice his concerns that their representatives were letting the Ogmore Gang make the running, and asked how the firm could be more proactive. Rottman deflected the criticism: as Claimants the Gang would be expected to run the show, and his tactics were 'subtly' proactive. He agreed with Max that they should not get sidetracked and should focus on getting the RICS surveyor instructed to see if his report confirmed that the Hammer plan was ambiguous. The Ogmore Gang was delaying any agreement on the selection of Jason Higgins as surveyor – three weeks had already been lost. They said it was because they were waiting for information from him about his litigation experience, but when Max phoned Mr Higgins he was assured that no such request had been made. So, another lie – this time to delay everything … but why?

Wolf Rottman again warned them that Ogmore might well expect to claim around £2,000 costs. Max suggested that Ethan Ganz might well want to minimise those unreasonable costs. He did not elaborate. They had already alerted the firm that they might decide to revisit the matter of costs incurred by Hannah Katz's inexperience, incompetence and lack of guidance. It would not be wise to engage in a full-blown battle with their Defenders, they needed them committed to their case; besides, until the survey was completed, no one knew what the overall costs situation would be. That would be a battle for another day.

Mr Rottman asked for comments on his draft. Max wrote four pages in response telling him to cut any expression of gratitude for the dishonest 'background information' replacing it with, 'Our clients will respond later and ask you meanwhile to re-read their letter to you of October 2007' which had set out a brief history of Ogmore's land grab and the Court shenanigans that ensued. Rottman had already agreed Max's proposal to write two separate letters: one relating to the survey and the other to the costs claim, but this must have been forgotten because the original draft was sent more or less unchanged: a bit more iron in the brief outline of events prior to Ogmore's latest injunction gambit but with the line 'We are grateful for the background information you have provided' still there.

The resumed hearing was listed for 11th June. The Ogmores were still delaying, 'We are not aware that we have agreed the identity of the joint expert.' And still objecting to a surveyor's report, and still insisting that the Hammer plan and the man himself were the ultimate authorities. Max and Lucy were confirmed in their view that the Ogmores did not want a survey because they did not want a fence demarcation showing the limitations of their land and preventing further encroachment by stealth. The Ogmores strongly objected to the survey including the one and only boundary with a fixed point: the boundary between Blackstone Cottage land and Dunroamin'. Max 'instructed' Rottman to inform Bulmers that if they didn't confirm Jason Higgins by the end of the month Ethan Ganz would apply to the Court to appoint a surveyor.

Max also wanted to know what was happening about the injunction application. It seemed to have faded away. Of course, as it had done its job and got the case on to the Court playground it now had to be forgotten, hidden from any scrutiny revealing that there was no just cause and that the whole court case was a waste of time and money. They continued to pay for EG's services as invoiced but at the same time alerting their service-provider that they intended to revisit costs.

As Bulmers would not budge, the second hearing before Judge Ten took place. Just prior to it Rottman had repeated the proposal that all other work necessary for trial purposes be suspended until the expert report was received. Again his clients wholeheartedly agreed. Again their opponents did not. Nor would they budge on an expert's report. Apparently their Mr Hammer *was* the expert, 'a very experienced chartered surveyor' (he was an architect and building surveyor). The letter included a further gem justifying the Ogmores' disappearance following the surveyors' proposals in November 2002, 'Our clients *acting on legal advice* [whose advice?] did not proceed [further] because your clients and *their surveyors* suggested some changes which would have resulted in a variation of the Hammer plan.' Hazel and Joe seemed to have forgotten that their estimable non-land chartered surveyor had shaken hands on the proposal he had agreed, and written to his clients promoting it.

Lucy took time to write a crib sheet for Mr Smythe in preparation for the costs hearing. It is likely she seriously overestimated the degree of knowledge, commitment and confidence their Deputy District Judge representative had. The four-page, carefully constructed commentary on the litigation ended: 'Please draw the Judge's attention to the Claimants' continuing delay on the survey and the fact the surveyor's report will be essential.' He never drew the attention of the Judge to anything. Despite requesting a later date for this hearing for his convenience, he did not show up. And nor did Wolf Rottman.

A week after the hearing Rottman came clean. Lucy and Max were represented by 'my colleague Hannah Katz as she *previously* had dealings with your file.' Interesting word 'previously' – was that 'previously' until she was sacked in early April? Or was that 'previously' rather more recently? It was not 'previously' at all. Hannah Katz had never taken her hands off the case. The bounced emails were the clue at that time, the time ledgers, invoices and attendance notes were the clinchers – but they came later. Yet again, their instructions had been ignored. Wolf Rottman had deceived them. His letter suggested this was a one-off, but the tone of 'his' letter had all the hallmarks of Katz: she 'secured the best possible outcome on your behalf ... she saved a considerable sum in costs. Nevertheless ... 'the costs of the amended Defence and Counterclaim to be paid by you. Please see attached interim invoice and attendance note.'

Her wordy attendance note reported that Ms Wormelow again resisted attempts to agree Directions before seeing the Judge. Hazel Ogmore was there to hold Tracey's hand so there must have been another reason. Ms Katz's four-page note recorded her own excellent performance, winning three out of the four clashes: (1.) Judge Ten ordered a preliminary report from the surveyor;

(2.) James Nunn's illustration on the Hammer plan of the splay of possible downhill boundaries persuaded him that it *was* open to dispute (DJ Dyer take note) and finally (3.) he agreed that the two costs hearings he had presided over should be costs in the case. He did not fully agree to suspend court action until the survey and report were in, but he did order that Witness Statements and all the paraphernalia (and costs) required for trial await the outcome of the survey. Unfortunately, he ordered that lists of documents the parties might want to show at trial be exchanged beforehand. According to Ms Katz's 'objective' report, she raised enough queries about the quantum of Ogmore's Claim for it to be talked out undecided – they had run over time. Just at the end the Judge referred to ADR as a means of reducing costs. We should perhaps give this Judge a name. Not Judge Ten but Judge White. Let's call him District Judge Hugo White.

If the case had come to him first thing back in January, it is possible that all the unnecessary litigation games – defences, counterclaims, responses, amended defences, amended responses, hearings, deferred hearings, letters, faxes, emails – quibbles and threats (that is to say costs, irritation and delay), could have been avoided and the Ogmore Gang confounded. But, only if he had insisted that both parties go away, agree an independent surveyor and only call on the assistance of the Court if they couldn't agree where a fence should go *after* the survey. Pity DJ White was not the Judge the papers went to first. He might have read them. He might have asked why the Ogmores had taken the dispute into court without warning or any of the pre-action procedures in Lord Woolf's new Rules and he might have spotted the deceitful pretext for the so-called injunction; he might have called Ogmore's bluff. He might even have seen through Ogmore's arrogant contention that information about Hammer's instructions, plans and (non-existent) reports were 'privileged'. Of course, there's no certainty he would have performed so well, but we'll give him the benefit of the doubt. In any event the papers did not go to District Judge White; they went to Judge With No Name Nine – who shall remain nameless. DJ White did feel obliged to follow up the hearing with a long list of precise orders with deadlines, all non-negotiable. So, not perfect.

One benefit of Court Orders was that the Ogmores could no longer prevaricate – Judge White *directed* the appointment of Jason Higgins. Wormelow's draft instructions for him were, true to form, contentious: Only two, not three boundaries to be marked out and no mention of a surveyor's report, merely a brief letter to the Court confirming the work had been done, no mention of the Land Registry plan and, above all, the survey to be based *solely* on the Hammer plan. She named Hannah Katz as the 'Defendants' representative'. As neither Max nor Lucy realised that Rottman was on the golf course again leaving it all to his 'colleague', they thought Wormelow had made another of her many mistakes, so they emailed *him* their commentary on The Gang's work correcting innumerable errors in the background information and 'relevant factual information' and instructing that all four boundaries would have to be surveyed and three marked out; that a report is required to include a commentary on both the Hammer plan and their rectified Title plan and that Mr Rottman not Ms Katz was their representative.

These conflicting draft instructions for Mr Higgins would have ensured several more months of litigation and considerably more costs but for the fact that Lucy had found out (O'Hare and Browne again) that in these situations if the parties don't agree instructions they can each send their own to the expert. If the Ogmores knew this they were not telling anybody and resisted it strenuously when officially informed. If Wolf Rottman knew he did not tell his clients. So they told him. This Civil Procedure Rule must have been frustrating for the Ogmores – not only were they denied further cost-generating litigation games, they were also forced to have the boundary between themselves and Dunroamin' included in the survey because that instruction was in the Ethan Ganz version. In fact, when Mr Higgins finally came to look at the site he confirmed what Max and Lucy had been saying for the previous six years – any survey would have to start at the third boundary: the carport wall provided the only fixed line. Mr Smythe, Ms Katz and Mr Rottman had copy of a recent Statement by Dick Ackroyd of Dunroamin' emphasising that undeniable fact – but neither Mr Smythe's doctored nor Ms Katz's self-laudatory notes made any mention of this essential fact. Indeed, despite Ms Katz's 'excellent' performance, District Judge White had been persuaded by the Ogmore Gang that only two boundaries needed to be surveyed.

They still had to use the unreliable email contact with Rottman and were not pleased that he had still failed to send *his* draft directions. When it finally arrived on the very deadline day, Lucy had to spend hours correcting and amending and trying to get her work back to him through his fortress walls. Even more urgent action was needed on disclosure documents. Even though Ethan Ganz LLP had known for a couple of weeks that a list had to be drawn up and exchanged, they did not alert Max and Lucy that they needed their help until a couple of days before the deadline. Their clients wearily accepted that their lawyers couldn't do the work, but they needed guidance on selecting from several thousand sheets of paper. Rottman's reply left them confused. On the one hand they had to list anything they might want to cite at trial (if it came to trial), on the other, they should only list items relating to the boundaries, but nothing prior to the date of the Consent Order, and leave out references to Ogmore's conduct. 'If you wish to adduce evidence relating to the misconduct of the Claimants' Solicitors [sic] it should be done under cover of a professional negligence claim in separate proceedings.' That really *was* confusing. How could they take out a professional negligence claim against a solicitor with whom they had no contract? Did Rottman know something they didn't? Of course he didn't. He had not written the incorrect 'advice' – young Ms Katz had. Masquerading as her boss, she told them they had to list everything supporting their case *and* items which did not. They could produce a supplemental list later if it appeared necessary, but, she warned, Ogmore could complain and demand costs, so, 'you should proceed on the basis that all documents pertinent to the issues in this case are disclosed at this stage.' It looked as though they'd have to add items to do with conduct just in case. More hours of hunting, collating and listing. They managed to type up a carefully pruned but detailed and referenced list of some 75 items. Had they seen their opponent's list they could have saved themselves most of the work. The Ogmores made no pretence of listing items not supporting their case, nor did they bother much with detail – just 'Correspondence – various', plus 10 referenced and familiar items.

The Ethan Ganz list came direct from Ms Katz – late again and full of seriously confusing errors. 'Not only do we have to pay these people, we have to write the draft and then correct the errors in their "final" version. We are doing nearly all the work,' said Lucy. They had just one day before the deadline to correct the mistakes and hunt for copies of documents their lawyers had lost or were too lazy to hunt down. Lucy did not get to bed until 2 am exhausted and then had to rise again early to re-type everything and send to both Katz and Rottman. A few hours later they received by email attachment Katz's attempt to complete the official online Standard Disclosure List, but the key item, Lucy's document list, was missing from the form which would now not be sent to meet the deadline – 'because you have included items which do not relate to the boundaries'! Ms Katz was in the blame game again. She had told them to list 'all pertinent documents' for a potential trial – and conduct would be an issue if costs were awarded against them. Besides, the Ogmores' list was vague – not even indicating *how many* documents let alone *what* documents, pertinent or otherwise, were included. More work for an angry Lucy now determined to ensure that Ms Katz was off their case as soon as this list was settled. The next version to arrive was even worse: the numbering was haywire and in duplicate, important plans were missing and documents solely relating to Ogmore's conduct *were* included, as were documents prior to the Consent Order. Lucy had no more time. She told Ms Katz to sign whatever was finally sent and, 'we must trust that the form is correctly completed in our best interests.'

Meanwhile, the Ogmores were pushing hard to force the third boundary out of the survey. They tried a familiar gambit – an application to the Court for an order from a Judge, *but* without a hearing 'to save costs'. 'To save costs or to avoid proper scrutiny?' wondered Max. But Lucy had already told them that they could dismiss this bullying because two separate sets of instructions would do and, moreover, would not need the Court's consent. Furthermore, eight feet of the third boundary was between *Homestead* and Blackstone Cottage. This last fact and Dick Ackroyd's Statement may be why the Ogmores decided to throw in the towel. The extra letters, faxes and emails had simply delayed the survey and added to costs. However, the Claimants did not take losing a battle in their stride; the correspondence with Ethan Ganz following that climb-down was as intolerant, unreasonable, aggressive and arrogant as ever.

The embarrassment created by Ms Katz's chaotic documents list was compounded by the opposition's demand for sight of some of the items and for an explanation of the abbreviations. A child of 11 could have worked out the abbreviations – but these were lawyers and these demands allowed costly bother. Ms Katz now wanted her clients to find, collate, copy and send the requested items so she could send them on to the opposition. All these documents had been sent months earlier to Ethan Ganz.

Frustrated by the blocking of her emails to Rottman and concerned about missed deadlines, Lucy was still copying emails to Ms Katz in the hope that somebody would respond. Then Max and Lucy were pleasantly surprised by a letter from the big man himself enclosing yet another version of the list which he had tidied up somewhat, together with a raft of letters from Wormelow. As suspected he had been neglecting his oversight role and ignoring his clients' instructions. He was now trying catch-up.

They were even more surprised to receive a call from him the same day, seemingly to justify passing the workload on to his clients: if his clients did the work, he pointed out; they would not incur any costs! Max could not challenge the logic, but couldn't help but feel that one engaged lawyers, at a cost per hour exceeding the weekly wage of many, to save doing the work oneself, and for their superior knowledge of the law and Civil Procedure Rules (about instructing experts, for example). Then the Head of Litigation (Dispute Resolution) got round to the real purpose of the call: Ms Katz was leaving the firm at the end of the week. Another lawyer, a Tim Pickles, a local man and a qualified solicitor who had recently joined the firm, had been getting up to speed on their case – *at no extra cost to them*. He insisted that he was still in overall control but he was a very busy person with other cases to deal with. The concept of 'no extra cost' was interesting. When Max and Lucy finally received the costs sheets which had been denied them for the months of April to July, they discovered that Ms Katz had been the sole lawyer defending their corner with no input from her boss, and also that they had been charged by both her and her replacement during the handover time.

Bulmers went over the top on Rottman's substitute document list, 'We have never experienced litigation being conducted in the manner of your firm.' Ms Wormelow refused to accept service because it was out of time. She complained that she had telephoned on two days and left messages but the calls were not returned. She demanded a document inspection appointment by a 4pm deadline, if not she 'would have no alternative but to ask for an order that your clients be debarred from further defending.' Nearly all the documents she demanded to see were in her file. Some were merely copies of letters addressed to her firm! Lucy hoped that not many litigators experienced litigation conducted in the Ogmore manner. She also hoped that their new representative was up to meeting the challenge.

Jason Higgins finally made it on site some six months after District Judge No Name (Nine) had made the Order. He could not complete the survey because he had a holiday booked and would be away until the middle of August, but he made a start. He discussed the two sets of directions with Max and Lucy and dismissed the idea that Blackstone Cottage land could be surveyed starting anywhere other than from the carport wall on the third boundary. He also found the Hammer plan amusing, but stifled the witty comments when Lucy pointed out that although everyone thought it a joke, apart from the Ogmores and possibly Royston Hammer and a few judges, this plan had tied them up in litigation for six years. Mr Higgins was not content to rely on it. He wanted digital versions of the Ordnance Survey plan. He then went on holiday for four weeks.

Now Max and Lucy had to get their new champion inducted. They hoped Tim Pickles would not take as long as his predecessor to grasp the set-up at Bulmers. By the time she was leaving Ms Katz was just beginning to understand that the constant warnings she had been given about the opposition were not just the usual demonising of the enemy. She had not curbed her desire to blame her clients for her errors and she never got as far as apologising for them, but there was evidence that she was learning much of what her clients had been telling her was reliable. They hoped she had passed on to the new man her assessment of Ms Wormelow, 'Out of her depth; a puppet of her lawyer clients.' They hoped that if she had he did not assume that this would make his job any easier. They were not sorry to see her go and both wondered – did she jump or was she pushed?

Most of Bulmer's documents were familiar but not the photograph of a severed baby conifer. This attempt to construct evidence of a dastardly crime was so cack-handed Lucy began again to worry not only about the judgement but also the state of mind of her next-door neighbours, and about the extent of Ms Wormelow's gullibility. The photo showed a flimsy conifer barely three feet high tied to the same part of the reed fence Lucy had photographed at the time the wire and post line was being constructed – not a conifer in sight. To compound the nonsense, the Ogmores accused Jarvis Jenkins, the woodland expert who had witnessed Kevin Swale's encounter with Hazel Ogmore back in 1999, of being implicated, possibly even the culprit, since his van had been parked in Homestead's drive at the time they decided the heinous crime had been committed. In fact he had been repairing the damage caused by three very large woodland trees that had been blown down over the path some 200 feet below the severed conifer. The little conifer could have been cut in half with a pair of secateurs. Why on Earth were they attempting this charade? Were they trying to discredit Mr Jenkins because he had written a Witness Statement back in 2002 which damned Mrs Hazel Ogmore?

Max decided that he would have to make the area of Homestead land near the boundary more accessible for Jason Higgins' next visit, and was in the process of scything through the brush and weeds on the very steep land when he became aware that Joe Ogmore was standing by the end of his roadside fence watching him. Just then Lucy arrived to help. She asked Ogmore if he wanted something. No. He wanted to make sure they did not set foot on his land. 'How do you know which is yours and which is ours?' asked Lucy. 'Mr Hammer's plan sets that out very clearly,' came the reply, which both Max and Lucy found amusing. 'So, why did Mr Hammer tell you to move your stretch of fence nearer the shed if all was very clear? Why did you get it wrong?' 'I'll call the Police if you step on to my land.' More laughter from his neighbours. Lucy could not resist a reply, 'You seem unaware that the local Police know all about you. They may not take too kindly to being bothered by you …' He left before she could elaborate further which she found frustrating but Max thought rather fortunate. Max never talked about the damage Ogmore's attack had done to him, but Lucy could see that neck movements were still painful and restricting, and she neither forgave nor forgot that Joe Ogmore had managed to escape justice.

Jason Higgins returned for his third visit in late August but, again, he did not finish the work. He arrived about noon and left at four but there was a torrential downpour for over half an hour. He had decided to ignore the Court Order that neither party speak to him; he needed to discuss the confusions between the two sets of background information and some conflicting dates. He wanted to know how the Hammer plan came about – what were his instructions? Max said that only the Ogmores and Royston Hammer himself knew what his instructions were, but any work would have to have been based on the original 1963 conveyance plan. Needless to say, that plan was not in Bulmer's pack – but then it was not listed in Ethan Ganz's pack either. It was only then that Lucy realised that Wolf Rottman and Tim Pickles had not sent him the version of instructions that she had painstakingly corrected and amended. She was able to provide the correct data – and the plan. Unsurprisingly, Mr Higgins saw little relationship between the Hammer plan, the 1963 plan and the various Land Registry Title plans and, like surveyors before him, regretted that the floating Hammer garden plan lacked any reference to adjoining properties. Lucy assumed that Jason Higgins had talked to the Ogmores during the downpour. A fairly safe and correct assumption.

Max and Lucy had assumed the work would be completed that day but the late arrival and early departure, aggravated by the downpour meant that he would have to come back again – and so far no boundary had been pegged out. Mr Higgins decided he would have to carry out a more extensive survey if he was required to come up with a reliable interpretation of the Hammer plan. He wanted more information from the Ogmore Gang; he had found inconsistencies between his survey and the Hammer plan which he would have to address as the Hammer plan 'is the key document'. Tim Pickles had become more and more encouraged by the expert's comments on the Hammer plan and even more so when he received Mr Higgins' report following the next survey visit: 'The Hammer plan does not accurately represent the relationship of features on the ground … the road frontage shows an error of magnitude of up to five feet.' 'The dimensions have not been used as I believe they should.' 'The Land Registry rectified drawing does not reflect the shape of the Blackstone plot.' 'If it is accepted that the dimensions should be used then the Hammer plan will need to be revised.'

The Ogmore Gang was not pleased. Ms Wormelow came back immediately to remind the expert that he had been instructed to mark out the shared boundaries based *solely* on the Hammer plan which showed three boundary measurements. Max reminded Tim to remind the unfortunate Mr Higgins that he had two sets of instructions of equal weight and that his prime duty was not to either client but to the Court. However, Max was far more interested in something else in Tracey's letter: the first admission that the Hammer plan was based on the 1963 conveyance plan. So, at last, the 'privileged' information so long withheld was revealed and Ms Wormelow's assertion that the 1963 plan showed measurements on *three* sides was revealed as a lie. It did not. It showed measurements on two – just as any oblong with equal sides would. She then compounded this assertion with another: she referred to 'the old telephone pole shown on the 1963 plan on the roadside.' On that plan no telephone pole was shown on the roadside. A pole was shown down the hill on the riverside. Any halfway decent surveyor who recognised his duty to the Court would have transcribed those measurements to his interpretation of the 1963 plan. Cain, Tweed and Scroggs had made no attempt to extract all this essential information from the squatters before they landed Max and Lucy in the mire with their Consent Order, but then neither had any judge, or any gentleman or lady at Her Majesty's Land Registry. Once they took back control of their case, Max and Lucy had tried and failed on more than one occasion. This unsurprising revelation was too late.

Max and Lucy found the expert's report interesting but could not check the pegs he had planted because they could not access Blackstone Cottage land. Also, they had to communicate through Tim who was having the usual off-site problems of sorting out his North, South, East and West. Too much time had already been wasted trying to get him to understand what so many other lawyers and judges had also failed to understand, not having seen the site, so in the end they abandoned all attempt to educate him in the basics of land surveying. Jason Higgins was having similar problems with both sets of lawyers but *he* could not duck them. He replied to Bulmer's letter pointing out that his problem was, 'that there are errors, which in land survey terms, would be described as gross errors with the Hammer plan,' and, 'The shed and the fence's as-built (i.e. real) position is different to the Hammer plan. The error is about two feet, which again in land survey terms is a gross error.' This expected rubbishing of the Hammer plan was comforting, but did not get to the heart of the matter for Max and Lucy. They wanted all their boundaries with Blackstone Cottage pegged out clearly and visibly so that they could finally get a fence up. They also wanted to know one way or another if the shed trespassed on their land.

The answer came with Jason Higgins' plan: the shed did not trespass; the boundary line did not cut through the shed, even though some of the paths and fence were trespassing. It was clear, however, that five of the 10 metal posts were on the wrong side. Not quite the answer Max and Lucy hoped for. Even though this might, at last, give them a line for their fence to follow, and add more strength to their various claims for recompense from those who had allowed the Hammer plan to cause so much damage, it was not a good answer for them from a litigation point of view. The Court would only be concerned to know who was trespassing on whose land the most. Being realists Max and Lucy had known that this was a possible outcome; they had repeated often enough that no one could know precisely where the boundary line was. After all, three surveyors had told them that by applying the Hammer plan to the real world the shed trespassed on Homestead land. By thwarting all attempts at a survey – until now – the Ogmores had ensured for six years that nobody could know where the boundary should be. The Ogmores were troublemakers, obviously, but that did not excuse the civil justice system failing to bring them to book. Judges, several judges, could have stopped their games. Above all, District Judge Dyer. By refusing to order an independent survey Judge Dyer had given *carte blanche* to the Ogmores to make trouble for a further five years.

SIXTEEN
October 2008–2010

Зако́н что ды́шло, куда́ повернёшь - туда́ и вы́шло

'The law is like a shaft. Whichever way you turn – you're still shafted.'

Interpretation of the Russian proverb

As the days went by Max and Lucy's initial satisfaction that a survey had finally produced a result slowly faded. The report had rightly trashed Royston Hammer's work but Max wanted to know, 'Where do we put our fence? There are too few pegs and we can't see most of them. We've no idea where in the undergrowth the riverside peg is and the other pegs are even more difficult to get at.' They should not have allowed their expert to leave the site without showing where the pegs were; after all, he had been asked to peg out all the boundaries in order to make clear where fences should go.

They were also disconcerted by the fact that Mr Higgins' plan plotted their wire and posts oddly. It was clear for all to see (and recorded in photos) that they had put the first post right at the end of the Ogmore's fence, but on his drawing that post was 18 inches further along the fence very firmly on Ogmore land. He had plotted their fence incorrectly. Moreover he had failed to include the Ogmores' reed fence altogether. It was becoming all too clear that if they wanted to they could challenge Mr Higgins's plan – but did they want to?

He would only come back if they paid him. Another unsatisfactory mess but not one the optimistic Tim Pickles recognised. For him Mr Higgins' report trashed the Hammer plan sufficiently to prove that it was not reliable. 'Not reliable, of course not,' said Max, 'we always knew that, but it is showing the shed on Ogmore land even if the flagstones and so on are not.' Mr Pickles told them to wait until they received the tracings which could be overlaid on the Hammer plan and the Title plan and show just how wrong both plans were.

According to Mr Pickles, 'Mr Higgins thinks he is going to have difficulty persuading the Ogmores to pay for his report as it is.' Lucy and Max thought that the real difficulty would be persuading the Ogmores to accept that the Hammer plan was defective and ambiguous. Sure enough, Ms Wormelow's next letter to Ethan Ganz written in a more than strictly necessary triumphalist style, ignored everything that damned the Hammer plan and went straight for the trespassing metal posts. The Ogmore Gang wanted the metal posts out, and £250 for the (non-existent) plants, adding tartly, that 'no *further* damage to plants be done in the process of removing the posts.' The Gang was considering an application for summary judgment.[1] The letter contained the requisite number of false assertions (Ogmore rules): (1.) 'The Hammer plan is not ambiguous' (!), (2.) 'your clients' fence which precipitated these proceedings' (!), (3.) Mrs Ogmore personally planted the missing [sic] plants which were damaged or disappeared after your clients put up their trespassing fence …' etc., etc. Inured to the provocative lies, Max merely observed the Ogmores no longer claimed that the Land Registry plan was an adequate interpretation of the Hammer plan regardless of the General Boundary Rules.[2]

When the transparencies eventually arrived they did indeed confirm that it was impossible to match any one boundary on Mr Higgins' transparency with the same one on the Hammer plan without throwing the others out of line. There was no way to get them to match either the Hammer plan or the HMLR plan. The best they could get were two matching boundaries, but then Jason Higgins' shed boundary-line cut through Hammer's plotting of the shed! However, Max and Lucy added another reservation about Mr Higgins' plan. They saw something odd about *his* plotting of the shed: it did not seem to reflect what they could see on site and important measurements were missing.

Nevertheless, this plan was an improvement on the Consent Order plan and they were not prepared to argue further, but they believed the Ogmores should pay for their vexatious litigation, for bringing the dispute to court on a pretence when it was quite unnecessary. Ethan Ganz LLP agreed with that and corresponded with the enemy accordingly. This predictably set off a storm of letters and yet more Ogmore variations on the *actualité*: the land by the shed 'has always belonged to our clients … the only difference between Mr Higgins' plan and the Hammer plan is the roadside boundary which is of no concern to your clients … for six years your clients never agreed with anything proposed by our clients … your clients failed to agree to an independent survey …' etc., etc.

They tried the same thing on with Mr Higgins but he was having nothing of it. His reply refuting their various assertions ended with, 'I confirm my opinion that we have a duty of care to successors in Title and an adequate, accurate drawing should be used to define the extent of Blackstone Cottage's Title. To use the Hammer plan, without amendments, would not fulfil this duty.'

The Ethan Ganz letters were now far more forthright and unequivocal, but this quality was wasted on the adversaries. Every Ethan Ganz statement was ignored or directly rebutted with yet more fanciful assertions. It was like fighting a mountain of spider webs. There was nothing for it; a judge would have to settle matters.

The judiciary started rather badly. A judge – number Eleven (who has a name but as he disappears from this play almost immediately we will not put him in the cast list), decided to allocate this simple boundary dispute to multi-track, that's the most expensive track usually dealing with cases of considerable value and complexity. His Orders cited trial dates for January 2009 and several time-consuming, expensive procedures. It is not clear what triggered this pointless intervention. Certainly Ethan Ganz LLP hadn't asked for it and the opposition did not want trial, they wanted summary judgment and indemnity costs. They provided a Witness Statement by Hazel Ogmore, most of it familiar Ogmore storytelling. The confusions were numerous, starting with the undeniable fact that the Ogmores wanted summary judgment (because some of the metal posts trespassed), but they had *not* issued a claim against trespass. They had issued an application for an injunction to prevent Max and Lucy dismantling any fence they might chose to erect and Max and Lucy had dismantled nothing. The Gang had never actually issued a claim for damages arising from the wire and post fence. Yet now they declared *that* as the 'cause of action' and the trespass was their right to damages and costs. There seemed to be no alternative: 'We'll have to go back to court. As if we have much faith in judges,' said Max, 'How long would it take?' asked Lucy. Less time with a summary judgment hearing apparently.

It was late October 2008. Max and Lucy returned a day early from London and Lucy went up the road to check the lie of the land. She was amazed to see a workman moving the Ogmores' reed fence – *again*. He told her that he had been instructed to run a string down the hill between the roadside peg and the peg marking the end of that boundary and in doing so found that the Ogmores' reed fence was trespassing! If Lucy had not caught him in the act, and taken several photographs, it is unlikely the move would have been detected. He moved it just over a metre, and if they had not come back a day early they would not have caught him in the act. So, the question arises: why had Mr Higgins omitted the Ogmores' reed fence on his plan even though he did delineate – inaccurately, the metal posts? The Ogmores had admitted moving their trespassing fence a year earlier and claimed to have moved it to a position, 'where there can be no question of it being on (Homestead) land,' and yet here they were a year later having to move it again, secretly, when Max and Lucy should have been in London. It had still been trespassing even after the move.

Initially Tim Pickles' diffident demeanour had not impressed, but in their view anyone would have been an improvement on Hannah Katz. *He* seemed genuinely concerned and committed. They regretted even more that Hannah Katz had ever come into their lives. He had visited Homestead (at a charge of £550!), but at least he knew the lie of the land and some of the lies of the opposition. Nevertheless, they were not sure he was the man to do the Court talking, particularly if Stoat was sitting in the other chair. They would need a good, competent, well briefed barrister. Mr Pickles agreed, not the least offended, 'Horses for courses.' They now knew of two recommended Chambers in the region and they finally decided on young, highly recommended Mark Christie who agreed to visit the site prior to the hearing.

The point of the summary judgment for the Ogmore Gang was to avoid a full disclosure of the facts. As no witnesses are permitted there would be no Jason Higgins to trash the Hammer plan and reveal the dilemma Max and Lucy had faced when it was applied to a Consent Order. No public untangling to lay bare Ogmore lies. Mr Pickles favoured a full trial to expose the Gang in court, but Max and Lucy preferred an end to court games. There followed some elaborate jousting between the Gang and Tim Pickles about Statements and other documents caused by the confusing still-on-the-table allocation to multi-track. Unlike his predecessor, Mr Pickles saw off the bullying at a very modest charge of £69.50 plus VAT. Witness Statements were needed a week before the summary judgment hearing and Lucy's left nothing out: it ran to 10 pages and 50 separate paragraphs; she knew it was unlikely any judge would read it in full, if at all, but she wanted to be sure that Mr Christie had as much background information as possible. Max's Statement was half the length and focussed on the actual pretext for taking the matter into court and the lies around it. He also, uncharacteristically, elaborated on Joe Ogmore's attack and the consequences for him.

Throughout this time the Gang involved the Court whenever possible in several attempts to wrong-foot the enemy and paint their ideal picture of the warring parties. Much against his good taste, Tim Pickles felt obliged to ensure that an alternative view was represented, so the Court and whichever judge was listed for the hearing found themselves pestered with correspondence not only from the Gang, but also from Ethan Ganz.

Mark Christie proved to be a very amenable young man and cheaper than the solicitor. Cheaper and sharper. Unlike the equally amenable Tim Pickles, he spotted immediately the discrepancy between Jason Higgins' tracing of their metal posts and what he could see on the land, and he was open to Max's suspicions about the expert's location of the shed, but both agreed that they should open as few cans of worms as possible and Max and Lucy were not unhappy to avoid a trial before yet another judge. The land was small matter, costs, on the other hand, were not and Mark Christie's initial advice was that as some of the metal posts clearly trespassed they would lose and as they would lose they would have to pay the Gang's costs. Lucy felt sick. She could not believe that all the evidence of bad conduct, vexatious, unnecessary litigation, the injunction gambit, the false accusations, Hammer's trashed plan and the recorded evidence that the Ogmores had moved their trespassing fence twice would result yet again in paying the squatters for their crimes. The hearing was just three days away and Mr Christie had one other court appearance and another case to review before then. He had not read their Witness Statements and had only the briefest of briefings when he made that shock announcement. By the time he left, having got up to speed with speed, he had a more optimistic view but not optimistic enough for Max and Lucy, who decided that they would now have to redouble their efforts to ensure that those who had been negligent paid for it.

When they arrived at the Court where all the damage had been done six years earlier, they were met by the ever optimistic Tim Pickles. He had spoken to Mark Christie who was now of the opinion that he had a good case to make in their Defence. A few hours earlier he had sent his skeleton argument to the Judge, a District Judge Green (Judge 12), drawing attention to their Witness Statement and citing key precedents and CPRs. Max wanted to know if he knew anything about this District Judge Green. Tim Pickles wasn't sure, he didn't think so. 'Well,' said Max, 'knowing your Judge is often more important than knowing the law.'

They were called several times but the other side was not to be seen. When they did finally make it into the hearing room, only Ms Wormelow was there. Lucy already knew Stoat was most unlikely to turn up; Tim had done his homework and found that Stoat's Chambers had not booked him for work that day, but where was Hazel Ogmore? How would Tracey Wormelow manage without her? Apparently her client was parking her car. 'It can take a long time in this city,' the Judge observed. The two Defendants silently concurred.

District Judge Green set a no-nonsense pace straight from the word go. He started by fulminating at length on being inundated with faxes and letters, 'The CPRs say you shall not send faxes and letters. I will not tolerate it. The Court staff are being repeatedly cut back so stop sending letters. I have not read all that I can assure you.' Mark Christie apologised immediately, he was guilty of sending in his skeleton argument that morning. 'Skeletons are a bit different; we are used to getting those at the last minute.'

'Now,' he continued, 'am I right that a surveyor has been involved recently and people agree where the boundary is according to this 2002 plan?' He held high the Hammer plan between finger and thumb as something distasteful, 'Doomed to cause problems it seems to me.'

Both representatives agreed the string line between two pegs was not in contention. District Judge Green heaved a huge sigh of relief. He was trying to deduce why they were in court. The answer: costs, litigation costs and damages costs.

Hazel Ogmore finally arrived and was seen through the glass door panel trying to get in. Failing, she went away and only finally made it through when she read the instructions to press the buzzer. She was seriously flummoxed. Not only parking problems, not only buzzer problems, but her mouthpiece had been on her own and floundering in her absence – although the Judge had done most of the talking. She made her way to sit next to her puppet, but Judge Green would not permit it. She had to sit some two metres behind with Max, Lucy and Tim. Too far back to whisper instructions. 'This could be interesting,' Lucy mouthed. 'He *hasn't* read the papers,' whispered Max, 'It will be six of one and half dozen of the other. We'll be tarred with the Ogmore brush as usual.'

'This war has gone on longer than World War One,' opined the Judge on cue to reinforce Max's fear. 'I'm not taking sides, okay? Each of you might think it is the other one hundred per cent I do not know, but this is barmy. If it goes to multi-track I would be terrified if I were in the shoes of either of you. Now let's get on but tread carefully because I will fly off the handle pretty quickly. I will tell you that for nothing.'

Lucy tried hard to ignore Tracey Wormelow's tired gypsy skirt, her elderly shoes and the ladder running up her navy tights. For some reason her inappropriate appearance for a solicitor in court gave Lucy hope, as did the furious scribbling by the Claimant two chairs away when Judge Green pointed out at length and forcefully that you could not have a summary judgment for an injunction. However, the next statement by Ms Wormelow was electrifying 'The Defendants admit in their amended defence that they have interfered with the Claimants' fence.' Where did that lie come from? Ms Wormelow, Ms Katz or the Usual Suspects? As Lucy was not permitted to speak it would just have to lie there in the Judge's head until they could contact Mark and kill it dead. Meanwhile the rapid-fire Judge had moved on. The injunction was effectively dismissed. Now it was the business of the loss of amenity from the wire and posts and the damage to plants. Tracey Wormelow estimated £1,000 in damages. The Judge was becoming impatient with Hazel Ogmore 'going up and down like a yo-yo' trying to get her spokesperson to say what she wanted her to say. He just wanted to know what the Claimant wanted him to do. 'Are you the Claimant or the Defendant?' He was also getting impatient with the Claimant's solicitor and she was getting more and more confused and confounded. Lucy observed her nervously shifting feet. The quick-fire questioning left her far behind. She rummaged through notes; she referred to Max's Witness Statement when she meant her client's. It was clear that she really was out of her depth and Hazel Ogmore, prevented from feeding her lines, was getting more and more frustrated. Judge Green was not making any allowances, 'Come on. You *are* a solicitor, are you not?' Ms Wormelow paused for breath, 'Yes I am, sir.' Hazel could stand it no more, risking Judge Green's ire she rushed to her unfortunate puppet and stubbed a finger at a note she had scrawled. It did not appear to be much help because her representative then started on about Ethan Ganz's refusal to exchange Statements for the multi-track case before this hearing only to have her efforts dismissed by the Judge, 'Would you please just tell me what figure you want me to write down on an order: £1,000, £29.59 or £20,000 or what? Then tell me where you get the figure from and what law supports you.'

Forty-five minutes too late Tracey Wormelow at last had a grasp on her role. She wanted a summary judgment not a trial – therefore her job was to say what she wanted in costs and damages and why. There ensued a slightly less confusing duologue leading Judge Green to inspect Hammer's year-old amended plan and noting the instruction that the Ogmores' fence should be moved nearer the shed. Wormelow had enough wits about her to distract him from that damaging evidence of her clients' conduct and got him to focus on Hammer's plotting of the post and wire fence. Judge Green could clearly see trespass and nobody seemed to think otherwise, so it was simply a question of how much the trespass should cost. He wanted a price. Flummoxed again Ms Wormelow wanted to take instruction, but the Judge thought she should have come prepared. It was her summary judgment application – 'and please show me how it can be more than the Small Claims limit (£5,000)[3] because I do not think it would be.'

'My client is seeking only nominal damages for the encroachment.'

'So, in simple language, you are saying a trial is totally unnecessary.'

'Spot on, Mr Judge,' whispered Max. Another competent judge arrives on scene too late.

Judge Green then returned to the moved fence and Mark got to speak. He pointed out that the reed fence had been moved twice. The second time just marginally (*de minimis*[4] in legal jargon) so, not worth fussing about. 'Quite,' said the Judge who then started to reminisce about boundary cases he had known and judges who had tried to get the warring parties to see sense, 'We are all used to these cases and people … there we are. I would get upset about my neighbours if they were to do something, I understand that. Right. Now I understand what it is that we are talking about.'

Mark pointed out his clients were very dissatisfied with the legal representation they had in 2002. 'For obvious reasons, the plan attached to that Order is completely incomprehensible. Any property lawyer worth his salt would say the same. The plan is useless for marking out the boundary line.' The Judge wholeheartedly agreed and referred to the role of Land Registry whereat Mark seized the opportunity to ask that any order he might make should also incorporate an order for Land Registry to correct their register to reflect the position on the ground as shown on the expert's plan. The Judge was not unsympathetic, but proposed they 'bounced it off the Registry first', to see what they thought. He was clearly happier dealing with Mark, who was having an easier ride.

'Both parties,' Mark said, 'were trespassing on each other's property,' but he did not clarify that the Ogmores' first trespass had triggered the chain reaction and the court case, and was more than *de minimis*. Added together both Ogmore trespasses were about the same as the trespass by the metal posts. Mark Christie missed that argument unfortunately, but in any event Judge Green was concentrating on something else. He was far more concerned to establish that this was a Small Claim case and damages would be ordered accordingly. Despite admitting he had not read any of the papers, he was fully convinced that this was a typical boundary dispute with two sets of goats squabbling over a few blades of grass and impoverishing themselves in the process. Lucy could see the advantage of summary judgment but the constraints worked against her side: no evidence could be admitted so no revelation of the Gang's litigation conduct and no way to challenge the Judge's pre-conceived notions.

When Mark described his clients' post and wire fence the Judge threw down his pen and leant back exasperated, 'How was *this* allocated to multi-track?' Mark seized the advantage, 'We are dealing with a pleaded case, sir, and my learned friend (Wormelow) has not pleaded for an injunction to remove this trespass, so I would be entitled to have this application thrown out.' He was now in full flow and the Judge was with him – most of the way. They both wanted to ensure that the case did not continue after that day and they both wanted to make sure that the litigants knew that costs would be serious if it did. They need not have worried: the Gang did not want it to continue as conduct might be revealed, and possibly because Mark Christie was doing rather well, and, of course, they knew all about costs. The Defendants did not want it to continue because they did not want to entrust their fate to yet another judge. This one talked too much and had not read the papers but he was fully behind the Woolf reforms. He had the makings of a good judge. As if to confirm Lucy's view, he then went on to quote extensively from the rules in Lord Woolf's 'New Landscape'.

He seemed to imagine that Mark and Tracey had engaged in the usual lawyer parley before the hearing but, of course, they had not. He also decided, looking at the litigants that, 'they do not come over as wanting to be aggressive, or wanting injunctions.' Lucy and Max exchanged wry smiles. Mark tried again to persuade him to make an order for Land Registry to rectify Titles, but he slid away from that, again. He wanted to know what the costs were: £10,000 on each side according to barrister and lawyer. 'Unbelievable!' according to the Judge. 'Nobody is going to get costs like that'. He de-listed the case from the multi-track trial. If they didn't come up with an agreement today he would list it as a Small Claim. He urged them to reach 1918, 11th November, 11am.

'We have a court mediator for Children Act cases but not for civil matters. I am not … I am almost doing it, aren't I? But I cannot enter the arena. It is a huge, huge sadness to me that you people have got stuck in this horrible rut and it really needs to be finished.' What a pity he hadn't read anything, it would have been so interesting to see how he would have managed this evidence-free summary judgment if he had had some idea of what had really been going on. He was an interesting judge. They adjourned for lunch and what Judge Green erroneously imagined would be lawyer negotiations.

When Lucy and Max met up with Mark and Tim after a tense lunch, they learned that Mark had failed to speak to Tracey Wormelow; she would not open the door. He tried again and she told him to go away. Next time he knocked and entered, and before the door was slammed shut again glimpsed her taking dictation from her client. He found this surprising. His clients did not. They waited. Lucy saw the Judge going back into the room and Mark let the opposition know, through the door, that the Judge was waiting. It stayed firmly shut. The Judge called them again and both women eventually appeared. Tracey's script was written in full in long-hand. Mark was bemused and very generously shared the blame for the delay suggesting that his 'friend' was taking instructions from her 'lay client' and may want a little more time. The Judge was prepared to oblige, he had various interlocutories. They had another adjournment. An hour passed as Ms Wormelow took not instruction but dictation. Mark, Tim and their clients were getting impatient. The clients particularly as they were paying for this frozen action, but not for Mark. He was on a fixed fee. Only Tim was happy.

The Judged called again and was displeased that there were no agreed orders, unaware that there had not even been discussions. Mark took the initiative. He repeated his clients' admission that there had been a technical trespass. Ms Wormelow emboldened by her 'lay' client's script stepped in openly reading the dictated words proposing that the question of costs be dealt with at a further hearing. Max groaned and hoped the Judge would refuse. The Judge was tired; he'd been hard at this sort of dingdong all day. He turned to Tracey Wormelow, 'The other side do not agree that there is a trespass …' He'd forgotten that only a few minutes earlier the Defendants agreed there had been a technical trespass.

Mark Christie let the memory lapse go and instead urged the Judge to assess costs then and there. Judge Green agreed. As Ms Wormelow was lost again with a redundant script, Mark proposed that she helped all concerned by saying how much the trespass is worth. She said it was worth £1,000 and £29.95 for damaged plants. She wanted to use Lucy's photos as evidence of the damaged plants, but her problem was a clear lack of evidence in any of the pictures. There was evidence of weeds, grass and the wire and metal-post fence, but the Judge could not understand how a bit of wire restricted Ogmore's enjoyment of her weeds and grass. 'Where is the inconvenience? Why didn't she just remove them and chuck them back? Are we going down the route of psychological damage?'

Ms Wormelow and her 'lay client' must have wished they had not introduced the photographs at all but she ploughed on, 'My client is not able to prune her plants, work her garden.' The Judge was now enjoying more photos, 'A couple of burly lads putting the posts in on the steep hillside, in rough grass and weeds. Photographs are helpful. They normally speak a million words.'

Mark seized another opportunity, 'The photographs you have been taken to, quite helpfully in my view (Tracey flinched) … show how steep the land is and any loss of use of this land is …' There was no need to continue. The Judge agreed.

He changed the tape and gave his Judgment. This wavered in and out of accurate and inaccurate record mixed with faulty guesswork on the relationship between the parties, but correctly noted the need for an agreed registered boundary. He was very concerned about the costs that he believed the parties had accrued. Max, having noted much valuable ammunition for his recovery task, was fairly certain that Hazel Ogmore was unlikely to have a £10,000 debt (down from the £20,000 previously claimed), so maybe the sympathy was misplaced. Judge Green dismissed the loss of amenity argument, but acknowledged that embroilment in a multi-track trial was an impingement on lives. 'Why anyone ever wants to come to court to litigate such matters is beyond me. I could think of far better ways of spending my money.' The Defendants wholeheartedly and silently agreed. 'However, there is a technical, real, if *de minimis*, trespass and I agree the assessment of damages for £1,000 (pause – a glance at Hazel Ogmore) except in one respect… It is one nought too many. My award is £100 for damages. The claim for damages to plants dismissed not proven.'

Lucy was amused by the theatrics but irritated by being tarred as a vexatious litigant. 'How,' she wondered, 'could *we* have got off the Court track altogether? Ethan Ganz insisted we had to stay with it. No one had proposed an escape route. Ogmore precipitated court action with her injunction and without any of the pre-action stuff. It was our idea to remove our "fence" as soon as we returned home and found the mess created by our lawyers.' She still liked this Judge and wished he had been the first to encounter the Gang's work back in January (he had overtaken Judge White, who they had never seen, in her estimation). He was playing the mediator role with a Small Claim, but at this late stage he was unlikely to do a good job without reading the background story and the Witness Statements.

Mark was now in full flow, 'The injunction has been abandoned, the damages are nominal (and less than offered before trial) and the counterclaim we have succeeded on. Two out of three we have won.' District Judge Green baulked at that, 'In a sense you have both succeeded on the counterclaim.' A statement that mystified both Defendants. Mark Christie pressed further pointing out that without the initial injunction application the case would never have been on multi-track. 'It wouldn't be in court at all,' muttered Max observing frantic scribbling by the Claimant a few chairs to his left.

Tracey Wormelow took the hurried note stabbed on the table by her rather heated advisor, 'We offered the appointment of an independent advisor before action, if they had accepted that …'

> Mark Christie: 'My clients agreed but proposed getting Land Registry to do it for free.'
> Wormelow: 'But Land Registry was not independent.'

Judge: 'Oh, come on now …'
Christie: 'Land Registry was offering a free service which would be the same as an independent surveyor. There is no suggestion Land Registry were in anybody's pocket.'

The Judge unwisely asserted that, 'They have had six years to sort that out with Land Registry and the Registry have not been out in the interim' (and was not corrected by Mark), continuing impatiently, 'I cannot spend ages on this. I have people who have been waiting an hour.' Turning to Ms Wormelow, 'You want costs of the action?'

'Absolutely,' she said, because her Gang 'had previously offered to resolve the matter without recourse to litigation'. (Sharp intake of breath from the Defendants.) Judge Green reminded her that she had applied for an injunction, she had not sought a declaration on the ground. 'So, you want about £10K off them?'

'Absolutely, sir.'

Mark made a last attempt to shift the Judge from his plague-on-both-your-houses approach by reading the section of a letter Lucy had sent prior to the Gang's injunction gambit, which not only asked for Land Registry to carry out the survey but referred briefly to Land Registry's attempt to carry out that task in 2005 (and in so doing gently corrected the Judge's earlier misconception). The Judge was not really listening he was rummaging through his papers. He had decided.

'The approach I am taking will not require a summary assessment of any of the bills. We have a £10,000 bulldozer facing a £10,000 tank in what was always Small Claims territory. The Claimants have established a trespass and shall have fixed costs for a Small Claim: £69.50 plus £70 plus £175 … £314.50 I think that is. I will now vacate the trial.'

Mark tried yet again to get Judge Green to make an order to get Land Registry to rectify the register (again), but he would only agree to make an order by consent. There was little chance of getting any consent from the Gang. The two in the courtroom were already objecting very loudly.

Lucy did not know what to make of this, but clearly it was a better result than had been threatened just a few days earlier and better, too, than one they might have achieved with most of the previous judges. Max was less relaxed, he would now have a heavy battle with the Registry. The Claimant was even less relaxed. The Defendants were dismayed to see her throw all her papers on the floor and as she scrambled to pick them up Max went over to her, not to help but to admonish, convinced she was annoyed by the costs result. Lucy did not hear him say anything but she did notice frantic, angry whispering from Hazel Ogmore to her somewhat flustered solicitor.

'Did you say something to annoy her?' Max did not reply but he did have the faintest hint of a smile. They were leaving the room for a post-battle conference with their team which was not as sombre as one might expect from the losing side. Mark had done a good job in his clients' view, on a different plane from the performances they had had to endure from his predecessors, particularly bearing in mind the very few hours he'd had for preparation, the other cases he'd dealt with in the previous two days and his well-prepared skeleton. They weren't so sure about Tim's contribution. He had been redundant but because he was there they had to communicate with Mark in his presence. Hazel Ogmore had direct access to her representative. Max and Lucy particularly regretted that Mark Christie was not a direct access barrister[5] when they got the timesheet and discovered that simply for Tim's travel and attendance on the day they were charged over half the amount their barrister charged for *all* his work including the site visit.

'You don't need litigation solicitors, they get in the way and overcharge, you just need a good direct access barrister,' said Max.

'As long as you don't spend six weeks researching in remote parts of the world,' replied Lucy, 'and as long as you don't have the Gang against you, or a Scroggs or Tweed as direct access barrister.'

'Or a District Judge Alfred Dyer judging,' added Max.

The following Monday Tim sent them copy of a letter of searing complaint from Tracey Wormelow. She demanded an immediate and written apology. Apparently Max had called her client a 'slut'. Lucy found this very amusing. She had several words to describe Mrs Ogmore, but 'slut' was not among them. Max was not amused, particularly as she reported that he had called Stoat a 'blackguard' (in fact he'd actually muttered 'scoundrel'). '"Blackguard", "scoundrel", both describe that man accurately in our experience of him,' Lucy consoled him. 'I don't think there's any evidence that she's a "slut". It's laughable. Nobody would believe it. She was furious that you'd patronised her with your "Tut tut" when she had her tantrum and threw her files on the floor. I suggest you don't confuse things, don't waste energy correcting her, just deny everything even though that is edging into Ogmore territory, we can live with that. I certainly can.'

Since nobody had heard or was even aware of anything Max said to Hazel Ogmore that is what they did. Tim advised them to ignore it as Ogmore would not be able to achieve anything if she wanted to make it an issue it. The Gang did try to take it further and threatened a defamation suit. Tim informed them that he 'had no knowledge of the grounds for this allegation', that Ogmore was clearly upset that she only got nominal damages and costs and threw her papers on the floor. The allegation was denied and would amount to no more than vulgar abuse in any event and not actionable. No one had been identified who had heard the word nor was any consequential damage cited. Neither he nor Counsel heard it and if the Gang wanted to take things further they would have to do so directly.

Ogmore replied to Ethan Ganz on Bulmer paper. Max was accused of being a liar (heavy, ironic laughter in Homestead), Max and Lucy were vexatious (more laughter), they had libelled Hazel Ogmore in the past (only *untrue* statements are libellous) and they had abused the Court process repeatedly over six years (louder laughter). She cited The Slander of Women Act 1891,[6] but finally landed a punch with the taunt that she was not troubled by any attempt to strike out her claim as, 'your clients have not been successful in any case between the parties.' Max suggested that Tim inform the Gang that if they continue writing to him he will neither accept correspondence nor bill his (ex-) clients for it. They heard no more.

Now they wanted their papers and documents back. Tim was all set to send them but Wolf Rottman returned to the scene. No documents until they paid their final bill which will be with them in a few days.

One of the first things Max and Lucy did in the New Year was get a transcript of District Judge Green's hearing. They wish they had done this for all hearings; not doing so was a false economy, not just for pursuit of recovery, but also for Lucy's report, which she had still to allocate to a project. They wrote to Tim Pickles asking for the promised – or, rather, threatened – final account now several weeks late, which meant the return of their file was several weeks late, to let him know that they were now acting in person, and to advise that although they believed it unlikely he would encounter such talented exponents of unscrupulous litigation in the future, what he had witnessed should prove useful to him and therefore his clients because he would know to retaliate quickly and forcefully if ever faced with similar 'bulldozer litigation'.

When the final invoice did eventually arrive it did not include the time ledgers and billing guides. An email prod resulted in a pack of ledgers including those for the months of April to June 2008. So they *had* been produced, they had just not been sent to the paying customer. Could this be because they revealed that Hannah Katz had been running the show all the time – after they had fired her? They also received a deduction for the original negligent defence, nearly a year after paying for it.

Then, in early February 2009, they received a claim for £3,600 from Bulmers for that same negligent defence. They forwarded it straight to Wolf Rottman warning him that this was not the first time the Gang had sent a bill well out of time. An order to pay the Gang's costs, despite Hannah Katz's self-declared triumph, had been made in June 2008, some eight months earlier, and the Civil Procedure Rules state that the latest time for costs claims is three months after the Order is made. The Gang was trying the same old trick: presenting a sudden, unexpected late claim which would cost more to challenge than to pay. Max repeated their view that Ethan Ganz was well placed and possibly duty bound to report Bulmers to the Law Society, but they also repeated their view that Ethan Ganz was liable for all costs arising from the negligent defence.

Rottman protested that his firm had done a good job for them bearing in mind that their adversaries were determined to cause them 'as much grief as possible'. However, he proposed a settlement offer of £1,900. Wolf Rottman was unlikely to take well to the idea that his firm should pay for his firm's negligence, but Max and Lucy decided it was worth another visit to that miserable town to put that proposal to him face-to-face and hear what he had to say in defence.

Rottman maintained his usual amiable demeanour throughout the meeting, with Tim Pickles taking notes. Perhaps he hoped to charm them into disappearing from his life and pay Bulmers whatever was finally agreed. According to Lucy, *they* also maintained a cool demeanour as they asked their awkward questions, finishing with the query: why did Ethan Ganz's Head of Litigation (re-titled 'Dispute Resolution'), fail to oversee the work of his paralegal? Until then Rottman had been batting away with aplomb but he took exception to that one insisting that he had advised Ms Katz at all times. In which case why did Ms Katz need to ask another Partner for advice and why did he do nothing while she was away when the enemy, having threatened an interlocutory, carried out the threat? The embarrassed smile this elicited was quite satisfying, but an answer would have been appreciated.

Max proposed that they pay the last invoice under duress, and as *quid pro quo* EG review invoices and payments and make an offer to compensate them for losses arising from the negligent defence. Mr Rottman did not concede that the defence was negligent, he apologised neither for the negligence, nor for the ill-mannered Ms Katz.

His main defence was that they could not now look back with hindsight and they should not ignore the nature of their opponents. He relied heavily on the unnatural character of the opposition and rule-bound, intransigent yet unpredictable judges incapable of using common sense. He claimed that the outcome was quite successful and their opponents had effectively failed as the posts and wire were found to be trespassing, yet the Judge only awarded them fixed costs for a Small Claim, 'As a way of punishment for their conduct.' He also emphasised the restrictions on Defendants, 'As Defendants to these proceedings there was a limit as to how far we could have avoided trial for you. In the light of such opponents there was little further we could have done on your behalf.' He agreed the Gang was way past the deadline for submitting a bill, but that particular CPR was rarely enforced. 'Why is it,' wondered Max, 'that the rules that have to be obeyed always apply to us and the rules that can be ignored apply to the Gang?' Ethan Ganz wanted money upfront for the costs battle to come. Max and Lucy saw this as adding insult to injury and said so, but did not think they had a choice.

The battle did not last quite as long as anticipated. Rottman sent Bulmer a detailed assessment of their costs leaving space for comments. Bulmer came back with comments handwritten by none other than the long-retired Hazel Ogmore and reducing their Claim to £2,500. Assured by several legal experts that Ethan Ganz LLP was guilty of negligence, Max and Lucy were confident that the end payer would be the solicitors, so they sent a cheque and requested their file back.

The irritation that remained was Rottman's repeated assertion that Max and Lucy had originally instructed him to 'defend the matter fully'. They had not. At their very first meeting with Rottman both Max and Lucy pointed out that although they could rebut the pretext for Ogmore's injunction, they couldn't know whether their posts were on Homestead land or not and the best thing to do would be to remove the posts, say why and offer no defence. Rottman had replied that as the matter was now in court they could be liable for Ogmore's costs if they did not offer a defence, and moreover they would not achieve the objective of an independent survey. So Ethan Ganz got the job and produced a defence even after the main objective of a RICS survey was back on track.

That was not quite the end of the matter. After they paid the final invoice there was something of a tussle to get all the papers back and Tim Pickles was charged with demanding 20p for each page copied. This would have been a substantial sum, but someone at the Law Society pointed out that since it was their file, those pages were their pages so, no charge. It was early June 2009 by the time Max returned again to those dreary offices to collect what they believed to be their full file free of charge. Max signed for it stating he had not and could not check it before leaving. They were not to know until the following year that the file handed to him was incomplete.

As for the fence both parties claimed to want, Max and Lucy were constrained by the invisibility and inaccessibility of most of Jason Higgins' pegs. The Ogmores did nothing until Max and Lucy went away for a couple of weeks. On their return they came back to find a close boarded panel fence part-built down from the road to the end of the shed. There was a space of nine inches between fence and shed at the top corner so the portly Ogmores would not be able to pass, and flagstones and shuttering were clearly on the Homestead side.

'Technical trespass,' Max observed.

'We had *offered* full access for maintenance,' Lucy observed. Max decided to creosote the section facing them so that it was less visible. A letter of protest from the other side of the fence arrived within days. Apparently Hazel had no objection to them painting their side but they should have sought permission. Pettiness flared occasionally on both sides. Hazel Ogmore upbraided Lucy's excellent gardener for throwing rubbish on her land. It was her rubbish and identifiable as such and it was Max who had thrown it back some weeks earlier. He wrote to let her know he would do so again if she did so again. These sadly predictable skirmishes continued. A month later they returned from work in Scotland and once again the Ogmores had taken advantage of their absence, this time to continue with wooden posts and wire downhill from the end of the newly-erected fence into the undergrowth, presumably to the higher of the two pegs Mr Higgins had planted to mark the two possible ends to that boundary, as their fence started at the higher roadside peg.[7]

It was not until August 2010 when their gardener had finished clearing land and building steps down by that boundary, that they realised that Ogmore had extended it to the lower peg and had then taken it for about 30 feet along the riverside boundary and was using the extra stretch for bonfires which had smoked some Homestead trees. It was a dry summer in 2010. This time they protested: 'Please remove the trespassing posts and move your unsupervised bonfires away from our trees. We intend to erect a fence along the riverside boundary between our two properties. If you want to discuss this further we are here throughout the rest of the summer.'

Well, that certainly triggered a response. Four pages of poisonous Hazel Ogmore rant and perverted history and ending with yet another injunction threat should they touch her posts. 'She doesn't want a visible fence marking that boundary. She's worried about the sort of fence we might put up,' Lucy explained.

They then received a polite letter agreeing to meet. 'Do you think she's bi-polar?' wondered Lucy, 'I thought it was Joe's mental state I should worry about'. The meeting produced nothing as usual. Hazel brought John, her fencer, who she had told was accused of moving the boundary marker pegs. No such accusation had been made. As Lucy pointed out, even if the pegs had been moved they would never have known since they had never seen them. They had brought a friend as witness just in case an Ogmore version of the encounter were broadcast later. John, unhappy about the disagreement, suggested they split the difference and put up a fence midway between the two pegs. 'Nice man,' said Lucy.

Following the meeting Max wrote advising the Ogmores to decide whether they wanted their downhill shed boundary to start at the road or where the telephone pole used to be and move the fencing accordingly, failing that he advised they should alert Land Registry that they had extended that boundary and that the extension was disputed. Should they ever wish to sell their property, they should alert potential buyers to this boundary dispute. They could, of course, buy the extra strip at a reasonable price.

A month later Lucy was walking past an estate agent in the nearby town and there was Blackstone Cottage centre window looking very pretty. Her initial whoosh of joy was dimmed somewhat by the ambitious asking price, 'They'll never sell at that.'

Having received no reply to his letter sent six weeks earlier, Max wrote again warning the Ogmores that if they didn't come up with a resolution to the problem of their extended fence *he* would inform both Land Registry and the estate agents that there was a boundary dispute. 'If we don't it will be a *fait accompli*[8] and once again you will have got away with taking more of our land.' No reply after another week (although she did move her bonfire), so Max wrote to the agents and the Registry. The agents had sold Homestead to Max and Lucy and knew about the land grab in the early years of the drama. They confirmed that they would make any potential buyer aware of the dispute. The Registry proposed they consult a solicitor!

It was the ugly Hazel Ogmore who next wrote, but a slightly more astute one: less tirade more smooth spin-doctor dismay at the bizarre and malevolent conduct of dominant, bullying Max and Lucy who were clearly attempting to extort money. The letter was quite impressive, and therefore upsetting, but she or Joe or both got carried away in the end and reverted to old-style ranting libel. They copied their letter to Land Registry and the agent so Max and Lucy copied their reply to both as well. Theirs was long and detailed. They now knew that spin-doctor Ogmore had successfully sullied their names with Bulmer and Wormelow and others. They suspected that Stoat had managed something similar with judges and barristers, so they dealt with the slurs and lies one by one and for the very first time gave a true report of the old fence post story. They added a record of Stoat's conduct and made very clear that they still had the records evidencing all their detailed accounts not only of the Ogmore theft of their land and dishonesty, but also of the fence-post saga.

The response from Land Registry was illuminating: essentially there is no way that the Registry would protect potential buyers of a property where there is a neighbour dispute.[9] The only protection comes from the SPIF when the buyer must rely on the honesty of the seller and if honesty is missing, the buyer should get the Court to deal with the consequences! The Registry files correspondence, but the public would not be aware of items filed. Max's response was succinct: 'We regret we cannot feel confident in future dealings in property in England and Wales as the provision of "up-to-date and guaranteed land information" as claimed on the Registry's website, is not, in fact, guaranteed or transparent and, as we have found to our cost, Title may not, after all, be secure … All we can say is that in this instance we have informed you of a dispute and done what we can. Please do not feel obliged to respond to this email.'

Obliged or not the Land Registrar replied at length, six mind-numbing pages explaining Land Registry rules, including the fact that the Registry does not offer protection if a registered property is physically encroached on by neighbours. Registered proprietors must deal with that themselves in the same way as unregistered Title holders. So, despite those large stamp duty payments you are on your own against squatting, trespassing or adverse possession. Not quite what one might expect from a 'Guaranteed Title'. There is just one flicker of potential help: all documents and correspondence are open to public inspection and copying. So, perhaps the best advice for any prospective purchaser would be to ask for copies of everything Land Registry may have on file for their selected property. The paying client must be proactive as the Registry is inert … unless, of course, the Rules require action.

Nothing in life is certain apart from death (not everyone pays taxes), but it would be nice if we could be reasonably confident that our civil justice service is programmed, above all, to serve *justice* civilly, and a government agency claiming to provide a guarantee were programmed, above all, to protect it.

The Ogmores didn't sell. They were asking too much was the general consensus in the village.

'Possibly,' says Max, 'but then again, who wants to buy a boundary dispute?'

THE SQUATTER SAGA

THE SQUATTER SAGA

'It is always the business of a judge in a trial to find out the truth.'
Cicero, De Officiis. *Bk ii, ch. 14 sec. 51*

PART TWO

SEVENTEEN
Recovery

Not a very impressive performance from the best justice system in the world is it? Lucy and Max buy a property and find that two rogue lawyers have stolen some of it. Although the rogue lawyers have an impressive talent for lying, Max and Lucy uncover the key facts fairly easily and manage to collect reliable evidence of the misdeeds, so when they are trapped in the justice system they quite reasonably expect the best justice system in the world to sort out the problem efficiently and quickly. Just look what happened! It is not as though it is a particularly complex case: the judges were not dealing with an elaborate city scam or an expensive, messy divorce involving child custody. The Ogmores claimed that they owned at least some of the land they had taken so all *the System* had to do was to look at the written and *physical* evidence and listen to the arguments from both sides and make a ruling. *The System* should never have indulged injunction games, consent order games or precedent games. It should have focussed on the job in hand – the actual land in dispute, without wasting too much of anybody's time … or money.

Of course, the Ogmore Gang was an uncommon band of lawyers, but a few pertinent questions asked in the early stages might well have avoided what happened later. Why, if there had been an 'argy bargy', did the Police arrest only one side? Why did nobody ask the Ogmores to explain their case – with supporting evidence? Why did only one judge, Her Honour Judge Gold, take account of the fairly odd double act played by Mrs Hazel Ogmore? Did it not strike any other judge that this was unusual? What about that level playing field? What about managing the case with due regard to time and costs?

Max and Lucy think that they should never have handed over to lawyers in the early stages. They should have remained Litigants in Person (LiPs) so that they retained control. They may be right and hindsight is, of course, a wonderful thing, but once Ogmore got it into court they would have needed judges who were trained to deal fairly and appropriately with LiPs. The Judicial Studies Board has offered such training from time to time but as Lord Woolf said, 'All too often the litigant in person is regarded as a problem for judges and for the court system rather than the person for whom the system of civil justice exists.'

It might have helped if one judge had stayed on the case, or a trio of magistrates or a few people with a modicum of common sense, a willingness to travel to the site and the authority to decide. Instead we have 12 judges, several court clerks, eight barristers, 20 or so solicitors, a few paralegals, three police officers, various Land Registry people, the Crown Prosecution Service and Her Majesty's Court Service. Max and Lucy still don't have an agreed boundary and the 'ex-con thug' (Max's description) who attacked them claims he was *found* not guilty of the assault. The system has failed them, it does not appear to be 'fit for purpose' as they used to say, it is 'broken' as they now say. It needs sorting. But that is not a job for Max or Lucy, that is a job for others; people who are paid, trained and have the power to do it, Lucy and Max would very much like to get on with their plans for retirement. Those who are paid and trained first need to recognise that they have a job which *must* be done, then they need to accept that blaming the client is not an available option. They might find that last bit rather difficult, blaming the client may prove a difficult habit to kick.

Meanwhile Max and Lucy are busy repairing the damage ... where possible. There are losses to be recouped: The gifted land is gone for good, but although patience and a sense of humour eventually returned, lost time is lost forever. That leaves money. It will take a lot of time, patience and humour to chase the tens of thousands owed as there is quite a list of donors to pursue, all with different degrees of obligation but all identical in their reluctance to donate.

There are the *conveyancing solicitors* who failed to follow Lucy's instruction to investigate possible disputes.

There are *the Swales* who lied on the SPIF.

There is *James Nunn*, surveyor, who consistently assured his clients that the boundary cut through the chalet/shed.

There is *Robin Cain* of *Cross & Cross & Co.*, who did not know that an order 'by consent' is invalid if the parties are litigants in person and hadn't signed it, who failed to act in time to prevent the second so-called 'Consent' Order being sealed, who failed to instruct Malcolm Scroggs to make amends for his negligence, who gave only intermittent service, and who overcharged.

There is *Robert Tweed*, who also did not know the rules about Litigants in Person and Consent, whose work was late and in need of serious corrections, who agreed to attend a crucial hearing and pulled out just days before. Who was happy for this simple case to be placed on the multi-track.

There is *Malcolm Scroggs*, who also did not know the rules about LiPs and Consent (apparently), did not master his brief (apparently), signed a deal which proved disastrous for his clients, ignored instructions about the Hammer plan and who either refused or failed to act when made aware he had signed the wrong plan saying that it was too late to do anything when, in fact, the Order had yet to be sealed and the Judge had asked for an agreed agreement. Who then shrugged off his responsibilities and walked away.

There is *Guy Castor*, who failed dismally to live up to either his reputation or his promises, lacked diligence, whose work was inadequate and late and who overcharged.

There is *Hannah Katz* and *Wolf Rottman of Ethan Ganz LLP*, who failed to focus on client care so obsessed were they with fees and income, who were professionally negligent, who bullied, insulted and misled their clients, and failed to keep the Court, various judges and their clients informed. Who were robustly adversarial to their clients but pusillanimous towards the opponents allowing them to rack up costs, bully and waste time. And who overcharged.

There are public bodies: *Her Majesty's Land Registry*; *Her Majesty's Court Service* and the *Crown Prosecution Service*. Only Land Registry admitted they might have created a bit of a bother and offered compensation, but they are allowed to admit that. It is in the rules.

All the above, apart from the Swales, owed Max and Lucy a duty of care. The Swales were guilty of misrepresentation, fraudulent misrepresentation according to Max, the serious kind.

Neither of them wants to add *Jason Higgins FRICS*, of Millett and Hunt Ltd to the list, even though his plan contradicted the physical evidence in places, and he failed to peg out the boundaries clearly and visibly as instructed leaving his clients vulnerable to later Ogmore games. They don't think his misdemeanours are serious, and their list is long enough.

It is all too obvious who is missing from the above: the Ogmores, Keith Stoat, Royston Hammer, Clive Vernon Bulmer and Ms Tracey Wormelow. None of them owed a duty of care to Max or Lucy. They did have a duty to the Court and to their own regulatory bodies, but that is not something Max and Lucy can pursue for recovery.

The other key players missing from the list are the various judges. They cannot be pursued for recovery either, although their actions could have been challenged by appeal. Lucy and Max had a go at an appeal even though they knew that statistically the odds were stacked against them. It was an unsatisfactory experience. However, there is a way judges can be subjected to scrutiny by their regulator, a department of the Ministry of Justice, and this the couple have pursued – in just one case. Max prioritised the claims and put James Nunn at the end. He took Guy Castor off altogether as he had reduced his bill and then his firm went into administration.

There are several options available to clients of the law business to help with paying for justice, and over the period of this story, from the autumn of 2001 to spring 2014, there have been several routes to damage recovery, some now defunct, some newly on-stream. Legal Aid[1] for a professional negligence claim has long been a no-no, and it is highly likely you will need help in persuading a member of the legal profession to reimburse you if they are reluctant to do so. Since October 2010 unhappy, dissatisfied clients have been able to complain to the new Legal Ombudsman[2] who can make awards as high as £50,000 (but rarely goes above £500). If your losses are greater than that maximum you may well find a lawyer with expertise in professional negligence very willing to take on a higher value case once persuaded you have a valid claim, possibly on a no win, no fee basis. In theory, Legal Expenses Insurance (LEI), taken out before the event (BTE) – often as an add-on to household or car insurance – or more expensively after the event (ATE), should provide the support you need, but as Max and Lucy have found, LEI can be more trouble than it's worth for certain types of cases and professional negligence claims for less than a six-figure sum against lawyers are just those sorts of cases. WHICH?[3] provides a good legal advice service for an annual fee, and Trades Unions usually offer legal help to members. If you are very lucky you may have a law centre[4] near you but law centres are becoming an extinct species and like Citizens Advice Bureau[5] (CAB) not really geared for traction in expensive, tricky, professional negligence claims especially if the sum claimed is less than the potential cost of claiming. You might persuade your lawyer opponent to agree to mediation in one of its various forms, but if the stakes are higher than the Legal Ombudsman's limit and your adversary resistant, your best bet for such combat is another lawyer, expert in the field, a solicitor or a direct access barrister.[6]

Max and Lucy's recovery campaign could not benefit from the new-style Legal Ombudsman. Until 2010 claims against lawyers, if informal negotiation failed, had to be pursued through the courts and/or through the complaints procedures offered by the various brands of legal service-provider. In Max and Lucy's case they were the solicitors' complaints service and the Bar Council, but, despite name changes, some structural changes and chameleon-like attempts to change with the changing legal landscape, those services are now defunct.

The legal services market and the justice system went through major transformations during the years of Max and Lucy's travails. In 2005 the Lord Chancellor's Department was reformed into the Department of Constitutional Affairs (DCA) and in 2007 having taken over prisons, probation and so on from the Home Office, was transformed again into the Ministry of Justice. In 2009 the Law Lords moved across Parliament Square to the expensively refurbished Middlesex Guildhall where they became its first Justices of the new Supreme Court with their judicial powers separated from the legislature. Although the Justices remain Members of the House of Lords, they are unable to sit and vote in the House. This is now the final Court of Appeal in UK civil matters. These reforms were viewed as controversial by some, but long overdue by the Government and others who saw the old intermingling of Government and Justice lacking transparency and confusing people. There was a need to make explicit the separation of powers. Besides, the House of Lords was (and is) terribly overcrowded.

When Max and Lucy first found themselves confronted by the court system and litigation in 2002, they had placed some hope in the changes brought in following Lord Woolf's 'Access to Justice' inquiry and recommendations as set out in the 1999 Act, hoping they would ensure that the nonsense Lucy and her family had had to tolerate 20 years earlier would be avoided. The Act was supposed to improve access to justice by making it cheaper, easier and quicker, but Max and Lucy have discovered that getting it more or less right on paper has not been enough. The new rules, together with the new and necessary mindset, had to be in the heads of all involved in providing the potentially improved service.

Until July 2004 barristers refused to take instruction directly from clients, only through a solicitor, potentially doubling the cost. Ethan Ganz billed Max and Lucy £600 for Tim Pickles' redundant attendance at the site meeting with Mark Christie, and £1,112 for his silent appearance at the final hearing in court, of which £556 was his charge for the 24-mile return journey from office to court. Barrister Mark could have managed very well on his own. This restrictive practice also made clients vulnerable to disasters arising from communication failures. Max and Lucy were excluded from the heated exchanges between both sides when Judge Blacker's letter arrived, and had to rely on Robin Cain to pass on the instruction to Malcolm Scroggs to 'make amends' for his deadly 'Consent' agreement. Perhaps the following 10 years and thousands of pounds in costs would have been avoided if they had contracted their own Counsel directly, and spoken to him or her directly. Unfortunately for Max and Lucy, talking directly to barristers was not an option in 2002. It *is* an option for clients today as the barrier to direct contact was officially removed in July 2004, and many barristers now offer their skills and expertise to clients without a solicitor intermediary. Mark Christie's Chambers didn't offer direct access in 2008 when Max and Lucy needed him, but now do. Bad timing. They could have dispensed with Ethan Ganz LLP altogether.

In March 2001, the Office of Fair Trading produced a report, 'Competition in the Professions',[7] which recommended that unjustified restrictions on competition in the legal business be removed.

The Government responded with a consultation paper and report into competition and regulation in the legal services market. The Government's report concluded that, 'the current framework is outdated, inflexible, over-complex and insufficiently accountable or transparent,' and in July 2003 Sir David Clementi, an accountant not a lawyer, was asked to carry out an independent review of legal services in England and Wales. In December 2004 Sir David published his recommendations.[8] The Government liked them and moved swiftly from Green Paper to White Paper to Draft Bill. This was introduced in the Lords where the proportion of lawyers to non-lawyers is far higher than in the general population. In the USA there is approximately one lawyer for every 265 citizens. In the UK it is currently approximately one for every 400, but the law schools are churning out law graduates at a prolific rate, we may soon catch up; there is already something of a glut in the market.

Several skirmishes between the Commons and the Lords ensured lawyerly delays with the Bill. Barristers, in particular, were deeply offended that they should lose control of complaints – 'Why get at us when 90% of the complaints are against solicitors?' They forced several votes in the Lords which were overturned in the Commons and sent back. Predictably the voting split along party lines revealing that the power of the Whips is just as strong in the Lords as in the Commons – unless it is true that Baroness Shirley Williams, a Lib Dem peer who in 1974 was the first 'consumer' minister, and Baroness Judith Wilcox, a Tory peer who was for six years Chairman of the National Consumer Council, really believed that consumers were well protected by the Bar's complaints system. The noble ladies voted to leave self-regulation and complaints handling firmly in the hands of the barristers' union, but in the end Parliament decided otherwise. After a rather dilatory game of ping-pong between the two Houses, in October 2007 the Bill became the Legal Services Act.[9] Its subtitle, 'Putting consumers first', possibly not having registered in the minds of the two Baronesses. The Act had been skilfully manoeuvred through the Lords by Baroness Ashton who seemed able to charm away opposition from some awesome Masters of the Universe (Legal Division). The Act was shaped and driven in the Commons by the then Parliamentary Under Secretary of State at the Ministry of Justice, Bridget Prentice MP, a school teacher in her previous life.

The Act lists eight objectives. First on the list is 'Protecting and promoting the public interest', which can mean different things to different people and possibly lead to lengthy, lawyerly debate on where that ill-defined public interest lies exactly. 'Improving access to justice' is more easily identified as is 'Protecting and promoting the interests of consumers', which is number four on the list, so – not quite 'Putting Consumers First'. Another objective is 'Increasing public understanding of the citizen's legal rights and duties'. If this leads to improved *public* legal education, very much the poor relation of *professional* legal education, we should all benefit, but only if we are also signposted to what we need to know when we need to know it. Raising public awareness of legal rights and duties might also improve those rights and duties to the benefit of the public, particularly when members of the public become consumers in the legal market.

The Act effectively removed that oxymoron, self-regulation, from the legal profession by establishing the Legal Services Board,[10] a new legal services regulator set up to provide consistent oversight and coordination of front-line regulators, with a non-lawyer Chair and a majority of non-lawyer members. This over-arching regulator devolves regulatory functions to front-line bodies, now called Approved Regulators, for example the Bar Standards Board, a body created when the Bar lost the battle over self-regulation and had to separate its often conflicting regulatory and representative roles. The

Act also established a consumer panel[11] of non-lawyers with responsibility to advise and research on behalf of the Board from the consumer perspective.

Until 2010 the regulators had their own complaints system, complex, confusing, rarely coordinated and often compounding client dissatisfaction. Most regulators doubled as business representatives promoting business objectives which, despite warm words, did not necessarily match client objectives, the business promotion role trumping the regulator role rather too often.

As well as removing complaints from Approved Regulators (ARs) and handing them to the new independent Legal Ombudsman, the Act freed up the market in legal know-how by establishing Alternative Business Structures (ABSs)[12] so that different types of lawyers and non-lawyers could manage and own legal practices, the so-called Tesco Law which, in fact, is Co-op Law or Halifax Law or AA Law. Tesco have not entered that market to date. It is early days as ABSs only came on-stream in March 2012 and are yet untested in the UK. Up until then non-lawyers were not permitted to be formally involved with the management of solicitors' firms or have a stake in their ownership. and although not everyone is in favour, the few ABS companies formed so far, have already opened up the law market to competition and enterprise with the promotion of fixed-fee contracts as an alternative to six-minute billing, and offering a one-stop-shop for important transactions like house buying.

Lawyers were and still are (in 2014) much exercised by the liberalisation of their market with the introduction of these new business arrangements. Consumers should be interested too. Like most people Max and Lucy were too rich and too poor to easily afford to buy the services of skilled law tradesmen. There are several reasons for this denial of service to so many people in need of help: restrictive practices allowing for cartel-style pricing being one; a sense of entitlement is another; a lack of transparency in the law business yet another; needless complexity leading to time-wasting and higher costs is possibly the clincher. More transparency and open competition may make legal services more accessible to the rest of us. After all, 'access to justice' is usually viewed as a must-have – usually viewed from an ever extending, just-out-of-reach distance.

All professionals commoditise knowledge to one degree or another. Some, like teachers, are not too good at profiting from their knowledge and skills; lawyers, on the other hand, can be master-class stars. So, Hannah Katz rated herself at over £100 an hour even though not a qualified solicitor: high on confidence, low on performance with flexi-billing to ensure an hourly rate five times that of a qualified, experienced classroom teacher. Most lawyers still add up their six-minute pay units without guaranteeing outcomes, and their failures are rarely as public as those of teachers or doctors, engineers or architects, but since the introduction of ABSs and other revolutions like direct access barristers, the Small Claim limit rise to £10,000 *and* free access to knowledge, information and guidance via the internet, competition has flickered into life in the legal services market. Still not a level playing field, but consumers do stand more of a chance.

The Legal Ombudsman now publishes online the names of firms and individuals complained about. The savvy consumer may find that shopping around will identify those lawyers who have entered the real world, who see how the market is going and are creating new law business models and more affordable, targeted services. On the other hand, reluctant clients of the legal profession may decide that they can do the litigation themselves. The very savvy Bar Council realises this and has produced an online guide for Litigants in Person (LiPs).[13] The unwelcome removal of Legal Aid in much of the justice market is likely to force many more to join the ranks of those who cannot afford legal services, channeling them to attempt DIY justice. Unless the judiciary make the essential revolutionary change of mindset to accommodate these new clients there will be trouble ahead. Few of the judges Max and Lucy encountered seemed to have even got as far as adjusting their minds to the 1999 reforms.

Previously, consumer complaints about lawyers went first to the lawyer, then if still dissatisfied to their complaints service and if still dissatisfied to the old-style Legal Services Ombudsman.[14] That pre-Legal Services Act Ombudsman would then investigate *how* the complaint had been handled, but very rarely the complaint itself. Although the Ombudsman had the power to do so, she rarely did. In 2004, she used this power in less than one per cent of cases, and client satisfaction with the old Ombudsman service was no higher than with the solicitors' complaints service, which was near ground level if not subterranean.

That was the field of battle for Max and Lucy's fight to recover something from the damage done to them by lawyers in various forms, and others. Despite the impact on their lives all they could recover were itemised financial losses on a 'not a penny more, not a penny less' basis. Unlike in the US where juries can deliver serious compensation to successful professional negligence claimants, the single-judge civil court system in the UK has no interest in the well-being of the grey-faced litigant seeking recompense, and as a rule rarely allows claims for loss of time and sleep, distress, frustration, anxiety or aggravation, and the impact these reactions may have had on the litigant's health, relationships and careers. The decision-makers acknowledge such reactions are likely *and foreseeable*, but ignore them 'on grounds of policy'. The courts reject claims for stress and the like for fear it would open the proverbial floodgates to even more litigation. If the same courts were dealing with a *libel* claim in the UK it would be a different story. The UK has (or had until the Defamation Act of 2013),[15] something of a reputation as the libel battleground of choice and compensated the rich and famous, often rather generously, for distress, anxiety and the like.

EIGHTEEN
Recovery 1: Solicitors Professional Indemnity Insurers

Lucy had never met face-to-face the young yet-to-fully-qualify trainee, Daisy Hoople, who had carried out the conveyancing for the sale of Lucy's house and the purchase of Homestead. Everything was done by telephone, fax or letter. Even in 2001 email had yet to be widely recognised as a respectable way for lawyers to communicate with clients. Daisy had carried out the prolonged and complicated sale of Lucy's mother's house just months before and Lucy's family had been so grateful for her patience and efficient service that, at Lucy's behest, they sent her a very large bouquet as a thank you. Not something any of them would normally do for a lawyer. By the time this second contract was made, Daisy was taking her final exams and there had been several communication problems. On a couple of occasions she had been forced to hand over the work to a senior colleague, and on completion day to the Finance Director, who had kept the money handed over by Lucy's purchaser for an extra 24 hours at great inconvenience to their clients and others but a neat little interest payment to them. On her return Daisy was able to offer the missing apologies but not the missing explanation. Lucy liked her. She found her easy to get on with. Daisy never attempted to bully or blame her client for problems and tolerated with good humour the irritating, patronising behaviour and nit-picking delays from the firm acting on behalf of Lucy's purchaser – which just happened to be the same firm that had acted for the Doyles some 20 years earlier.

So Lucy was not happy when urged to make a claim for negligence against Daisy's firm. This was unlikely to do Daisy's career much good and Lucy thought that unfair; she saw her as yet another victim of the squatters. But she had to admit it was likely that Daisy had failed to investigate any possible neighbour dispute as requested. Worse, she thought that Lucy was fussing quite unnecessarily and Lucy did not see herself as a fusser.

When Max and Lucy first suspected trouble they had chased the firm (The Firm) to get their Title documents. By December 2001 they were convinced they had a nasty problem with the next neighbour along the road and fired the first shot at The Firm: 'Please advise what enquiries you made on our behalf on a dispute with a neighbour and what the results were. A serious dispute has now come to our attention.' Lucy hoped that Daisy had written to the Swales' solicitor so that the other side would be found culpable and not Daisy. In the New Year, Daisy sent them a copy of the Swales' SPIF[1] with their 'We have not been notified of any' response to the questions on disputes and adverse possession. They already knew that but not what action, if any, had been taken on Lucy's written request. As they were still stymied by the fact that so many earlier deeds were missing, in particular the 1963 conveyance, they needed more help from Daisy and The Firm. Ominously neither Daisy nor The Firm replied to that initial call for help, so Max decided to take it to the top and wrote to a senior partner proposing that The Firm, Lucy and he had been victims of a disingenuous reply by the vendors. Moreover, Max had inferred from the wording on the SPIF that the solicitor acting for the Swales was complicit, 'We have not been notified of any', sounded lawyerly to him and only the lawyer had signed the form.

The senior partner did not reply. After several weeks and several reminders fielded by his secretary, he passed the problem on to his Client Liaison Manager who eventually let them know that responsibility for any incorrect information on the SPIF would lie with the Swales and not their solicitor, and if Max and Lucy wanted The Firm to take the matter further they would have to pay on account first. However, The Firm did agree to follow the trail of the missing conveyances as part of their original contract. They did not do so with any sense of urgency and it took several prodding phone calls to persuade them to act by which time it was March 2002 and their discontented (ex-) clients were becoming entangled in Ogmore shenanigans. The Client Liaison Manager informed them that the Swales' solicitor was not obliged to obtain or supply any missing deeds, but if he found and forwarded them, the correct certified copy of the 1963 sale of the Black Hut and the land sold with it should be among the bundle. Max and Lucy pinned their hopes on this copy conveyance being found. As we now know it has never been found.

Although most of the old deeds eventually ended up in the safe at Homestead, that one deed disappeared for good some time after the Swales' purchase. The Client Liaison lady had offered to chase up the missing deeds and to write to Land Registry at no charge but if, as suspected, they had a claim against the Swales and wanted her firm to pursue it, a payment on account was required.

Max and Lucy now confronted one of the main challenges that was to dog them for recovery. They could not recover more than their itemised financial losses and Land Registry was offering to compensate for any lost land and any 'reasonable' financial costs. All unknowns. Did they really want to get embroiled in another legal contest? There seemed to be little to be gained for a lot of hassle. Besides, if the Swales' solicitor was deemed to have clean hands and only the Swales themselves held responsible for the misinformation on the SPIF, Lucy for one was disinclined to chase them, 'Unless we find Land Registry renege on their offer.' Not that Lucy felt warmly towards the Swales. They had taken the quality bathroom and kitchen taps and a very fancy toilet seat with them leaving cheap replacements, and it had taken Lucy some time to forgive them for that. Now she was sure the Swales had just wanted the sale to go through without delay and persuaded themselves that their disingenuous response to the SPIF question was not actually a downright lie. They had gambled on Hazel Ogmore not doing anything stupid or dishonest – telling themselves that as she had not contacted them after that 'friendly' meeting when she failed to show them her deed plan, it was not unreasonable to assume she had thought better of claiming their land and it had all blown over.

The Firm did try to locate the missing deeds and gave monthly updates on their attempts, but by August 2002 Lucy herself had succeeded in recovering them from the solicitors the Swales had used when they *purchased* Homestead, on first registration. It seemed likely that this was when the crucial 1963 copy conveyance had disappeared as all earlier extracts referred to it. In August 2002, just before the Ogmores manoeuvred their antics into court, Lucy wrote to alert The Firm to what had happened and let them know that they were chasing recovery of costs. She only tangentially referred to The Firm's possible negligence.

It was not until January 2003, having finally realised that the Ogmores were not satisfied with their ill-gotten gains and intended to force the Hammer plan all the way, that Max and Lucy began to suspect the shenanigans were going to be prolonged and that Land Registry could not be relied on to fully compensate for losses. As The Firm had not provided any evidence that Daisy had probed further on the Swales' SPIF answers, they wrote to the senior partner again, this time specifying the allegations and enclosing a schedule of losses. That letter brought a prompt reply. The Firm was treating the matter as a possible negligence claim and liaising with their insurers. The need for urgent action must have exhausted them as nothing further was heard for months despite several reminders. Only when Max threatened to send the file to the Law Society's Office for the Supervision of Solicitors (OSS) did they get a response. The Firm explained that they needed their permission to send the file to their insurers so would they write granting that permission? How long would it have taken to get round to that request without the threat of the OSS?

From now on the battle for recovery was between Max and Lucy and The Firm's insurers, and for the first time Max and Lucy heard of the very important distinction the legal professionals made at that time between 'inadequate professional service' and 'negligence'. The former was dealt with by the various legal bodies – the Law Society, the Bar Council, at no cost to the complainant, but if negligence was suspected the claim went to litigation via professional indemnity insurers skilled in the dark arts of resisting claims but at least free of charge to the complainant – unless and until the dispute was taken to court. So the objective for the client was to get a satisfactory settlement out of court. One of the little known but significant changes brought about by the Legal Services Act avoids this elephant trap for unhappy clients of legal services. The Legal Ombudsman (LeO)[2] makes no distinction between levels of bad service, so the complainant can apply for compensation up to the limit of £50,000 (currently) for any degree of damage – from inconvenience caused by delay or failing to inform, to serious losses caused by negligence. Unfortunately for Max and Lucy, LeO was yet to be born and they had to go with the old system. The Law Society made no charge for investigating Inadequate Professional Service (IPS) but the compensation on offer was very low, usually far less than the losses actually incurred. Complaints against solicitors ran to around 17,000 a year before all were removed from self-regulation and passed to the new, independent Ombudsman. If the Law Society Complaints Service or its later incarnation, the Legal Complaints Service (LCS), decided that the complaint fell into the negligence category they would not look at it and the hapless complainant would have to battle with the insurers, or pay and do battle through (and possibly with) a professional negligence lawyer. Negligence was a court matter with all the costs and stress the courts can supply. Max and Lucy acknowledge that something like the authority of the courts may be needed on occasion, but they are not fans of court-style dispute resolution.

The Firm's insurers behaved like most insurers resisting a claim. They asked for more information, lots more and copies of everything. They questioned what would have been gleaned had Daisy actually delved further on disputes and, of course, they delayed. A stiff letter of protest from Max at the work their demands implied was met with an equally stiff letter from the Canadian lady dealing with the claim. In the end, in order to make any progress the couple decided that alongside the main Ogmore action they would have to allocate several more hours – possibly a few days to finding, collating and copying hundreds of documents. The Canadian lady offered to pay for the copying and postage. She did not offer to compensate for the time and irritation.

In reply to a letter from Lucy, the Law Society wrote at length explaining that if they were alleging negligence by The Firm neither the Society nor The Firm could deal with the matter or even access the file until the insurers finished their work, and if they wanted to complain to the Society about the Swales' solicitor, the service could only consider an accusation of professional misconduct – and no compensation was on offer. Complex and mystifying. Presenting the equally unattractive choices of insurers or court, the system devised by the professionals was guaranteed to dissuade all but the most robust from pursuing a claim. The new service from LeO is certainly more attractive as long as the claim is within the maximum compensation allowed, but it is early days and satisfaction levels are currently (2013) higher among lawyers than among complainants[3] – with all that that implies.

They sent 18 files by special delivery. The Canadian lady promised a reply within 21 days. More than a month later, Max wrote to remind her of that promise and two weeks after that another reminder – and an updated claim. Still no reply, so Max called in help from the Law Society and finally got one. Apparently the delay was caused by the Canadian lady's other workload and the 'extensive amount of documentation provided by you'. It was their fault. The lawyer tactic of blaming the client (or complainant in this case) was not confined to England and Wales, apparently ex-colonies had adopted a similar approach.

She wanted yet more documents, and plans amended to show the different assertions to land ownership. The papers were tracked down, copied and collated, and the plans and claim carefully amended. Max also let the Canadian lady know that Land Registry had now started to make offers and they were not seeking to recover more than the quantum of their losses – whatever that might turn out to be in the end. The Canadian lady eventually informed them that as they were recovering losses from Land Registry she would await the outcome of those negotiations and if then there were items on the schedule they still wanted reimbursed, 'no doubt you will revert to me.'

So here were the recovery challenges: how much should they expect to recover bearing in mind the shenanigans were still in full flood, and who could say when the business would be over, and how much it would all cost? They would have to bear the losses until some settlement was reached. Also, who should they pursue … and, how should they pursue them? Their claim against The Firm was garrisoned with well-armed insurers impervious to all attempts to force a settlement.

Negotiations with Land Registry were still in flux by July 2004, the tussle with the rectified plan was delaying everything and The Firm's insurers were still refusing to budge, insisting that the Registry's settlement must come first. As the couple saw it, The Firm had been negligent and had not denied it, nor had the insurers, so the claim against them was a separate issue and they should make an offer. The Firm insisted that their hands were completely tied as they were under their insurers' direction. Despite the myriad of rules and regulations made by law firms intertwined with insurers, there was not a single one which insisted that one claim had to be settled before another. It was all down to tactics and Max and Lucy had no tactical weaponry except to threaten to add the General Insurance Standards Council to the list of agencies set up to deal with complaints. Max mentioned it in his next letter.

Canadian Lady decided it would be better to talk, first at her London office and then at Homestead. Max and Lucy wholeheartedly and immediately agreed. No response. More prodding and finally a date was fixed for the London meeting. Canadian Lady had softened; she understood their frustration, she offered to contribute towards the cost of a Land Registry survey, and assured them that an offer to settle would be made … in the near future. Lucy wondered if this was because she was very pregnant and about to go on maternity leave and hand the whole business over to her colleague, a Dagenham lady. As usual with solicitors, Dagenham Lady assured them she was fully apprised of everything, so there would be no back-tracking or time wasting as she got up to speed, but, of course, she was not, in fact, fully apprised of everything so there was, indeed, back-tracking and time wasting as she established her own delaying tactics. Canadian Lady had not even been pregnant when she took on their claim and the two-year delay meant Max and Lucy had to deal with Dagenham Lady who was beginning to look like trouble. Her strategy was to await the results of the Land Registry survey but, as we know, that survey did not materialise as planned in 2004. In early 2005, nearly four years after Daisy had failed to do what she should have done, Lucy decided they should invest in one of these new direct access barristers she had come across in some newspaper article by one who reported that he was not 'plagued by nutters' as some of his confrères warned, but, on the contrary, found that direct access clients spending their own money were more focussed on the need for realistic advice rather than angling to be told what they wanted to hear, as some solicitors spending their clients' money often expected. She asked him to review their claims against the Swales and The Firm.

The direct access barrister, Mr D. Barr, grasped most but not all the facts. Significantly, he failed to see Lucy's letter to Daisy asking her to check up on the Swales' answers on their SPIF or note that there had been no denial that Daisy had thought Lucy was fussing unnecessarily when she raised the issue a second time. However, he was pleasant to deal with and gave the useful warning that they must avoid compromising one claim against one party by settling with another. This made sense in theory, but how could they manage their various claims in practice when everything was so fluid, uncertain, with so many unknowns? They also had to factor in the six-year limitation barrier for nearly all civil court claims. Mr Barr drafted a letter referencing a recent case which had ruled that Land Registry should be the insurer of *last* resort, so other potentially liable parties should be pursued first. They reproduced his letter in full adding a revised itemised claim and confidently sent it to Dagenham Lady. Dagenham Lady firmly rebutted everything declaring that they should continue negotiations with Land Registry and that Canadian Lady had not believed The Firm in any way liable – a view she shared. As Canadian Lady had more or less conceded in writing several months earlier that The Firm *had* been negligent, their suspicions about this new adversary were confirmed. They should have demanded to know why, if that had been Canadian Lady's view, she had not mentioned it to them at the meeting, but had simply said that their claim was 'premature', and repeated her proposal that they settle with Land Registry first. What possible reason could she and her successor have to clear The Firm of negligence? What was their argument?

If they had had the time they should have persisted, but they were too involved in other matters, not least more Ogmore games and Land Registry challenges, to find time for that war and did nothing for several months. It was not until July 2005, following the thwarted, inconclusive Land Registry survey of the previous March and the ensuing sterile correspondence, that they got round to picking up The Firm claim again.

Several delaying letters followed and Max wearily decided that they would have to pay for more of Mr Barr's time to help decide how best to juggle with all three interlocking claims (The Firm, Land Registry and the Swales), leaving the targets with enough negotiating room for compromise and avoiding a tangle in what could prove to be a fruitless pursuit of recovery from all three. More Mr Barr meant more costs; however, he charged less and gave far better value, in Max and Lucy's view, than the solicitors they had encountered (and they had yet to encounter Ethan Ganz LLP). He advised a Part 36 offer to settle with The Firm and an offer of mediation to the Swales.

Their Part 36 offer was duly sent to Dagenham Lady and was duly rejected. She informed them that neither her company nor The Firm admitted any liability. Lawyers and insurers, of course, usually advise their clients to deny liability and, naturally, can be expected to take their own advice. Once again she informed them that they should resolve their claim against Land Registry first. First? Did this imply there was to be a second settlement – possibly with The Firm? Was there not a contradiction between the forceful denial of any liability and the intimation that following a first settlement with Land Registry there might be another … with The Firm?

Lucy asked for clarification, 'If you do indeed now deny liability for negligence … will you please set out clearly the basis for your denial?' Dagenham Lady ignored the invitation, she merely repeated herself at greater length seemingly unaware of any internal contradictions. Max's response was more robust the next time. He intimated that as the insurers and The Firm had turned down mediation it was beginning to look as though Lucy and he would have to take the matter to court. Dagenham Lady played a mean hand at poker. Realising that if it came to court action she would need to communicate court-style, she came up with an explanation for denying liability: 'Even if our insured had enquired further, the response would have been the same.' What psychic powers gave her such confidence? Had she not seen (or was she choosing to ignore) the Swales' admission in writing that they knew just months before they put Homestead on the market that Ogmore had challenged their Title? Neither Max nor Lucy believed the insurers genuinely considered The Firm free of liability, but were playing a tactical game to wait for someone else to pick up the tab – or at least most of it, and they had marked Land Registry to pay.

The limitation period gave them until July 2007 for court action against either the Swales or The Firm, or both, so Max and Lucy let the claim against The Firm hang in order to make time to deal with more urgent matters. They did not pick it up again until August 2006 when they reverted to their original proposal to mediate and also corrected the key errors in Dagenham Lady's letter. There followed the familiar delaying tactic of a series of letters promising a reply, and only in late October did they receive a non-reply reiterating precisely the same position, ignoring the corrected errors of fact and the mediation proposal. In her view any claim against her insured would fall on the issue of 'causation' as the Swales would have given the same answer on disputes if Daisy *had* made further enquiries. Psychic powers obviously still intact. Causation can keep lawyers entertained and financed for quite a time: would Max and Lucy have avoided loss from entanglement with the Ogmore Gang *but for* Daisy's failure? Did they lose out *because* Daisy failed to follow up Lucy's request? Who (apart from Dagenham Lady) can say what would have happened? Clearly they would have avoided the previous six years of legal battering *but for* a series of interlocking failings and misdemeanours on the part of a number of people, but they just might have avoided the expensive, time-wasting entanglement with the squatters if the Swales had not misled both them and Daisy, *or* if Daisy had responded correctly when her attention was drawn to the possibility of a dispute, and insisted on evidence it was sorted before the sale went through. Causation is a malleable legal construct which is interesting for lawyers but expensive, time-wasting and distressing for claimants.

By early June 2007 they had finally reached a part-settlement with Land Registry and wrote to inform Dagenham Lady. She wanted to know the terms and repeated her view that any claim would fail on causation. They did not waste time arguing. They mistakenly believed they had come to the end of the Ogmore Saga and were focussed on tying up loose ends, so when the Land Registry payment went into their Recovery Account, Max was able to make his calculations and propose a much reduced claim against The Firm on the 'not a penny more, not a penny less' basis. It took another month for Dagenham Lady and her clients to finally agree. Max suggested they also added reimbursement of the conveyance charges paid to The Firm six years earlier. Again they agreed. In September 2007, six years after Daisy's conveyance work, the cheque arrived. It was accompanied by the assurance that it, 'in no way reflects an admission of liability on the part of our Insured.'

NINETEEN
Recovery 2: The Law Society's Complaints Service (dec'd)

By early March 2003 they had decided to dispense with Cross & Cross & Co. and go it alone. Robin Cain was possibly relieved, but, of course, there were fees yet to be paid. They had already made clear that they had no intention of paying either barrister's fees: Cross & Cross had selected them and briefed them, so Cross & Cross would have to pay them if they thought the fees had been earned. Max and Lucy were not going to pay for two representatives who, after just two hearings, had placed them in a worse position than they had been in before. Mr Cain had to 'reluctantly' advise them that the file would not be released until all fees had been paid. They wanted the file for the ongoing Ogmore action and the various claims, and therefore responded by drawing attention to Ogmore's repeated assertion that Cain had written to the Court agreeing the terms of the Consent Order. That brought a prompt reply. He 'did *not* write to the Court specifically agreeing the terms of the Consent Order.' Alarmed by that 'specifically', Lucy made further investigations and found that he had not written any sort of agreement to the Court, specific or otherwise and Ogmore had told yet another mischievous lie.

By September 2003 the Bar Council had involved Cain in their claims against both barristers and he had sought his ex-clients' agreement to assist in the investigations. They had been on a French canal at the time but managed to fax agreement pointing out that his information would be essential to any enquiry. They had no expectation that he would help their cause, but in the event the good Cain was on form and his evidence was cautious but fair. However, the later demand for a further payment, albeit small, without an invoice was not fair, particularly as the 'invoice' when it arrived after several requests was darkly opaque. Even Ethan Ganz LLP managed a more transparent job. Not surprisingly it was the invoices and bullying meted out to any reluctant payer, above all, which earned Cross & Cross their poor reputation locally, and it is no surprise that they have not survived the recent earthquakes in legal services following the 2007 Act. The building has a new name above the door, though Cross Senior is still around as a consultant. Back in 2003 Lucy was more interested to see Robin Cain's reference to Ogmore's version of the 'Consent Order' as a *draft*, which confirmed her memory of the scribbled document Scroggs had shown her. They agreed they should refuse to pay the barristers' fees, 'Adding injury to injury,' as Max put it. Despite the fact they had paid the dubious Cross & Cross part of the claim, the file remained locked away. They decided they could manage without it. They would have to.

Over the following months Cain and his firm had to deal with a flurry of letters with the barristers' chambers chasing fees, and the Bar Council chasing opinions and documents, with the addition of confusing statements about the status of Max and Lucy's formal complaints. They heard nothing from the Crosses for several months, but in October 2004 the Chambers' Clerk made another request for payment which prompted another demand from Cross & Cross with a new signature on the letter and the information that Robin Cain had left the firm to 'pursue his career closer to home'. Max let the new man know that the claims against the barristers were now with the (old) Ombudsman for legal affairs. Silence from C&C until January 2005 when the firm renewed their efforts to extract payment, reporting that Tweed had reduced his claim by half and that neither Chambers nor they were aware of any investigation by the Ombudsman. Max made them aware that they had raised the matter of consent orders with the then Chairman of the Civil Procedure Rules Committee, a Very Senior Judge, who confirmed unambiguously that consent orders not signed by litigants in person are invalid. Not one of their expensive legal experts realised this – apparently. He copied the Judge's letter to the new man and he also copied a letter from the Ombudsman.

Silence from the new man. A whole year passed. There was a lot of action on the complaints against the two barristers and The Firm but no action with Cross & Cross, and they still wanted their file back. Scroggs was continuing to insist that Cain had never asked him 'to make amends' and as Cross & Cross had never offered any evidence that Cain had, they decided to add Cross & Cross to the Recovery list. They wanted their file back.

Mr Cross Junior took over the correspondence and agreed to meet these difficult ex-clients at his office. He had not read the very large file, but he smoothly avoided any challenge on details. Apart from establishing that they would only get their file back on payment of the latest invoice, he had no other objective. The meeting was designed to be unproductive and lawyers are rather good at unproductive meetings. Cross Junior intended a meeting for the records not one for resolution and had no intention of handing over his best bargaining tool, the file, without profit. His ex-clients wanted proof that C&C (Cain) had instructed Scroggs to 'make amends'; instead they got alarming intimations that there was no such proof. They needed to know what Cain and Scroggs had discussed after the Judge's letter was received and they wanted to know why Scroggs had returned the file without warning in January 2003 while the matter was still ongoing. Cross Junior, having failed to read the file, knew nothing. He did offer to contact Cain to see if he could help.

Yet again silence. They tried another letter in July 2006 pointing out they had engaged Cross & Cross the firm, not specifically Cain, the solicitor. They wanted answers: 'We are sure that you will want to do everything to permit the investigation to proceed to a just conclusion.' It took another prompt to get a non-reply telling them nothing other than that Cain had a rather rusty memory. Further prompts went unacknowledged and so they started two lengthy processes for recovery against Cross & Cross: one using their own Legal Expenses Insurers, and one with the Law Society's complaints procedures. They complained that no evidence had been forthcoming that Cain had ever passed on their instruction to Scroggs, and the invoice Cross & Cross were using to ransom their file had first appeared without warning three years after the termination of their contract and contained no breakdown of costs nor any other explanation of the charges.

A fanciful costs 'breakdown' did eventually appear but amounted to no more than the number of telephone calls in and out, letters likewise, notes to file and so on, which could easily have been made up in a quiet coffee break: No dates, no time sheets, no names, no evidence. Max wanted copy of their complaints procedures and properly recorded work; he also proposed another meeting. He waited a couple of weeks and when no response arrived activated a Law Society complaint.

Lucy's online research into the Law Society's record for dealing with complaints was not encouraging. In-house, self-regulating complaints procedures are rarely satisfactory for the complainant, even less so when 'the house' represents lawyers, masters of argument, who have constructed their own complaints rules. This one-sided, biased scheme and the distress it caused already unhappy complainants was one of the main motivators behind the Legal Services Bill then going through Parliament.

Cross Junior was not happy. He protested that their correspondence was unnecessarily indignant and repeated his threat of court action if they did not pay up. He claimed to include his firm's complaints procedures – which should have been provided when they first engaged the firm – but it was not to be found.

Max and Lucy now faced another recovery dilemma. Land Registry was pressing to finalise the indemnity account and make a final settlement. The dubious Cross & Cross invoice would be covered by the indemnity, as would have been the two barrister invoices had Max and Lucy not successfully resisted paying. They knew enough about the reputation of Cross & Cross locally to feel duty bound to resist Mr Cross Junior too, but they wanted their file back. Should they pay the invoice and recover the cost from Land Registry or should they fight on without the file essential for their other recovery actions? They still feel mildly ashamed that they paid up ... under protest.

Mr Cross Junior indulged in a piece of pettiness on the day they went to hand over the cheque and collect their file. They had let him know in advance that they had a tight schedule that day, but he kept them waiting nearly an hour. How long does it take to locate a recently viewed file? He did not apologise for keeping them waiting. When they finally got it home they could see that certain items were missing and feared that others might be too. Could he have filleted their file? They asked for confirmation that they had the full file and the payment they had made was in full and final settlement. The Cross & Cross reply, no doubt mindful of an impending Law Society investigation, re-structured recent dealings with the couple casting them as bad payers, and also indulged in an imaginative analogy, 'Would you demand free food from a supermarket where you owed a substantial sum of money and then complain about the manner the food was handed to you?' Lucy quite enjoyed that and responded in kind, 'You would not expect a customer to pay for goods which had not been supplied, or itemised or had been faulty and caused serious damage.' Both she and Max were far less amused when they found documents in the file which would have been useful had they had them in time, particularly for the complaints against the barristers.

When Lucy reviewed the Cross & Cross file in late 2004, she was stunned. She regretted that they had been forced by the Ogmores' pre-emptive strike in 2002 to engage these solicitors knowing nothing about them, or any other local firm. By 2004 they had been living in the area long enough to become aware of the reputation of local law firms. Apparently there were two firms to avoid. Cross & Cross was not the worst of the two, but the reputation of the worst was spread wide enough for that single-practice firm to close its office locally and move to a larger town where few people had heard of it, so Cross & Cross then topped the list of firms to avoid.

The file revealed, to Lucy at least, a solicitor who's 'best' was satisfactory but, sadly, whose second best was dismal. Cain had not been at the firm long when they first encountered him, and over the months of dealing with him they had been frustrated by the dismal Cain but gratified by his performance when giving his best. Lucy was sure he had too much on his plate. He lived a long way from the office, he had problematic family demands and Max was convinced he was being harassed to stack up his six-minute charges.[1] To do the job well he needed time but there wasn't enough time to satisfy the demands of all the clients he was expected to take on. Would he have failed so catastrophically when they needed him if he had given their embroilment with the Ogmores his full attention? Would he have attempted to claim over £1,000 a week for at most 10 hours' work if his new bosses had not been breathing down his neck to generate income? Possibly but not certainly; both Lucy and Max were prepared to give him the benefit of the doubt.

Unfortunately, there was no doubt in their minds that he had made gross errors when it came to Scroggs. The list of misdemeanours was long:

- To start with he should have known that the first Order could not be described as a 'consent' agreement because Max and Lucy hadn't signed it.
- Then he should have copied them Tweed's availability list so they would know to reject a hearing date Tweed could not make.
- Having failed at that he should have ensured that he accompanied them to court, knowing what he did of the nature and conduct of their adversaries, and the fact that Scroggs was an unknown.
- Having failed at that he should have ensured that another lawyer from the firm went in his place.
- Having failed at that he should have advised them to agree nothing on the day, but to wait to discuss any proposals with him.

- Having failed to do that, after the drastic failures at the hearing he should have acted with the forcefulness he had shown previously to scotch the Hammer plan as soon as he heard that it had been finessed into the agreement.
- Failing that, he should have checked whether the agreement had in fact been made an order on the day.
- Failing on that, he should have responded quickly and correctly to the Judge's letter.
- Failing that, he should have acted on Max's instruction to tell Scroggs to 'make amends', – even if it did mean the barrister would have had to eat humble pie.

Lucy expected delays from the main Leamington Spa-based Law Society Complaints Service (LSCS). She had read about them online, and she did not have high expectations. However, in January 2007 their complaint against Cross & Cross was handed to a caseworker not at the Leamington Spa office but in London, who, to their surprise, did not match the deeply unpleasant image of the LSCS conveyed online by dissatisfied complainants.

Nevertheless, their complaint did take a long time to be processed and once again, just as with their claim against The Firm and, their complaint to the Complaints Commissioner about Land Registry, their caseworker moved on. She had spent 10 months on it, mainly due to Cross Junior's delaying tactics. The constraints on caseworkers meant that she could not take further anything that might be deemed 'negligence' nor could she comment on what would have been correct legal procedure as, for example, challenging so-called consent agreements with LiPs that had not been signed by them.

They were pleasantly surprised, therefore, when, after just one month, their new caseworker informed them that she was upholding the majority of their complaints, placing them in the 'serious' category of four category levels of inadequate professional services. She let them know that she would endeavour to secure compensation at the top end of that category and she did just that. It wasn't much but it was most gratifying to add another cheque to the Recovery fund. Their persistence placed them among the very small percentage of complainants to the LSCS who actually got a satisfactory result. The cheque arrived from Mr Cross Junior with the predictable denial of any admission of liability.

TWENTY
Recovery 3: The Bar Council's complaints service (also dec'd)

In 2003 client complaints about barristers were sent to the General Council of the Bar's Complaints Department which went through a few transformations and name changes before they finally closed down and reluctantly handed over to the new, independent Ombudsman in 2010. The system devised by the professionals was as complex as an IKEA floor plan but, unlike that plan, was designed to get the client out the door as soon as possible. The Bar itself raised internal complaints against its members usually for failing to obtain, and pay for the necessary practising certificate or compulsory training hours. External complaints first went to the Complaints Commissioner who either dismissed the complaint or sent it on to the Professional Conduct and Complaints Committee, which either dismissed the complaint or sent it on to the Adjudication Panel for an informal or summary hearing, or a disciplinary tribunal and then either dismissed the complaint or found against the barrister who could then appeal. It was rare for external client complaints to make it all the way and still come out with a positive result. Few made it past the first hurdle. Internal complaints managed a higher success rate. In 2003, of 123 *internal* complaints only 25% were dismissed. In the same year, of the 541 *external* complaints 85% were dismissed and those external complaints came not just from disgruntled clients but also from judges, magistrates, Heads of Chambers, the Lord Chancellor's Department and solicitors. A mere 27 (five per cent) of all external complaints were upheld after a final hearing. The statistics provided in the Bar's Complaints Department's Annual Report for 2003 do not say how many of those 27 complaints actually came from ordinary members of the public – or 'lay clients' as the law professionals label them. In that year just *one* complaint went as far as an appeal.

Lucy already had some idea of the challenge ahead when they completed the standard complaints form in July 2003. At that stage they believed the problems stemmed mainly from Scroggs' failure to master his brief and subsequent failure to advocate it vigorously in court. They believed that if he had read the papers he would have rejected the Hammer plan and applied the OS plan Lucy had negotiated to use. He not only signed a defective Consent Order and compounded that error by signing the Hammer plan; he made no effort to obtain payment for the land given to the squatters. Moreover, he did this without his clients' knowing agreement or even showing them the documents in draft form. He then refused or failed to act when the error was exposed in the following days and weeks. At the time of lodging these complaints neither Max nor Lucy realised that Cain was complicit in the failures, nor did they know that Scroggs' failings were not limited to a failure to master his brief since they did not know what was in their file held hostage by Cross & Cross until they paid the ransom some three years later and retrieved it.

A significant item they retrieved was a note in Scroggs' hand fixed to the brief he had suddenly returned in January 2003, unbidden and without explanation, describing the Consent agreement as a 'draft' – just as Lucy insisted she remembered. Had they had that evidence right from the start they could have sent it with their original claim, together with other evidence they found in the retrieved file: for example Scroggs *did* know about the Judge's letter, in fact he had been sent a copy of it, and he had been made fully aware from the start that his clients were less than happy about his 'Consent' agreement. Perhaps most important of all, they could have included evidence that the brief he returned contained several references to the common rejection of the Hammer plan. Throughout the lengthy processing of the complaint against him Malcolm Scroggs sustained his claim that he knew nothing of any of these, apart from some mild criticism of the Hammer plan which he had discounted. If only they had been able to send that evidence then, before the barrister chose to gamble on the risky strategy of setting his word against theirs. That evidence might have persuaded him to select another strategy. He might not have decided to employ the old standby of blaming the clients on the safe assumption that in the Court of the Bar Council, the judges would believe the word of an experienced barrister with a clean record over a pair of lay clients indulging in a boundary dispute.

A couple of months after they sent the completed forms to the Bar Council's Complaints Department, they went on the long research trip with a heavy tome of O'Hare and Browne's *Civil Litigation*,[1] and found the other significant failure by Mr Malcolm Scroggs. He had been in court on the fateful day *not* to settle a boundary dispute, *not* to remove squatters, but to vary a Consent Order that should never, would never, have been made had somebody known the rules: Civil Procedure Rule 40.6 making clear that the 'binding, non-revertible' Consent Order was invalid. Malcolm Scroggs should have known that the Order was invalid, Robert Tweed and Robin Cain should have known, a couple of judges should have known. If anyone in the Ogmore Gang had known they kept very quiet about it.

Their complaint went to the Bar's Complaints Commissioner (a non-lawyer) who asked for more papers. In those days their paper copying had to be done at a shop or library and was a time-consuming process particularly as they lived in the country. Some 70 pages were found, collated, copied, packaged and sent – a minimum of 10 hours' work. But the package lacked the potent revelations trapped in the offices of Cross & Cross.

At least this work got them past the first hurdle. Their complaint was to be investigated. Seventy per cent of all external complaints against barristers fell at that first hurdle. Scroggs was informed and asked for his views. He was warned that his complete response would normally be seen by the complainant. He was also informed that a number of barristers were prepared to offer on a *pro bono*[2] basis, confidential, sympathetic advice on how to respond to a complaint. That service may still be available today to barristers in need of help with a complaint to the new Ombudsman. Such a service was not, of course, available to 'lay' complainants. Tweed and Cain were also asked for their opinions.

Tweed knew where his loyalties lay and perhaps the *pro bono* assistance had guided him on the stance to adopt to help his fellow member. His report was a challenge to read for his ex-clients: the case was a 'boundary dispute'; the injunction had been made 'by consent'; Lucy was 'a difficult client' but only in the context of the case, 'I found her otherwise to be very pleasant.' He was surprised and pleased that Scroggs had effected a compromise, 'Where I had failed.' As Tweed had never proposed a compromise, in fact they had suspected he had wanted to milk the case way into the future, both his ex-clients realised just how nasty this business could become; nastiness was not exclusive to the Ogmore Gang. Max, who was referred to only once by Tweed and not by name (he was merely Lucy's 'partner'), deplored Tweed's work and, instead of being daunted by the unpleasant distortions, both Max and Lucy hardened in their resolve – Ogmore's earlier attempts at character assassination had hardened them.

So they were prepared for Scroggs' response when they saw it. First, he wanted to be assured that Stoat would be contacted, because Stoat 'would recall the length of time I spent in conference with my clients before the compromise was agreed.' Then he wanted to be assured that Cain was contacted, because he would confirm that no request was made to provide a written explanation or advice. His response was rather more subtle than Tweed's. He was 'disappointed' that a complaint had been lodged against him, since this had never happened before in two decades in the profession. He distanced himself from Tweed, but was somewhat inaccurate on details, confusing the Circuit Judges for District Judges, showing ignorance of Land Registry's costs indemnity and, of course, ignorance of the rules on consent orders and litigants in person.

When he claimed to have spent a great deal of time explaining everything to 'the lay clients' about costs and about use of the Hammer plan, the ugliness was made concrete: His word against theirs. According to him they had kept the opponents and the Court waiting for 'well over an hour' while they discussed the detail. He also reported that in the days and weeks following the hearing no request had been made to him to provide any further clarification, explanation or advice. The evidence contradicting this was locked away in the Cross & Cross file.

No surprise, of course, that Stoat confirmed the story. According to him, Scroggs disappeared for 'about an hour' to discuss the compromise agreement. 'From time to time I went to see where he was but he was still consulting them.' Stoat and Scroggs decided that this hour-long discussion had taken place before they went into court. An impossibility.

On 31st October 2002 Max had finally met up with Lucy and Scroggs in court just before 10 o'clock. His very late arrival meant that after introductions and the explanation for his late arrival, he had needed a rapid update on the state of play. He needed to hear what Scroggs had to report on the character and prejudice of the Judge. Despite the information they had just received from the police officer that their claim to the rectification land was very strong, they decided that if the Judge was hostile they would abandon the purpose of their attendance in court that day (to set aside the non-Consent Order) and agree Scroggs' proposal: they would abandon their Claim to the rectification land if Ogmore abandoned her Claim to any land by adverse possession. And that would be the end of the matter. After they had come to that unwise decision, Scroggs had left to speak to Stoat. He had been gone for about 15 minutes before he rushed back holding the Hammer plan. It was the first time that plan had appeared in their discussion. He wanted to get their agreement to let the shed stay. It was then past the due time for the hearing – 10.30. Max and Lucy discussed Ogmore's obsession with her shed and finally decided that since it would add just a few feet more and they would be compensated for any land lost by Land Registry, they would agree. Scroggs had then left a second time. It was nearly 10.45. Seven to 10 minutes later he was back to ask if they would agree to add the other strip of land in the opposite corner of the plot to the package. They had agreed within a minute and he was gone again. He returned to tell them to get into court. It was 11 o'clock. Five minutes after they had settled in court the Judge arrived. Max had had barely 15 minutes to discuss any compromise with Scroggs before they went into court to tell the Judge what had been 'agreed'. Stoat shared his co-Counsel's talent for expanding time, and, true to form, he reported that he found Max and Lucy very difficult and was pleased he did not have to deal with them directly!

Cain took quite a time to respond. His main contribution was that he considered it was clear that the Hammer plan should not be used in any agreement, but he could not comment on how it came to form the basis of the Consent Order as he had not been present. He also expressed the view, that given the Ogmores' conduct in the matter, one would have expected Counsel to have included in the Order itself some machinery/timescale for agreement to be reached, and for resolving the matter if agreement could not be reached. He had little else to say because he hadn't been there. Whether Cain had seen Scroggs' submission implying that he had failed to pass on Max's instruction to the barrister to 'make amends', is an unknown.

Back from their working trip and refreshed and fired by the information on CPR 40.6 in the *Civil Litigation* doorstopper, Lucy wrote a forthright letter in response to the two barristers' 'evidence'. She also expressed her disappointment in the post-Woolf reformed civil justice system they had encountered. She wanted to know what the Bar Council[3] was going to do about monitoring the implementation of the reforms and she wanted an explanation for the barristers' failure to recognise CPR 40.6.

Her enquiries were ignored. There was to be no dialogue between lay persons and the Bar Council on such matters. They should just respond to what Scroggs, Stoat, Tweed and Cain had to say. Lucy was not prepared to reply until she had some explanation for the barristers' failure to recognise Rule 40.6. A sniffy reply from the Secretary of the Professional Conduct and Complaints Committee made clear she was not going to get an explanation. 'The Bar Council cannot comment to you on the operation of the Civil Procedure Rules.'

The Bar Council had the stronger hand and won the stand-off. Both Max and Lucy responded to the oppositions' various submissions adding a formal complaint against Robert Tweed. They had copy of the transcript of the hearing at the Royal Courts of Justice when Stoat had engineered Ogmore's land grab into court by persuading a High Court Judge to issue the first injunction. Lucy and Max had urged Tweed and Cain to get that injunction discharged. In fact, the Judge had decreed that they should be at liberty to apply to vary or discharge it, but none of their advisors had proposed taking advantage of that liberty. Lucy started with a description of Stoat's conduct, dismissing his evidence as inaccurate, distorted and totally unreliable. She then commented on Robert Tweed. She said it was ironic, bearing in mind his unfair and dishonest description of her, that she had persuaded Max not to lodge a complaint about the younger barrister. All the evidence showed that she did not have any obsession with the land as he asserted – after all, she had taken no time to agree to give some away, but she admitted to 'well-founded and serious concerns about abuse of the legal system – *our* legal system'. She advised Tweed to learn to focus on the needs of those he was paid to represent rather than his own career opportunities. 'Unless he listens to and understands the "end client" he will not provide the service required.'

She was more restrained in her comments on Scroggs since, unaware of the facts, she suspected he had been misled by Tweed and inadequately briefed, but she could not forgive his untrue description of the length of time their discussions had taken nor his ignorance of the crucial CPR. She outlined how she thought a competent representative should have acted and suggested that he should reflect on how he had managed to end by handing their land to the squatters, without payment or costs, and producing an 'agreement' which continued to cause problems. What exactly had he or Tweed achieved? 'How have we benefitted from their services?' She ended by drawing attention to her discovery that the Head of their Chambers was also a member of Stoat's Chambers. She could not avoid observing that the result of the two barristers' work was a far better outcome for the Ogmore Gang than they had any right to hope for, and far worse for Max and herself.

In his commentary Max had more than a few words to say about Stoat's conduct, detailing, for example, the fact that he had withheld from them that Ogmore had withdrawn all plans and papers from Land Registry when he got their agreement to let the Registry decide on the registration land. Robert Tweed's letter was subjected to a cooler, more forensic commentary and Malcolm Scroggs' response was given similar treatment but neither commentary masked Max's indignation.

Robert Tweed's response to their complaints against *him* was far more measured and extensive than his report on the Scroggs complaint. Perhaps he had benefitted from some *pro bono* assistance. He wrote that he had no concern to make much of this 'very ordinary, common, everyday boundary dispute with no new points of law.' He dealt with such cases regularly. Clearly he had forgotten that in his Scroggs commentary he had described the case as 'difficult'. He acknowledged the shouting match with Stoat who he had found difficult. He argued that if he had successfully had the injunction set aside under Rule 40.6, the Judge would have imposed another because of Joe Ogmore's attack! His clerks were responsible for misleading his ex-clients about his availability, and two days is more than adequate for a barrister of Malcolm Scroggs' talents and experience to fully master his brief. He offered no explanation for, nor made any reference to Master Scroggs' failure to master a key element in his brief: the OS plan and not the Hammer plan was to be used in any settlement.

The assertion made by Malcolm Scroggs that they had fully discussed and agreed to use the Hammer plan had shocked and depressed Max and Lucy. They wished he had not lied. Once embarked on the lie he could not retract, it would be professional suicide. It was a declaration of war on them: his word or theirs – there was no room for compromise. He must have been very confident. His second submission repeated the lie and elaborated further claiming that it was agreed the plan identified sufficient physical features for the surveyors to mark boundaries. Yet it was precisely because the plan failed to do that job that all the problems ensued. In his second submission he added another: they had fully discussed costs, he claimed, and were 'also aware that the opponents would not concede any element of costs in negotiation'. There had been no discussion on costs with Max and Lucy. Lucy had mentioned it much later while waiting for Max to return and Scroggs had merely shrugged. Another depressing lie allowing no room for manoeuvre.

He quoted extensively from the fax Lucy had sent to Cain the day after the hearing, extensively and most selectively. By ignoring completely her statement that they wanted to use the agreed OS plan 'from now on', he tried to convey the impression that the fax confirmed her acceptance of the Hammer plan for the survey. On the one hand he asserted that he had fully explained and they had fully understood the terms and conditions of the 'binding compromise', on the other he suggested that they had failed to understand what was agreed. He did the standard demolition job of describing their letters and emails and the complaint itself as evidencing the strong emotions 'generated by the litigation'. He, like Cain, seemed to find it hard to relinquish the cost threat method of herding clients into his chosen result, despite being made aware that his clients would not be picking up the tab.

As for CPR 40.6: according to Mr Scroggs, Lucy's reference to it was, 'with respect, of course misconceived.' Nothing else, no explanation, with or without respect of why 'of course' it was misconceived.

One small gleam of honesty: he admitted that Max had left the building before seeing the scribbled draft and curiously he reported that he and Stoat had 'outlined' the terms of the agreed order to the Judge. Was he aware that the Judge had not sealed his misconceived agreement when he advised Cain, days later, that nothing could be done, the Hammer plan ruled?

His final flurry took their breath away. 'It appears to me inconceivable that any Counsel could compromise a dispute of this nature by reference to a plan without the lay clients seeing and approving the plan.' There was no way out. The Bar Council would have to choose whom to believe: one of their own with 20 years of faultless record or a couple embroiled in a standard, 'very common' boundary dispute with added 'strong emotions'.

Max and Lucy combined their responses to the latest hatchet job and managed to restrict it to four sides of A4, even though they included an update on the sorry consequences of the barristers' work. They described Malcolm Scroggs' various inexactitudes as 'quite simply untrue' (Lucy's choice), but added that they could express themselves more forcefully (Max's preferred option). They asked to be assured that no papers would be passed to Stoat because the litigation was ongoing. They pointed out that *they* had not had any professional advice on their responses.

In February the Secretary to the Complaints Committee decided to refer their papers to a practitioner on his Committee, because the Commissioner was a layman and advice might be needed on legal or procedural issues. He promised a response in two weeks. By April it had not arrived and the costs hearing with Judge Dyer was imminent. Polite apologies were offered, the practitioner member had been very busy. They wrote again after Dyer's costs hearing to report that Stoat maintained throughout the hearing that Scroggs' signature on the Hammer plan 'established the agreement' and their attempt to persuade the Court to order an independent survey was actually an attempt to resile from it. They received a holding reply from the Secretary and had to write a month later to find out when they would get a real one. Could the accruing costs lie behind the Commissioner's failure to meet any of his deadlines? Finally, a response. The Commissioner decided to pass their complaint on to the next stage – the Professional Conduct and Complaints Committee. They would be informed of the Committee's decision as soon as it was to hand. They congratulated themselves; they had made it past two of the firewalls.

The Committee, made up of eight QCs, 11 standard barristers and two 'lay representatives' met in May 2004 to consider their complaints among others. A week later Max and Lucy were informed that the Committee had concerns about certain aspects of the case. Mr Tweed had been summoned to attend the Chairman to discuss the concerns and be advised as to his future conduct. Scroggs, on the other hand, had been found not guilty of anything. So, clearly his version of events was believed, theirs was not. The Bar Council avoided such plain speaking and informed them that the Committee 'did not presume to make a preference for Mr Scroggs' account as it would plainly be wrong to do so. The basis for the decision was the lack of any realistic prospect of a finding being made that Mr Scroggs would make a compromise without your instructions.' This looked like a 'presumed preference' to Max and Lucy. The Committee also bought the rest of Scroggs' package: it was unrealistic to expect him to get the Ogmores to pay costs; if he had attempted to set aside the first misnamed Consent order on the basis of Rule 40.6, the Judge would have made an identical replacement order. So, no suggestion now that their understanding of the Rule was misconceived, but how fortunate that Mr Scroggs and all the Committee members, including the lay members, could confidently predict, like the Canadian Lady, what a judge would do when so often lawyers would warn clients that judges were unpredictable.

Max and Lucy knew the statistics so they were not surprised at the outcome. There was no mechanism to appeal the decision, but Lucy did extract some facts and figures: The Committee had considered 14 complaints in two hours! Each one guided by a single practitioner member acting as a sponsor for the complaint (or should that read 'for the barrister'?). No minutes were taken of the discussions and the meeting was not taped. The Secretary could not reveal the identity of the sponsor nor report what was said. Nor could he forward the sponsor's notes. So, around 10 minutes' discussion on a complaint with 100 pages of documented evidence and only the decision itself minuted. It was not difficult to see why so many complaints were dismissed and why so many complainants despaired.

Max and Lucy decided on a detailed response. They first drew attention to the fact that they had originally complained of inadequate professional service (IPS), not professional misconduct which had to satisfy the criminal standard of proof (beyond reasonable doubt), but the Committee had chosen to review it as a claim of professional misconduct. They suggested that it would have been interesting if they and Scroggs had been invited to attend so all could hear Scroggs' report of the hour-long discussions he claimed to have taken place. They finished by proposing that the Bar Council introduce a rule to ensure that clients sign any agreement deemed to be by consent, thus allowing the clients to see it first and avoid being misled and also, possibly avoid misleading the Court. They asked if anyone on the Committee could identify any net benefit they had received from the barrister's representation, because they couldn't. The Secretary forwarded their letter to a senior member of the Committee for a detailed response which would be with them by 8th September 2004. Lucy had to write to remind them of that promise at the end of September. Finally, in October they learnt that the two complaints had been referred back to the Professional Conduct and Complaints Committee (PCCC). Their letter had succeeded in reopening the fire door just a little. The Secretary reported that Robert Tweed had accepted that he bore responsibility for his clerk and had been warned not to allow a similar incident to occur again. His clerk was sacked. Their interpretation of Rule 40.6 was correct (not misconceived), but the Committee repeated the confident prediction that the Judge would have immediately made a new identical order. This, apparently, cleared Robert Tweed of inadequate professional service.

As for Scroggs and the diametrically opposing reports of what had taken place in October 2002: the Secretary repeated that the Committee was not attempting to decide who was to be believed, but it was 'clear that extensive discussions took place', so their dissatisfaction with the Hammer plan would have been made obvious to their Counsel who would not have incorporated it in the compromise without their agreement (!). So, it was confirmed, the Panel did decide who to believe after all.

They had asked to see the mysterious sponsor's notes, but transparency was a word yet to be added to the Committee's dictionary and the request was rejected as was their proposal that clients sign any binding agreement before anything is put in front of a judge. Finally, their request that any benefit they had received from the two barristers' work be identified was ignored. Wearily they decided to take their dissatisfaction with the Bar Council's complaints procedures, delays and lack of transparency to the 2004 version of the Legal Ombudsman.

In July 2004 Max and Lucy had started to firm up on their understanding of the rules on consent orders, not just those involving litigants in person but rules governing all consent orders. It seemed patently obvious to them that clients of the civil justice service should see any agreement they were deemed to have agreed. After all they would be held to it. They also thought it would be a good idea if the Civil Procedure Rules included one similar to the cooling-off period that applied to consumer agreements in the financial sector. The Deputy Head of Civil Justice did not agree. In his view it was essential to the smooth running of civil litigation that legal representatives should be recognised by law as having 'apparent' or 'ostensible' authority to do things in the course of litigation which binds their clients *vis-à-vis* opposing parties. If they do something they are not authorised by their clients to do they would be in breach of their professional duty ... and liable for any adverse consequences. So, in such circumstances this very Senior Judge would be content to let the client battle it out with the lawyer after the error had been set in stone ... an unequal battle that could end in an even more unequal battle in court. As for the cooling-off period: in the very senior Judge's view, such a rule would cause chaos in the service with delays and confusions. 'There is no analogy between financial services and litigation.'

This sad display of judicial blindness to the fact that judges are supposed to be running a service, not some 2004 version of Kafka's *The Trial*, had not deterred the two hardened litigants from one final attempt to get written clarification of CPR 40.6. The very Senior Judge replied in writing that, 'The order must be expressed as "by consent" *and signed by the litigant in person.*'

The Ombudsman circa 2004/5[4] saw her responsibility limited to investigating how the Bar Council had dealt with their complaint. They sent a detailed report and commentary in November 2004. They heard nothing more about it until April 2005 when they received, to their surprise, her detailed response and commentary. They were surprised because the Ombudsman service was reported to be in disarray due to caseload outsourcing and a backlog of cases, but they were far more surprised because their complaint was upheld. The Bar Council was 'asked' to reconsider their complaint against Mr Scroggs. The statistics had not encouraged them to believe it a likely outcome. Few complaints handled by the Law Society were referred on to her – just nine per cent of the original 17,000 or so in 2003, whereas of the 541 external complaints handled by the Bar Council, 40% of the complainants were discontented enough to go further. The Law Society failed to persuade the Ombudsman in around half of referred complaints. The Bar was far more successful: 90% of complaints about barristers referred on to the Ombudsman were dismissed. Max and Lucy were among the 10% to be accepted.

They decided to make sure that the next 'senior practitioner' of the Council's Professional Conduct and Complaints Committee was well informed. They sent yet more papers including copies of all the emails between Lucy and Ordnance Survey seeking permission in 2002 to use the agreed OS plan. Once again they asked for the name of the QC who would be 'sponsoring' their complaint and a copy of his or her report, and once again their requests were refused: it was a confidential document purely for the benefit of the Committee – but it would be seen by the Ombudsman! It just would not be seen by them.

As long as the Council avoided any reference to the facts underlying the complaints and merely stuck to procedures and decisions, they were on safe ground, but they were now forced to venture out into unknown territory – unknown to them but all too familiar to Max and Lucy. The Council's attempt at background information was lamentable – they started by confusing Tweed for Scroggs and went downhill from there. The lamentable record called for detailed, time-consuming and sensitively polite corrections. The case was handed to the Secretary of the Adjudication Panel who wanted further comments from both sides. Scroggs did not budge from his claim to have spent an hour persuading his clients to agree the Hammer plan. His confusion with dates was inexplicable but not too significant; his attempt to redefine the rules on consent orders was not excusable. He complained he had not been paid. Lucy was forced yet again to write correcting errors and falsehoods, and yet again to urge the Council to consider an open meeting with both parties present, or, even better, a mediated resolution if only to cut down on the casework.

At the end of 2005 the Bar Council had to put all Panel hearings on hold because of a challenge to their disciplinary procedures. They had to reconfigure the whole process and hand the administration to the Council of the Inns of Court. The delay went on for months. Meanwhile, new evidence came to light of further consequences from the fateful Consent Order in the form of a copy of Joe Ogmore's Witness Statement for the criminal trial of March 2003 (when he had been merely bound over). His unchallenged Statement claimed that the Hammer plan had been totally vindicated; that 'what we deemed was our land indeed belonged to us' and the shed was determined as 'lying totally in our land'. All false claims endorsed by Malcolm Scroggs' signature on the infamous plan.

Finally a date was set for the Panel hearing in early February 2006. The Bar Council did not require their attendance but it did want to compensate them for the delay. A cheque duly arrived in the post – another surprise, a rare, pleasant surprise.

They heard nothing more until five weeks after the hearing date. The Panel found that Mr Malcolm Scroggs had provided inadequate professional service. He was directed to make a formal apology, remit his fees and pay £1,500 compensation. Malcolm Scroggs had 28 days to appeal. And appeal he did.

His letter of appeal repeated his insistence that he had had full knowing agreement from his clients to use the Hammer plan and he could see nothing wrong with it. Only one boundary was relevant and surveyors would have no problem marking it out. His clients could have gone back to court but chose not to. So, his appeal was based on one untruth and two unknowns: his clients *did not* knowingly agree to use the plan and said so in a fax to their solicitor the day after Scroggs signed it; Scroggs had not seen the site and, as reported by the expert surveyor in 2008, *all* the boundaries interrelated and *all* were relevant; they had tried to go back to court but the attempt was thwarted – by Mr Scroggs' Consent agreement. He wanted an oral hearing and he wanted to be represented by leading Counsel. Both wishes were met but the same right was accorded not only to Max and Lucy but also to the Chair of the Committee that had found him guilty.

In his appeal notice Scroggs had referred to a well-known recent (2005) boundary case and Lucy observed that that case had become an expensive soul-draining experience for both parties, not least because of the difficulty in understanding land disputes without plans. She sent plans. She also sent a minute-by-minute record of events on the day showing that there were barely 10 minutes, let alone an hour, when both she and Max were with Scroggs to agree to proposals that had never been suggested before.

The Appeal hearing took place on a long, hot September day in a stuffy room overlooking Chancery Lane. They had arrived early with a close friend for moral support and waited. There were a dozen or so people in the anteroom also waiting, but they could not see Malcolm Scroggs. They asked the Secretary if he had been delayed. 'No,' she replied indicating a tall man on the other side of the room. This was a very different Malcolm Scroggs: gone were the red-rimmed glasses; gone was the alarming hair; gone was the sharp suit; above all gone was the shark-like flash of a cold smile. This Malcolm Scroggs was a quiet gentleman, with conventional brown hair, sober suit and slightly worried expression. 'My God!' whispered Lucy. 'He's an actor *par excellence*. Either he was putting it on for us or he's putting it on now.' 'Most likely both. Performances selected for the likely audience,' whispered Max.

Since the main performers were to be the two QC representatives – one for Scroggs and one for the Chair of the Conduct Committee – neither Lucy nor Max had seen the need to brief their own Counsel, at a cost to them – something Scroggs and the Chairman would avoid. Counsel for the Chair, Mr Simon, impressed. He did not waste time on irrelevant arguments or on whether they had or had not spent an hour agreeing to use the Hammer plan. Having first satisfied himself with the Complainants about the conditions for surveying on site, he concentrated exclusively on the terms of the compromise which were unclear, ill-conceived and had failed to resolve the dispute. The Order plan was hopeless. It should never have been applied no matter how long discussions had taken.

Counsel for Scroggs decided on personal attacks on the Complainants, first as uncompromising litigants and then as confused litigants. They were the problem not the Order, not the plan, not the Ogmores and certainly not the lawyers or the Civil Procedure Rules. The hot day wore on and finally the Panel Chair asked if the Complainants had anything to say. All Lucy could think to contribute was to repeat the record of timing of the encounters with Malcolm Scroggs showing that there had been no time for an hour-long discussion, and to reinforce the arguments put by Mr Simon. She did add that she was fairly certain she would think what she should have said on the bus home, as indeed she did. She noted that one piece of information about timings had pricked Scroggs' attention. She had reported that she had been given the times for the Judge's arrival in court and for his departure by HM Court Service, but that other arrival and departure times had been recorded on CCTV and the film had been wiped by the time she realised she needed corroboration of her record. She said this was a pity since it would have given conclusive evidence of Max's arrival and departure. A pity for the

Complainants, but helpful for the Appellant. Scroggs had not known that they had been too late to get a record of Max's departure until he heard it at his appeal. Maybe that was why he had admitted that Max had left early.

The Appeal Panel of four, two QCs and two 'lay' experts, dismissed the Appeal. Mr Simon was quite pleased with himself in a restrained, mature QC sort of way. Lucy and Max were pleased with him too, especially when he told them that the Appeal was 'fairly unique' and the dismissal a complete one-off, he had never known it happen before. They were quite pleased with themselves for a while. It really did look as though they had jumped all the hurdles and beaten the system.

Good job they had learnt to be wary of phantom success. The Panel Chair had not elaborated on the dismissal at the hearing but promised a full report in a few days. It took over three weeks. Scroggs was still found guilty of inadequate professional service, he still had to apologise and forgo his fee but he did not have to pay compensation. That was not a disappointing financial loss since the compensation ordered was as inadequate as the service provided, but the commentary which accompanied the decision was deeply unpleasant. It began by describing a 'boundary dispute' between two equally intransigent, unwise neighbours who had been fighting for many years (actually nine months of correspondence and two months in court) before Mr Scroggs came on the scene. Scroggs would not have known from his brief, it continued, that the Hammer plan was unacceptable as there was nothing in it to warn him (there was – a lot, and Max had warned him anyway); they commended Scroggs for acting to minimise costs (his clients had not been vulnerable to costs since they were not paying at that time, he saved nothing *at that time* but he caused many ensuing costs); the amount of land in dispute was no more than a few square feet (in fact it was over 8,000 square feet). The commentary went on and on with similar errors to paint a dishonest, insulting picture of Max and Lucy. Classic legal profession defence: the silly, unreasonable clients were to blame; the noble lawyer had done his best in very difficult circumstances. The Panel had ventured way out into unknown territory unapologetically displaying ignorance all the way. In lavishing sympathy on Scroggs, accepting his record of events on 31st October 2002 and by implication accusing Max and Lucy of lying, they displayed blatant bias. Clearly something had been going on during the extended three-week delay between Appeal and written decision. Lucy remembered the look on Scroggs' face when he heard the decision. She remembered the angry glance at Max and herself from both Scroggs and his

QC as they left the hearing room. The two barristers had not expected the result perhaps, but they did know how best to mitigate the potential threat to Scroggs' career. The written decision did a good job for Scroggs. It did a bad job for the reputation of the Bar.

Before they received the written decision they had proposed a mediated resolution of the Claim they intended to pursue. On receipt of the decision Scroggs was emboldened: There was nothing to mediate, he had done nothing wrong, they had reneged on the agreement, lied about his representation and all ensuing costs were due to their subsequent actions. As for his formal apology – it was strictly limited to a minor failure to mark measurements on the plan (a new and unexplained idea). He referred their Claim to his indemnity insurers. Max replied in constrained fury, feeling vindicated in his deprecation of Scroggs. Lucy had given the barrister the benefit of the doubt for the previous four years and was deeply shocked at what she saw as an ill-judged display of truculent bad manners and dishonesty. They copied his churlish letter and Max's reply to the Secretary together with their commentary on the Panel's written decision. The Secretary thanked them and asked if they would participate in a review of the Bar Council's complaints handling. 'Your comments would be most gratefully received.' If so it would be a first – their comments to the Panel and to Scroggs were quite clearly *not* gratefully received.

TWENTY-ONE
Recovery 4: The Bar's Professional Indemnity Insurance

By December 2006 action with the indemnity insurers was beginning to follow a familiar path. It had started very civilly. Lucy felt she could do business with Charles Waterhouse and despite experience with The Firm was hopeful of reaching a settlement within six months. Then Mr Waterhouse retired and by January 2007 Muhammed Saif had taken over. He could see no reason to compensate them one penny. The Appeal Panel's report exonerated his client completely.

They were prepared for this. Of course he would delay as long as possible, they replied, neither he nor Scroggs was vulnerable to personal material loss and he could indulge in time-wasting argument unhindered by facts. As for the written decision and other Statements by various Bar Council bodies, they were shamefully full of bias and error. This was somewhat surprising since in early 2007 the Council was fighting fiercely at Parliamentary level to retain control of complaints in the Legal Services Bill. The record of the Bar's conduct of Max and Lucy's complaint confirmed (to them and others) that self-regulation in legal services could not work to the public good. The professional skills of lawyers, acquired in an adversarial system, militated against objectivity and therefore fair determinations and just outcomes.

It must have been something they said. Mr Saif disappeared and Mr Waterhouse came out of retirement to retrieve the file and suggest a meeting at Homestead. He visited in early April, agreed their Title was encumbered should they wish to sell, had sight of a menacing Hazel Ogmore when he went to see the site, sympathised fully with everything, but feared that few if any of their Claims were legally enforceable if they went to court. They would fall, he thought, on the familiar 'causality' and a new 'remoteness' argument. Scroggs had not caused the subsequent losses, they were too 'remote' from anything he did or failed to do. He proposed binding arbitration and suggested two arbitrators he knew and trusted. This was somewhat naive on his part. Charming though he was, he had not fully gained their trust, not least because he persisted in avoiding a few of their most compelling questions and using a Latin phrase that did not translate meaningfully and did not appear in any legal glossary. How could they address the point if they didn't know what it meant? Although he was prepared to make an assumption of negligence by Malcolm Scroggs, he was not prepared to name a number when it came to the *ex gratia*[1] payment he was continuing to dangle promisingly – just out of their reach.

By October 2007 Mr Waterhouse was fading back into retirement, but after a sharp prod from Max he refocussed to offer to pay for legal advice on liability and quantum. They wrote for clarification but he then disappeared completely and a Jack Dyson took over. Mr Dyson confidently informed them that he had read the file fully (where had they heard that before?) and would need some convincing any of the costs Max and Lucy were trying to recover could properly be said to have been caused by the acts or omissions of any member of the Bar. A year on from the Appeal decision and five years from Scroggs' negligent conduct in court they were back to square one.

They decided that it takes a lawyer to deal with lawyers – especially those who become judges, they seem to have a different mindset from ordinary people, added to which the six-minute billing clock was in action again with the Ethan Ganz-Tracey Wormelow (aka Ogmore) jousts and it was now 2008 and another ticking clock was set with an alarm – the six-year limitation rule was just months away. They decided to accept the offer Mr Waterhouse had made to pay for legal advice.

Lawyer selection was delayed by dealing with the consequences of Hannah Katz's misdeeds. In April 2008 they had a look at the Chambers and Partners[2] website again and identified a leading firm of London solicitors. Once again they were instructed to find, copy, collate and list papers and yet more papers. They delivered a large plastic crate of them to their new champion in London, had an encouraging discussion and, after another large batch of papers was forwarded by post, felt confident that all was going well (unlike their dealings with Ethan Ganz & Co.) until their champion proposed that an expert property barrister be contracted to advise on 'mitigation'. They asked for clarification. He insisted that they needed Counsel's advice on what should have been done about the Consent Order. He intimated that their attempt to get an independent survey could be deemed negligent and so let Scroggs off the hook. It might be that they should have gone back to court to get the Consent Order dealt with first. They, or rather the lawyer who had advised them on the independent survey application, Cynthia Buxton, could be held negligent.

This was not new. Two years earlier when they were still battling with the Lady from Dagenham and The Firm, they had decided to get an expert's view on their Claims against both The Firm and the Swales. The trouble with both Claims was that they had been advised to wait until their Claim was settled with Land Registry. Time was passing and all Claims appeared to be frozen. They decided to get advice from the super breed of solicitors who had achieved the Lexcel[3] quality mark, which is only awarded to legal practices meeting the highest management and customer care standards. This time they would choose the best.

Mr Excel had agreed they should do nothing about the Swales until the Land Registry Claim was settled, but he had been interested in the role of Mrs Buxton. He had suspected negligent advice. They were dismayed. Mrs Buxton may have lacked charm but in their view she had given good advice, besides which they had specifically said in writing that they only wanted her advice and would take responsibility for any problems that might arise from their subsequent actions. Her advice, in their view, had been sensible and she could not be held responsible for their subsequent actions and District Judge Dyer's misjudgments. Mr Excel had been insistent, so they had written a background report and sent a pack of papers. In the accompanying letter they had repeated their misgivings about any culpability on her part and asked, in words they underlined, for him to contact them by phone to discuss the reasons for their misgivings *before* looking at the papers. He might agree with them and they did not want to pay for advice they already had in their heads.

He had phoned. They had drawn attention to the specific words in the contract they had had with Cynthia Buxton but he had dismissed their concerns. Then he had looked at the papers. He informed them that due to the contract they had with Mrs Cynthia Buxton they would not have a claim against her! Mr Excel Lexcel sent his bill with his opinion. They paid it adding a few opinions of their own.

Now their new Chambers and Partners recommended lawyer was following the same line and they were sure that after he had spent rather too many six-minute slots investigating he would come up with the same result.

They did not want him to waste his time, a barrister's time and their money on a dead end. But he was not prepared to continue with their case unless they played it his way and so eventually they parted company. He felt he had lost their trust. They felt the same but it was trust in his judgement not in his honour which proved to be sound. He did not bill them for the considerable time he had spent among the thousands of pages they had sent.

It was now June 2008 and the six-year limitation period for making a claim against Scroggs would run out in months. They still had the Professional Indemnity Fund's offer intact. They decided that there was little point looking for another solicitor and that their best bet was to engage a barrister by direct access. Direct Public Access[4] has mushroomed since it was sanctioned by the Bar Council in July 2004. Of the 12,000 self-employed barristers roughly a third can be contracted directly by members of the public to do most things a member of the public would want a legal expert to do if they suspected they were not up to a DIY approach. Chambers and Partners came up with a top leading set offering direct access, in the premier division for professional negligence claims, and the Chambers' Clerk came up with Harvey Rishus.

His first advice was to get agreement to remove the limitation threat. They hadn't realised this might be possible (none of the solicitors had suggested it), so he scored a goal from first whistle. He drafted a letter to persuade Jack Dyson to enter into a 'standstill' agreement so that a defence of limitation against Max and Lucy would not be raised. Armed with the evidence found in the Cross & Cross file, together with part of the transcript from their Appeal before Judge Pelt when the Judge agreed he was dismissing the Appeal because of Scroggs' negligence, Mr Rishus was able to hint that the insurers and their client might be wise to avoid a court claim and to start negotiating. He tackled head-on the defence position on causation and foreseeability. Jack Dyson must have wondered if honouring Mr Waterhouse's offer to pay for expert opinion had backfired. Far from discouraging the Claimants, the advice had provided accurate weaponry for the attack. Mr Dyson agreed to the 'standstill' until Christmas.

Mr Rishus was pleased. In his view Dyson would not have agreed a standstill if he had not already decided to make an offer. He proposed a meeting or mediation 'which, we may hope, will resolve this dispute.' They copied his next draft letter and included his first invoice. The Indemnity Fund paid it promptly but refused to pay any more. Apparently the offer was to pay for 'advice' not for '*ongoing* advice'. They objected that they had had advice on liability but the offer had been for advice on liability *and quantum* which Mr Rishus had yet to give. Mr Dyson would not budge and they could not waste time arguing and so they decided to gamble on recovering Mr Rishus' fees in the settlement. Jack Dyson intimated that he would make an offer early in the New Year.

A deciding factor in selecting solicitors first rather than a barrister for their Claim against a barrister was that all members of the Bar were indemnified by Jack Dyson's firm and therefore all barristers had a vested interest in minimising claims against their fellow members. Mr Rishus now drew attention to this ironic fact which Lucy thought rather charmingly open and Max thought an astute guess that they knew anyway.

They sent Jack Dyson a detailed list of the losses they wished to recover. Perhaps he needed time to recover from the shock because he asked if they would agree to extend the limitation period to the end of February 2009, seven years and four months and three court cases on from when Malcolm Scroggs' signature appeared on the Hammer plan. Dyson then managed to extend it further, dangling the desirable prospect of a settlement without an encounter with yet another judge. Deadline February became deadline March. The offer he finally sent was less than half their Claim. Clearly he was in no hurry to settle: the strategy was to drag it out and wear them down. His justifications for rejecting the various heads of Claim were provocative and illuminating. In his view they should not have done what they did to sort out the boundary mess Scroggs had left them, nor should they have attempted to set the record straight about Joe Ogmore's attack (or learn something of the mental state of the fat man along the road). Although he was content to say what they should not have done, he was not prepared or, more likely, able to say what they should have done. Presumably they should have suffered the consequences of Scroggs' negligence without protest, remedy or recompense. Despite the clarity of Harvey Rishus' dismantling of the causation defence, Dyson bulldozed on with this one weapon: it was for the Claimants to show the direct connection between the now admitted negligence and the two cases that had been struck out as abuse of process.

General insurers can be intransigent, unreasonable on occasion; barrister insurers are in a class of their own. It is not part of their professional mindset to be reasonable and compromising when the opponent is weak, as all non-barristers will be regardless of the strength of their case. Had the new independent Ombudsman scheme been available to them, Max and Lucy might have achieved an acceptable outcome within months, but luckily for Messrs Dyson and Scroggs, that Ombudsman had yet to open shop so they were forced into an expensive, uneven battle holding only one weapon with any potency, a weapon they did not want to use because they did not trust it. It could blow up in their faces. Their only weapon was court action – before a Judge – who could turn out to be another Judge Dyer, or Carmine or Pelt rather than another Judge Gold or Green. They would be gambling ... again.

Harvey Rishus advised an end to argument with the deaf: action was called for. They lodged a claim in the High Court of Justice, Queen's Bench Division on 7 May 2009. The 'standstill' ran out the following day. They let the opposition know and offered to defer further moves in litigation if there was agreement to negotiate a settlement through mediation. A series of blustering letters followed from a firm of solicitors in a distant city denying that the indemnifiers were in any way responsible for dragging out negotiations. However, their client did finally agree to mediation. No doubt he considered a secret mediation was preferable to a public court appearance. Pity he had not agreed three years previously when they had first proposed it so avoiding delays, work and expense. Another stay was proposed until the end of September, more delay. And more expense: Mr Harvey Rishus' bills were rising inexorably.

TWENTY-TWO
Recovery 5: Mediation

Before they had experienced any mediation, and for very different reasons, both Max and Lucy had become enthusiasts. He, because he had hated to see small companies taken to the cleaners by large companies with a full battalion of expensive lawyers; and she, because of her bitter experience with the Doyles and the fence-post saga.

Lord Woolf and quite a few other judges shared that enthusiasm and now and then the Ministry of Justice, under whatever name applied at the time, would invest a little in a little promotion exercise, and were often mystified by the unimpressive take-up. A disappointingly low proportion of disputants were encouraged to abandon the court route. This should not have been so surprising as it was usually left to lawyers, mindful that ADR stands for Alarming Drop in Revenue, to persuade them.

However, each puff of expenditure did generate more interest among an increasing and increasingly threatened legal profession. A number, fearing the future for old-style lawyers, took up training in one form of mediation or another from one of the several accrediting companies like the Centre for Effective Dispute Resolution (CEDR)[1] and UK Mediation.[2] A government promotion exercise had been taking place when Max and Lucy tried to mediate resolutions to their disputes with the Swales and Joe Ogmore which is how they got caught by Elaine Boyd and the newly-formed BetweenOurselves, unaware at first that Mrs Boyd was a solicitor working in the same small county town as Hazel Ogmore. Judge Carmine decided that was the reason Mrs Boyd pulled out of the planned mediation with Joe Ogmore. Max and Lucy were not so sure. They suspected it might also have had something to do with their comments on the feedback form after the failed mediation with the Swales.

A mediator is a detached outsider who helps people reach agreement on a dispute they have been unable to resolve between themselves. Mediated negotiations offer a structure, timetable and dynamic that unplanned negotiations lack. The parties agree voluntarily to a process which is private and confidential, but which can be enforced by law, the mediator acting as a neutral third party who *facilitates* rather than *directs* the process; unlike an arbitration where the arbitrator decides.

Mediators use various techniques to open, or improve dialogue between disputants aiming to help them reach an agreement. So, much depends on the mediator's skill, training and independence. Acting as a neutral facilitator, she guides the parties through the process helping them to think outside the box for possible solutions, broadening the range of the possible.

While a mediator may charge a fee comparable to that of a lawyer, the mediation process generally takes much less time than moving a case through the usual legal tunnel. While a case in the hands of a lawyer or a court may take months or, as in Max and Lucy's case, years, mediation usually achieves a resolution in a matter of hours once the limited preliminaries are sorted.

Court hearings are public, mediations remain strictly confidential. No one but the parties to the dispute and the mediator know what happened. Confidentiality in mediation has such importance that in most cases the legal system cannot force a mediator to testify in court as to the content or progress of mediation. Many mediators destroy any notes they take. The only exceptions to such strict confidentiality usually involve child abuse or other actual or threatened criminal acts.

For Max and Lucy the main attraction was control. Mediation increases the control the parties have over the resolution. Control resides with them rather than a judge, barrister or solicitor, so in theory mediation is more likely to produce a result that is mutually acceptable – if it results in agreement. Solutions can emerge in mediation that a court could not provide. The Court could not order an apology from Joe Ogmore or the Swales even if the Court (that's to say, Judge Carmine) had wanted to. It is possible that a skilled, trained mediator, preferably with a background in psychology or counselling rather than exclusively law, might have eased an apology from Joe Ogmore and the Swales. Nobody, apart from the parties and the mediator, would know but it would have allowed Max and Lucy some 'closure' and 'move on' – the irritating, patronising words of advice to clients who have been badly served by courts and lawyers.

Because the parties working together reach a mutually agreed resolution, compliance is usually high which further reduces costs, as the parties do not have to engage a lawyer and possibly the Court to enforce it. If enforcement problems do arise the mediated agreement is fully enforceable in a court of law. No one, not even a judge, can force anyone to mediation, but courts can use costs sanctions as a prod to reluctant disputants, and legislation is up-coming from the EU to ensure that all disputes for goods and services are mediated by some form of ADR initially.[3]

Mediators are trained to work with difficult situations and all the disputes Max and Lucy were embroiled in were difficult one way or another

The Swales had handed control to their lawyer, the solicitor they had used to sell to Max and Lucy, who ensured that meaningful dialogue ceased. Lucy had found it hard to believe the Swales would lie on the SPIF if only a year earlier they had been told by Hazel Ogmore, solicitor of the Supreme Court, that she disputed their ownership of some Homestead land. Max had put their man in the firing line because of the wording, 'We have not been notified of any' (disputes) until he was informed that only the Swales would be held responsible. The solicitor was very insistent that Max and Lucy find (and pay for) their own lawyer to do business with him. Instead, in 2002 they wrote directly to the Swales proposing mediation, but *they*, unfortunately, handed the matter back to their lawyer who insisted that Max and Lucy engage in a proper legal dispute through lawyers so they could endure proper legal games.

The Swales were persuaded to invest in Counsel's opinion. Apparently Counsel told them they were innocent of all charges and should fight on. A court case looked inevitable especially when their lawyer refused to respond to Max's perfectly drafted pre-protocol letter. But then the Swales agreed (again) to mediate.

They correctly rejected Max's cheeky proposal that they pay for it in full, but wrongly proposed who the mediator should be, where the mediation should take place, the fee, remit and length of time. Having been harassed for several years to 'seek legal advice' by this pompous solicitor, Max and Lucy now advised him to seek advice himself on mediation and helpfully provided references. The solicitor did not appreciate their advice any more than they did his. He threatened to strike out any claim they might choose to make in court. His reference to their '*late confirmation* to agree to mediation' was pure Ogmore.

Max wanted to know if this solicitor had any previous connection with the two mediators he proposed. He admitted he had so they proposed half a dozen of their own including one from BetweenOurselves and that was the one the Swales (or their mentor) selected. Max did not think to check any connection between him and their selection. He would attend the mediation of course, in fact, at first there was the suggestion that *only* he would attend.

Max and Lucy were surprised at the flimsiness of the Swales' position statement. They had expected something with a bit of bite but all they got was a repeat of the argument that the Swales did not believe there was any dispute when they answered the questions on the SPIF and that, besides, Max and Lucy had learnt from the forestry expert, Mr Jenkins, that there was a dispute and still went ahead with the purchase. They did not think there was a dispute with Ogmore, but apparently Max and Lucy should have realised there was.

The Swales' solicitor did not simply attend the event in December 2005. He took over. Max and Lucy did not get to speak to the people they had come to speak to. They only glimpsed them briefly through an open door. The lawyer mediator by contrast was hardly present. When it was all over, after it had dismally failed, neither Max nor Lucy could remember much about him. He certainly could not be accused of directing but he did not facilitate much either, apart from encouraging Lucy to show to the other side Mr Barr's opinion that the Swales were guilty as charged and why. The Swales could not reciprocate with their Counsel's opinion because he or she had not put it in writing. So they had been relying on an opinion from a barrister who had not been prepared to put it on paper and sign it. It was beginning to look as though the Swales were a 21st-century version of the Doyles, foolishly allowing themselves to be blindly led by business-generating lawyers, who, no doubt, assured them that they would recover their payments from Max and Lucy.

Max and Lucy want to respect the confidentiality of what actually took place that day, as agreed, but they are prepared to report that they saw it as a waste of time and money. It would have been better chancing it in court with a Small Claim. Unfortunately, by the time they had settled other matters and were able to draw up an arguable and much reduced Claim against the Swales, they had come up against the limitation rule. Their first experience of mediation had taught them one or two things including don't delay, be all set to try the Court route if mediation fails.

When they found out that they could not extend the six-year limitation period, which they had thought possible (for technical reasons), and had to abandon any claim against the Swales, Lucy was not too concerned. They had by then put sufficient money into the Recovery Fund and obviously the Swales had had to make several contributions to their solicitor's pension fund. In her view they had suffered enough for their lies. Not a view shared by Max.

So the mediation with Scroggs was a second test of what both Max and Lucy had long argued was a dispute resolution process far preferable to what the Courts could offer. Unfortunately, this time they would be opposed exclusively by lawyers, and lawyers of a far higher grade than the Swales' man or Tracey Wormelow or even Stoat. Not exactly a level playing field. Mediations can perpetuate power imbalances and this was shaping up to be litigation without wigs, but there was nothing they could do to avoid it – apart from reverting to their court Claim and adding the intimidating wig. It would very much depend on the skills and judgement of the mediator. The general advice that either all or none of the parties have professional legal support forced them to consider inviting Mr Rishus to hold their hands on the day, despite their misgivings about costs. But their misgivings underestimated just how much Harvey would charge. Far too much. In fact, comparable to a court appearance, which for a brief moment they began to reconsider – until the spectres of Judges Dyer, Carmine and Pelt loomed. Harvey offered a more economical but far less helpful emergency telephone support which they accepted. They were encouraged, however, when the friend who attended Scroggs' appeal with them agreed to attend the mediation for moral if not legal support.

A mediation will usually be a one-off for most non-lawyers and so they will have no first-hand experience to go on. They are unlikely to know the mediator, let alone have a commercial connection with him. Lawyers fighting their own case rather than a client's would be in an entirely different position.

The distant solicitor, Lucas Skolski, nominated a mediator. Lucy asked if his firm or Malcolm Scroggs had used the nominated man before and also for confirmation that all parties – Malcolm Scroggs, Jack Dyson and Mr Skolski himself would attend the mediation. The answers were not encouraging. The firm had worked with their nominated mediator before (and no doubt he would want to work with the large international law firm again) and Malcolm Scroggs would not be there. They could deal with the first problem by proposing a few mediators of their own and they did finally get Mr Skolski to agree a very high-profile, well-reputed, experienced mediator. They could do nothing about the second which Mr Skolski assured them was no problem at all, 'As far as you are concerned,' he informed them,'the priority is to know that we will be attending with someone with full authority to settle the claim, Jack Dyson.' They could not agree; they saw it as a denial of the whole principle of mediation. 'If the only purpose is to barter compensation, similar to wrangling at the Court door, what need do we have of a mediation? If the mediator is there merely to rehearse all the legal arguments without adding meat to the bones, as only we and Malcolm Scroggs can do, what is the point of showing up for a quasi-litigious confrontation?' The reply made clear that, whereas there would be no dispute about Scroggs' negligence, there would be plenty of argument around that get-out litigation tactic: causation, allowing lengthy dispute on quantum. Since it is likely that such arguments would be even more expensive and lengthy if pursued in court, even if only at the Court door, Max and Lucy decided mediation would be a better bet. But would it be a true mediation? What about truth and reconciliation?

Again, Max and Lucy want to observe confidentiality and can therefore give no details of the eventual agreement. The day-long mediation involved just 20 minutes talking to the other side. Which, in view of the extraordinary number of errors of fact in Scroggs' position statement Lucy felt obliged to correct, was nowhere near long enough. Lucy and Max expected to meet them again but that was the one and only contact they had. The rest of the day was spent in conventional court-door manoeuvering. The other side raised their settlement offer but not enough for Max who, with an in-built calculator and an up-to-date statement of the Recovery Account, was able to name his very bottom line to the mediator. His bottom line was not Lucy's. Hers was rather higher, but then she had neither the in-built calculator nor the account statement. Both sets of disputants went home without an agreement. Their friend was dismayed. Although he knew something of the Scroggs debacle from attending the barrister's appeal, he had not realised how strong his friends' case was until he heard their discussions with the mediator. Like Lucy he suspected Max's very bottom line was too low. He feared it had all been a wasted effort and they would, after all, have to gamble in the Court casino.

Lucy was not so sure about that. She thought the private poker game was not yet over. The mediator would continue negotiations for a while, giving Scroggs time to contemplate the challenge of fighting the case in open court which, win or lose on causation, would make public his negligence – and possibly a bit more he would prefer to keep confidential. Certainly, a half-competent barrister should be able to pulp his error-filled 'Position Statement'.

Sure enough a week later Max's offer was agreed. Lucy wanted to know whether it was Jack Dyson or Scroggs who had called it a day – but that information was privileged. They would never know.

The cheque arrived in due course – with the anticipated denial of any liability.

So, despite their efforts and enthusiasm Max and Lucy did not attend a single, face-to-face mediation. Joe Ogmore pulled out – Lucy doubts he was ever in; the Swales and Malcolm Scroggs refused to face them. They still do not know what motivated Malcolm Scroggs: why his work was so negligent; why he claimed to have discussed his 'agreement' with them for an hour. The process that took place, in both instances, lacked two essential ingredients – truth and reconciliation.

TWENTY-THREE
Recovery 6: Legal Expenses Insurance (LEI)

Access to civil justice like access to the Ritz is open to everyone – as long as you can find a way to pay for it. Legal Aid, introduced in 1949, used to help around a third of litigants in England and Wales, but as Legal Aid costs exploded to become among the highest per capita in the world and some lawyers accumulated very impressive bank accounts from tax payers, successive governments decided something must be done and in 2012 a new Act was introduced which radically reduced the scope of Legal Aid, so many more joined the ranks of those denied it. Restrictions on Legal Aid have also impacted on the few remaining Law Centres, closing some and limiting the remit of others. Even high profile chambers working in the criminal law sector have closed.

No win, No fee, or Conditional Fee Agreements – CFAs (not to be confused with *Contingency* Fee Agreements), were given formal recognition in 1990 and seemed to be a liberating idea until certain 'refinements' were introduced and ambulance chasers and claims farmers moved in on the Act. Among the casualties was the NHS, forced to pay out millions to lawyers and claims management firms. CFAs fuelled the compensation culture which was itself fuelled by increased insurance premiums for everybody. Governments tried to clamp down on this unhealthy ballooning culture and eventually new rules were introduced in 2013, which quickly succeeded in weeding out a third of the ambulance chasers. Now the winning side, rather than the losing side, pay from their compensation their lawyers' success mark-up fee – which can be as high as 100%. Even though the loser pays the winner's basic legal fees (less mark-up), if the fees are challenged in court and the Court agrees they are too high, and if the lawyer insists on payment as per contract, the winner also has to make up the difference. Moreover, the winner may not be entitled to recover any extra fees for barristers, experts and so on. If you disagree with your lawyer and either fail to do as he says or abandon him for another, you may still have to pay him even if you've taken out insurance to cover failure. If you succeed with another lawyer you may have to pay the first abandoned one's success fee – even though he did not himself succeed! It all rather depends on the agreement you have with your chosen lawyer. So, read that contract carefully – and negotiate.

CFA litigants are often urged to take out 'After the Event' (ATE) insurance. This is usually rather expensive. Far less expensive is Before the Event (BTE) insurance tagged on to general house and car insurance for an additional £20 or so. Both Max and Lucy had BTE insurance so when the Ogmore games began they immediately contacted their insurers, but then abandoned the idea when they received Land Registry's indemnity offer as that promised more reliable and less troublesome cover. Over the following years, as they pursued claims against The Firm, Cross & Cross & Co and Malcolm Scroggs, they adopted a two-prong approach: claiming through their Legal Expenses Insurers and complaining to the respective complaints services backed by the now deceased old Ombudsman service. Whereas the complaints services could identify wrongdoing, they offered little to nothing for the Recovery Fund, and the defunct Ombudsman offered even less.

Max was the first to encounter the Byzantine complexity of Legal Expenses Insurance when he innocently decided to follow up the report by the Law Society's Complaints Investigator on their complaint against Cross & Cross & Co. In the Investigator's opinion the solicitors had denied him and Lucy the chance to set aside the Consent Order by failing to act in time to correct Scrogg's errors and Ogmore's lies to the Court, but because that might be *negligence* it fell outside her remit, so Max turned to their insurers for the Claim. First, he had to find the right house insurance company. The errors had occurred in 2002 and in each of the four intervening years Max had shopped around for the best house insurance deal. When he identified the correct one the insurers tried to dismiss his Claim because of the delay – any claim should be made within six months of the event, but reinstated it when he pointed out that until he gained access to the file and received the investigator's report he did not realise he had a claim against Robin Cain's old firm. The insurers sent it to a Panel firm in the East Midlands for a Mr

Alan Thorne to determine whether there was a valid claim with a fifty-fifty chance of success. Without that it would not be supported by LEI.

Alan Thorne's name did not turn up on the Law Society's 'Find a solicitor' webpage which caused Lucy some concern, but Mr Thorne insisted that he was qualified and registered and sent them copy of his certificate. His inevitable and impossible demand for copy of every single piece of paper that had accumulated over the years followed. In the end they proposed he visit Homestead and check the files on site. He spent a comfortable day in pleasant surroundings with a good lunch supplied free of charge, went away and several weeks later informed them that they had no claim against either Cross & Cross & Co. or Malcolm Scroggs, so he could not recommend to the LEI company that they take on the claims. However, he very kindly offered to take on the Claims himself … for his hourly rate. As the report he based his assessment on was even more full of holes than they had come to expect (and they had learnt to expect a lot) they did not respond. Mr Thorne viewed his business relationship with the LEI insurers as an opaque referral scheme, but seemed unaware of the holes not only in his report but in his logic. If they did not have a case, why would they pay him to take it further? He sent a reminder two months later. And another reminder two months after that. A year later he informed them that he was closing their file. By that time they had received compensation for Scroggs' negligence so a negligence claim against Cross & Cross & Co. would be not just difficult but redundant. Perhaps they should have charged for the lunch.

As soon as they sent payment to Bulmers via Ethan Ganz for Hannah Katz's negligent Defence, they started the lengthy process to get it back. The lady herself had long since left the firm, but Wolf Rottman was still Head of Dispute Resolution (Litigation) *and* Complaints Manager. He dealt with their complaint against him in the style they predicted: delaying, denying, distorting and ignoring most of what they wrote, but they had to go through the necessary, time-wasting pretence of seeking 'resolution' with him until they felt justified in lodging a long list of his misdeeds with the straggly remains of the soon-to-be-obsolete Law Society Complaints Service (LSCS).

This time they got the advertised service. That is to say the service advertised online by so many dissatisfied complainants who had innocently expected something a little more impartial and competent from the Law Society. Apart from failing to alert his clients about the increase in fees from the estimated £3,000 to the actual £14,000, Mr Wolf Rottman had done no wrong according to the slowly dying LSCS who saw this failure as IPS – Inadequate Professional Service. The investigator could not comment on any possible negligence because the LSCS didn't deal with negligence. Nor did they explain how they differentiated between the two. However, Max and Lucy could comment and passed their comments, together with a report, on to their Insurers who took six weeks and several packs of documents to tell them they were the wrong insurers because they were not the insurers at the time the contract with Ethan Ganz was agreed, even if they were when the Defence was found to be negligent. So, it was back to square one. More forms, more packages and the Claim eventually ended up with the same Panel solicitors in the East Midlands Alan Thorne worked for.

Although this did not augur well, the lengthy process began rather encouragingly with a quite different solicitor from the Panel firm. Mr Thorne had moved on. Melissa Pugh proved to be far more of a terrier than her weak telephone voice suggested. She was not fazed by the Rottman style and blocked his various attempts to divert, delay and intimidate her. He stalled everything he could hope to stall, in particular refusing to send her the full file. Some items were eventually recovered from the LSCS, but she knew more were missing. Rottman tried to get her to pay not only for the photocopying but also for his time at his hourly rate. She threatened court action citing the Civil Procedure Rule obliging him to provide the full file free of charge and organised provisional funding with the LEI providers for any such action. He caved in.

Meanwhile Max and Lucy had returned to the Court to check the file for the hearing before District Judge Green and found yet more documents they had never seen. It was only when they combined their findings with her successfully retrieved ones, that they got to see the attendance notes, time sheets and other documents revealing Mr Wolf Rottman's IPS and negligence in full. Ms Pugh then arranged funding for Counsel's opinion on their negligence Claim. In late August 2010 Max and Lucy learnt that Counsel agreed they had a good claim for professional negligence against Ethan Ganz LLP. Max and Lucy were relieved but not surprised. They did not see how any other conclusion could be drawn: either the Defence was negligently written or Rottman's response to Bulmer's (i.e. Ogmore's) accusation of negligence was … negligent.

The next stage was to agree the quantum of their Claim but then something happened to Melissa Pugh. Her draft Claim mystified them and then she became unavailable. Throughout the month of November 2010 Lucy tried to urge the Legal Expenses team to find out what was going on but they claimed to be as mystified as she. Max was getting impatient. He had checked their insurance document which clearly stated that once it was confirmed that a claim was valid they could choose who they wanted to represent them. Both Max and Lucy were agreed who they wanted for the job.

Five years earlier Lucy had discovered another error in their Land Registry Title plan. Nothing to do with the Ogmores this time and no dispute that a small bit of land registered to Max and herself actually belonged to another neighbour. The Registry offered compensation which Max and Lucy thought totally inadequate. A couple of different valuers agreed. Land Registry refused to increase the offer so Max and Lucy called for help from their legal expenses insurers at that time, which sent them to a large firm in the city where they encountered David Burke. Bright Mr Burke provided a perfect service, with perfect manners, in perfect time. Lucy could hardly believe it when he telephoned the news after a month that he had achieved exactly what they wanted and he had achieved that with minimum input from them. In their view he had provided what every legal-service client wants. And now they wanted him to take this Claim over.

The Team at the legal expenses insurers did not. Mr Burke's firm was not on their Panel list and would not agree their terms. The Team Leader proposed another Panel firm in Liverpool. But Lucy had discovered that LEI clients were entitled by UK and EU law to use the lawyer of their choice once it was established they had more than 50% chance of a successful claim and the insurers had agreed to start legal proceedings. Different insurance companies have different rules, but Max and Lucy's household insurance policy actually confirmed: 'Unless there is a conflict of interest, you can choose an appointed representative by sending us the suitably qualified person's name and address. We may choose not to accept the choice of representative, *but only in exceptional circumstances*.' 'No conflict of interest and no exceptional circumstances. We tick all the right boxes,' Lucy thought. The Team Leader disagreed, 'It's rather more complex than that.'

The insurers would not budge. How many more letters and emails and holding on to the phone – how many more battles did Max and Lucy want? Should they now take on The Team by turning to the Financial Services Ombudsman overburdened with PPI claims, and delay yet more months? Or should they just sigh wearily and hope that Liverpool man was up to the job? They decided he would have to be.

By Christmas 2010, after several telephone conversations and a few letters, they had formed a good impression of Tony Willis of AWA Solicitors LLP. He followed the narrative easily and was quick to grasp the case without requiring constant repetition. But he was constrained by having limited documentation because The Team had yet to send him the full file. Nevertheless, they became hopeful that their negligence Claim would be done, dusted and paid within the first few months of 2011.

Imagine Lucy's surprise when in the morning of 6th January 2011 she received a call from a Mr Adrian Wilson of AW & Co., solicitors in an outer London zone, enquiring about the Claim and interrogating her for details. She had a houseful of sleepover guests to deal with, but tried to help as best she could and soon realised he had confused their negligence Claim for over £7,000 with the £250 compensation the LSCS had awarded them for Ethan Ganz's IPS which he assured her confidently was all her negligence Claim was worth. She thought this a mildly interesting mix of ignorance, confusion and arrogance. He told her that the file had arrived on his desk that morning. Lawyers pride themselves on their speed-reading skills but to master that file in a couple of hours would be miraculous. She thanked him, put the phone down and thought no more about him.

Whoever sent the file to the wrong firm certainly messed up the next two years of their lives. Mr Adrian Wilson's judgement was (apparently) forwarded in a brief note to The Team along with his invoice, drawn up on 5th January before he'd even touched the file. His invoice was paid – promptly – and his note was (apparently) taken seriously by The Team – for a long time. No amount of arguing would persuade Team Leader to pass the case to Tony Willis or David Burke. Mr Wilson had failed to provide any rationalisation for his instant judgement, but Team Leader thought him the man for the job. Team Leader did agree to get his man to put some meat on the bones (complaints to the Ombudsman were an irritating bore to be avoided). Perhaps he tried, if so he failed. Nothing more was forthcoming from Mr Wilson.

Calls and emails to The Team increased, a different Team player responding nearly every time adding to the frustration. At the end of February Max sent Team Leader a report of how poorly their Claim had been handled and attached copy of the letter Lucy had found online from the Financial Services Authority (FSA) to all LEI providers asking for confirmation that they were complying with EU and UK rules on choice of legal representative.

It took Team Leader's boss three weeks to digest it and inform them that the 'Panel solicitors' (Adrian Wilson) had written to advise based on Counsel's opinion, they did not consider their case had 'sufficient chance of the matter proceeding forward'. No wonder the insurers paid Mr Wilson's invoice promptly. He was prepared to say what he knew the insurers wanted to hear to get them off a potentially expensive claim. Max notified Team Leader's boss that they were referring the matter to the underwriters and the FSA and needed the file back together with a copy of Mr Wilson's letter. They finally got some of the file but none of the possibly non-existent letter.

The insurance business can be confusing, and legal expenses insurance even more so. Quite apart from the complex rules, there are numerous parties in the chain, Lucy counted seven in theirs, and during the lengthy processing of a claim the players may change. Lucy found out later that The Team and Melissa Pugh's firm had severed relations, which was probably why Ms Pugh had faded from the case. When they embarked on their complaint that they had not been treated fairly by their LEI providers, they were informed by the helpful man at Lloyds that the underwriters and the insurers had also parted company, but he told them nevertheless to liaise with Mercury Claims who had dealt with complaints about The Team prior to the divorce. Six weeks later, through a circuitous route, their complaint finally reached Henry Jackson at Mercury. Mr Jackson turned out to be one of the good guys, but as connection with The Team had been severed, Mercury had less leverage.

Mr Jackson decided, possibly correctly, that The Team's lack of cooperation stemmed from a combination of David Burke's refusal to budge on his rates and a desire to avoid battling with the likes of Mr Rottman – they'd far rather fund combat with someone other than a bullish, troublesome litigation expert. Mr Jackson was very sympathetic and dogged in Max and Lucy's cause. In his view they had a valid claim, knew who they wanted to pursue it, the rules supported their right to choose their lawyer, so the insurers should cover it. After all, these LEI providers were protected by the prospect of winning the case and recovering costs, and at the end of the line their exposure was restricted to the £50,000 limit.

Henry Jackson eventually came up with a negotiated compromise: The Team foot the costs at The Team's £125 per hour rate (plus VAT), with Max and Lucy making up the difference of £25 per hour plus VAT, 'all of which will be awarded against Ethan Ganz when you win the negligence case'. Simple? It's likely to be rather more complex than that, they thought, but as time was passing and they wanted to close the Recovery Account, they agreed. They felt they could trust David Burke.

It started with a repeat of the chase-the-file game. That took a couple of weeks of almost daily calls and emails. Adrian Wilson of the non-existent letter did not respond. Then the Team decided to change the agreement and tried to reduce their cover to £90 per hour. That took a weary Henry Jackson several more hours on the phone to sort out. Then David Burke decided he wanted to double check the barrister's opinion (even though it had been reviewed by a QC) and wanted up-front payment for 10 hours' work, a request Team Leader sent to a committee for consideration, wasting more time. Mr Jackson finally prevailed: the hourly rate reverted and Team Leader agreed to fund 10 hours for files review. More file chasing, email exchanging, document copying and forwarding, and eventually a second opinion appeared agreeing they had a claim. It was not written by David Burke. He had handed the Claim over to a new recruit, Nathan Groome. They so wished young Mr Groome had been able to inspire their confidence. They found they had wasted 10 months waiting for second-rate work and now they had to waste more time politely correcting errors of fact. They arranged to see him.

They met Natham Groome at the large glass and steel office of his large national law firm. He grasped some of their polite corrections and amended the quantum of their Claim upwards to around £6,500 with interest (costs extra). It was at that meeting they finally saw the hidden attendance note by Aubrey Smythe expressing his concern about inadequate monitoring of Hannah Katz's work. Somehow it had shown up in Nathan's version of the file. A few days later they received the contract with David Burke's firm which was clearly a pro-forma contract Mr Groome had failed to amend properly from an employment claim to theirs – with quite amusing results.

It was late June 2012 by the time Wolf Rottman was obliged to respond to their Claim. Over the years Max and Lucy had developed an aptitude for Zen-like calm when provoked by lawyers and Rottman's letter contained some gems of provocation: 'This was a boundary dispute in which sadly common sense did not prevail between these respective parties.' Several deep breaths and they were able to ignore the insulting distortion and agree that a Part 36 offer be made. Nathan was of the 'it is impossible to predict what a judge's decision will be' school, but was confident they would not be awarded the entirety of their losses (no contradiction spotted). He proposed an offer to settle for 75% of the Claim plus costs and interest. He named Mark Christie as one of three recommended barristers should the Claim go to trial. How would Mr Christie feel about opposing his previous contractor? Apparently he would feel quite happy. Max and Lucy were not so happy about the lowered Claim. It was perilously close to the (then) Small Claim limit. They could have lodged a Small Claim three years earlier and saved themselves an awful lot of bother, besides they had quantified their losses meticulously listing losses arising exclusively from the negligence. Why should Ethan Ganz LLP retain any income from their own incompetence? Surely this only encourages income-generation from bad work.

Nevertheless they instructed Nathan to go ahead with the Part 36 offer which he did – and at the same time he told them he was leaving the firm. The Claim was handed to yet another young solicitor and so, despite the assurance 'Your file will continue seamlessly with my replacement', the time-consuming tutorials had to begin all over again.

Whereas Nathan Groome appeared to be sympathetic to their case, his replacement, Julia Cox, was far more interested in costs, that is to say her income. She amended Nathan's draft Part 36 offer and sent it off. Wolf Rottman replied with an offer to settle which did not include costs, VAT or interest. Max and Lucy rejected it immediately. But it was not up to them.

Ms Cox 'advised' them to accept – thus making Max and Lucy vulnerable to a £30 hourly charge. She made clear that if they did not accept her 'advice' they would be on their own and liable for all her firm's costs, which she estimated at £1,000. Three times their estimate. She had issued a 'no win' ultimatum. At that stage neither the clients nor the insurers knew how many hours she would claim. If Max and Lucy argued, if they rejected Ms Cox's advice, she informed them, they would be vulnerable for all £180 per hour costs plus 20% VAT. They were left with no option. So much for client care, so much for legal service, so much for trust in David Burke. Rottman had gauged Ms Cox correctly and between them they had painted Max and Lucy into a corner with consequences rather more serious than paint-covered shoes.

Wolf Rottman's extraordinary lack of concern for truth and accuracy and his casual attempt to demolish their reputations intimated his confidence that a judge would be similarly unconcerned with truth and justice, and no lawyer would waste much time quibbling about facts on such a 'low cost claim'. As all the lawyers involved in the Ogmore Claim, apart from Rottman himself, had left Ethan Ganz, he, as Head of Litigation *and* Complaints Manager – two diametrically-opposed skill-sets – could run this negligence Claim against himself without fear of contradiction … or exposure.

Ms Cox negotiated her way through complex maths to justify assuring her clients that the outcome was an overall victory: they had succeeded in 'punishing' Wolf Rottman/Ethan Ganz and also in forcing The Team to give them cover, 'I understand that itself was a notable victory.' She claimed the result a moral victory.

Needless to say, like most 'successful' litigants awarded less than they had lost, Max and Lucy did not see it as any kind of victory. Victory over Rottman was not their objective. Justice and money in the Recovery Fund was. Most judges in most civil litigation mark down awards to successful litigants, Max assumed this was because the judges take for granted that the Claim had been marked up. 'But we didn't. We were claiming back itemised costs arising from negligent work. We were not claiming compensation for stress, time, defamation.' Why, one wonders, is this 'mark-down' practice not challenged – or at least investigated. In failing to recover all losses in full Ms Cox ensured that Ethan Ganz through Wolf Rottman, retained income derived exclusively from the firm's own negligence. Now that *is* a nice little earner!

Ms Cox proposed that the award be forwarded to her and she deduct her fees and send them what was left. They did not think this such a good idea. They proposed that she ensure the cheque be made out to them and forwarded to them, she could then send an itemised bill for them to consider. It is likely that Ms Cox's proposal was frowned on by others since theirs prevailed. The six-minute billing records that eventually arrived were scrutinised carefully by Ms Cox's ex-clients – and contested.

Affordable costs are still not very high on the agenda of legal service-providers. Legal Aid, which never aided all who needed help in any event, has proved near impossible to police and finance, and access to justice on level playing fields remains out of reach for most. If it is hoped Legal Expenses Insurance (LEI) in its current state will provide a better, more universal service there is likely to be disappointment. Unless the LEI market is robustly regulated and clients feel confident in an efficient, transparent and simplified complaints service, this style of financing justice will not work to the benefit of paying clients. Fixed costs contracts are being offered by some lawyers, reluctantly and warily – mindful of what happened to income when conveyancing opened up to competition and fixed costs for that service became the norm. Some of the new Alternative Business Structures[1] which have come on-stream in the last couple of years have gone down that route. As have some other forward-looking firms.

It is a pity the reforming government of 1945 did not find some way of overcoming powerful vested interests to establish a National Law Service. It might possibly have transformed the law business to something approaching a Truth and Justice Service.

PART THREE

TWENTY-FOUR
Who judges the judges?

The final payment into the Recovery Fund was a contribution to the cost of incidentals like travel, printing, copying, postage and the odd medicinal gin and tonic. The final tally did not even touch the cost of Max and Lucy's time which, over 10 years, must have equalled at least two years' full-time work for each of them. If that were costed at the average solicitor's annual remuneration in, say, 2007, half-way through the saga, it would total well over £200,000. As for stress, physical assault, irritation, libel, slander, etc., etc., … well, as we now know, that is of little concern to anybody but Max and Lucy, their family and friends, and people gifted with a trace of human empathy, who, before hearing the story, had thought the civil justice system in England and Wales was OK … on balance … most of the time.

Why all this about money and hardly a mention of justice? Truth and justice featured prominently at the beginning of this book. Well, unfortunately, neither truth nor justice got much of a look-in as the story developed. Few of the full-time professionals Max and Lucy encountered in the free-market civil justice business showed much concern for truth or justice.

Of course, Max and Lucy may have been unlucky in the professionals they selected – or had foisted on them, but then they had looked for help from quite a range: 19 or so solicitors, a few paralegals, seven barristers and 12 judges. Perhaps they were not just unlucky, perhaps they were incompetent. But, then again, they did try to make sensible choices where choice was an option; they did look online at the rated people and ask around for recommendations. They reckon they found one solicitor and one barrister they could give four or five stars – Harvey Rishus spoilt his previous good rating by overcharging at the end when they most needed him onside and could not argue the account. They also reckon they came across a couple of good paralegals who Lucy hopes stayed good if they later moved into the full professional role, and were not contaminated by others in the business.

They also reckon they came across two or three potentially good judges but that, of course, was and has to be the luck of the draw.

The bad drives out the good. That's a line Lucy had heard several times over her professional life – often from lawyers. So, how do we drive out the bad? How do we get the civil justice service refocussed on the hard slog of truth and justice and prise it away from the bright lights of legal games and money? There's no lack of lawyers to tell you what is wrong with their business. They can be very eloquent and witty. Some find it all rather amusing. They have to make a living; they've spent a lot of time learning the trade. They don't want another major overhaul, and certainly not scrapping it all to start again. Truth and justice are so difficult and time consuming but profit is so tantalisingly attainable – and measurable.

Lucy does not think there is any mileage in tinkering with rules and regulations. If overhauls worked, the Woolf reforms would have directed the battle with the Ogmores in a different direction right from the start and, most likely, brought the war to an end after the first court skirmish. To be applied to good effect, rules and regulations have to be internalised by *all* the key players. Above all, the *key* key players – the judges – who, in the UK, have reached their powerful status after years in the law trade, and we know what they say about old dogs and new tricks.

For the first 10 years of this century targets were the fashionable tool for shaking-up or reshaping, public services. They worked for a while in the mostly *free-to-the-consumer* health and education services, but civil justice is not free to most clients, it is a business and quite a profitable one, particularly in the commercial sectors. These sectors are often viewed enviously by practitioners in others like family, housing, consumer and neighbour law, and poor-relation lawyers can be observed measuring their rewards against the target they see hit on the gold by their colleagues in commercial law. Who can blame them? As for lawyers working in the criminal sector post the remodelling of Legal Aid – let's just say they are not happy.

When Aneurin Bevan fought to create the NHS, he met serious opposition from the service-providers and declared he had had to stuff the complaining doctors' mouths with gold to get them onboard. That was in immediate post-war pull-together Britain. There is not enough gold in the world to persuade the legal profession of the 21st century, within or without the Big

Society, to adopt a salaried, public-service approach to *their* essential service, so something else is required.

The Legal Services Act is a step in the right direction – were it to finally succeed in putting consumers first, and we are a long way off achieving that at present. In the meantime, the market traders need constant policing.

The only people with the power to do that on a day-to-day basis are judges. The fact judges in the UK are drawn from the profession itself has advantages: 'It takes a thief to catch a thief' you might say (if there are no judges around), but it also has disadvantages if the objective is to establish a *justice* service and transform the age-old sclerotic traditions of the legal advice and advocacy trade. The mind-forged manacles are fused in the shape of the business model by the time they join the judiciary. If a judge loses his good judgement – or never really had it in the first place – there is little the consumer or the politician can do about it. The man-made laws of *Henderson* v *Henderson* and Consent Orders are as immutable to them as the laws of physics.

Among the many attempts to improve the civil justice service during the decade of the Ogmore Saga was an attempt to address the problem of who guards the guardians, who judges the judges. In April 2006 the Government's Department of Constitutional Affairs (DCA) – now the Ministry of Justice – transformed the judicial complaints structure and created an Ombudsman as a third-tier overseer of complaints about judicial conduct and appointments, all part of a package of measures 'to ensure integrity and transparency in the judicial system.'

Max and Lucy deemed only one of the seven Judges they had encountered by 2006 worthy of complaint and decided to test the transparency and integrity of the newly-configured service with a complaint about District Judge Alfred Dyer. As this was its first year of operation, Max and Lucy were among the guinea pig complainants.

It had been their bad luck to encounter Mr Dyer at a pivotal time in their dealings with the squatters. They had attempted, in June 2003, to get Judge Blacker to help sort out the mess created by the barristers and Ogmore, and failed. They had had to withdraw their possibly doomed application to set aside the Consent Order when that route was closed by Land Registry's revised Title plan – which left Max and Lucy none the wiser about where to put up a protective fence on the shed boundary. On the advice of Mrs Buxton they had decided to try to get a court-ordered independent survey based on the despised Hammer plan – as the Consent Order stipulated.

At the brief directions hearing, Mr Dyer had perversely refused to order the independent survey. He had ignored the fact that they had reluctantly accepted the authority of the infamous Hammer plan and told them to show on that plan where they 'thought' the boundary should be. He then ignored the unvalidated work they did, and at the following three-hour hearing threw out their Claim on Stoat/Ogmore's *Henderson* v *Henderson* assertion. They were mystified why they could not persuade him otherwise. As far as they could see they were not revisiting the Consent Order (Stoat admitted as much at one stage), but problem-solving in changed circumstances. Despite their experience of judges, they really had expected the Court to help. Dyer delayed a decision on costs for yet another long hearing – adding yet more costs, and granted Ogmore costs on the standard basis ignoring all that had been revealed of her misdeeds including her lie to Judge Blacker. This then required a further expensive costs hearing where he forgot that he had ordered costs on the standard basis and granted it on a reduced indemnity CFA basis.[1] Four hearings in all for a perfectly simple and valid application for a court-ordered independent survey to determine where the boundary fence on the stolen land should go. Bad management and bad decision-making, something that could only be challenged by appeal, and he had refused permission to appeal.

His illogical management and decision-making were not, however, what caused them to test the system for judging the judges. It was his conduct at the costs hearing. At that hearing, Lionel Knapp, their costs lawyer, who viewed Dyer as hostile, read out the libellous comments Ogmore had written on her own CFA form – a form normally completed by a solicitor who is not her own client.

Her responses to the pro-forma CFA questions were shocking: Next to the query 'Knowledge of the opponents' she had written 'Untruthful, liars, manipulative, selective in what they disclose ... the Claimants are totally unpredictable and regarded as loose cannon; evidence of fact is likely to be an issue; "your" [she wrote to herself] opponent has in previous proceedings demonstrated a lack of veracity and has shown a willingness to mislead the Court.' Lucy says she still finds the shamelessness takes her breath away.

Lionel Knapp had his suspicions about Alfred Dyer and therefore asked for confirmation that the District Judge did not believe the libels. Alfred Dyer changed the subject. Lionel Knapp read some more and repeated his request. Lucy says that Alfred Dyer looked at them both and changed the subject again.

Mr Knapp managed to say he was very surprised since he and his clients' solicitor found this to be most untrue ... but before he could finish, Ogmore's costs expert spoke over him – and that was that. Ogmore had needed to offload her own sins on to her opponents not only to divert the accusations against her but also to encourage her boss, Clive Vernon Bulmer, to sign the 100% CFA success uplift agreement. A little later under questioning from Lionel Knapp, Ogmore's expert admitted Mr C. V. Bulmer, Head of the small law firm, was 'not familiar with the regulations for Conditional Fee Arrangements and left such matters to his Associate'. One Mrs Hazel Ogmore!

That Ogmore was capable of such sickening dishonesty did not shock Max or Lucy. What shocked them was Dyer's response. He could not have had any *verified* independent evidence to support her libel; even if he *had* been force-fed the lies, he had made no effort to check them out. Max and Lucy found him guilty of irresponsible, embarrassing and disrespectful conduct. Later, when Lionel Knapp asked for an adjournment so that he could discuss matters with his clients, Dyer expressed the view that he would not expect any compliance on their part. Apart from the fact that Dyer did not know what Lionel intended to discuss, he could not possibly know what these clients (who had agreed to *give* land to abusive, aggressive land thieves) would or would not agree.

His behaviour still rankled a year later and therefore, when they discovered the Judicial Correspondence Unit (JCU),[2] the Agency then dealing with complaints about the conduct of judges, they wrote a letter of complaint about Judge Alfred Dyer's odd conduct at the costs hearing. They also briefly outlined their experiences at the three previous hearings.

For some reason Mr Barry Sutton of the JCU, who had been handed their complaint, decided he would review Dyer's conduct during the *second* hearing – when he dismissed their application for an independent survey. Since most complaints were rejected without a review, they were pleased that at least theirs had got that far. But why review and listen to the tape for the second hearing when the conduct they complained about happened in the fourth and last? They hadn't liked Dyer's attitude at any of the hearings, but could not think of anything they could strongly object to in his *conduct* at the first three – strongly enough to make a formal complaint. They had quite a few complaints about his *decisions* of course.

Mr Sutton refused to be persuaded and persevered with his uncalled-for investigation into the second hearing, retrieving the tapes and requesting a response from Judge Dyer. He conflated other conduct references they had touched on from other hearings and piled them all under the heading of conduct at the second hearing. However, no mention was made of their objection to Dyer's response to Ogmore's libels. No mention was made of the costs hearing.

The heavily redacted version of District Judge Alfred Dyer's response to Mr Sutton focuses almost exclusively on justifying his decisions: they should not have applied for an independent survey; they should have applied to set aside or vary the Consent Order, 'On the grounds that there was no real consent at all.' If that is what he thought, why didn't he say so at the very first hearing, or the second, or the third? And why were they confidently assured by several lawyers that they should never attempt such a thing?

Needless to say, Mr Sutton found nothing on the tape of the second hearing that could be described as bad conduct. 'I doubt if we would either,' says Max. So now it was a question of why Mr Sutton refused to investigate the costs hearing. Did he contact the Judge before or after he decided to investigate a hearing they had not formally complained about? He assured them that he made that decision beforehand. He kept repeating that he could not look at the Judge's decisions only his conduct. They had understood that from their first reading of the JCU's website.

Mr Sutton's response was a challenge to the rationally minded: 'I cannot ask District Judge Dyer to explain remarks he made in a judicial capacity.' All judge conduct in a courtroom could be said to be 'in a judicial capacity'. Could it be that if he had pursued their actual complaint, Judge Dyer would have had to explain both his response to Lionel Knapp's enquiries and his comment that he would not expect Max and Lucy to comply with anything Lionel Knapp might propose?

With such Jesuitical arguments it is not surprising the statistics for that year showed that of the 2,295 complaints received by the Unit, all but 273 were dismissed uninvestigated and just four were upheld to some degree. There must have been an awful lot of people that year who either couldn't read the guidance or couldn't follow Mr Sutton's logic. Not just that year but most years since. Despite several overhauls and a name change to OJC, in the year 2011/2012,[3] of 1,615 complaints 1,245 were dismissed uninvestigated. The name change did not change anything – 867 were dismissed because they were deemed to be complaints about decisions. It looks like unhappy litigants are taking a long time to understand the mystifying judicial complaints mindset.

Max and Lucy failed to make much of an impact from then on. They wrote a long letter to the Head of the Unit voicing their concerns about the system purporting to protect clients from the 'arbitrary abuse of the uniquely protected power accorded to judges'. They pointed out that complainants cannot gain materially if their complaint is upheld – there's no money incentive; it is highly *un*likely that some 80% of complainants did not check the guidance available to them before taking the time and making the effort to lodge a complaint and that as the Unit is not widely promoted and few people know about it, it is highly *likely* that the recorded complaints understate the level of dissatisfaction. Their letter continued:

'An overwhelming proportion of complaints are rejected on the basis that they concern *decisions* rather than *conduct*. This would suggest not that the majority of those who elect to make a complaint are intellectually deficient, but rather that the criteria for determining what is "*conduct*" and what is a "*judicial decision*" are specious.' Was Mr Sutton suggesting that the Judge, not having investigated anything, was ill-mannered and offensive because he *decided judicially* to be ill-mannered and offensive? If their actual complaint had been investigated, Judge Dyer might have been obliged to explain himself. He might then have learnt, just a bit, how to be a better judge.

Things dragged on for months. Their letter to the Head of the Unit was ignored until, three months later, it was rebuffed by her Deputy: Mr Sutton was absolutely correct not to investigate the costs hearing. 'Unfortunately', they could not forward Mr Dyer's redacted letter – he did not want them to and it was agreed that he would not have to expose his response if he did not want to. All four pages of his background report were redacted so they could not see any of that.

The letter concluded with the suggestion that Lucy might like to join her local Court User Group. In fact Lucy had briefly joined her local Court User Group and had been warmly welcomed. She did not stay. The first meeting was chaired by none other than District Judge Alfred Dyer. Lucy had been misled by the title, Court User Group, and assumed it was like other specialist consumer groups whereas in reality it was a liaison group between service-providers and service users playing quite another role.

That was 2006. The era of openness; of Freedom of Information. It took two more months and research into the FoI rules and the Data Protection Act to squeeze out a few more drops of information: Dyer had provided some 'personal observations about the history and background to the case'. That would have been an interesting read – were they able to read it. They just might have found the odd error of fact – and the odd omission. The Deputy Head of the new Office for Judicial Complaints (OJC) told them to pay the £10 processing fee to acquire 'full subject access' under the Data Protection Act.

Three more months passed. Scroggs' Appeal was approaching and they wanted whatever they were permitted to see of Dyer's work. They wanted evidence that Scroggs' negligence had exposed them to the vagaries of 'judicial decisions'. A year after they requested it, they finally received the redacted version of Dyer's letter under FoI. They were refused one under the Data Protection Act – but did get their £10 back.

Of course, they got none of the fully redacted, four-page 'background report' District Judge Alfred Dyer helpfully provided for Mr Sutton and his team. When they wrote expressing their dismay and criticism of the set-up, they were informed that in future judges subject to complaints would have to reply to the OJC in open correspondence; no hidden, redacted information. This might be helpful or it might be of dubious value. Lucy asked for copy of any protocol or guidance the newly-formed OJC produced for complainants. The reply indicated that a change of name was not enough, 'I am sorry that *you are still unable to understand* why we could not investigate Judge Dyer's conduct at the costs hearing.' Lucy had a well developed imperviousness to patronising stupidity by then and simply asked again for copy of any protocol or guidance the newly-formed OJC produces for complainants.

The next stage was to refer the matter to the Judicial Appointments and Conduct Ombudsman.[4] Max thought they had already wasted enough time testing the State's protection for court users from the arbitrary abuse of judicial power, but for Lucy the wrangling, arrogance and incompetence exposed by their efforts tempted her further. She knew she was uniquely placed to delve deeper, to take it as far as it goes. The urge for further research into who guards the guardians was irresistible. If their experience was anything to go by, this was yet another expensive Government-sponsored safeguarding-the-citizen agency not fit for purpose.

The Ombudsman had been set up under the Constitutional Reform Act of 2005 and started business in April 2006, so, again, in September 2006 there was no past performance to indicate the likelihood of success. Max and Lucy's original complaint had started at the old Judicial *Correspondence* Unit (JCU). Nobody thought to ensure that the changeover to the new Office for Judicial Complaints (OJC) allowed complaints to move smoothly from one Government agency checking judge conduct to its successor agency doing exactly the same thing. Moreover, some decision-maker had decided that the Ombudsman should not comment on the actions of the unlamented Judicial *Correspondence* Unit which was unfortunate because that is where Mr Sutton decided to look at Judge Dyer's conduct at a hearing Max and Lucy had not complained about, rather than the one they had. Nobody was going to investigate that bizarre decision by Mr Sutton.

It soon became clear that the Ombudsman would also be debarred from looking at the way the OJC dealt with their request for non-redacted versions of Dyers contributions: 'This is a matter for the Freedom of Information Commissioner.' This did not leave much for the Ombudsman to do. Well, at least that avoided the usual lengthy delays. It had taken two years to get that far but it took only a week for the investigator to go through the papers and write her report. Lucy reckons she could have anticipated the outcome in less than an hour, bearing in mind the self-imposed restraints: the OJC had asked Judge Dyer to give permission to disclose fully what he had written and he had refused. Not the OJC's fault. The Judge had been offered the opportunity to withhold some of his contribution before the OJC existed and he had seized it. The Ombudsman's report did reveal the letter Mr Sutton's next-up-in-command, Ms Snype, wrote to the Judge asking if he would change his mind. Her letter was hardly persuasive, 'Mrs Graham has returned to the fray to ask again' and the usual errors of fact: from the silly (a misspelling of Max's name), to the worrying 'We had informed them we were unable to consider the *earlier* hearings.' Mr Dyer was unlikely to be worried enough to change his mind. The OJC had a duty of confidence, bordering on connivance to District Judge Alfred Dyer, but not a duty of transparency to Max and Lucy.

The Ombudsman himself managed to get Lucy's name wrong – completely, she became Mrs Bromley. Lucy sometimes wonders what Mrs Bromley was unhappy about and whether the Ombudsman called *her* Mrs Graham and whether *she* was impressed with the Ombudsman's work. Well, it was early days; perhaps the Ombudsman has had some terse feedback since then and upped his game. He got no feedback from Lucy. His annual reports include a few quotes from satisfied complainants but never a word from the unsatisfied, or even the mystified.

Over a year later, in June 2008, they discussed the sorry business with their local MP who urged them to write about the redacted papers to Jack Straw MP, then Lord Chancellor and Secretary of State for Justice. Jack Straw, he assured them, was very keen on Freedom of Information. They were promised a reply to their letter to the Minister within 20 days. Three months later it had not arrived, so they delved deeper and discovered to their dismay that it had been sent on to the very same Ms Snype who had written the inaccurate error-filled and patronising letter from the Judicial Complaints Unit (JCU). Apparently she was now charged with investigating her own work at her Department at the Ministry of Justice (MoJ). On the very day they tracked down their letter to her, the very same lady wrote to them. It would appear their delving had ruffled the nest. Her letter was longer and contained an apology for the three-month delay. That was as far as she was prepared to go. Had Dyer's letter been revealed in full, she declared, it might have disclosed information that might have been relevant to an appeal and, 'It would be quite wrong for one party to the proceedings to have access while the other party or parties did not.' It clearly did not occur to Ms Snype that the problem she identified would be easily solved if the Judge's letter were made available to all concerned. 'Transparency' is a word that appears frequently on the MoJ's website; it joins the glossary of words abused in the legal context Max and Lucy have been compiling over the years. Besides, what did the Judge write that might have made him open to a very late and most unlikely appeal?

She concluded with a clumsy attempt to repeat the tired, threadbare justification for investigating the wrong hearing: the caseworker (Mr Sutton) made the decision based on his opinion and explained why. His opinion and his 'explanation' remain uninvestigated or explained.

Ms Snype's letter went straight to Jack Straw's office. Whoever in the Lord Chancellor's Department wrote the brief reply for Mr Straw to sign, was fully satisfied that his colleagues in the same Ministry had carefully considered, responded to and reviewed *Mr* Graham's concerns, and the brief letter was placed on the pile of letters for signing that day. Jack Straw duly signed that he was fully satisfied that all was correct.

A year later their MP tried Mr Straw again following a failed attempt by Max to get non-redacted copies of Dyer's work through the Information Commissioner's Office. The attempt had again been stonewalled: Mr Dyer did not want them to know what he said to influence Mr Sutton so they regretted they could not help. Once again Mr Straw signed a reply to the MP saying that all was as it should be and he was satisfied. It would be interesting to know whether he would still be satisfied if he knew something about the limitations of his (then) Judicial Complaints Unit – and the skewed constraints on his Freedom of Information Act.

Over a quarter of a century earlier Felix and Lucy had been urged by friends and family to write to their MP about the fence-post saga. They were reluctant to waste time on what they believed would be a fruitless exercise, but under pressure eventually wrote a robust letter expressing their dismay at the shambles of the civil justice system they had experienced. Their much respected and senior local MP took the letter seriously and forwarded it to the then Lord Chancellor (they hadn't asked him to and they were not even party supporters). So, here was the first example of that most scorned of species – a politician – taking the matter seriously. Nevertheless, they had few hopes of anything much from the Lord Chancellor, the theatrical High Tory, Quintin Hogg (Lord Hailsham). They expected no more than a few emollient but patronising and dismissive lines drafted by some lowly gopher in the Department, which ignored the main purpose of their letter: the unforgivable mismanagement of their case. In fact, they got a long letter signed by the Big Man himself (no doubt drafted by the gopher). As expected, he could not comment on judges' judgments and 'his' attempt to record the history of the case was almost as bad as Ms Snype's attempt in 2009. Possibly these failures arose from the same misplaced confidence in the accounts provided by the two principal judges in the two cases 25 years apart.

However, Lord Hailsham of Marylebone did express his sympathy with their feelings of frustration that the matter had been pursued through the Court. The Chief Lawyer was not at all pleased with the delays or with the manners of some of the players. These were not acceptable. An apology was called for and an apology was made. But the real news that he thought they'd like to hear was that in 1985, he had 'set up a major review of the system of civil justice in England and Wales. The object of the review is to consider and bring about reform that will cut the cost, delays and complexity of civil litigation and they may be interested to know that the Civil Justice Review, as it is called, will be completed by the end of this year.'

In fact it took three years to complete the review (the 63rd review in a hundred years) and a further 11 years to get Lord Woolf's 'Access to Justice' reform of the Civil Procedure Rules and Practice Directions up and running. Well, limping at least. As revealed here, the new rules did not do much for Lucy second time round.

Right from the start of the Ogmore story friends and family assumed Max and Lucy would ensure that Ogmore's antics were exposed in the press and later, as the explosion in communication technology progressed, online. The Law Society might consider Ogmore's schizoid representation of 'our client' by 'my solicitor' perfectly acceptable, most normal people thought it both shocking and hilarious. They had assumed she would be unable to claim her hourly rate and would be treated as a litigant-in-person. When they heard how the legal fraternity, particularly the judges, responded to her conduct and mismanaged a straightforward squatter-cum-boundary dispute, they urged Max or Lucy to let the world know. Lucy had no intention of doing so. She knew first-hand just how contaminating and dangerous the Fourth Estate could be.

During the five-month wait in 1985 for the old Judge's judgment, Lucy had come across an article in a national newspaper telling the story of a man who had been destroyed by the poisonous alchemy of certain lawyers, the civil justice system and various members of the judiciary. She got in touch with the editor and let him know that his story was not a one-off, although she admitted that the one Felix and she had to tell was not quite so sad, in fact it would be funny if The System did not make the consequences for the losing side so serious. He sent a jobbing journalist to interview them and attend court on Judgment Day. The young freelance had the necessary talents of her trade so she easily gained the confidence of both Felix and Lucy. She tut-tutted at the fence post and sympathised fully with their frustration. Felix was at work most of the time so Lucy talked to her alone. They were getting on well except for a moment when Lucy had a flash suspicion that the journalist might have come with the story already formed in her head. Lucy had read out to her Paul's warning that the Doyles' attack could cost them a lot of money – as much as Lucy would take home in a year, 'But we couldn't back down in the face of their bullying,' she said, 'If we gave in, the fence would obstruct the passage and I'd have to hand over my annual earnings to their bullying, tricksy lawyer.' The journalist started writing furiously and Lucy unwisely continued, 'What do you do? You can't just give in and pay up, can you? Not sums of money like that. Not without reason.'

Before the journalist's confused and confusing report was published in the national newspaper she offered to let them see it. Apparently she had seriously upset a lady she had written about in an earlier item she'd produced for the same newspaper, and the lady was deeply offended by a mistake she had made in her report, accused her of damaging her life, so the freelance was wary of repeating the offence. Despite this warning, Felix and Lucy insisted that they should not interfere particularly as the Doyles had refused to speak to her and it would be just their side of the story. Most unwise. She had failed to follow the old Judge's ramblings and her piece implied that they had been found guilty of trespass by two inches. Worse, she ascribed to them views which were diametrically opposed to those they held by taking Lucy's unwise statements out of context and ignoring all she had said about The System, which had served not only them but the Doyles so badly. She made no reference to their proposals for dealing with boundary disputes – judges on site at the earliest opportunity. They had hoped the story would expose the need for reform of the judicial process: instead, all it did was reinforce the generally held prejudice that all parties in neighbour disputes are equally obsessive. Her piece added to their exasperation. They wrote to the paper to correct the errors of fact, pointing out that if either one of them had *stolen* a fence post, the potential punishment, bearing in mind their previous good character, would have been considerably less than the 'fine' they had been threatened with.

Some time later Lucy took an excited call from her mother. A leading columnist in another leading national newspaper had taken up the story and her mother was impressed that it had reached such illustrious heights. Lucy happened to hold that particular columnist in low esteem; she had heard some unpleasant stories about his working practices and she hated the way he used his power and influence to batter the unfortunates in life. Now she found he was doing just that to batter her and Felix – and the Doyles. He made no attempt to check his version. He wittily explained that he had to write about their court case – 'to exorcise the demons' lest he end up as 'mad as them'. Having rambled on at length from a very high horse about several irrational obsessive personal wars he 'knew' of, he finally returned to Felix and Lucy, quoting Lucy's now infamous line, 'You can't just give in can you?' He thought she could – but then the purpose of the piece was to exonerate some of his 'best friends' – the lawyers and judges upset by Lucy's published letter – which had not only corrected the journalist's mischief-making report, but also described the trap defendants can be placed in by professionals working the civil justice market. 'What can the lawyers do if the client insists?' he asked. Lucy could have given him a few ideas, but he went incommunicado the very day his piece was published.

A good friend drafted a complaint on their behalf to the Press Complaints Commission (PCC) which they endorsed only to discover what is now common knowledge about the PCC: it is the poodle of the Press. 'You were not named so what are you complaining about?'

The columnist is long dead, but although some journalists, like some lawyers, *are* interested in truth and justice, neither Max nor Lucy had any intention of allowing themselves to be betrayed by journalists of any kind.

Over the years of the Ogmore Saga Lucy had come across a number of boundary dispute stories in the media as well as ones that never made news anywhere but locally. There was the story of the seller who had misled his buyer on the SPIF, resulting in a much cited case (the *McMeekin*[5] case) with serious costs for the seller and unsatisfactory compensation for the buyer. There was the story of the litigant who altered a '3' to an '8' on a plan (and then tried to accuse the other side of the misdeed), resulting in financial disaster for the forger despite 'winning' the boundary dispute. There was the story of an elderly couple who, having already lost all their life savings, had to sell their much loved home to meet huge legal bills after losing an 18-year battle with their neighbour over an insignificant strip of land worth only £200. There was the 11-year dispute over a virtually worthless six foot-wide strip of land which occupied the time of 12 judges and where costs totalled in the region of £200,000 for each side. There are stories of boundary disputes which have divided families, led to divorce and, in one particularly upsetting case, to suicide.

You might think that those 12 judges would have objected to a system that occupied so much of their valued time. You might think that they would question whether they had managed the dispute efficiently and if, like ordinary non-lawyer people, they thought they had managed it rather badly indeed they would want to do something about their failure. Could the judge or judges involved in the dispute leading to suicide have been in part to blame?

From the experiences of Lucy, Felix and Max, it can be seen that judges do indeed allow vexatious litigation; that they can ignore their own rules; they can indulge in prejudice and whim; they can ignore serious wrongdoing by lawyers; they do not always read what is painstakingly prepared for them and that the various protections for victims of their failings – appeals, the Office of Judicial Complaints, the Judicial Complaints Ombudsman, freedom of information, the Lord Chancellor, the press – can also fail. If the statistics are any guide the statutory 'protections' fail more often than not.

Perhaps the answer lies in training, in judge education. In the European civil law system judges can be selected straight from law school to be trained as judges rather than work as solicitors or barristers, whereas in common law jurisdictions like the UK they are usually drawn from a pool of experienced lawyers. Comparative studies do not yet suggest that one system produces a better outcome for the public than the other, and in fact the two different approaches are melding: some European judicial recruitment programmes now allow late entrants from practising lawyers and some appointments in the common law (UK) system are being made from younger, less experienced (contaminated?) lawyers. In both systems it is recognised that judges face increasing public scrutiny, so some quality control measures have been introduced to provide them with more than just updates on the law … some, but not nearly enough.

It is likely that such developments will always be behind the curve, reactive rather than proactive, and in the meantime a poor service is a poor and damaging service. So the question arises – is it a service that *always* has to be provided in the end by judges working in an adversarial, legalistic arena?

Different civil disputes call for different resolution processes. What may be best for family disputes may not be appropriate for consumer, employment or housing disputes. Lucy and Felix had a straightforward boundary dispute, Lucy and Max had a squatter problem which they thought they'd solved by giving the squatters some land, but which became a boundary dispute. In both cases the lawyers and the judges made a mess: a painful, expensive, time-consuming, stressful mess which damaged not just neighbour relations, but in the Doyles' case health, permanently, and in the Grahams' case family harmony, temporarily, not to mention the collateral damage to extended families and the neighbourhood.

General practitioner judges sitting in a courtroom are unlikely to resolve a boundary dispute fairly and efficiently even without the interference of expensive lawyers playing games with the law. Other skills are required, so other paths to resolution should be considered. A couple of genuinely independent land surveyors working from a plan either agreed by the parties or identified by Land Registry, could study the facts on the ground and mark a boundary. Land Registry staff have not given a stellar performance in this book, but the Registry is the specialist agency with more expertise (potentially at least) and so is far better placed than most judges to understand plans, terrain and the compass. The potential could be realised by more appropriate training and careful vetting. Funded by stamp duty, Registry staff should be able to provide a cost-free investigation; no lawyers' fees allowed. Anxiety about costs has to be removed from boundary disputes. That alone should save a few sleepless nights, even, possibly, some neighbour relations. The Registry's remit should be enlarged to encompass any claim by adverse possession, and squatting on land should be a criminal offence just as squatting in private property has recently become – it is theft, after all. Land Registrars should not be allowed to wash their hands with 'a plague on both your houses' shrug, exposing people to the vagaries of the courts. They should have the final authority, apart from the dreaded judicial review, to encourage good behaviour in the property market.

Of course, lawyers will tell you it's not as simple as that; boundary disputes can be far too complex for Land Registry people and surveyors to sort out. Well, it is facts on the ground and documentary evidence that matter and Land Registry already has its own free-of-charge legal experts in land disputes. That was a service Mr Beige was hoping to offer Max and Lucy before Ogmore jumped the gun to avoid it with her first spurious injunction. The court option allowed her to make mayhem. Judges were at best redundant and lawyers dangerous. Together they worked a system not fit for purpose. It was not broken, it was never whole and justice leaked out through the cracks lawyers entered.

'Openness is fundamental to the political health of a modern state.'
Freedom of Information Act. *Introduction*

'Access to information helps the public make public authorities accountable for their actions.'
'What is the Freedom Of Information Act?'
(Information Commissioner's Office website)

PART FOUR

SO, WHAT'S TO BE DONE?

This is not a book for lawyers or would-be lawyers; there are plenty of books for them, about them, by them. Nor is it a book against lawyers, there are enough of those, both fact and fiction. This is a book targeted primarily at people at the bookends of our civil justice system: individual citizens or small and medium-sized businesses in dispute, and judges – dispute resolution providers of last resort. The purpose of the book is to encourage the former to avoid having anything to do with the latter – if at all possible. And it is often possible as there is a growing number of less challenging routes to dispute resolution. It could be made more possible if the people with the power to make the necessary changes, make the necessary changes. Our civil justice system is a human construct, after all, and not the outcome of some immutable law of physics.

If avoidance is not possible and the citizen or small business becomes a claimant or defendant, they will usually look to professional experts for help, and the usual source of that is still a lawyer. As the stories in this book show, lawyers of all kinds can get in between litigants and their objective – justice. Sometimes to lead their clients into the mire as the Doyles, and Max and Lucy found to their dismay, but sometimes to save their clients from falling off a cliff. Most of the time they provide a useful service, allowing us to get on with our lives without undue hassle, let alone setting foot in a courtroom. Their job is not all about litigation, or even resolving disputes – it can be, and certainly should be, about avoiding disputes altogether.

The fact that the two stories reported here show the profession in a less than glowing light could unfairly distort the picture: after all, the Ogmores are not run-of-the-mill litigants, nor Scroggs, Stoat et al. average lawyers, nor Judges Lethe and Dyer typical members of the judiciary ... it is to be hoped! But they are all real people (names and descriptions altered somewhat) and they played the roles described (the records are still available to check). It is unlikely they are unique.

Our early ambition to describe the *anatomy* of two sets of litigation from the perspective of clients has been frustrated by the need to avoid the level of detail required for such an exercise – this was not intended to be a legal doorstopper running to several volumes, but the details kept building over the years, as did major changes in the civil justice landscape. Lucy's records began in 2003 with the working title, *The Squatters' Handbook – how to get the courts to help you steal*, but as more of the challenges facing service-users were revealed, and as the justice landscape changed, she refocussed on the objective of encouraging the target audiences – litigants and the judiciary – to think how best to avoid the mistakes, traps, pitfalls, and misjudgements she managed to record.

The target audiences will no doubt decide for themselves what to do or not do, but that doesn't prevent us from making a few suggestions of our own. Suggestions for people with a dispute to resolve and for those advising them, and for the judiciary and those who make and shape the civil justice system: the senior judiciary and parliamentarians – especially non-lawyer Members of Parliament.

Perhaps the makers and shapers could start by looking at the abuse of injunctions: the Ogmore Gang's smart way to get their quarry entangled in the court system. Then they could revisit Lucy's proposal to that Very Senior Judge that the *client* should have the authority to decide what they agree and don't agree in a binding Consent Order. The V. S. Judge rejected her proposal as time wasting, but look at the time wasted since those two non-consent orders were signed off by others without the paying customers' agreement. They might also revisit her cooling-off period proposal to ensure that any claimed agreement is genuine. The rule-makers might even consider radical action on *Henderson* v *Henderson*-type precedents. Too many in the law business are mesmerised by precedents which they see as the bedrock of our common law system, but fail to see as possible threats to a just outcome. Jonathan Swift complained about the consequences of overindulgence in precedents centuries ago:

> 'Lawyers take special care to record all the decisions formerly made against common justice, and general reason. Under the name of *precedents* they are produced as authorities to justify the most iniquitous opinions; and the judges never fail to direct accordingly.' (*Gullivers Travels* Part iv, Ch. v)

So, what has changed?

Perhaps those with the power to do something will give more than a dismissive glance at the proposal to remove land ownership disputes from the civil courts and beef up and retrain Land Registry to do the job instead. Perhaps they will then review the Courts' current remit to see if other types of dispute would be better placed in other, more expert hands, and in the process check if tribunals are becoming rather too like courts. Maybe they could ask themselves why litigants are prohibited from recording trials and hearings they attend – what possible objection could they raise to this customer-friendly proposal for greater transparency and efficiency? Maybe they will decide that if a litigant lodges a claim in the Small Claims Court, that is where it stays unless *the customer* agrees otherwise – or withdraws altogether. And perhaps they will have a long, hard look at how hearings on the Small Claims track are managed. Do they really have to mimic the intimidating formality of fast and multi-tracks?

What are the chances that they will decide to do something about lawyers acting for themselves unsupervised and rampaging through the justice system unchecked? Lawyers delight in saying that the litigant in person has a fool for a client. If this was apt in Hazel Ogmore's case, as lawyer-client she was a *dangerous* fool.

It would be most helpful if judges were regularly reminded of the overriding objective of the Civil Procedure Rules: to deal with cases justly, and of CPR 3.1(2)(m), which provides the Court with 'an unfettered discretion', to quote senior Judge Sir Henry Brooke, 'to make *any* order to manage cases in furtherance of that objective'. Lord Woolf and colleagues wanted the Rules to be simple, clear and certain, but by 2013 they, with supplementary directions, protocols and so on, extend to over 7,000 pages of such complexity that professionals are daunted and laymen confounded.

If the resolution of disputes between citizens cannot be wrested from the hands of judges, they are going to have to reconfigure their mindsets to deal fairly, justly and politely with litigants in person, since there are certain to be more of them. The near demise of Legal Aid for civil cases, adjustments to CFA ('no-win, no-fee') and claims management rules, lawyer costs and the present legal expenses insurance market, mean more will be faced with the choice of representing themselves or abandoning any attempt to access justice through the courts. Encouraged by online information and advice, and, lately, the increasing availability of McKenzie Friends[1] many will choose DIY justice, despite dwindling help from previous support agencies like law centres.

This calls for new skills in dealing with a changed cast of players. Skills that teachers, doctors, social workers and other professionals who deal directly with the public have to develop. Like listening to the client, speaking everyday English – and patience. LiPs may seem to take more time, but they are the clients the courts and judges are there to serve, not the other way round, and besides, there is the chance that freed from an overload of law and rules and ritualised procedures, judges may get to justice more efficiently using client-friendly techniques. For example, reading the Statements and looking at the documents *before* the court hearing – and asking questions. This may seem rather too Napoleonic, too inquisitorial for some, but the adversarial approach does not fit the nature of most civil disputes. Whether they admit it or not, judges, like referees, *are* in the arena when required to settle arguments between citizens. There are rumours that a few do a good job in the less adversarial, mainly cost-free, mainly lawyer-free, Small Claims Courts when they play the part of effective, non-patronising mediator or arbitrator. The raising of the Small Claims limit to £10,000 should rescue more clients from chilling adversarial combats on fast and multi-tracks, but *only if* the Small Claims judges adopt the mediator approach. A fear at the moment is that things are moving in the opposite direction and that mediation is becoming more like court-door haggling.

As for Her Majesty's Court Service (HMCS), it needs the resources to allow it to fully enter the 21st century online world and ensure that relevant information is available to all who need it on time. Data which would be valuable to litigants and their advisors is still elusive in 2014. Even the judiciary complains about a lack of data on litigants in person. Max and Lucy would have appreciated up-to-date data on boundary disputes and easily accessible data on appeals. We all need the evidence, the cold facts on which corrections and improvements to our civil justice service should be based.

There has been some limited progress in providing online forms (although they can be less than user-friendly on occasion), including money or possession claims online, but there are still vast areas of the civil courts service that need to be more technologically efficient and client-aware. The time and place for any judicial decision should be agreed for everyone's convenience. No decision should be made without clear warning that decision-making is planned, unless a party refuses to cooperate. There should be no cause for litigants to pay for transcripts of hearings they were unaware they needed to attend, nor should they have to rummage through mountains of files in distant court houses to find, too late if at all, what they needed to know. If a

Circuit Judge reverts a case back to a colleague, that is what should happen. No client should have four different judges for four consecutive hearings of the same claim ... in three different courts.

All professionals involved in attempting to deliver a just outcome should always remember that the civil courts are designed to resolve differences between citizens. They are not criminal courts designed for something else.

Powerful gusts of change have swept through the civil justice landscape in recent years. Full-time professionals find it hard to keep up. What was Legal Aid in 2000 is not Legal Aid today; Woolf has been superseded by Jackson and legal services radically altered by the Legal Services Act 2007. There is talk of a revolution taking place. There was certainly a need for one, but so far there is scant evidence that the turmoil has benefitted the peasants.

Nevertheless, thanks to that little known Legal Services Act, we have the hope, at least, of a nicer law business, which may in time match the image the lawyers like to project: a friendly, efficient, economical, client-caring legal service. Thanks to the Act we now have an *independent* Ombudsman to investigate complaints and feed information and recommendations drawn from investigations to both consumers and service-providers. We also have an independent oversight regulator (light touch) to keep an eye on how the market is operating, ostensibly directing it to benefit consumers and advised to that end by its Consumer Panel. All these new statutory agencies have a preponderance of non-lawyers in key positions.

There is no guarantee that any consumer guidance given here would be accurately targeted for five years or even five months hence, so clients and potential clients should access advice and information on a timely need-to-know basis. Some advice holds good at all times: always try talking first; keep calm, polite and listen to what the other side actually says. Check the current legal position on your problem (see 'Blogs, books and contacts' for some sources of information). Keep audio and paper records of everything you can, including telephone calls and face-to-face interviews (dated and timed), and file paper copies twice: chronologically and by source. It may seem tedious and unnecessary, but you cannot predict what may happen and what may be important and useful. If using a solicitor, insist that attendance notes are copied and agreed with you and that time-billing records are sent monthly. And above all, negotiate that contract – remember how Max and Lucy put their misplaced trust in David Burke, you really do not want to write a blank cheque for six-minute billing which could result in a charge of £25 plus VAT (or more) for a 15-second answerphone message, saying they will ring again! Fixed fees are preferable. If acting for yourself in court consider finding support from a McKenzie Friend. Whichever dispute resolution route you are on whether it is a neighbourhood mediation scheme or the High Court, collect evidence and witness statements as soon as you can. Don't precipitate, but do not delay, hoping the unresolved problem will fade away. And always remember, if it goes to court – the Judge decides.

Apart from conventional support from fee-earning solicitors and barristers, there are the free advisory support agencies like law centres (rare), Citizen Advice Bureaux (overburdened), online legal advice sites (some good, some dangerous[2]) and books (soon outdated – like this one!). Some solicitors still offer a 30-minute or one-hour free introductory session often as a loss leader, but now there are also the interesting, new Alternative Business Structures (ignore the catchy title) which offer innovative ways of doing legal business and look like being more client-focussed – so far. It is early days. The intention is to free-up adventurous law firms with the injection of new management skills and finance. Many offer fixed fees so clients can escape the shock of the unexpected invoice at the end of the contract, and flexible, extended office hours so clients can avoid the dispiriting frustration caused by strict nine-to-five, five days a week contact. Some will see clients in their home or workplace or wherever convenient. Some work closely with vetted, economically-priced barristers. Some will encourage appropriate ADR routes to dispute resolution and new types of contract like Damage Based Agreements.[3] They are mushrooming exponentially at present – but they are still as yet untested.

However, two essential ingredients are missing: (1.) savvy and confident law-service customers collectively playing their regulatory role, by selecting the best option on service and price and negotiating the best deal *before* contract and (2.) a vehicle for *the laity* to influence decision-makers on the nature and quality of our civil justice services.

For markets in goods and services to work efficiently and effectively to benefit not just consumers and providers but the whole community, consumers need to play their role as regulators. They need to feel confident that their reasonable needs will be met, that the market is transparent and that there is a fair system of redress if things go wrong. The civil justice service is unlike all other essential services, in that the courts themselves are the final arbiters – all the more reason for consumers to play their essential regulating role. They lack confidence because they are intimidated by costs, mystified by language and customs and excluded from influence on the service – and their own fate. Parliament can and must play its part, but if civil justice remains an intimidating ordeal for clients, with providers cocooned from the consequences of their actions, it will fail to be the accessible public service to which we all have a right: one which many of its proponents claim it to be – despite evidence to the contrary.

There are serious obstacles in the way: legal services are rarely repeat purchases for the average buyer, so there's little opportunity or need for individual clients to develop consumer expertise, and public legal education is a faint ghost of what is required, directed mainly at providing basic information on laws and rules and identifying agencies offering help and guidance. The market is opaque so each new client, ignorant and vulnerable as a newborn, must blindly trust that trained, experienced and networked professionals will put service to them first. Such trust is not yet much in evidence. Potential clients would feel more confident if they had clear guidance on what standards of service to expect not just from front-line lawyers and ADR providers, but also from the judiciary.

No 'lay' person in their right mind goes happily or willingly to court not least because they lose control, as, for example, when they are 'deemed' to have consented to an agreement which they most emphatically reject. When the adversarial precedent-driven civil courts fail they can be an expensive way of messing up the lives of ordinary people, people who have to rely on them as problem solvers if all other attempts fail, either that or abandon any attempt to access justice. If the courts create more problems than they solve, perhaps radical alternatives should be considered. Judge-free and lawyer-free alternatives. Lucy and Max still favour ADR, mediation in particular, but know that it, too, can be corrupted or fail just like courts when in the wrong hands. The legalistic mindset is seeping increasingly into the mediation service as legalistically-minded lawyers, aware of the changing legal marketplace, look for back-up careers.

How to change a nasty business into a good public service? As things stand, litigants cannot do it, they are stuck with the service as it is and have little chance of playing their regulator role. Front-line lawyers are unlikely to do it; they have a living to make from their lengthy and expensive training.

Things are unlikely to change until a critical mass of those who have first-hand consumer experience of the present set-up, collectively find a voice, informed and reasonable, and organise to make that voice heard.

Fathers4Justice and Families Need Fathers have fought long and hard to make their voices heard in the Family courts and are pioneering models for the generalist organisation we would like to see covering all areas of civil dispute. They offer advice and support (including McKenzie Friends) to anyone – not just fathers – entangled in a family dispute. And they lobby the decision-makers to make changes they have found from experience to be necessary.

We need a specialist Which?-style consumer organisation for our civil justice services, financed independent of government and the profession, to deliver the missing ingredients for confident consumers of this essential service: information, guidance, support, education and representation. Such an organisation would build a body of knowledge and expertise from the collective experience of service-users and lobby to make it fit for purpose: accessible, transparent and balanced – favouring neither providers as at present, nor users.

In the absence of any effective, well-resourced, high-profile consumer organisation exclusively for *clients* of legal services, the internet becomes the essential tool, but some valuable internet services like the quality website ADRnow which, until 2012 was run by the Advice Services Alliance (www.asauk.org.uk) disappeared when their funding disappeared, hence the need for independent finance. And we should not forget that the internet can be used to trap the unwary.

There is a need for one, single, effective, well-resourced and independent organisation for consumers, covering all our different civil dispute-resolution services. An organisation which could provide targeted support and advice as well as general information for the public and so enable consumers to play their regulatory role in the dispute-resolution market. An organisation which could build a body of knowledge about how the market is operating and feed their views and ideas to the decision-makers. With such an organisation, one may hope that all those involved in providing our civil justice service – from judges and parliamentarians, to ADR providers, lawyers and court staff – will be persuaded, one way or another, to put service to their clients, the public and justice first.

BLOGS, BOOKS AND CONTACTS

There are innumerable blogs by lawyers. Our favourite is *BabyBarista* by Tim Kevan (http://www.babybarista.com), not least because his site links to Alex William's *Queen's Counsel* cartoons and other lawyer blogs, some serious, some witty, some both. *BabyBarista* has spawned two wicked, laugh-out-loud books: *Law and Disorder* and *Law and Peace*.[1] The site also promotes books by other writers including reader-friendly advice books and heavy but useful legal tomes like *The English Legal System*[2] by Gary Slapper and David Kelly. The site provides links to video clips from films, lectures, comedy shows, discussions and to other websites, most notably the Incorporated Council on Law Reporting (ICLR online[3]) which could be useful for litigants in person as well as lawyers and is not quite as dry and dreary as it sounds, having created the entertaining HHJ Pennyweather and providing a portal to a wide range of online legal websites.

There are few books chronicling a consumer's experience of the nasty side of the law business, but Terence Frisby's *Outrageous Fortune*[4] records in poignant detail the damage that nastiness in the divorce courts can do and records the bad conduct of some of the key players he encountered as he fought for custody of his son. His play *Rough Justice*[5] draws on his experience of the court system, and gives voice to the genuine anger our uncivil justice service can generate.

There is an ever-expanding library of books on the future of legal services mostly aimed at professionals who find themselves in an alarming new marketplace. Non-professionals with more important things in their life may nonetheless find two by Richard Susskind: *The End of Lawyers?* (2008) and *Tomorrow's Lawyers* (2013),[6] both published by OUP, readable and thought-provoking.

If you find yourself in a dispute and want help always bear in mind that relevant information must be up to date, so the main source of advice post-2013 has to be the internet. Citizens Advice will provide face-to-face guidance when they have time, as will Law Centres if you can get to one near you, and there are still some *pro bono* lawyers and high street solicitors offering free, half-hour advice sessions, but accessibility is a problem, so we would advise that the first port of call be the reconfigured Citizens Advice website: www.adviceguide.org.uk.

If the dispute escalates beyond talking, emailing and letters, towards some form of ADR, (ombudsman, mediator, arbitrator, etc.), and looks like it is heading for the courts or tribunals, two recent guides for litigants in person are worth the homework-time whether you intend to represent yourself or engage professional help, or if you are helping someone else – as a McKenzie Friend[7] perhaps.

A Handbook for Litigants in Person (www.judiciary.gov.uk) was compiled by a team of judges just before enactment in April 2013 of the somewhat misleadingly titled Legal Aid, Sentencing and Punishment of Offenders Act (LASPO[8]), which is the outcome of Lord Justice Jackson's research into civil litigation costs, and the latest quiet mini-revolution in our civil justice service. This handbook is directed at helping LiPs who find themselves in court on the challenging multi-track, but it is helpful to anyone looking at the options for resolving otherwise intractable disputes. It begins with useful guidance on where to find cost-free or near cost-free advice, describes the dispute-resolution options and provides advice on contracts with professionals, including the new Damage-Based Agreements (DBAs),[9] and fixed costs as opposed to hourly (six-minute) billing. Things change so fast that even the judiciary cannot always keep up, as evidenced by the reference to the outdated £5,000 limit on Small Claims in the early pages. Nevertheless, as we finalise this book this is the most reliable up-to-date consumer guide to the civil justice system which incorporates the Jackson reforms and amends accordingly the 1999 Woolf reforms that applied during the Ogmore Squatter saga. Whether you would find the detailed advice on pursuing a multi-track case more intimidating than encouraging, it is too early to say. The advice is sound no doubt, but the dispiriting insistence on the complex rules they want *us* to learn for DIY justice suggests that they have no plans at present to make the system created by the professionals more user-friendly.

The Bar Council's *A Guide to Representing Yourself in Court* (www.barcouncil.org.uk/instructing-a-barrister/representing-yourself-in-court) is a more attractively presented and shorter version covering the same ground with added targeted advice on some areas of law (not including boundary disputes or squatter removal) and a glossary (not including 'Consent Orders' or 'Abuse of Process'), but also useful advice on how to conduct yourself in front of a judge and how to examine a witness. Both publications wisely urge caution when considering court action – which may be redundant advice.

To check on current Civil Procedure Rules the eBook edition of O'Hare and Browne's *Civil Litigation* is now available … at a price.

For news and gossip on current legal stories, *The Telegraph*, *The Guardian* and *The Independent* have law sections; *The Times* has too but behind its firewall.

Finally, here are some further useful web addresses. (Note: Only for England and Wales which share the same legal system. Scotland and Northern Ireland have their own variations.)

The Legal Ombudsman (LeO): www.legalombudsman.org.uk. For guidance on making a complaint, the names of lawyers and firms complained about and Ombudsman decisions.

The Legal Services Board (LSB): www.legalservicesboard.org.uk. The Board is independent of Government and the legal professions and is responsible for overseeing the Legal Ombudsman and eight Approved Regulators (e.g. the Bar Council and the Law Society), which in turn regulate seven frontline regulators. The frontline regulators have a website for the public (www.legalchoices.org.uk) 'To help you with decisions about legal issues and lawyers. Putting you in the driving seat with your lawyer'.

The Legal Services Board Consumer Panel (LSBCP): www.legalservicesconsumerpanel.org.uk. The Panel has a lay membership, is independent of the LSB, carries out its own research and advises and scrutinises the Board's work on behalf of consumers. The Panel has legal powers to publish its advice and the Legal Services Board has a legal duty to explain its reasons when it disagrees with the Panel. The Chair (currently Elisabeth Davies) publishes a regular blog on the website which is well worth the read.

The Judicial Conduct Investigations Office (JCIO): www.judicialconduct.judiciary.gov.uk. Took over from the OJC in October 2013 and publishes disciplinary statements on investigations into judicial conduct.

The Civil Court Users Association (CCUA): www.ccua.org.uk. A consumer group with 26 years' experience of lobbying for improvements in court services. NOT a *liaison* group similar to the one Lucy was persuaded to join!

Solicitor.info: www.solicitor.info. 'There are many good solicitors – the trick is finding one.' This is an independent rating website with the goal of finding the best solicitor for individual consumers by providing reviews and opinions directly from clients. The site also reports Ombudsman decisions and remedies, and decisions by the Solicitors' Regulatory Authority (SRA). It is owned and managed by non-lawyers. Note: there are several rating sites which are worth a look – but with the usual warnings about the independence and availability of such sites (e.g. reallymoving.com for comparison of house purchase costs and checkaprofessional.com, part of checkatrade.com).

The Free Representation Unit (FRU): www.thefru.org.uk. Provides free representation for employment and social security cases but only from referrals from listed organisations.

Advice Services Alliance: advicenow.org.uk. For free advice and support including advice on ADR.

Advice UK: adviceuk.org.uk. Site for the coordinating body for independent advice providers.

The Bar Council: www.barcouncil.org.uk. For the Bar Directory, the barristers' *Pro Bono* Group and the Public (direct) Access Directory, and 'A Guide to Representing Yourself in Court'.

The Civil Justice Council: www.civiljusticecouncil.org.uk. For 'A Guide to Bringing and Defending a Small Claim'.

The Law Centres Network: www.lawcentres.org.uk. Specialises in social welfare law offering legal advice, casework and representation to groups and individuals.

The Law Society: www.lawsociety.org.uk. To check out registrations of lawyers and firms ('Find a solicitor') and Alternative Business Structures such as Co-op Legal Services and AA Law Limited.

Lawworks: www.lawworks.org.uk. The solicitors' *Pro Bono* group.

Ministry of Justice: www.justice.gov.uk. For statistics and information on such matters as the regulation of claims management companies, tribunals, mediation, LiPs, court fees, etc.

Trading Standards: www.tradingstandards.gov.uk. To check out the law on consumer disputes.

The Justice Gap: www.thejusticegap.com. A site with items from many contributors on the theme of justice, edited by Jon Robbins, a journalist who campaigns to improve access to justice.

FOOTNOTES

Part One

Chapter 1

1. Title documents are now issued online by Land Registry (www.landregistry.gov.uk). Absolute title in registered freehold land is guaranteed by the registration as vested in the proprietor of the land, except in rare exceptional circumstances.
2 SPIF: Seller's Property Information Form. The responsibility for the accuracy of responses on this form lies with the seller, not the solicitor or the estate agent.
3. The new rules that came with the Land Registry Act (LRA) 2002 have shifted the balance in favour slightly of the registered Title holder. After 10 years the squatter can apply to be registered as the Title holder, but the Title holder will be notified of the application and if they object the application will be rejected except in certain specific circumstances.
4. Adverse possession: squatters' rights have no fixed specific meaning but squatters can apply for adverse possession if they meet specific requirements. Squatting in residential property is now illegal.

Chapter 2

1. See page 8 for rules prior to the LRA 2002.
2. Registration of properties in England and Wales at time of sale became compulsory from 1990.
3. *ex parte*: applications to the Court are usually made after notifying the other party in advance, but in emergency cases the application can be made *ex parte* – without warning the other party. In this instance there was no emergency and Max and Lucy should have been told an application was being made at the Royal Courts of Justice.

Chapter 3

1. *Mea culpa*: my fault.
2. See Chapter 1, footnote 4.
3. Vexatious litigation is legal action which is brought, regardless of its merits, solely to *harass* or subdue an adversary. Filing vexatious litigation is considered an abuse of the judicial process to be subject to sanctions.

4. Legal Aid was originally established by the Legal Aid and Advice Act 1949. In 2009, Legal Aid in England and Wales cost the taxpayer £2bn a year – a higher per capita spend than anywhere else in the world – and was available to around 29% of adults. Until 31 March 2013 Legal Aid was administered by the Legal Services Commission, and was available for most criminal cases, and many types of civil cases. A new Act, The Legal Aid, Sentencing and Punishment of Offenders Act 2012 (LASPO) abolished the Legal Services Commission, and replaced it with the Legal Aid Agency, a new executive agency of the Ministry of Justice. The new Act finally removed financial support for most civil cases including housing, welfare, medical negligence, employment, debt and immigration.
5. 'No-win, no-fee' or conditional fee arrangements (CFAs) usually meant that a solicitor would take a civil case on the understanding that if lost, the client would not be liable for the lawyer's fees and if won, the losing side would pay all the winner's fees plus a 'success fee', with a mark-up which could be as high as 100%. In January 2010 Lord Justice Jackson published his 'Review of Civil Litigation Costs' and some of his key recommendations have been adopted in LASPO (see footnote 4 of this chapter): success fees and after the event (ATE) insurance are no longer recoverable from the losing party. If the client agrees a success fee, they pay it from their award.
6. They would act without professional help.

Chapter 4

1. Summary judgment: a judgment entered by the Court for one party against the other without a full trial.
2. Counterclaim: a claim by a defendant opposing the claim and seeking some form of relief from the claimant.
3. Plaintiff: the title given to a claimant at that time.
4. Lord Woolf published his 'Access to Justice' report in July 1996 which identified rules intended to ensure that the civil justice system is 'accessible, fair and efficient', with the overriding objective of enabling the Court to deal with cases justly by, for example (as far as practicable):
   - ensuring the parties are on an equal footing
   - saving expense
   - dealing with cases in ways which are proportionate to the amount of money involved to the importance of the case; to the complexity of the issues; to the financial position of each party
   - ensuring that it is dealt with expeditiously and fairly
   - allocating to it an appropriate share of the Court's resources, while taking into account the need to allot resources to other cases.

   The parties are *required* to help the Court to further the overriding objective and the court must *actively manage* cases by, for example, encouraging and facilitating the use of ADR if considered appropriate; fixing timetables and controlling the progress of the case; making efficient use of technology.

   The draft rules granted wide management powers to judges and proposed that cases be allocated to one of three tracks: Small Claims Track, Fast Track or Multi-Track. The Civil Procedure Act of 1997 which came into force in April 1999 also allowed for the gradual introduction of 'pre-action protocols' for different types of disputes to encourage cooperation in identifying the main issues. Failure to cooperate can lead to cost penalties, regardless of the eventual outcome.

5. The inquisitorial system applies in certain jurisdictions with *civil legal systems*, for example France, where the Court or a part of the Court is actively involved in investigating the facts of the case, as opposed to the adversarial system that applies in England and Wales with our *common law system* where the role of the Court is primarily that of an impartial referee between the parties.
6. Legal Executives evolved from managing clerks in law firms who had become knowledgeable about certain areas of the law and who were allowed to manage their fellow clerks. In 1963 the Law Society sponsored the creation of the Institute of Legal Executives (ILEX), and in 2012 the Institute received its Royal Charter. A law firm clerk can now study to qualify as a Chartered Legal Executive and is eligible to become a partner in the law firm.

Chapter 5

1. See Chapter 4, footnote 4.
2. See Chapter 2, footnote 3.
3. *American Cyanamid* v *Ethicon* [1973] AC 396: set a precedent that arguably the court should not prejudge the merits of the case, but merely take into account the balance of convenience when granting an interim injunction as a *provisional* remedy.
4. Particulars of Claim: the court document setting out the essential factual details of the Claim and the 'relief' the Claimant is asking the Court to award.
5. Fair market value is an estimate of the market value based on what a knowledgeable, *willing* and unpressured *buyer* would probably pay a knowledgeable, *willing* and unpressured *seller.*
6. Alternative Dispute Resolution (ADR) covers a wide range of processes for resolving disputes without litigation. The four main types in the UK are adjudication, arbitration, conciliation and mediation. There are also increasing numbers and varieties of ombudsman schemes. Less well known is Early Neutral Evaluation, where a third party, often an expert in the subject of the dispute or an expert in law, gives an evaluation or opinion on the dispute to both sides which is not legally binding. An EU Directive on ADR is due to come into force in July 2015 and the Directive on ODR (Online Dispute Resolution) in January 2016. The Directives should give consumers the chance to resolve their dispute without going to law regardless of product or service or place of purchase.
7. *Chamberlain* v *Lindon* (1998) 1 WLR 1252. This precedent upholds a 'lawful excuse' defence of damaging property in order to protect other property, allowing the defendant to destroy an obstruction that was blocking his right of way.
8. Wayleave is a right of way granted by a landowner (usually for payment) for purposes such as the erection of telephone or electricity poles.

Chapter 6

1. Consent Order: this is a legally-binding document that confirms agreements between parties, most frequently used in settling family matters. Once a court has approved a draft Consent Order it is legally binding and cannot be changed unless an appeal is upheld by a senior judge. If one or both parties breach a Consent Order then the Order can be enforced by the Court, a breach of a Consent Order is effectively a breach of a court order – something that courts look upon very unfavourably. Where one or both parties to an agreement is a Litigant in Person, the agreement is only valid if signed by the LiP(s).
2. The correct way to address a judge in court: judges in higher courts such as Courts of Appeal: My Lord or My lady; Circuit judges: Your Honour. District and other lower courts: Sir or Madam.
3. See Chapter 5, footnote 7.

Chapter 7

1. The court circuit: there are six court circuits. In 2002 they were Midland, Northern, North Eastern, South Eastern, Wales and Chester and Western. In 2005 these were rearranged into: Midlands, North West, North East, South East, London, South West and Wales. Circuit judges are senior judges in England and Wales who sit in the Crown Court, county courts and certain specialised sub-divisions of the High Court of Justice. They sit below High Court judges but above district judges. Some more senior circuit judges are also eligible to sit in the Criminal Division of the Court of Appeal.
2. See Chapter 2, footnote 3.

Chapter 8

1. Solicitors in England and Wales with practising certificates: 134,447 (source: LSB statistics April 2013), Solicitors on roll: 163,514 (source: Law Society statistics Dec. 2013), Barristers: 15,355 (source: LSB statistics April 2013), Chartered Legal Executives: 7,947 (source: LSB statistics April 2013).
2. See Chapter 1, footnotes 1 and 3; Chapter 2, footnote 2 and www.landregistry.gov.uk/public/boundaries. Note on the same web page the emphatic rejection of any role for Land Registry in settling boundary disputes.
3. The court seal is applied to a document (usually an order) to authenticate it is issued by the Court.

Chapter 9

1. See Chapter 8, footnote 2.
2. Skeleton argument: a document summarising the main issues and arguments for one party in the case.

Chapter 10

1. The latest edition as we go to press is O'Hare, J. and K. Browne *Civil Litigation*. (London: Sweet and Maxwell, 2013) 16th edition [ISBN L15578-E16]. Also available as an eBook.

Chapter 11

1. A Witness Statement is a formal document containing your own account of the facts relating to your dispute. Comments made in the Statement should be limited to fact; those based on opinion should be kept to a minimum. It is important to ensure that the Statement is accurate and comprehensive. It must be in your own words. If you wish to attach supporting documents (exhibits), number them and reference them in the Statement. Once you are satisfied with it, you should sign and date it as your 'proof of evidence'. Copies of Witness Statements are normally exchanged between parties at the same time. You should state when signing and dating the Statement that you believe the facts in it are true and accurate. You could be held in contempt of court if you make a false statement which you do not believe to be true.
2. *Henderson* v *Henderson* (1843) 3 Hare 100; [2002] 2 All ER 850 CA.
3. See Chapter 5, footnote 3.
4. At the time of publication the most recent (2013) version of *Civil Court Practice*, the Green Book, is the (rather pricey) set published in an eBook and hard copy ISBN/ ISSN 9781405778640.
5. *Dunnett* v *Raitrack Plc* [2002] EWCA Civ 302; [2002] 1 WLR 2434; [2002] 2 All ER 850; 2 All ER 454 CA: Costs were denied to Railtrack, the successful party, because it had earlier flatly refused to mediate. This case was a benchmark towards the requirement to mediate and followed earlier cases warning of likely costs sanctions if a party refuses mediation.
6. OS: Registered Title plans are based on the relevant Ordnance Survey plan.
7. A Part 36 offer to settle ('compromise') a claim sets out the costs and other consequences that a party will face if it refuses a reasonable settlement offer. Such offers should not be seen as a sign of weakness but an appropriate way of putting pressure on an opponent to settle and conclude the dispute. They must be genuine offers made on a 'without prejudice save as to costs' basis. If an offer is not accepted and at trial, the judgment is at least as advantageous as the terms on offer, an additional sum for damages in respect of a money claim or an additional sum for costs in respect of a non-money claim, can be added.
8. See Chapter 2, footnote 3.
9. Chambers and Partners: www.chambersandpartners.com. The most popular online

directory of lawyers (solicitors, firms, barristers and chambers) recommended and ranked by region and specialism.

10. Civil Procedure Rules: the court rules that all civil cases must keep to (see Chapter 4, footnote 4).The civil procedure rules make up a procedural code whose overriding aim is to enable the courts to deal with cases justly. There are also criminal procedure rules which give courts explicit powers to actively manage the preparation of criminal cases and avoid unfair and avoidable delays, and family court procedures governing practice and procedure in the family courts.
11. 'Without prejudice' communications: a rule which prevents evidence about ADR and settlement discussions being disclosed to the Court except at the end of the case when costs are being considered.
12. See Chapter 9, footnote 2.
13. See Chapter 8, footnote 3.
14. Success fee: the uplift to costs paid to a successful litigant with a CFA ('no win, no fee') agreement. The rules governing such agreements changed on 1st April 2013 following the proposals in Lord Jackson's report on litigation costs.
15. See Chapter 5, footnote 6.
16. See Chapter 3, footnote 5.
17. *The Examined Life* by Stephen Grosz (London: Chatto and Windus, 2013) [ISBN 9780701185350].

Chapter 12

1. Form N460.
2. The Independent Complaints Reviewer (ICR) investigates complaints about four organisations: Land Registry, the National Archives, The Northern Ireland Youth Justice Agency and the Children's Commissioner for Wales. The current ICR for Land Registry is Elizabeth Derrington. ICR reports are not made public.

Chapter 13

1. See Chapter 12, footnote 2.
2. See Chapter 11, footnote 10.
3. See Chapter 5, footnote 4.
4. Track: see Chapter 4, footnote 4. The judge allocates each case to one of three tracks: (1.) Small Claims when the value of the claim is less than £10,000 (previously £5,000), (2.) Fast track when the value is between £10,000 and £25,000 (previously £5,000 and £15,000) and (3.) Multi-track when it is above £25,000. Claimant and defendant complete an allocation questionnaire stating which track they consider appropriate and which court should hear the case.
5. Pleadings: The court documents setting out the parties' cases.

Chapter 15

1. See Chapter 10, footnote 1.
2. Unless the client negotiates alternative contracts, for example, a set fee (as currently offered for most conveyancing and wills and probate work and increasingly for other legal services), solicitors will normally bill in six-minute units (one-tenth of the hourly rate) so that the client is billed at least a tenth of the rate for each action the lawyer takes – even if it is a brief answer-phone message lasting less than a minute.

Chapter 16

1. Summary judgment: see Chapter 4, footnote 1.
2. See Chapter 1, footnote 1 and 3; Chapter 2, footnote 2; Chapter 8, footnote 2.
3. Small Claims limit: see Chapter 4, footnote 4; Chapter 13, footnote 4.
4. *de minimis*: trivial.
5. Since 2004 anyone can go directly to a barrister without having to involve anyone else (e.g. a solicitor). Barristers can advise you on your legal status or rights. Barristers can draft documents for you and can represent you in court and at tribunals or mediations. Barristers can also negotiate on your behalf and can attend employment or investigative interviews and hearings where appropriate. Because the barrister's role is unchanged and there are limits on the types of work that a barrister can do, there are still some cases and situations in which you will need to instruct a solicitor or another intermediary as well as a barrister. Nevertheless, for many cases the public access scheme allows you to go directly to the expert barrister for advice, representation and drafting. Not all barristers accept public access work; those who do are listed on the public access directory. You can search the directory by town or city, area of practice or the barrister's name from the Bar Council's website Direct access barristers: www.barcouncil.org.uk, tel: 0207 6111472.
6. Slander of Women Act 1891, replaced by the Defamation Act 2013.
7. The land surveyor, Mr Higgins, pegged two alternative boundaries downhill at the back of the shed: one starting on the roadside at the end of the roadside fence, the other at the point two and a half feet downhill from the roadside where the old telephone pole had been (until October 2003) and where Hammer's plan (the 'Consent' Order plan) started the 60 foot downhill boundary. Ogmore had selected the roadside peg so it was assumed she had run this new stretch of fencing to end two and a half feet higher uphill than the alternative in order to comply with the 60 foot measurement on the Consent Order plan.
8. *fait accompli*: done deed/established fact.
9. LR and boundary disputes: see Chapter 1, footnote 1 and 3; Chapter 2, footnote 2; Chapter 8, footnote 2.

Part Two

Chapter 17

1. Legal Aid: see Chapter 3, footnote 4.
2. Legal Ombudsman: www.legalombudsman.gov.uk. Established under the Legal Services Act 2007; started investigating legal complaints October 2010.
3. WHICH? Legal Service: www.which.co.uk, tel: 01992 822 828. For an annual fee of £86 households and small businesses can have telephone advice from qualified lawyers on consumer problems with goods and services and a wide range of legal issues including neighbour disputes, tenancy and employment matters, holiday and travel problems.
4. Law centres have existed since the early 1970s and work within their communities to help local people. Specialising in social welfare law, they have an in-depth knowledge of the issues their communities face. They use this knowledge to help people save their homes, keep their jobs and protect their families. All law centres are independent and operate on a not-for-profit basis. They are also accountable to their communities, with local people acting on their management committees. There are around some 50 centres around the UK. To see if there is one near you go to www.lawcentres.org.uk.
5. Citizen Advice Bureau: www.citizenadvice.org.uk. Provides free, independent, confidential and impartial advice dealing with any issue, spanning debt and employment to consumer and housing. CAB also uses clients' stories anonymously to campaign for policy changes that benefit the population as a whole.
   There are over 3,300 community bureaux in England and Wales, run by 338 individual charities. Citizens Advice is the national body and is a registered charity in its own right. Information and advice is offered face-to-face, by phone and email services, and online via Adviceguide.org.uk. Citizens Advice Bureau also makes face-to-face advice available from other locations including community centres, doctors' surgeries, courts and prisons, helping people to access advicewhere they need it most.
6. Direct access barristers: see Chapter 16, footnote 5.
7. Office of Fair Trading. 'Competition in the Professions' (March 2001). www.oft.gov.uk. Publication reference: oft328.
8. The Clementi Report December 2004: 'A Review of the Regulatory Framework for Legal Services in England and Wales'.
9. Legal Services Act 2007: www.legislation.gov.uk/ukpga/2007/29/contents.
10. www.legalservicesboard.org.uk. There are eight Approved Regulators: Solicitors' Regulatory Authority (Law society); Bar Standards Board (Bar Council); ILEX Professional Standards Ltd (Chartered Institute of Legal Executives); Council for Licensed Conveyancers; Intellectual Property Regulation Board (Trade Marks and Patent Attorneys); Costs Lawyers Standards Board (Association of Cost lawyers) and Master of Faculties (Notaries).
11. Legal Services Board Consumer Panel: located within the Legal Services Board, the Panel's role is to provide independent advice to the Legal Services Board by investigating issues that affect consumers of legal services and by seeking to influence decisions about how lawyers are regulated.

12. Alternative Business Structures (ABS): at the time of publication (spring 2014) there are 245 ABSs licensed by the Law Society's Solicitors' Regulatory Authority.
13. Litigants in Person: two guides for litigants in person (LiPs) have been produced; one by the judiciary: *A Handbook for Litigants in Person* (www.judiciary.gov.uk), and one by the Bar Council: *A Guide to Representing Yourself in Court* (www.barcouncil.org.uk/instructing-a-barrister/representing-yourself-in-court). Both a recommended read for anyone considering representing themselves in court.
14. The Legal Services Ombudsman for England and Wales between 2003 and 2011 was Zahida Manzoor, CBE. During this period Baroness Manzoor made improvements in the way legal professional bodies, such as the Law Society and the Bar Council, dealt with complaints from members of the public. She also instigated an investigation into the handling of personal injury claims for coal miners, resulting in redress for the miners and some solicitors being barred from practice. In 2004 she took on the role of Legal Services Complaints Commissioner for England and Wales acting as the Statutory Regulator responsible for overseeing the handling of complaints by the Law Society and was given powers to set performance improvement targets and impose financial penalties of up to £1 million for failure to meet those targets.
15. See Chapter 16, footnote 6.

Chapter 18

1. See Chapter 1, footnote 2.
2. See Chapter 17, footnote 2.
3. Legal Ombudsman Annual Report March 2013: 72% satisfaction recorded among customers; 80% among lawyers.

Chapter 19

1. See Chapter 15, footnote 2.

Chapter 20

1. See Chapter 10, footnote 1.
2. *pro bono publico*: for the public good. Work carried out by lawyers unpaid for the good of the general community.
3. Bar Council: see www.barcouncil.org.uk.
4. See Chapter 17, footnote 14.

Chapter 21

1. *ex gratia* payments are payments *not* required to be made by a legal duty.
2. See Chapter 11, footnote 9.
3. Lexcel is the Law Society's international practice management standard. It is a scheme to certify that certain standards have been met following independent assessment.

The Lexcel practice management standard is awarded to solicitors who meet the highest management and customer care standards.

4. See Chapter 16, footnote 5.

Chapter 22

1. CEDR provides access to expertise in a range of problem-solving disciplines used to achieve resolution of conflict in business and offers the services of mediators and skilled expert neutrals worldwide together with mediation training and coaching.
2. UK Mediation was formed in 1999 dedicated to the use and promotion of mediation, and mediation training. Members of the Civil Mediation Council (www.civilmediation.org), provide trained and experienced *non-lawyer* mediators and educators.
3. The EU ADR/ODR Directive is expected to give all EU consumers the chance to resolve their disputes without going to court, regardless of product or service type or place of purchase. In order to address the particular needs of online consumers, once implemented, the Directive will allow disputes to be resolved online and within a set period of time. Ultimately it is hoped that these proposals will improve competition within the EU, and give consumers better access to, and confidence in non-litigative means of redress. (See also Chapter 5, footnote 5.)

Chapter 23

1. See Chapter 17, footnote 12.

Part Three

Chapter 24

1. See Chapter 3, footnote 5; Chapter 11, footnote 14.
2. Judicial Correspondence Unit: Now known as the Ministerial Correspondence Unit of the Ministry of Justice (www.justice.gov.uk).
3. Changed again on 1.10.2013 to Judicial Conduct Investigations Office (JCIO).
4. The name, The Judicial Appointments and Conduct Ombudsman (JACO) stays at time of publication. The online complaint form can be found via the Ministry of Justice website (see footnote 2) and assistance is offered with completing it.
5. *McMeekin* v *Long* [2003] 29 EG 120.

PART FOUR

So, what's to be done?

1. McKenzie Friend: a Litigant in Person (LiP) may be helped in court by a McKenzie Friend. This is not an automatic right, but a judge would only refuse to allow a LIP to have the help of a McKenzie Friend for a very good reason. McKenzie Friends can help in preparing the case beforehand and sit alongside the LiP to provide moral support, take notes, help with case papers, quietly give advice on points of law or procedure, advice on issues the LiP may want to raise and questions they may wish to ask witnesses. The Friend may or may not be legally qualified. There are now online firms offering a McKenzie Friend service for a fee – which is considerably less than the fees charged by solicitors, but such firms are unregulated and do not offer the protection of the Legal Ombudsman.
2. The Solicitors from Hell website was taken down in November 2011 but almost immediately similar sites appeared based abroad outside UK jurisdiction. Complaints about lawyers should be sent to the Legal Ombudsman (LeO) for investigation. LeO's Annual Reports can be accessed on-line as can data on firms complained about together with reports on anonymised cases and current issues of concern in the legal services market.
3. Damage Based Agreements (which were unlawful except in employment claims until April 2013), are agreements between lawyer and client where the client agrees to pay the lawyer a percentage of any damages awarded in a claim but not any legal fees (except expenses, such as expert's fees), until recovery. Costs paid out of damages are capped at between 25% and 50% depending on the nature of the claim and if the case is lost you will not have to pay your own legal fees – but you will be liable for your opponent's costs.

Blogs, books and contacts

1. *Law and disorder* (2010) [ISBN 978-1408801147] and *Law and Peace* (2011) [ISBN 978-1408814215] by Tim Kevan both published by Bloomsbury.
2. *The English Legal System* by Gary Slapper and David Kelly published by Routledge (2013), 14th edition [ISBN 978-0415639989].
3. ICLR online: www.iclr.co.uk. The Incorporated Council on Law Reporting offers an online case law service which includes all case reports published by ICLR since 1865. The useful service is open to non-lawyers on a single case basis at a small charge. Tel: 020 7242 6471.
4. *Outrageous Fortune* by Terence Frisby. Published in 1998 by First Thing Publications [ISBN 0-9532208-0-X].
5. *Rough Justice* a play by Terence Frisby. First performed at the Apollo Theatre, London in 1994.
6. *The End of Lawyers?* (2010) [ISBN 978-0199593613] and *Tomorrow's lawyers* (2013) [ISBN 978-0199668069] by Richard Susskind, published by OUP.

7. See 'So, what's to be done?', footnote 1.
8. Lord Justice Jackson's proposals to rein in civil litigation costs came into effect on 1st April 2013 with LASPO (see Chapter 3, footnote 5) and changes to CPRs, and could arguably be described as having effect on civil litigation equivalent to both the Woolf reforms and the Legal Services Act. Lord Jackson began his investigation in January 2009, and a year later presented his proposals which include reforms to CFAs (the losing party no longer pays the winning party's success uplift), bans referral fees in Personal Injury (PI) claims, permits DBAs (see So, what's to be done?, footnote 3) and makes amendments to CPRs to limit other litigation costs, for example the costs of disclosure. (See also Chapter 3, footnote 6; Chapter 8, footnote 3.)
9 See Part 4, footnote 3.

CAST LIST

The Fence-Post Saga

Barrister, Ms: the Doyles' barrister.
Britton, Mrs: elderly vendor to the Grahams.
Builders 1 & 2: removed and replaced the Grahams' fence.

Doyle, Mr Reg & Mrs Thelma: Plaintiffs (Claimants).
Doyles' surveyor.

Gee, Mr: the Doyles' solicitor.
Goode, Ted & Dorothy: next door neighbours to Lucy and Felix who sold to Charlene Payne.
Graham, Felix & Lucy: Defendants.
Graham, Clair & Emma: their daughters.
Grahams' surveyor.

Hassle, Costa & Grabbe: Mr Gee's firm of solicitors.

Legal Executive (Mr): Legal Executive at Hassle, Costa & Grabbe.
Lethe, His Honour Judge: final Judge for the Doyles' claim.
Longlegs, Miss: Assistant solicitor to Mr Gee.

Payne, Charlene: noisy, difficult neighbour who replaced the Goodes.
Paul: solicitor & Mackenzie Friend to the Grahams.

Registrar 1 (Desiccated): first Judge for the Doyles' claim.
Registrar 2 (Twinkly Eyes): second Judge for the Doyles' claim.

V.E. Solicitor: very expensive solicitor the Grahams consulted.

The Squatter Saga

Ackroyd, Dick & Alice: owners of *Dunroamin'* next door to *Blackstone Cottage*.

Beige, Mr: Assistant District Registrar, HM Land Registry.

BetweenOurselves: local mediation service.

Blacker, His Honour Judge: final judge for Mrs Ogmore's first court action, 2002 (Judge 5).

Boy Barrister: counsel for the CPS in Joe Ogmore's criminal assault case, 2003.

Boyd, Elaine: solicitor and coordinator of mediators BetweenOurselves.

Brown, Mr: Senior District Land Registrar, HM Land Registry.

Bulmer, Clive Vernon: Head of Bulmer & Co. solicitors. Mrs Ogmore's firm to 2004.

Burke, David: Partner in large law firm, engaged to act for M&L in their LEI claim against Ethan Ganz LLP, 2011–2014.

Buxton, Cynthia: solicitor, advised M&L on various claims, 2003–2004.

Cain, Robin: solicitor at Cross & Cross & Co., engaged to act for M&L in Mrs Ogmore's first court action, 2002–2003.

Canadian Lady: first negotiator at The Firm' insurers in M&L's claim for losses arising from The Firm's negligent conveyance work.

Carmine, Andrew, District Judge: presided at M&L's assault claim against Joe Ogmore. (Judge 7).

Castor, Guy: solicitor, expert in ADR. Represented M&L before Judge Dyer, 2004.

Cox, Julia: second assistant solicitor appointed by David Burke to represent M&L in their LEI claim against Ethan Ganz LLP.

Christie, Mark: barrister who represented M&L at the summary judgment hearing, 2008.

Cohen, Ruby: lawyer, HM Land Registry Agency Case Review Team.

Cross & Cross & Co.: Robin Cain's firm of solicitors.

Cross Junior: Partner, Cross & Cross & Co.

Cross Major: Senior Partner, Cross & Cross & Co.

D. Barr, Mr: Direct Access Barrister who advised Max and Lucy on their claims against The Firm and the Swales.

Dagenham Lady: second negotiator who took over M&L's claim against The Firm from Canadian Lady.

Dyson, Jack: second senior negotiator, barristers' indemnity insurers, who dealt with M&L's claim against Malcolm Scroggs for professional negligence.

Deputy District Judge Not Dyer: Judge at redundant directions hearing, August 2002. (Judge 2)

Dyer, Alfred, District Judge: presided at hearings 5–8 of M&L's independent survey application and claim. (Judge 6)

Edwards, Police Sergeant: arrested and charged Joe Ogmore for the attacks on M&L.

Excel, Mr: Lexcel quality solicitor M&L consulted briefly on their claim against the Swales.

The Firm: M&L's solicitors for the purchase of *Homestead,* 2001.

Ganz, Ethan LLP: Solicitors for M&L in Mrs Ogmore's second court action, 2008–2009.

Gold, Gloria, Circuit Judge: Judge for third hearing M&L attended September 2002 (Judge 4).

Goodchild, Max: joint owner of *Homestead.*

Graham, Lucy: joint owner of *Homestead.*

Green, District Judge: presided at final hearing of Mrs Ogmore's second court action, 2008 (Judge 12).

Grey, Circuit Judge: presided at second hearing M&L attended, September 2002. (Judge 3).

Groom, Nathan: assistant solicitor to David Burke acted for M&L in their LEI claim against Ethan Ganz LLP, 2012.

Hammer, Royston: Mrs Ogmore's surveyor/architect, creator of the Hammer plan.

Higgins, Jason: surveyor with Millett and Hunt Ltd., engaged for independent survey, 2008.

High Court Judge: Judge at Royal Courts of Justice, granted Mrs Ogmore's first temporary injunction. (Judge 1).

Hoople, Daisy: trainee solicitor with The Firm. Acted for M&L in the purchase of *Homestead,* 2001.

Jackson, Henry: Client Care Manager, Mercury Claims, Underwriter for The Team.

Jenkins, Jarvis: forestry expert who witnessed Ogmore's illegal tree-felling, 1999.

Katz, Hannah: paralegal, Ethan Ganz LLP. Initial lawyer to act for M&L, 2008. Wrote and signed negligent defence.

Kerociewk, Stanislav: Replacement Investigations Officer, Independent Complaints Reviewer.

Knapp, Lionel: costs lawyer acted for M&L at costs hearing before Judge Dyer, 2004.

Loach, Caspian: owner and renovator of *Blackstone Cottage,* 1964–1970.

Mercury Claims: Underwriters for The Team.

MiC: man in charge at HM Land Registry Agency Case Review Team.

Millett and Hunt Ltd.: surveyors, Jason Higgins' firm.

Nelson, Mr: bailiff.

Nunn, James: M&L's surveyor post purchase of *Homestead.*

No Name, District Judge: Judge for Ogmore's second court action, 2008. (Judge 9.)

Northcote, P.C. Steve: Police Constable and amateur expert on squatting.

Ogmore, Hazel: owner of *Blackstone Cottage.* Assistant solicitor Bulmer & Co to 2004.

Ogmore, Joe: owner of *Blackstone Cottage*. Ex-solicitor.
Open Talk UK: national mediation service.

Pelt, His Honour Judge: High Court Judge for appeal hearing of assault claim. (Judge 8).
Pickles, Tim: assistant solicitor to Wolf Rottman, who replaced Hannah Katz, 2008.
Pilling, Julian: first solicitor M&L consulted about Mrs Ogmore's trespass, 2002.
Priest, Colin: Senior Investigations Officer at the Independent Complaints Reviewer.
Pugh, Melissa: first LEI panel solicitor to act for M&L in their claim against Ethan Ganz, 2009–2010.

Rishus, Harvey: Direct Access Barrister. Advised M&L on their professional negligence claim against Malcolm Scroggs.
Rottman, Wolf: Head of Litigation and Complaints Manager at Ethan Ganz LLP.

Saif, Mohammed: negotiator, barristers' indemnity insurance firm. Opposed M&L's claim against Malcolm Scroggs.
Scroggs, Malcolm: second barrister to represent M&L. Attended fourth hearing of Mrs Ogmore's first court action and signed the 'agreement' and plan, October 2002.
Severn, Tony: owner of *Blackstone Cottage* to 1988 and vendor to the Ogmores.
Shah, Sameer: assistant solicitor to Robin Cain.
Skolski, Lucas: solicitor, represented Malcolm Scroggs' at the mediation of M&L's professional negligence claim.
Smythe, Aubrey: Partner at Ethan Ganz LLP and Deputy District Judge.
Snype, Ms: Deputy Head, Office for Judicial Complaints.
Stoat, Rex: barrister, advised and represented the Ogmores.
Stone, Rick: owner of *Homestead* 1984 to April 1999.
Sutton, Barry: Judicial Correspondence Unit complaints investigator.

Swales, Kevin and Kate: owners of *Homestead* 1999–2001. Vendors to Max & Lucy.

Thorne, Alan: solicitor at LEI panel firm who reviewed M&L's claims against Cross & Cross & Co. and others, 2006.

The Team: M&L's Legal Expenses Insurers for the Ethan Ganz LLP negligence claim.

Tweed, Robert: barrister who represent M&L at the third hearing of Mrs Ogmore's first court action and drafted their defence and counterclaim, September 2002.

Waterhouse, Charles: first senior negotiator for the barristers' insurers, represented Malcolm Scroggs in M&L's professional negligence claim.

Willis, Tony, AWA Solicitors: second LEI panel solicitor for M&L's negligence claim against Ethan Ganz LLP.

Wilson, Adrian, AW & Co. LLP: third LEI panel solicitor for M&L's negligence claim against Ethan Ganz LLP.

Windsmoor, PC: investigated Mrs Ogmore's assertions prior to her first court action, 2002.

White, District Judge: a judge in Mrs Ogmore's second court action, 2008. (Judge 10).

Wormelow, Tracey: Associate then Partner at Bulmer & Co. Solicitors.